FIFTH EDITION

Strategies and Models for Teachers

Teaching Content and Thinking Skills

Paul D. Eggen

University of North Florida

Donald P. Kauchak

University of Utah

Boston ■ New York ■ San Francisco
Mexico City ■ Montreal ■ Toronto ■ London ■ Madrid ■ Munich ■ Paris
Hong Kong ■ Singapore ■ Tokyo ■ Cape Town ■ Sydney

Executive Editor and Publisher: *Stephen D. Dragin*
Editorial Assistant: *Meaghan Minnick*
Marketing Manager: *Tara Kelly*
Composition and Prepress Buyer: *Linda Cox*
Manufacturing Buyer: *Andrew Turso*
Editorial-Production Service: *Omegatype Typography, Inc.*
Cover Administrator: *Kristina Mose-Libon*
Electronic Composition: *Omegatype Typography, Inc.*

For related titles and support materials, visit our online catalog at www.ablongman.com.

Between the time website information is gathered and published, some sites may have closed. Also, the transcription of URLs can result in typographical errors. The publisher would appreciate notification where these errors occur so that they may be corrected in subsequent editions.

Library of Congress Cataloging-in-Publication Data

Eggen, Paul D.
   Strategies and models for teachers: teaching content and thinking skills / Paul D. Eggen, Donald P. Kauchak.–5th ed
      p. cm.
   Rev. ed. of: Strategies for teachers. 4th ed. 2001.
   Includes bibliographical references (p.) and index.
   ISBN 0-205-45332-5
      1. Teaching. 2. Education—Experimental methods. 3. Thought and thinking—Study and teaching. 4. Learning, Psychology of. I. Kauchak, Donald P. II. Eggen, Paul D., Strategies for teachers. III. Title.

LB1027.3.E44 2006
371.102—dc22
                                                                    2004060212

Printed in the United States of America

10 9 8 7 6 5 4 3 2 1   10 09 08 07 06 05

CONTENTS

PREFACE

The field of instruction continues to evolve rapidly, and we remain immersed in one of the most exciting periods in the history of education. Cognitive views of learning are now the primary guide for instruction, and this foundation is reflected in greater emphasis on social interaction as an essential factor in learning, the importance of learners' prior knowledge, the influence of context on learning, and the general acceptance that learners construct their own understanding of the topics they study. In addition, the interdependence of learning and motivation is more fully understood.

Teachers continue to use the effective teaching literature popular in the 1970s and 1980s as a foundation, but they now apply principles of learning and motivation to help their students acquire a deep understanding of the topics they study while simultaneously developing their critical-thinking abilities. In addition, technology, as well as standards and accountability, are having an increasing influence on instruction. To reflect these advances and influences, the following are new to this edition:

- A new Chapter 2, "Learning, Motivation, and Models of Teaching," that reflects the increasing influence of cognitive learning and motivation theory as foundations for instruction.
- A discussion of the influence of standards on planning and implementing instruction.
- Tables that outline the learning and motivation functions of each phase of each model.
- New figures in each chapter intended to make the content more readable and meaningful.
- Sections describing how technology can be used to make the models more effective.

In writing the fifth edition, we relied on four primary sources. The first is the continuing advance of cognitive learning theory as a framework for guiding instruction. The implications that our understanding of learning has for teachers is reflected in each of the models in the text. The second is the influence of cognitive motivation theory and the implications it has for the way we design instruction, implement it, and interact with our students. The third is research on classroom instruction, which continues to identify essential links between teacher actions and student learning. The fourth is our own experience in schools. As with previous editions, we continue to work in classrooms, observing teachers and students and studying the complex interactions that take place between them. This experience has helped us realize that, although an understanding of cognitive learning and motivation theory is essential for expert instruction, teaching is fundamentally a personal process that requires an enormous number of individual decisions. Though guided by the structure of a model, we repeatedly note that teachers must continually make decisions about the best course of action in a particular context. This is what makes teaching so rewarding and challenging.

As with previous editions, the fifth edition focuses on instruction, using a models approach. This approach links the models to specific content and thinking objectives, while acknowledging that no approach to instruction replaces the wisdom and judgment of an expert teacher. Reflecting research suggesting that in-depth study of carefully selected content in detail is preferable to broad, superficial coverage, we have consciously decided to avoid examining every topic typically found in methods texts. Instead, we have chosen to present and illustrate specific models in detail—those we believe are most useful to classroom teachers.

The book exists in two main parts. Chapters 1 through 3 provide a frame of reference by outlining advances in our understanding of learning and motivation, essential teaching strategies that support all models, and the teaching of thinking. Chapters 4 through 10 are devoted to detailed descriptions of the individual models, including suggestions for modifications that make them adaptable to a variety of teaching–learning situations.

In doing our revision, we have attempted to ground the models in the most recent theory and research, making it a conceptually sound yet highly applicable text. We hope it provides you with opportunities for professional growth.

Acknowledgments

In preparing this manuscript, we want to thank the people who have supported its development, particularly Steve Dragin, our editor, and the reviewers for this edition: Judith L. Martin, University of Texas at San Antonio; Susan L. Mintz, University of Virginia; and Sharon Tettegah, University of Illinois, Urbana-Champaign. We want to thank especially the many teachers whose classrooms we've worked in and visited, and on whose instruction the case studies in the text were based. This experience has brought to the book a reality and authenticity that would have been otherwise impossible.

P. E.
D. K.

CHAPTER

1

Models of Teaching and Developing as a Teacher

This is a book about teaching strategies. Some are general, such as skilled questioning, clear communication, and effective feedback, which apply in virtually all teaching situations. Other, more explicit strategies, called *teaching models,* are grounded in learning and motivation theory and designed to reach specific learning objectives. As you study this book, you will read about both the general strategies and the specific models. All are designed to help students develop a deep understanding of the topics they study and improve their critical-thinking abilities. When you have completed your study of this chapter, you should be able to:

- Describe the different kinds of knowledge expert teachers possess.
- Identify the important elements of the teacher-effectiveness research.
- Describe the characteristics of teaching models.
- Identify factors influencing the choice of a teaching model.

To begin this discussion, let's look at a fourth-grade teacher who is working on adding fractions with unlike denominators with her students.

Entering the kitchen, Jim Barton sees his wife, Shirley, working at the kitchen table. "What are you doing with those cake pans? We've already eaten dinner."

"What do you think?" she grins at him. "Do they look like cake?" she asks holding up cardboard pieces drawn to resemble cake cut into squares in the two pans.

"Actually they almost do," he responds, a bit impressed.

"My kids didn't score as well as I would have liked on the fractions part of the statewide assessment test last year, and you know how important those tests are. The kids had trouble adding fractions with unlike denominators, and I found that they didn't understand the concept of equivalent fractions as well as they should have, so

I'm going to be more thorough there. We're starting right at the beginning, like what equivalent fractions are and how to find them."

"But you said that the kids aren't as sharp this year."

"I don't care. I'm pushing them harder. I think I could have done a better job last year, so I swore I was really going to be ready for them this time. They're going to knock the top off the test this year. . . . And they're going to get over their fear of math."

Jim mumbles something about thinking that teachers who have taught for 11 years were supposed to burn out and walks back into the living room with a slight smile on his face.

Shirley has 25 fourth graders in her class and usually schedules the day as follows:

8:30–10:00 A.M.	Reading
10:00–10:55 A.M.	Math
10:55–11:05 A.M.	Break
11:05–11:35 A.M.	Science
11:35–12:00 noon	Lunch
12:00–1:25 P.M.	Language Arts (spelling, writing, grammar)
1:25–1:35 P.M.	Break
1:35–2:00 P.M.	Social Studies
2:00–3:00 P.M.	Resource (art, music, physical education, computer)

As we join her class, Shirley is walking up and down the aisles, at times stopping for a few seconds to comment on a student's work or offer reassurance as they complete their reading seatwork.

Glancing at her watch she sees that it's 9:58 and announces, "Let me have your reading papers and please get out your math homework. It's nearly time to begin math."

The students stop their writing and pass the papers forward. She collects them from the first person in each row, and, as she walks by Shelli on the way to the chalkboard, she pauses and asks, "How are you feeling today, Shelli? Is your cold better?"

"A lot better," Shelli replies looking up at her. "I've just got some sniffles now."

Shirley puts the papers in a folder on her desk and steps to the chalkboard as she watches students put their reading materials away and pull their math books out of their desks. She writes the following problems on the board:

$$\frac{3}{8} + \frac{2}{8} = \qquad \frac{3}{7} + \frac{4}{7} = \qquad \frac{5}{12} + \frac{6}{12} =$$

At 10:01 the children have their math books out and are waiting.

"Now," she begins, "we've been adding fractions, so for a moment let's look again at what we've been doing. What does the eight mean in the first problem? . . . Safar?" and she walks to the board, taps it with her chalk, and then pulls out the following drawings from behind her desk.

"We have eight parts of something altogether."

"And what kind of parts? . . . Joe?"

". . . Equal."

"Okay, good observation, Joe. You recognized that the parts are equal."

Shirley continues asking Andrea what the top numbers mean, and then continues on, "What is the sum in the first problem? . . . Hakim."

"Five eighths."

"What do the rest of you think?" Shirley probes.

"I don't think so," Adam says. "It looks like five-sixteenths to me."

"No, look," Natasha counters. "We have only eight pieces altogether. . . . See, if we put these two pieces on top of the others, we have five, five out of eight."

Shirley watches for a minute as other students join this discussion and the class finally concludes that Natasha's argument makes sense.

She then continues with the second and third problems on the board and finishes by saying, "Now remember everyone, this is very important. Each of these problems has the same denominator," as she points respectively to the eights, the sevens, and the twelves.

"Now," she continues, striding vigorously across the front of the room, "we're going to shift gears to where we want to add fractions when the denominators are not alike."

She then pulls the two cardboard rectangles drawn to resemble the cake that she had made the night before from the shelf, one divided into thirds and the other divided in half.

"Now suppose I want to add half of this cake to a third of this one." She points to a shaded half and third respectively. "How much cake will I have? How am I going to figure it out?" She pauses for a couple seconds and continues, "That's where we're going to begin today."

She then points to the shaded third of the cardboard and asks, "How much cake do I have here? . . . Raymond?"

". . . A third."

"Okay, fine, . . . but now look," and she folds the cardboard in half along the opposite axis. "How many pieces do I have altogether now? . . . Karen?"

". . . It looks like six," she responds uncertainly.

"Yes, good Karen. So, . . . what portion is now shaded? . . . Michael?"

". . . Two sixths."

"Excellent, Michael," and she moves to the board and writes

$$\frac{1}{3} = \frac{2}{6}$$

She then says, "Watch what I do here," and she demonstrates for the students how they can write

(2) $\frac{2}{3} = \frac{4}{6}$
(2)

and refers again to her cardboard cake as she does it.

She then does another example with one fourth, again folding her cardboard and writing

(3) $\frac{1}{4} = \frac{3}{12}$
(3)

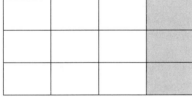

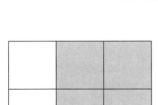

After the two examples she asks, "Now, let's stop for a moment. How do we know that the two thirds and the four sixths are the same? . . . Ken?"

". . ."

"How much is shaded here?"

". . ."

"Look at the cardboard, Ken," Shirley smiles encouragingly. "Tell me what you see here."

". . . Some of the cardboard is a different color."

"How much?"

". . . Two thirds."

"And how about this way? . . . Serena?"

". . . Four sixths."

"So how do they compare? . . . Latrell?"

"They're the same."

"Outstanding!" Shirley smiles and glances at Ken to see if he appears to understand.

Shirley continues with the process for another 15 minutes, and then says, "Now everyone, let's look and see what kind of pattern we have in these examples. Give it a try. . . . Ron?"

". . . Well, we're finding fractions that are the same as other fractions."

"Explain that a little further, please."

". . . The one third and the two sixths were the same, and the one fourth and the three twelfths were the same, and the two thirds and the four sixths were the same."

"Excellent, Ron," Shirley smiles. "And why do we need to do this? . . . Eddie?"

". . ."

"Think about what we did in our last lesson. What were the fractions like there?"

". . . They all had the same denominators," Eddie blurts out.

"Super Eddie," Shirley responds.

She then continues, "So, what is the purpose of doing what we've done here? . . . Kelly?"

"To get fractions with the same denominators so we can add them."

"Exactly," Shirley smiles. "Now I'm going to give you the name for these. They're called *equivalent fractions.*"

"Now let's see what we have here. What have we been doing here? . . . Toni?"

". . . We're finding equivalent fractions."

"Good, Toni, and why do we want to find them? . . . Gary?"

". . . So we can add fractions when the denominators are not the same."

Shirley praises Gary and the rest of the students for their good work and gives them an assignment that involves finding equivalent fractions. "Everyone, do the first one on your sheet."

As the students work the first problem, Shirley walks up and down the rows, checking each student's progress as she goes. Periodically, she stops to point something out to an individual, then moves on.

"Let's take a look at the first problem," Shirley suggests when everyone has completed it. "What's the first thing you noticed? . . . Michelle?"

". . . The denominators aren't the same."

"Good! So what did we do?"

Shirley guides the class through an analysis of the first problem and has them do the second problem.

She analyzes the second one with them, and they work a third one. After reviewing the third problem, she has them work independently for the remainder of their time in math. As they do their seatwork, she circulates around the room, looking over their shoulders, offering assistance to different individuals.

At one point Shirley turns as she hears Jimmy and Karen whispering rather loudly behind her. Stepping over to them, she touches Jimmy's shoulder, and looking directly at Karen puts her finger to her lips signaling "Shh."

The students quickly stop.

The students continue their work until 10:52 when Shirley says, "It's nearly time for science. Put your math papers away and we'll have our recess break."

Teacher Knowledge and Developing as a Teacher

Education has changed significantly since the previous edition of this book was published. The increased emphasis on standards, accountability, high-stakes tests, and federal mandates, such as the No Child Left Behind Act all have increased the need for teachers who are knowledgeable and highly skilled in the classroom. Let's look a bit more closely at these changes.

Standards and Accountability: The Increasing Need for Teacher Knowledge

Those of you who are already teaching do not have to be told about the influence of standards on your work. **Standards,** *statements that describe what students should know or be* *able to do at the end of a prescribed period of study,* are a part of every teacher's daily life. They influence your thinking by suggesting content, learning objectives, and, in some cases, the way you assess your students' learning. Shirley's comment about the statewide assessment test is an example of this influence.

The "standards" movement resulted from concerns about Americans' and American students' lack of knowledge about their history and their world. Some of this concern is well founded. Research suggests, for example, that 60 percent of adult Americans do not know the name of the president who ordered the dropping of the atomic bomb, 42 percent of college seniors can not place the Civil War in the correct half century, and most Americans can not find the Persian Gulf on a map (Bertman, 2000). These examples are in social studies, and even greater concerns have been raised about math, science, and writing. Although the standards movement is highly controversial, with critics (e.g., Amrein & Berliner, 2002; Paris, 1998) and proponents (e.g., Bishop, 1998; Hirsh, 2000) lining up on opposite sides, virtually every professional organization in education, ranging from those involved with core subjects, such as math and English, to those concerned with the arts, foreign language, and physical education, has prepared lists of standards (e.g., Consortium of National Arts Education Associations, 1994; Geography Education Standards Project, 1994; National Association for Sport and Physical Education, 1995; National Council of Teachers of Mathematics, 2000; National Standards in Foreign Language Education Project, 1999). Even support organizations, such as the National Parent Teacher Association (2000), have created standards. In addition, the District of Columbia, Puerto Rico, and every state except Iowa have set academic standards for students. The following are some examples:

- *Science.* In science, students in Missouri public schools will acquire a solid foundation, which includes knowledge of . . . properties and principles of force and motion (Missouri Department of Elementary and Secondary Education, 1996).
- *Math.* Instructional programs from prekindergarten through grade twelve should enable all students to compute fluently and make reasonable estimates. In grades six through eight all students should:
  - Work flexibly with fractions, decimals, and percents to solve problems;
  - Develop meaning for percents greater than 100 and less than 1 (National Council of Teachers of Mathematics, 2000, p. 214).
- *Geography.* Students will know physical and human criteria used to define regions (for example, hemispheres, mountains, deserts, countries, city boundaries, and school districts) (Florida Educational Tools, Inc., 2003–2004).

These standards are then used to hold both students and teachers accountable for student learning.

As we can see from the examples, standards are written with varying degrees of specificity. This means standards must first be interpreted, and then appropriate teaching strategies much be selected to help students meet the standards. All this requires professionals who are highly knowledgeable about their work. Let's look at this professional knowledge in more detail.

Teacher Knowledge

About the middle of the twentieth century, views of learning experienced a major shift away from an emphasis on specific, observable behaviors and toward internal, mental processes (Mayer, 1998). This shift, commonly described as the "cognitive revolution," has resulted in a greater emphasis on teachers' knowledge and thinking in the process of developing as expert teachers.

Studies of expertise in a variety of fields confirm the importance of knowledge in the development of expert performance (Bruning, Schraw, Norby, & Ronning, 2004), and this is true for teaching as well. "The accumulation of richly structured and accessible bodies of knowledge allows individuals to engage in expert thinking and action. In studies of teaching, this understanding of expertise has led researchers to devote increased attention to teachers' knowledge and its organization" (Borko & Putnam, 1996, p. 674).

Research indicates that at least four different kinds of knowledge are essential for expert teaching. Each helps teachers make professional decisions, such as determining the most effective ways to help students reach standards, which we discussed in the previous section, as well as a host of others. These different types of knowledge include:

- Knowledge of content
- Pedagogical content knowledge
- General pedagogical knowledge
- Knowledge of learners and learning (Peterson, 1988; Shulman, 1987)

Our goal in writing this book is to support your development as a teacher by helping you acquire knowledge in each of these areas, and particularly in the last three. Let's look at them.

Knowledge of Content.   We can't teach what we don't understand. Although this statement appears self-evident, it is also well documented by research examining the relationships between what teachers know and how they teach (Shulman, 1986; Wilson, Shulman, & Richert, 1987). To effectively teach about the American Revolutionary War, for example, a social studies teacher must know not only basic facts about the war but also how it relates to other aspects of history, such as the French and Indian War, our relationship with England before the Revolution, and the characteristics of the colonies. Shirley obviously understood the concept of equivalent fractions and why understanding them is essential for understanding how to add fractions with unlike denominators. A thorough understanding of the topics we teach is essential for all teachers in all content areas.

Pedagogical Content Knowledge.   Shirley didn't simply explain equivalent fractions to her students. Instead, she used her cardboard cakes and folded papers as examples that allowed the students to see that two thirds and four sixths, or one fourth and three twelfths are equal. Her ability to create examples such as these demonstrates her **pedagogical content knowledge,** which is the *understanding of "ways of representing . . . the subject that make it comprehensible to others" and "an understanding of what makes the learning of specific topics easy or difficult"* (Shulman, 1986, p. 9 [italics added]). The difference between content knowledge and pedagogical content knowledge is similar to the difference between knowing *that* and knowing *how*. Pedagogical content knowledge depends on an understanding of a particular topic, such as understanding the factors leading to the American Revolution (knowing *that*), but it goes beyond this understanding and includes being able to explain and illustrate these factors so they make sense to students (knowing *how*).

Teachers who possess pedagogical content knowledge also recognize when topics are hard to understand and illustrate these difficult-to-teach ideas with concrete experiences that make them meaningful. This is what Shirley did with her cardboard cakes and folded papers.

Concrete representations of topics, such as equivalent fractions, are important because they make abstract ideas meaningful, which not only helps students learn the ideas in the first place but also allows them to apply their understanding in a variety of real-world settings (Mayer & Wittrock, 1996). Intuitively, it isn't obvious that one fourth and three twelfths are equal; so many students mechanically perform the operation of finding equivalent fractions with little understanding. This is why teachers' abilities to create effective illustrations of abstract topics are so essential. Without the examples, students grasp what they can and memorize as much as possible. Little understanding develops. (We examine different types of examples in detail in Chapter 5 when we discuss the Inductive Model.)

Paradoxically, researchers have found that teachers with high levels of content knowledge sometimes have trouble representing topics for novice learners (Nathan, Koedinger, & Alibali, 2001). Because of their own personal deep understanding, they have trouble "putting themselves in learners' shoes." Expert teachers both thoroughly understand the topics they teach and are able to represent those topics in ways that are understandable to students.

General Pedagogical Knowledge. Knowledge of content and pedagogical content knowledge are important in teaching but they have one limitation—they are domain specific, that is, they depend on knowledge of a particular content area, such as equivalent fractions, the concept *density,* the Crusades, or our judicial system. In comparison, **general pedagogical knowledge** involves *an understanding of general principles of instruction and classroom management that transcends individual topics or subject matter areas* (Borko & Putnam, 1996).

Instructional Strategies. Regardless of the content area or topic, teachers need to understand and know how to apply different ways of promoting learning, including involving students in learning activities, using techniques for checking their understanding, and using strategies for running lessons smoothly. Questioning is an important example. Shirley recognized that asking questions that engage all students is important, and she developed her entire lesson with questioning. The importance of actively involving students through questioning is confirmed by research (McDougall & Granby, 1996), and it is a teaching strategy that applies to every area of teaching. Similarly, teachers must also be able to communicate clearly, provide effective feedback, and use a variety of other strategies to maximize learning for all students. We examine these aspects of general pedagogical knowledge in detail in Chapter 3.

Classroom Management. Regardless of the content area or topic being taught, teachers also need to know how to create orderly classroom environments that promote learning

(Emmer, Evertson, & Worsham, 2003; Evertson, Emmer, & Worsham, 2003). Understanding how to keep twenty to thirty-five or more students actively engaged and working together in learning activities requires that teachers know how to plan, implement, and monitor rules and procedures; organize groups; and react to misbehavior. It is virtually impossible to maintain an orderly, learning-focused classroom if we wait for misbehavior to occur. Teachers who create productive learning environments prevent most misbehavior from occurring in the first place, rather than stopping misbehavior once it begins.

The ability to create and maintain order was illustrated in Shirley's work with her students. She was well organized; she had her materials ready, and she began her math class when it was scheduled to begin, for example. In addition, she immediately reacted to Jimmy and Karen's whispering, quickly helping them get back on task. All of these abilities reflect general pedagogical knowledge.

Knowledge of Learners and Learning.   Knowledge of learners and learning is also essential to effective teaching and is "arguably the most important knowledge a teacher can have" (Borko & Putnam, 1996, p. 675). This knowledge influences the way we teach by reminding us that we do not teach content, we teach students.

Shirley understood both how her students learn and how she could facilitate their learning. For example, evidence overwhelmingly indicates that people don't behave like tape recorders; they don't simply record in memory what they hear or read. Rather, they interpret information in an effort to make sense of it (Bransford, Brown, & Cocking, 2000; Mayer, 2002). In the process, meanings can be distorted and misconceptions can occur.

We saw this illustrated in Shirley's lesson. Hakim concluded that two eighths plus three eighths was five eighths, but Adam believed that the answer was five sixteenths. Shirley didn't teach this misconception; in all probability neither did any other teacher. Adam constructed this idea on his own because it made sense to him. Only after Natasha's argument and some additional discussion did Adam change his mind (and even then we can't be sure he truly believed it). Teachers' abilities to adapt their instruction based on what learners' know is essential for effective teaching. Shirley also demonstrated her understanding of learners by creating examples that provided all the information the students needed to understand the topic—equivalent fractions—and she also promoted involvement, which is so essential for learning. Each of the forms of knowledge—knowledge of content, pedagogical content knowledge, general pedagogical knowledge, and knowledge of learners and learning—is essential for teaching expertise. (We examine learning in more detail in Chapter 2.)

Professional Organizations Respond to the Need for Knowledge

Professional organizations have responded to the renewed emphasis on teachers' knowledge. Two organizations with the most widespread influence on teaching are:

- The *Interstate New Teacher Assessment and Support Consortium* (INTASC), an organization committed to increasing the professionalism of beginning teachers
- The *National Board for Professional Teaching Standards* (NBPTS), an organization whose goals are to strengthen teaching as a profession and raise the quality of education by recognizing the contributions of exemplary teachers

Let's look at them.

The INTASC Principles.   In response to the increased emphasis on professional knowledge in teaching, a number of states collaborated to create the Interstate New Teacher Assessment and Support Consortium (INTASC). INTASC has set rigorous standards in each of the four areas of teacher knowledge that were discussed in the previous sections. These standards describe what teachers should know and be able to do in each of these areas, and are organized around ten principles, which are outlined in Table 1.1.

TABLE 1.1   The INTASC Principles

Principle	Description
1. Knowledge of subject	The teacher understands the central concepts, tools of inquiry, and structures of the discipline(s) he or she teaches and can create learning experiences that make these aspects of subject matter meaningful for students.
2. Learning and human development	The teacher understands how children learn and develop, and can provide learning opportunities that support their intellectual, social, and personal development.
3. Adapting instruction	The teacher understands how students differ in their approaches to learning and creates instructional opportunities that are adapted to diverse learners.
4. Strategies	The teacher understands and uses a variety of instructional strategies to encourage students' development of critical-thinking, problem-solving, and performance skills.
5. Motivation and management	The teacher uses an understanding of individual and group motivation and behavior to create a learning environment that encourages positive social interaction, active engagement in learning, and self-motivation.
6. Communication skills	The teacher uses knowledge of effective verbal, nonverbal, and media communication techniques to foster active inquiry, collaboration, and supportive interaction in the classroom.
7. Planning	The teacher plans instruction based on knowledge of subject matter, students, the community, and curriculum goals.
8. Assessment	The teacher understands and uses formal and informal assessment strategies to evaluate and ensure the continuous intellectual, social, and physical development of the learner.
9. Commitment	The teacher is a reflective practitioner who continually evaluates the effects of his or her choices and actions on others (students, parents, and other professionals in the learning community) and who actively seeks out opportunities to grow professionally.
10. Partnership	The teacher fosters relationships with school colleagues, parents, and agencies in the larger community to support students' learning and well-being.

We address most of the principles in this text, with particular emphasis placed on strategies and the ability to adapt instruction to best meet particular learning objectives and students' needs.

The National Board for Professional Teaching Standards.   The National Board for Professional Teaching Standards (NBPTS) was created in 1987 and mostly is composed of teachers of students in kindergarten through twelfth grade, but it also includes union and business leaders and university faculty. NBPTS seeks to strengthen teaching as a profession and raise the quality of education by recognizing the contributions of exemplary teachers, compensating them financially, giving them increased responsibility, and increasing their roles in decision making (Serafini, 2002).

National board certification is based on standards that are directed by five core propositions about professional educators. These propositions and descriptions of how they are implemented in practice are outlined in Table 1.2. The INTASC principles are designed for beginning teachers, and the NBPTS is aimed at veterans. Both, however, focus on the types of professional knowledge that we discussed in the earlier sections of the chapter.

PRAXIS™ Exams Assess Teacher Knowledge

Increasingly, teachers are being asked to pass competency tests that measure their readiness for working with learners. The most frequently used test is the *PRAXIS™ Series* (*praxis* means putting theory into practice), which is required in thirty-five states (Educational Testing Service, 1999).

An important part of the PRAXIS™ Series is the Principles of Learning and Teaching (PLT) tests, which are specifically designed for teachers seeking licensure in kindergarten through grade six, fifth through ninth grades, and seventh through twelfth grades. The PRAXIS™ exams are closely aligned with the INTASC standards previously discussed, and this book addresses many of the topics covered on the tests. Consistent with the INTASC principles and NBPTS propositions, the PRAXIS™ exam is designed to measure teachers' professional knowledge. Many of the items on the exam are based on case studies, which PRAXIS calls case histories, similar to those you are studying in this text. People who take the PRAXIS™ exam are asked to analyze those cases in much the same way that cases are analyzed in this book.

Research and the Teacher's Role in Learning

A large body of research underscores the importance of the teacher in helping students learn (Good & Brophy, 2003; Shuell, 1996). Findings from this research consistently indicate that the teacher is the most important educational factor affecting student learning and development. This was illustrated in Shirley's lesson. Teachers with less expertise likely would have explained the concept of equivalent fractions and briefly modeled a procedure for finding them. They might then have assigned seatwork in which students were to find equivalent fractions, and the students' levels of understanding would have been much lower. Research consistently confirms this assertion.

TABLE 1.2 Propositions of the National Board for Professional Teaching Standards

Proposition	Description
1. Teachers are committed to students and their learning.	■ Accomplished teachers believe that all students can learn, and they treat students equitably. ■ Accomplished teachers understand how students develop, and they use accepted learning theory as the basis for their teaching. ■ Accomplished teachers are aware of the influence of context and culture on behavior, and they foster students' self-esteem, motivation, and character.
2. Teachers know the subjects they teach and how to teach those subjects to students.	■ Accomplished teachers have a rich understanding of the subject(s) they teach, and they appreciate how knowledge in their subject is linked to other disciplines and applied to real-world settings. ■ Accomplished teachers know to make subject matter understandable to students, and they are able to modify their instruction when difficulties arise. ■ Accomplished teachers demonstrate critical and analytic capacities in their teaching, and they develop those capacities in their students.
3. Teachers are responsible for managing and monitoring student learning.	■ Accomplished teachers capture and sustain the interest of their students and use their time effectively. ■ Accomplished teachers are able to use a variety of effective instructional techniques, and they use the techniques appropriately. ■ Accomplished teachers can use multiple methods to assess the progress of students, and the teachers effectively communicate this progress to parents.
4. Teachers think systematically about their practice and learn from experience.	■ Accomplished teachers are models for intellectual curiosity and they display virtues—honesty, fairness, and respect for diversity—that they seek to inspire in their students. ■ Accomplished teachers use their understanding of students, learning, and instruction to make principled judgments about sound practice, and they are lifelong learners. ■ Accomplished teachers critically examine their practice, and they seek continual professional growth.
5. Teachers are members of learning communities.	■ Accomplished teachers contribute to the effectiveness of the school, and they work collaboratively with their colleagues. ■ Accomplished teachers evaluate school progress, and they use community resources. ■ Accomplished teachers work collaboratively with parents, and they involve parents in school activities.

Educators have not always been optimistic about the ability of research to guide classroom practice. Before the 1970s both research and teachers themselves were given little credit for contributing to student learning. This pessimism was caused by a number of factors, including faulty research designs and inefficient research procedures (Gage & Giaconia, 1981; Rosenshine, 1979).

One of the oldest traditions in research on teaching focused on teacher characteristics: the implicit assumption that teachers are "born" and not "made." (This idea is no longer popular today.) This research examined teacher characteristics, such as warmth and humor, and tried to determine whether the presence or absence of these characteristics influenced student learning. However, the researchers often failed to establish whether these characteristics, typically measured on paper-and-pencil tests, produced any differences in actual teaching behaviors, let alone differences in student achievement. As we would expect, this approach proved unproductive and was ultimately abandoned.

Another line of research originating in the 1960s and continuing into the 1970s focused on the relationship between home- and school-related factors and student learning (Coleman et al., 1966; Jencks et al., 1972). Largely refinements of earlier work, these studies searched for factors that correlated with student achievement. Results suggested that the most important variables impacting school learning were factors outside the control of classroom teachers and even school environments, such as parental income and educational background. Needless to say, both researchers and teachers were discouraged by the results. The data seemed to suggest that the most important variables in learning were beyond educators' control. In addition, these results led to sharply reduced national and state funding for educational research. With reduced economic support, research efforts became even more difficult.

Teachers Make a Difference: The Teacher-Effectiveness Research

Fortunately, two converging lines of research led to a new and more productive paradigm, one focusing on teachers' actions in the classroom. The first was a reanalysis of the data gathered by Coleman and his associates (1966). This reanalysis focused on individual schools and teachers and found that there were large differences in the effectiveness of both. Some promoted much more student learning than did others (Brophy & Good, 1986; Good & Brophy, 1986).

The second emerged when researchers began to observe the teachers whose students learned more than expected for their grade and ability levels, compared to those whose students scored as expected or below. The researchers found wide variations in the ways the two groups taught, and a *description of these patterns—the patterns of teacher skills and strategies that influence student learning—makes up the body of knowledge that we now call the* **teacher-effectiveness research.** The inescapable conclusion from this research is that teachers make a "profound impact" on student learning (Marzano, 2003). (We examine specific teacher-effectiveness strategies in Chapter 3.)

Beyond Effective Teaching

The literature on effective teaching made an invaluable contribution to education because it both confirmed the essential role teachers play in student learning and provided "education with a knowledge base capable of moving the field beyond testimonials and unsupported claims toward scientific statements based on credible data" (Brophy, 1992, p. 5). It provides, however, only a threshold or a base line for all teachers. Experts, such as Shirley, go well beyond this threshold to design and implement lessons that result in deep student understanding.

Teaching for Understanding

The concept of *teaching for understanding* may seem ironic; no teacher teaches for lack of understanding. However, when we examine the concept of *understanding* closely, we see that it isn't as simple as it appears on the surface. Experts describe understanding as "being able to do a variety of thought-demanding things with a topic—like explaining, finding evidence and examples, generalizing, applying, analogizing, and representing the topic in a new way" (Perkins & Blythe, 1994, pp. 5–6). The teaching models and other strategies described in this text are designed to help teachers ensure that their students' learning extends beyond mere memorization, which is so prevalent in schools today.

Teacher questioning provides a foundation for this process, with questions such as:

"Why?"
"How do these compare?" ("How are they alike or different?")
"What would happen if . . . ?"

and particularly,

"How do you know?"

Questions such as these can do much to promote student understanding. Surprisingly (and disturbingly), teachers ask thought-provoking questions like these less than 1 percent of the time (Boyer, 1983).

Teaching for understanding requires that teachers possess the different types of knowledge discussed earlier in the chapter, which includes understanding the research on teacher effectiveness. Armed with this knowledge effective teachers achieve deep student understanding by:

- Identifying clear learning objectives for students
- Selecting teaching strategies that most effectively help students reach the objectives
- Providing examples and representations that help students acquire a deep understanding of the topics they study
- Encouraging students to become actively involved in the learning process
- Guiding students as they construct their understanding of the topics being studied
- Continually monitoring students for evidence of learning

Although the focus is on learners and learning, these strategies demonstrate the essential roles that teachers, as well as teacher knowledge, play in guiding this process.

A repertoire of effective teaching strategies is essential for teachers to promote deep understanding. Teachers must be able to select and use strategies that are most effective for different learning objectives. We analyze this idea in the next section.

The Need for Instructional Alternatives

What is the best way to teach? The answers to this question have been debated since the beginning of formal education. Discussions have focused on authoritarian versus democratic techniques (Anderson, 1959), discovery versus expository approaches (Keislar & Shulman, 1966), teacher- versus student-centeredness (Dunkin & Biddle, 1974), and direct versus indirect approaches to teaching (Peterson & Walberg, 1979). Thousands of studies have been conducted in an attempt to answer the question in its various forms. The most valid conclusion derived from this research is that *there is no single best way to teach.* Some learning objectives are better understood using teacher-centered approaches, for example, whereas students are more likely to understand others with learner-centered approaches.

Bruce Joyce and Marsha Weil first introduced the notion of varying procedures for different teaching situations when their book *Models of Teaching* was published in 1972. At that time the idea was new and perhaps even controversial. Since then, however, the view that teachers should be able to use different instructional strategies to meet different objectives has become so widely accepted that it's no longer an issue. The acceptance of this view is reflected in both the INTASC principles: "The teacher understands and uses a variety of instructional strategies to encourage students' development of critical thinking, problem solving, and performance skills," (Interstate New Teacher Assessment and Support Consortium, 1992, p. 20) and the NBPTS proposition: "Accomplished teachers command a range of generic instructional techniques, know when each is appropriate and can implement them as needed" (National Board for Professional Teaching Standards, 2004, p. 3). In addition, a comprehensive review of this topic concluded, "More effective teachers use more effective instructional strategies. . . . Effective teachers have more instructional strategies at their disposal" (Marzano, 2003, p. 78). Although having a repertoire of teaching strategies is essential for effective teaching, knowing when to use the different strategies is also important. Although a number of factors influence the choice of strategy, three are at the heart of the decision-making process:

- The teacher
- The students
- The content

Let's look at them.

Selecting Teaching Strategies: The Role of the Teacher

Teachers, themselves, are one of the most important factors influencing the question of how to teach. Directing student learning at any level is a personal enterprise. How we teach depends to a large extent on who we are (Kagan, 1992). The learning objectives that we select, the strategies that we use to reach the objectives, and the way that we relate to students all depend on what we bring to the classroom as human beings.

Attempts to identify an ideal teacher type have proved fruitless. Hundreds of research studies investigating different types of teachers have indicated that there is no one kind of effective teacher. Energetic, thoughtful, humorous, serious, traditional, and unorthodox teachers have all proven effective in different situations. Much of teachers' effectiveness lies in understanding their own strengths and preferences and adopting compatible teaching strategies.

You personally will find some of teaching models discussed in this book effective, whereas a colleague might feel just the opposite. You will also feel more comfortable with some than with others. Having a repertoire of strategies and models to choose from gives you the flexibility to select those most compatible with your personality and teaching style.

Selecting Teaching Strategies: The Impact of Learners

Students are a second factor influencing the choice of teaching strategies. They differ in academic ability, background experience, personality, and motivation. Some are outgoing; others are shy. Some are confident and others are uncertain. In addition, students' cultures, including the values, attitudes, and traditions of a particular group can also have an important influence on learning (Banks, 2001, 2002).

Because of these differences, individual students respond differently to various teaching strategies (Marzano, 2003). This effect has been called by some researchers an "aptitude-treatment interaction," with aptitude reflecting what students bring to a learning situation, and treatment describing our attempts to accommodate these differences (Schunk, 2004). In some instances, practices found effective with one type of student are ineffective with others (Brophy & Good, 1986).

Selecting Teaching Strategies: Content and Learning Objectives

The topic being taught is a third factor influencing the choice of teaching strategy. For example, a social studies teacher may want the class to remember basic facts concerning the American Revolution in one lesson, to understand the assimilation problems encountered by immigrants to a country in another, and to analyze the strengths of a democracy compared to a more authoritarian society in a third. Though these tasks all involve American history, the learning objectives for each are different. The teacher is trying to teach factual information to one class, have the students understand the process of assimilation in the second, and develop analytical skills in the third. Because the objectives are different, the strategies needed to reach the objectives are also different; we don't, for example, teach factual information in the same way that we teach analytical skills.

Teachers' objectives vary even within a class period. In a single lesson, for example, a literature teacher discussing "The Raven" might want students to remember the poem's author; to relate the poem to the author's life; and to learn the concepts of *meter, rhyme,* and *imagery.* These objectives are different and each requires a different teaching strategy.

Similar situations exist in elementary schools. In teaching reading, for instance, the teacher will want students to be able to correctly pronounce words, identify the major theme of a story, explain cause-and-effect relationships, and predict the consequences of certain events in the story. Again, the teacher's objectives are different for each situation. Trying to reach each in the same way is both ineffective and impossible.

A Models Approach to Teaching

In this chapter we've used both the terms *strategies* and *models.* They are closely related, but not identical. Let's look at this relationship.

Strategies and Models

Strategies are *general approaches to instruction that apply in a variety of content areas and are used to meet a range of learning objectives.* For example, questioning, organizing lessons, providing feedback, and ending lessons with review and closure are strategies. These strategies are general and apply across instructional settings; regardless of the grade level, content area, or topic, teachers use questioning, for example, to help students reach learning objectives. (We examine general strategies in detail in Chapter 3.)

By comparison, **models** are *specific approaches to instruction that have four characteristics:*

- They are designed to help students acquire deep understanding of specific forms of content and to develop their critical-thinking abilities.
- They include a series of specific steps that are intended to help students reach the objectives.
- They are grounded in learning theory.
- They are supported by motivation theory.

The relationships among these characteristics are illustrated in Figure 1.1.

General strategies are incorporated within each of the models. For instance, questioning is essential for the success of all the models in this book, as is careful lesson organization, feedback, and other strategies.

To examine teaching models more closely, we can compare the role of a teacher using a model to that of an engineer. In considering a project, an engineer first identifies the type of structure to be built, for example, a building, a bridge, or a road. Having selected a project, an appropriate design or blueprint is chosen. The specifications of the blueprint deter-

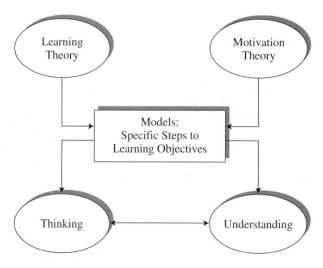

FIGURE 1.1   The Characteristics of Teaching Models

mine the actions the engineer will take and the kind of building that will result. Similarly, teachers considering a model first identify what is to be learned and then select a model to reach that learning objective. The model then determines, in part, the actions of the teacher.

Using this analogy, a teaching model, then, is a type of blueprint for teaching. Just as a blueprint provides structure and direction for the engineer, the model provides structure and direction for the teacher. However, a blueprint does not dictate all of the actions of an engineer, and a model cannot dictate all of the actions taken by a teacher. A blueprint is not a substitute for basic engineering skills, and a teaching model is not a substitute for basic teaching skills. It cannot take the place of qualities good teachers must have, such as sensitivity to students and the different types of knowledge we discussed earlier in the chapter. It is, instead, a tool designed to help teachers make their instruction systematic and efficient. Models provide enough flexibility to allow teachers to use their own creativity, just as engineers use creativity in the act of construction. As with a blueprint, a teaching model is a design for teaching within which teachers use all of the skills and insights at their command.

The number of possible learning objectives is so large and diverse that it is impossible to discuss them all in depth in one book. Each of the models discussed in this text is based on cognitive learning theory, and they are designed to reach cognitive objectives. (We discuss cognitive learning theory in Chapter 2.) Let's examine this cognitive dimension of learning.

Cognitive Learning Objectives

To begin this section, let's review Shirley's objectives. She wanted her students to:

- Know what equivalent fractions are
- Be able to find equivalent fractions
- Add fractions with unlike denominators

Each objective is in the **cognitive domain,** which focuses on *objectives that address the development of the student's intellect and understanding.* However, meeting each of the objectives requires different forms of knowledge and different cognitive processes.

In response to these differences researchers have developed a system to classify different objectives (Anderson & Krathwohl, 2001). A revision of the famous "Bloom's Taxonomy" first published in 1956 (Bloom, Englehart, Furst, Hill, & Krathwohl, 1956), the system is a matrix with twenty-four cells that represent the intersection of four types of knowledge with six cognitive processes. The revision reflects the dramatic increase in understanding of learning and teaching since the middle of the twentieth century, when the original taxonomy was created, and it now more nearly reflects the influence of cognitive learning theory on education (Anderson & Krathwohl, 2001). The revised taxonomy appears in Table 1.3.

Now, let's look at Shirley's objectives again and see how they relate to the taxonomy. Knowing what equivalent fractions are, for instance, simply requires that students are able to remember factual knowledge, so it would be classified into the cell where the *factual knowledge* intersects with the cognitive process *remember.* By comparison, being able to find equivalent fractions would be classified into the cell where *conceptual knowledge*

TABLE 1.3 A Taxonomy for Learning, Teaching, and Assessing

The Knowledge Dimension	The Cognitive Process Dimension					
	1. Remember	*2. Understand*	*3. Apply*	*4. Analyze*	*5. Evaluate*	*6. Create*
A. Factual knowledge						
B. Conceptual knowledge						
C. Procedural knowledge						
D. Metacognitive knowledge						

intersects with the cognitive process *apply* because equivalent fractions is a concept, and students have to *apply* understanding in order to find them. And her third objective would be classified into the cell where *procedural knowledge* intersects with *analyze* because adding fractions requires a procedure, and students must analyze problems to determine whether they can add the fractions directly or whether they must use equivalent fractions.

The taxonomy reminds us that learning is a complex process with many possible outcomes. It also reminds us that we want our students to do much more than remember factual knowledge. Unfortunately, a great deal of schooling focuses as much on this—most basic—cell as it does on the other twenty-three combined. Moving to the other forms of knowledge and more advanced cognitive processes is even more important in the twenty-first century as student thinking, decision making, and problem solving are increasingly emphasized. These advanced cognitive processes are also involved in the development of critical thinking, which is an essential feature of developing deep understanding of the topics students study. (We discuss critical thinking in more detail in Chapter 3.)

Although most of the focus in schools is on cognitive outcomes, teachers have many implicit objectives that don't fit that domain. For example, in her conversation with Jim, Shirley said, "And they're going to get over their fear of math." This is an objective in the **affective domain,** which *focuses on attitudes and values and the development of students' personal and emotional growth.* Also although they are not so apparent in Shirley's case, teachers sometimes have **psychomotor objectives,** which include *acquisition of manipulative and movement skills,* such as learning to write on a computer or to skip rope.

Each domain is important. Although Shirley focused explicitly on cognitive objectives, she was always aware of her students' self-concepts and their personal and emotional development. The ability to work with peers and the willingness to listen to other people's ideas, for example, falls within the affective domain. And Shirley's students needed to be able to use rulers, protractors, and compasses to create accurate drawings for topics she would teach later in the year. These are psychomotor skills.

The three domains are interdependent. For instance, although we focus on cognitive objectives in this book, we also emphasize the importance of a classroom environment in which students feel safe to respond to questions and describe their thinking without fear of embarrassment or criticism. The focus is never on one domain to the total exclusion of the other two. We examine all of these topics in more detail as we discuss the specific models throughout the book.

Summary

Teacher Knowledge and Developing as a Teacher

With increased emphasis on standards, high-stakes tests, and accountability, the need for teachers who are knowledgeable professionals has never been greater. Expert teachers thoroughly understand the topics they teach, know how to represent the topics in ways that are understandable to students, are able to organize classrooms and guide instruction, and understand how students learn.

Professional organizations, such as the *Interstate New Teacher Assessment and Support Consortium* and the *National Board for Professional Teaching Standards,* have recognized the need for knowledgeable professionals and have described the knowledge teachers need in their principles and core propositions.

Research and the Teacher's Role in Learning

Teachers are the single most important educational influence on student learning. Effective teachers promote learning to a much greater extent than do those who are less effective. They understand the research on effective teaching and are able to apply it in the classroom.

The Need for Instructional Alternatives

Research consistently demonstrates that there is no one best way to teach. Teachers themselves, the type of learners, and the topics being taught all influence the strategy that will be most effective in producing learning in a particular classroom.

A Models Approach to Teaching

Because learning objectives differ, the teaching strategies that we use to reach those objectives also must differ. A teaching model is a specific teaching strategy that is grounded in learning and motivation theory and is designed to help students reach specific learning objectives. It prescribes the general actions that help students learn, but it doesn't dictate a teacher's every move. A model is a general guide for instruction, but it doesn't replace the skill and professional judgment of an expert teacher.

The models presented in this text are designed to help students reach objectives in the cognitive domain, which focuses on thinking, problem solving and intellectual development. Attitudes and values—objectives in the affective domain—are important, however, as are those in the psychomotor domain, which deals with physical abilities. The three domains are interdependent, and a focus on the cognitive domain doesn't mean that the others should be ignored.

IMPORTANT CONCEPTS

Affective domain (p. 20)
Cognitive domain (p. 19)
General pedagogical knowledge
  (p. 9)

Models (p. 18)
Pedagogical content knowledge
  (p. 8)
Psychomotor objectives (p. 20)

Standards (p. 6)
Strategies (p. 18)
Teacher-effectiveness research
  (p. 14)

DISCUSSION QUESTIONS

1. Describe a class in which you've been. Give at least one example of each of the types of knowledge discussed in the chapter that your instructor displayed in teaching the class.

2. One criticism of effectiveness research is that teaching effectiveness was defined in terms of student performance on standardized achievement tests. What other important school outcomes might be missed or ignored by these tests?

3. Choose two different content areas of the curriculum (e.g., science versus language arts). Discuss how the content in each area might influence the choice of teaching method.

4. Briefly describe your own personal goals for teaching, and discuss how these might influence your choice of teaching methods.

5. How does the age or ability of a student influence the selection of a teaching strategy? Imagine that you are responsible for teaching the same basic content to three different classes ranging from remedial to accelerated. How would your teaching methods differ?

6. Identify an objective for the class in which you are now. Classify the objective into one of the cells of the taxonomy table discussed in the chapter.

2

Learning, Motivation, and Models of Teaching

In Chapter 1 we said that understanding learners and learning is one of the four types of knowledge that expert teachers possess. This makes sense. Understanding the way students learn and what motivates them is essential for designing instruction that maximizes student achievement. The key to effective teaching is understanding how our actions as teachers influence student learning. In this chapter we examine learning and motivation and the implications they have for designing and implementing effective instruction. When you have completed your study of this chapter, you should be able to:

- Describe the principles of cognitive motivation theory.
- Identify the characteristics of our cognitive architecture.
- Discuss the relationship between learning and motivation.
- Identify the factors that influence students' motivation to learn.

To begin our discussion, let's look at a teacher working with his students on the concepts *force* and *work*.

Javier Lopez's students are struggling to understand the concept *work,* which is movement resulting from a *force* (any push or pull). They struggle because the scientific definition of work differs from the one most people use in their everyday lives. Javier first defines *force* and gives several examples of pushes and pulls, such as pushing on the board, pulling on the door knob, and having the students turn toward each other and press their hands together.

Javier also defines the concept *work,* and, as examples, has Eduardo pull Melissa's chair with Melissa in it across the front of the room, and has each member of the class push a book across a desk. He notes that Eduardo is exerting a force on Melissa's chair and that the chair and Melissa are moving, so Eduardo is doing work. He also explains that they are all doing work when they exert a force on the books and the books move.

"You sure like science don't you, Mr. Lopez," Melissa says, as she moves her chair back into place.

"Yes I do," Javier smiles. "It's interesting and helps us understand our world."

Javier then holds up a chair in front of the class, and, standing still holding the chair, asks, "Am I doing any work?"

"Yes," Anya says assertively.

"Explain why you think I'm doing work," Javier responds.

"You'll get tired if you keep doing that."

"Is anything moving?"

"No," Anya responds.

"Am I doing any work?" Javier asks again.

"Yes," Anya repeats. "My mom was holding something for my dad, and she said, 'Please hurry, this is hard work.'"

Javier then puts the chair back down on the floor and slowly lifts it up, so the students can see it moving.

"What am I doing now? . . . Disideria?" he asks.

"Lifting the chair."

"Am I doing any work? . . . Tamika?"

"Yes."

"Explain how you know."

"You're pulling on the chair, . . . which is a force, and it moved . . . up."

"Now, am I doing any work?" Javier asks as he holds the chair but does not move. ". . . Devon?"

"No."

"Why not?"

"The chair isn't moving."

"So, . . . can I get tired without doing any work? . . . Anya?"

"I . . . guess so."

Javier then has Damien stand up and they grasp hands as if they are in a tug-of-war. He has Damien pull but doesn't allow any movement.

"Is either of us doing any work? . . . Anya?"

". . . No," she responds hesitantly.

"How do you know?"

". . . Neither . . . one . . . moved."

"Good thinking, Anya. . . . So, now everyone, I want you each to describe in writing three examples of doing work in your everyday life, and three more examples where a force is involved, but no work is being done. Go ahead now. You have about ten minutes. We'll discuss them when you're done. You should be able to finish in that time."

Learning: The Evolution from Behaviorist to Cognitive Views

In Chapter 1 we said that each of the models in this text is grounded in cognitive learning theory. What does this mean? What are the differences between cognitive views of learning and other perspectives? We begin the chapter by answering these questions.

The first half of the twentieth century was dominated by a view of learning that focused on specific, observable behaviors and the factors that influenced those behaviors, which is where the term *behaviorism* originated. According to behaviorism, **learning** is a *change in observable behavior that occurs as the result of experience.* According to behaviorism, learning has occurred, for example, when students consistently give specific, observable, desired responses to questions. The way they learn to give these responses is determined by reinforcement and punishment. (Being reinforced or punished is the *experience* that changes the behavior.) For example, if a teacher asks, "How do you spell *Tennessee?*" and the student responds "T-e-n-n-e-s-s-e-e," the teacher smiles and says, "Right!" Spelling *Tennessee* is a specific behavior, the teacher can observe (hear) the correct spelling, and the teacher's smile and comment reinforce the student. Consequently, the response is strengthened, and learning from a behavioral perspective has occurred.

However, if the student responds, "T-e-n-e-s-s-e-e," the teacher corrects the student saying, "Not quite" or "You'd better check your list." Saying, "Not quite," or "You'd better check your list," are punishers because comments such as these decrease the likelihood that the student will give the same response in the future.

The goal of instruction, according to behaviorism, is to increase the number, or strength, of correct student responses. The amount of learning is measured by observing changes in behavior, such as seeing that a student correctly spells twelve of twenty words on a list on Monday but correctly spells sixteen on Friday.

When using behaviorism as a guide for planning and conducting instruction, the teacher designs learning activities that require students to produce specific, observable responses to questions and exercises. Then, during these learning activities, the teacher's job is to reinforce desired responses, as we saw in the correct spelling of *Tennessee.*

However, behaviorism is unable to explain a variety of things that occur in classrooms, as well as everyday life. For instance, it can't explain why Anya continued to believe that Javier was doing work when he held the chair without moving, in spite of the fact that she wasn't reinforced for that belief. She developed it on her own, based on previous experiences. Behaviorism also cannot adequately explain how students learn language (Chomsky, 1959), nor can it explain how students reach some important school goals, such as critical thinking and problem solving.

These problems, or inadequacies with behaviorism, resulted in the "cognitive revolution" which marked a shift away from behaviorism and toward cognitive views of learning. It occurred some time between the mid-1950s and early 1970s (Bruning, Schraw, Norby, & Ronning, 2004), and it's influence on education has steadily increased since that time (Greeno, Collins, & Resnick, 1996; Mayer, 2002). Let's look at some principles of cognitive learning theory.

Principles of Cognitive Learning Theory

In contrast with behaviorism, **learning,** according to cognitive learning theory, is a *change in an individual's mental structures and processes that may or may not result in an immediate change in behavior.* Cognitive learning theory can help explain tasks as simple as remembering a phone number or as complex as solving ill-defined problems. Cognitive learning theories are grounded in six basic principles:

- Learning and development depend on learners' experiences.
- Learners construct understanding in an effort to make sense of experiences.
- The understanding learners construct depends on what they already know.
- Constructing understanding is facilitated by social interaction.
- Learners learn to do well what they practice doing.
- Learning experiences that are concrete and connected to the real world result in deeper understanding than those that are more abstract and disconnected.

Let's examine each of these.

Learning Depends on Learners' Experiences

To begin this section, consider the following example.

> You have learned to drive vehicles with automatic transmissions, and you can comfortably drive in a variety of situations. One day a couple who are friends of yours ask you to help them move. They drive a moving truck to the new location, and they ask you to drive their car. It has a stick shift, however, and you struggle with driving it, repeatedly killing the motor. Finally with jerks and lurches you're able to get to your destination.
> After a few trips, though, your driving improves significantly, and by the last trip you are actually quite comfortable with the stick shift.

You initially had experiences driving that were limited to vehicles with automatic transmissions. However, then you added some experience; you were forced to *learn* to drive a vehicle with a stick shift. As a result of this experience and learning, your ability to drive, as well as your understanding of the process, changed; you're now able to comfortably drive vehicles with both automatic and stick shift transmissions. Your experiences allowed you to change not only how you think about driving but also your capability of driving different kinds of cars.

The same is true for all learning. The more experience students have with reading, for example, the better readers they become, and the more experiences they have with solving word problems in math, the better they become at solving word problems. Our roles as teachers are to establish meaningful learning objectives for students and then to provide the experiences the students need to meet the objectives.

Learners Construct Understanding

Look at the following statements. Each was actually made by a student.

- It's warmer in the summer than in the winter because we're closer to the sun in the summer.
- Coats keep us warm by generating heat, like a fire.

- Trousers is an uncommon noun because it is singular at the top and plural at the bottom.
- A triangle that has an angle of 135 degrees is called an obscene triangle.
- Most houses in France are made of plaster of Paris.

Information learners receive from their teachers, what they read, and what they encounter on the Internet are experiences. However, learners don't behave like tape recorders, recording in their memories—in the form in which it is presented—what teachers tell them or what they read. Instead, they interpret new information in a way that makes sense to them (Greeno, Collins, & Resnick, 1996; Mayer, 2002). This helps us understand how students acquire misconceptions and come up with sometimes "off the wall" conclusions. Although they appear silly—and often funny—to us, they make sense to students.

We saw this process illustrated in Javier's lesson. Javier didn't teach Anya the idea that holding up the chair was *work,* and he didn't reinforce her for that conclusion. She constructed the idea on her own. A major task facing teachers is to provide experiences to students that allow them to construct correct and meaningful ideas about the world. A related task is to help students correct the misconceptions that they bring with them to the classroom.

Constructing Understanding Depends on What Students Know

In their attempts to understand how the world works, learners interpret new experiences based on what they already know—their background knowledge. For instance, Anya defended her conclusion that Javier was doing work as he held the chair by saying, "My mom was holding something for my dad, and she said, 'Please hurry, this is hard work.' " This was part of the background experiences she used as a basis for constructing her understanding of the concept. Only when she was provided with additional experiences, did she change her mind, and reluctantly at that. Similarly, as people move their hands close to a hot stove burner or move closer to a fireplace, it feels warmer, so concluding that we're closer to the sun in summer is very sensible.

In a similar way, we've all had the experience of becoming warmer after we put on a coat or jacket. A natural misconception that many students have is that the coat actually generates heat, rather than simply capturing or insulating it.

The tendency of people to connect new information with what they already know or believe in an attempt to make sense of the world has important implications for teaching and learning. First, if we are to build on or change students' ideas, we need to know what these ideas are. Second, rather than teaching items of information in isolation, students should learn them as they relate to other ideas. For example, Javier connected the concept *work* to the concept *force,* and his end-of-class assignment was an attempt to further relate the ideas to events in the real world. Hopefully, the end result will be a coherent system of interconnected ideas that not only are accurate but also make sense to students. A simple illustration of these relationships is illustrated in Figure 2.1.

Similarly, though we primarily focus on cognitive learning in this chapter and the next, we include a brief discussion of behaviorism in an attempt to provide context for cognitive learning theory (i.e., to relate the two to each other). This attempt to organize information and link items to each other is important for all learning.

FIGURE 2.1   Relationships between Force, Work, and Movement

Constructing Understanding Is Facilitated by Social Interaction

Although individuals construct their own understandings, the process is enhanced by social interaction. In fact, social interaction is so important that valid knowledge construction often won't occur without it. To illustrate this point, let's look again at some dialogue from Javier's lesson.

> **JAVIER:** Am I doing any work?
>
> **ANYA:** Yes . . . My mom was holding something for my dad, and she said, "Please hurry, this is hard work."
>
> **JAVIER:** What am I doing now? . . . Disideria? (as he slowly lifts a chair)
>
> **DISIDERIA:** Lifting the chair.
>
> **JAVIER:** Am I doing any work? . . . Tamika?
>
> **TAMIKA:** Yes.
>
> **JAVIER:** Explain how you know.
>
> **TAMIKA:** You're pulling on the chair, . . . which is a force, and it moved . . . up.
>
> **JAVIER:** Now, am I doing any work? (as he holds the chair) . . . Devon?
>
> **DEVON:** No.
>
> **JAVIER:** Why not?
>
> **DEVON:** The chair isn't moving.
>
> **JAVIER:** So, . . . can I get tired without doing any work? . . . Anya?
>
> **ANYA:** I . . . guess so.
>
> **JAVIER:** Is either of us doing any work? (as he grasps hands with Damien in a tug-of-war, but neither moves)
>
> **ANYA:** No. (hesitantly)
>
> **JAVIER:** How do you know?
>
> **ANYA:** . . . Neither . . . one . . . moved.

Without this discussion, it is unlikely that Anya's thinking about work would have changed. Social interaction allows teachers to get into students' heads to find out what they are thinking. It also provides opportunities for students to experience other perspectives, so they can calibrate their ideas against others'. Teacher explanations, combined with concrete examples, are powerful ways to help students construct and reconstruct their ideas (Eggen & Kauchak, 2004).

Learning Requires Practice

Earlier we said that learning depends on the experiences students have. In order to thoroughly understand complex tasks, however, learners must systematically practice those tasks. It is analogous to young boys and girls learning to play basketball. They don't learn to play simply by "experiencing" basketball. They must systematically practice dribbling, shooting, and passing, and ultimately put those skills together on the court in competition.

Similarly, to learn to read with comprehension, learners must develop reading skills and practice comprehension techniques in order to become skilled readers. The same is true for any academic area. This cognitive principle reminds us that our jobs as teachers are not done when we first introduce an idea to students. We need to provide extensive practice to allow ideas to solidify and connect. Javier did this when he asked his students to think about additional examples of work and force from their own lives.

Concrete and Real-World Tasks Result in Optimal Learning

We know that learners benefit from experiences, and these experiences form the building blocks or raw materials for constructing understanding. But what kind of experiences do students need to effectively construct understanding? To answer this question, let's think again about the way Javier ended his lesson. Not only did his assignment provide practice for his students but it also put the concepts in the context of concrete, real-world events. Research indicates that in-school learning is most effective when students are able to link the topic or the kind of thinking required to the real world (Putnam & Borko, 2000). Following are some classroom examples:

- A math teacher relates the concepts of area and perimeter to the school playground and the classroom, asking students to describe how the two ideas are similar and different.
- To teach the concepts *adjective* and *adverb,* a language arts teacher presents students with a written passage about their school in which she has embedded a number of examples of each concept.
- A science teacher links the concept of *symmetry* to the bilateral symmetry of our bodies and discusses the advantages animals with bilateral symmetry have over those with radial symmetry or no symmetry.
- A history teacher describes the loyalty the students have to their school and neighborhood, the slang they use, and the out-of-school activities they enjoy as an analogy to the developing nationalism prior to World War I.

In each case the teacher was attempting to make an abstract topic more concrete by linking it to the real world with examples or analogies. Attempts such as these make information meaningful for students regardless of the grade level or topic being taught.

Our Cognitive Architecture

In the previous section we saw that learning and development depend on learners' experiences, and people construct understanding in an attempt to make sense of those experiences. But how does the process of constructing understanding occur, and how is understanding stored so it can be retrieved and linked to new experiences?

Experts in the field of cognitive psychology describe learning in terms of a model similar to the one presented in Figure 2.2 (Eggen & Kauchak, 2004; Mayer, 1998). This model describes how experience and information are processed and stored using the computer as an analogy. We can think of the various components of the model as our "cognitive architecture" (Sweller, van Merrienboer, & Paas, 1998). Just as the architecture of a building is the structure in which its activities occur, our information processing system is the framework within which information is acquired, moved, and stored. The model has three major components:

- Information stores
- Cognitive processes
- Metacognition

Information stores are *repositories that hold information,* analogous to a computer's main memory and hard drive. The information stores in the model are *sensory memory, working memory,* and *long-term memory.*

Cognitive processes—*intellectual actions that transform information and move it from one store to another*—include *attention, perception, encoding,* and *retrieval.* They're analogous to the programs that process information in computers.

Metacognition, the third component of the model, is *people's awareness of and control over their cognitive processes* (Hiebert & Raphael, 1996). Metacognition is the mechanism we use to monitor our learning.

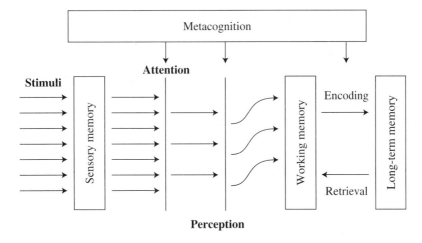

FIGURE 2.2   A Cognitive Model of Learning

Let's look at these components in more detail.

Information Stores

Information stores hold experiences sequentially and for different lengths of time, and include sensory memory, working memory, and long-term memory.

Sensory Memory.   From Figure 2.2 we see that stimuli from the environment enter **sensory memory,** *the part of our cognitive system that briefly holds information until we attend to it* (Mayer, 1998). For instance, when we read, we briefly retain the words at the beginning of a sentence in sensory memory until we have read the entire sentence. If we didn't, we wouldn't be able to understand the sentence, because the words at the beginning would have been lost before we could make sense of it.

Working Memory.   **Working memory,** historically called *short-term* memory, is *the conscious, "thinking" part of our cognitive learning system.* It is the workbench where information is organized and where understanding is constructed.

The most significant characteristic of working memory is its limitations (Sweller, van Merrienboer, & Paas, 1998), and some researchers suggest that the limitations of working memory are the most important feature of our entire cognitive architecture (Bruer, 1993). It can hold only about seven items of information at a time (Miller, 1956) and does so for a relatively short period (about 10 to 20 seconds for adults), particularly when new information is being received (Greene, 1992). Selecting, organizing, and otherwise processing information also take up working memory space, so the number of items that can be dealt with is much less than the seven that can be passively held. "Humans are probably only able to deal with two or three items of information simultaneously when required to process rather than merely hold information" (Sweller, van Merrienboer, & Paas, 1998, p. 252).

The limited capacity of working memory has important implications for teaching and learning. For example:

- Learners' writing often improves more rapidly if they are initially allowed to ignore handwriting quality, grammar, and spelling (Graham, Berninger, Weintraub, & Schafer, 1998; McCutchen, 2000).
- Students write better-quality essays using word processors if their word processing skills are well developed. If not, handwritten essays are superior (Roblyer, 2003a).
- In spite of research about its ineffectiveness and enormous staff development efforts to promote more sophisticated and effective forms of instruction, lecture persists as the most common teaching strategy (Cuban, 1984).

The limitations of working memory can be used to explain each case. In the first, for example, focusing on handwriting, grammar, and spelling occupies so much working memory space that little is left for the construction of quality products. In the second, students lacking word processing skills use too much of their working memory capacity on the mechanics of word processing, leaving too little to compose high-quality essays. And, in the third, sophisticated strategies, such as guided discovery, place a heavy load on teachers' working memories. Monitoring student understanding and behavior, keeping learning objectives in mind, and questioning students all occur simultaneously. For many teachers, this working memory load is too great, so they reduce it by reverting to lecture, a much simpler strategy.

The limitations of working memory also help us understand why lecturing can be so ineffective. When teachers lecture, they can easily overload students' working memories, and important information is often lost before it is processed into long-term memory. In contrast, interactive questioning prevents the lesson from being paced so rapidly that students' working memories are overloaded, that is, the teacher can move only at a pace that allows students to answer the questions.

Overcoming the Limitations of Working Memory: Schemas.   The fact that working memory has limited capacity is another reason for learning information in complex networks instead of isolated pieces because "although the number of elements is limited, the size, complexity, and sophistication of elements [are] not" (Sweller, van Merrienboer, & Paas, 1998, p. 256). In other words, each interconnected relationship is recorded in memory as one item of information. As an example, look again at Figure 2.1. There we see that the five individual items—push, pull, force, work, and movement—are all interconnected, so instead of occupying five bits of working memory, it occupies one.

These five items organized into a unit can be described as a schema. **Schemas** are *interrelated networks of information constructed in working memory and recorded in long-term memory.* Schemas represent the way our understanding is organized and stored in memory. The more connections among the individual items of information that make up our understanding, the more meaningful it is. We discuss schemas in more detail in Chapter 7.

Overcoming the Limitations of Working Memory: Automaticity.   **Automaticity** *results from overlearning a skill to the point that it can be performed with little conscious effort,* and it is important because it reduces the demand on our limited working memories. As an example, consider again the research result we cited earlier that students write better-quality essays using word processors but only if their word processing skills are well developed. If word processing has been developed to the point of automaticity, using these skills don't take up working memory space, so all of working memory can be devoted to constructing the essay. If the skills are not automatic, they occupy too much working memory space, and the quality of the essays is decreased. Similarly, if teachers are to use sophisticated forms of instruction, such as the models described in this book, their basic teaching skills, such as classroom organization, questioning, and clear communication, must be automatic, or they will take up too much working memory space, leaving too little space to execute the model.

Long-Term Memory.   After understanding is constructed and organized in working memory, it is recorded in **long-term memory,** which is *our permanent information store.* It's like a library with millions of entries and a network that allows them to be retrieved for reference and use. It differs from working memory in both capacity and duration. Whereas working memory is limited to approximately seven items of information for a matter of seconds, long-term memory's capacity is vast and durable. Some experts suggest that information in it remains for a lifetime (Schunk, 2004). How information is stored in long-term memory determines whether we'll be able to find it when we need it (retrieval) as well as our ability to apply it to different situations (transfer).

Cognitive Processes

Cognitive processes are the intellectual actions that move information from one information store to another. They include *attention, perception, encoding,* and *retrieval.*

Attention. Consider the room you're in right now. A variety of stimuli exists—pictures, furniture, other people moving and talking, the whisper of an air conditioner—even though you may not be aware of some of them. Others, however, attract your **attention,** which is *the process of consciously focusing on a stimulus.* Attention is where learning begins; all subsequent learning depends on the extent to which learners pay attention to appropriate stimuli and ignore distractions.

Because attention is the beginning point of learning, attracting and maintaining student attention are crucial. Effective teachers plan their lessons so students attend to what is being taught and ignore other irrelevant stimuli. If the science teacher introducing bilateral symmetry has a student stand on a box and hold his or her arms out to illustrate the concept, even the most disinterested student is likely to pay attention. Similarly, if students are actively involved in learning activities, they're much more likely to be attentive than if they're passively listening to lectures (Blumenfeld, 1992). This is the reason high levels of student involvement are so much a part of all the models discussed in this book.

Perception. Look at the two horizontal lines in the accompanying diagram. Which is longer? Does the top line appear longer? To most people, at first glance, it does. (The lines are actually the same length.) This classic example illustrates the nature of **perception,**

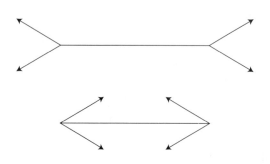

which is *the process people use to attach meaning to stimuli.* The "meaning," that is, the perception, most people have is that the top line is longer than the bottom one. Accurate perceptions in classroom learning are crucial. Students' perceptions of what they see or hear are what enter working memory, and if these perceptions aren't accurate, the information that is ultimately stored in long-term memory also will be inaccurate.

One way to determine whether students are accurately perceiving the information we display is to actively engage them in questioning. Again, this is why interaction is so important in teaching and learning, and why lecture is generally ineffective.

Encoding. **Encoding** is *the process of representing information in long-term memory* (Bruning, Schraw, Norby, & Ronning, 2004). The accuracy of this encoding process is crucial because what gets encoded will become what is remembered. For instance, Anya had originally represented the concept *work* in her long-term memory as anything that makes us tired. Only with considerable effort and discussion did she reconstruct the concept to include both effort (force) and movement. Then, it was reencoded accurately.

When encoding information, our goal should be to make it as meaningful as possible. **Meaningfulness** describes *the number of connections or links between an idea and other ideas in long-term memory* (Gagne, Yekovich, & Yekovich, 1993). We increase the meaningfulness of the ideas we teach by helping students connect them to other concepts. When the concept *work* was linked to pushes, pulls, and movement, as we saw in Figure 2.1, it was more meaningful than it was as an isolated idea. This is the case with all learning, and this is why we emphasize that relationships among ideas should be taught instead of teaching items of information in isolation.

Retrieval.   **Retrieval** is *the process of pulling information from long-term memory back into working memory,* and the key to retrieval is the extent to which the information is meaningfully encoded. For instance, if a student is attempting to remember the names of the Great Lakes and has them linked to the acronym HOMES (Huron, Ontario, Michigan, Erie, Superior), remembering them is much easier than attempting to remember them by themselves. The same is true for all retrieval, so the key is to help students meaningfully encode it in the first place.

Metacognition

Have you ever said to yourself, "I'm going to sit near the front of the class, so I won't fall asleep," or "I'm beat; I'd better drink a cup of coffee before I go to class"? If you have, you are being metacognitive. Earlier we said that metacognition is awareness of, and control over, your cognitive processes. You are aware of your attention (a cognitive process), and you exercise control over it by moving to the front of the class or drinking a cup of coffee.

Research indicates that students who are aware of the way they study and learn, and take conscious steps to maximize their learning, learn more than those who are more passive about their study (Bruning, Schraw, Norby, & Ronning, 2004). One of our goals in teaching is to both model metacognition and to encourage students to be metacognitive in their studies. The result will be more learning for all students.

Motivation and Learning

In the previous section we examined principles of cognitive learning theory and examined the architecture of our cognitive structures. For effective learning to occur, students must be motivated. It's very difficult to promote learning in students who don't care about learning in general or the topics taught. In fact, some researchers argue that learning and motivation are so interdependent that a person can't fully understand learning without considering motivation (Pintrich, Marx, & Boyle, 1993). This is why we examine motivation in this section of the chapter.

Motivation is *a force that energizes, sustains, and directs behavior toward a goal* (Pintrich & Schunk, 2002), and researchers have found a high correlation between motivation and achievement (McDermott, Mordell, & Stoltzfus, 2001; Weinstein, 1998). "Children's motivation to learn lies at the very core of achieving success in schooling. Given rapid technological advances, an ever-changing knowledge base, and shifting workplace needs, a continuing motivation to learn may well be the hallmark of individual accomplishment across the lifespan" (Weinstein, 1998, p. 81). In general, motivated students:

- Process information in depth and excel in classroom learning experiences
- Persist on difficult tasks and cause fewer management problems
- Have more positive attitudes toward school and describe school as satisfying (Stipek, 1996)

Not surprisingly, motivated students are a primary source of job satisfaction for teachers.

Extrinsic and Intrinsic Motivation

Motivation occurs in two forms. **Extrinsic motivation** refers to *motivation to engage in an activity as a means to an end,* whereas **intrinsic motivation** is *motivation to be involved in an activity for its own sake* (Pintrich & Schunk, 2002). Extrinsically motivated learners study hard for a test because they believe studying will lead to high test scores or teacher compliments, for example; intrinsically motivated learners study because they want to understand the content and view learning as worthwhile in itself. Researchers have determined that learners are intrinsically motivated by activities or experiences that

- *Present a challenge.* Goals are moderately difficult, and success isn't guaranteed (Lepper & Hodell, 1989; Ryan & Deci, 2000; White, 1959).
- *Give the learner control.* Learners believe they have some command or influence over their own learning (Lepper & Hoddell, 1989; Perry, 1998; Ryan & Deci, 2000).
- *Evoke curiosity.* Experiences are novel, surprising, or discrepant with learners' existing ideas (Lepper & Hoddell, 1989).

In addition, some researchers suggest that experiences with aesthetic values—those that evoke emotional reactions and particularly those associated with beauty—may be intrinsically motivating as well (Ryan & Deci, 2000).

Though we think of extrinsic and intrinsic motivation as two ends of a continuum (meaning the higher the extrinsic motivation, the lower the intrinsic motivation and vice versa), they are actually on separate continua (Covington, 2000; Pintrich & Schunk, 2002). For example, students might study hard both because a topic is interesting and because they want good grades. Others might study only to receive the good grades. The first group is high in both extrinsic and intrinsic motivation; the second is high in extrinsic motivation but low in intrinsic motivation.

Motivation to Learn

Although creating intrinsically motivated students who want to learn everything is a laudable goal, it might not be a realistic one.

> In short, intrinsic motivation cannot constitute a sufficient and stable motivational basis for schooling in general or a predesigned curriculum in particular. It . . . encourage[s] an orien-

tation toward activity based on immediate satisfaction rather than on values. Contrary to claims made by some psychologists, intrinsically motivated students will not be consistently motivated. Certain aspects of the curriculum will interest them, while others will not; at times they will study, and at times they will not. Thus students who rely exclusively on intrinsic motivation are likely to neglect a large part of their school work. (Nisan, 1992, p. 129)

Experts suggest that *motivation to learn* is a more meaningful concept. **Motivation to learn** *describes a "student's tendency to find academic activities meaningful and worthwhile and to try and get the intended learning benefits from them"* (Brophy, 1998, p. 162 [italics added]). Students with a motivation-to-learn orientation make an effort to understand topics regardless of whether they find the topics intrinsically interesting or the process of studying them enjoyable. They maintain this effort because they believe the understanding that results is valuable and worthwhile. Our goal as teachers should be to maximize students' motivation to learn, and the models that are discussed in Chapters 4 through 10 are grounded in this perspective.

Three sets of factors influence students' motivation to learn. They are outlined in Figure 2.3 and discussed in the sections that follow.

Teacher Characteristics That Increase Motivation to Learn

Teachers set the emotional tone for the classroom, design and implement learning activities, and assess student learning. Their personal characteristics strongly influence both learning and motivation.

Four teacher characteristics have an especially powerful influence on motivation:

- Personal teaching efficacy
- Modeling and enthusiasm
- Caring
- Positive expectations

Personal Teaching Efficacy.   Let's look back at Javier's lesson. He identified a clear lesson objective, he created examples (e.g., having Eduardo pull Melissa's chair across the

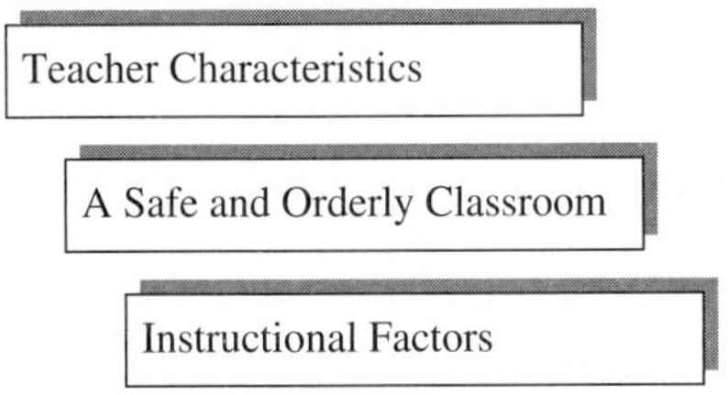

Teacher Characteristics

A Safe and Orderly Classroom

Instructional Factors

FIGURE 2.3   Factors Influencing Students' Motivation to Learn

floor, lifting the chair, and having students push books across their desks) designed to help students understand his topic, and he guided students' involvement throughout the learning activity. He had a positive, proactive orientation, based on the belief that it was his responsibility to ensure that all students learn as much as possible. Javier was high in **personal teaching efficacy,** which is *the belief that teachers can help all students learn, regardless of their backgrounds or abilities* (Bruning, Schraw, Norby, & Ronning, 2004). Teachers high in personal teaching efficacy use their time effectively, accept students and their ideas, use praise rather than criticism, and persevere when students have misconceptions. For example, when Anya persisted with her misconception about the concept *work* Javier didn't give up on her nor did he simply explain the concept an additional time. Rather, he used examples and questioning to guide her to a valid understanding.

In contrast, low-efficacy teachers are less student centered, spend less time on learning activities, "give up" on low achievers, and use criticism more than do high-efficacy teachers. High-efficacy teachers also tend to be more flexible, adopting new curriculum materials and changing strategies more readily than do low-efficacy teachers (Poole, Okeafor, & Sloan, 1989). As we would expect, high-efficacy teachers have students who learn more than the students of low-efficacy teachers.

Modeling and Enthusiasm.   **Modeling** is *the process of imitating behaviors people observe in others* (Bandura, 1986). Student motivation is virtually impossible if teachers model lack of interest or even distaste in the topics they teach. Statements such as the following serve no useful purpose and are devastating for motivation:

> "I know this stuff is boring, but we have to learn it."

> "I know you hate proofs."

> "This isn't my favorite topic either."

In contrast, if teachers display a pattern of statements, such as, "but what's most interesting about all of this is that what we're studying has ramifications for the entire world, even today," motivation and learning increase (Pintrich & Schunk, 2002; Stipek, 2002).

Teachers model enthusiasm by communicating their own genuine interest in the topics they teach (Good & Brophy, 2003). Melissa's comment, "You sure like science don't you, Mr. Lopez," is evidence of Javier's enthusiasm. He didn't give the students a pep talk or go into unnecessary theatrics; he simply demonstrated his own interest in the topic and explained why he thought it was important. A teacher's goal in projecting enthusiasm is to induce in students the feeling that the information is valuable and worth learning not to amuse or entertain them.

Caring.   A growing body of research confirms the importance of learners' relationships with their teachers in both learning and motivation (McCombs, 1998; Stipek, 2002). "Learners' natural motivation to learn can be elicited in safe, trusting, and supportive environments characterized by . . . quality relationships with caring adults that see their unique potential" (McCombs, 1998, p. 399).

Some researchers suggest that caring teachers help meet the need for belonging (Maslow, 1968, 1970), or relatedness, in students (Connell & Wellborn, 1990). **Relatedness** is *the feeling of connectedness to others in one's social environment resulting in feelings of worthiness of love and respect.*

Teachers who are available to students and who like, understand, and empathize with them have learners who are more emotionally, cognitively, and behaviorally engaged in classroom activities than teachers rated lower in these areas (McCombs, 1998; Skinner & Belmont, 1993). Further, students who feel as though they belong and who perceive personal support from their teachers report more interest in their class work and describe it as more important than students whose teachers are more distant (Goodenow, 1993).

The importance of caring is captured in a fourth-grader's comment, "If a teacher doesn't care about you, it affects your mind. You feel like you're a nobody, and it makes you want to drop out of school" (Noblit, Rogers, & McCadden, 1995, p. 683).

How do teachers communicate caring? Although individuals differ, two factors are essential. The first is time. We all have 24 hours a day, and the way we choose to allocate those hours communicates a great deal about our priorities. Willingness to spend time with students, talking about personal problems, helping them with assignments, or calling parents after hours, communicates that students are important enough to teachers that they will allocate some of their 24 hours to helping those individuals. Nothing communicates caring more effectively.

Let's look at a letter a ninth-grade student wrote to her geography teacher as an example from an actual classroom. (The teacher's name has been changed, but the student's note is verbatim.)

> Mrs. Hanson,
>
> I want to thank you for everything you have done for me this year. I think that you're the only teacher I've had who believed in me and gave me the confidence I really needed. In a sense, I went to you when I couldn't turn to my own family and I want to thank you for always having time for me and my problems.
>
> I don't want this letter to sound "cheesy" or "sucking up." It's just that I would have never gotten through the year without you and your advice.
>
> You never treated me just as a student, but as a person, unlike most teachers have and that's what makes a great teacher, and Mrs. Hanson you certainly are a great teacher.
>
> Sincerely,
> Lisa Zahorchak

By sharing their valuable time with students, teachers communicate their care for the students as human beings.

The second dimension of caring is respect, and the best way to demonstrate to students that we respect them is to hold them to high standards.

> One of the best ways to show respect is to hold students to high standards—by not accepting sloppy, thoughtless, or incomplete work, by pressing them to clarify vague comments, by encouraging them to not give up, and by not praising work that does not reflect genuine effort. Ironically, reactions that are often intended to protect students' self-esteem—such as accepting low quality work—convey a lack of interest, patience, or caring. (Stipek, 2002, p. 157)

Respect is a two-way street, however. Teachers should model respect for students, and in turn they have the right to expect students to respect them and each other. "Treat everyone with respect" is a rule that should be enforced in every classroom. Occasional lapses in terms of rudeness can be overlooked, but teachers should clearly communicate that chronic disrespect will not be tolerated.

Positive Teacher Expectations

Mrs. Cummings watched as her new fifth-grade class filed into her room. She noticed a girl named Nicole and recalled that she had had Nicole's brother, Mike, 2 years earlier. Mike had been an above-average student with excellent study habits, and he was a pleasure in class. Their parents were very involved in their children's schoolwork, and the home environment was positive.

Mrs. Cummings didn't know, however, that Nicole had few of her brother's study habits. She was a happy-go-lucky girl interested in socializing, and she was already developing an interest in boys. Schoolwork was not a high priority for her. Mrs. Cummings greeted Nicole with a big smile, told her it was nice to have her in class, and that she was sure that they would have a very good year.

Part way through the grading period, Mrs. Cummings was scoring some math papers and noticed that Nicole's was missing. In checking her book, she found that two other assignments were also missing and that Nicole had been scoring a bit lower on the tests than Mrs. Cummings had anticipated.

The next day she called Nicole to her desk before class, put her arm around her, and said, "Nicole, I can't imagine what happened to your homework papers. Please find them and turn them in. If you get them in by tomorrow, you'll get credit."

To be on the safe side, she called Nicole's parents that evening. They had been unaware of the missing homework and commented that Nicole had been rather vague when they asked if she had any homework for the next day.

Nicole's parents took immediate action. They postponed TV and telephone conversations until they saw that all her homework was finished and correct, and they called Mrs. Cummings, at Mrs. Cummings's request, to check on Nicole's progress. Mrs. Cummings reported that things were much better and that Nicole had improved considerably on the last test (adapted from Kauchak & Eggen, 2003).

Because of her experiences with Nicole's brother, Mrs. Cummings had positive expectations for Nicole and her behavior. She greeted Nicole warmly, and when she found that Nicole was less industrious than Mike had been, she acted immediately. As a result, Nicole's work improved. Mrs. Cummings expected Nicole to learn and took actions that promoted that learning.

Teacher expectations are *inferences that teachers make about the future behavior, academic achievement, or attitudes of their students* (Good & Brophy, 2003). They strongly influence teachers' behaviors, which in turn influence student motivation and achievement.

The effects of expectations on the ways teachers treat students can be grouped into four areas: emotional support, teacher effort and demands, questioning, and feedback and

TABLE 2.1   **Characteristics of Differential Teacher Expectations**

Characteristic	Teacher Behavior Favoring Perceived High Achievers
Emotional support	More interactions; more positive interactions; more eye contact and smiles; stand closer; more direct orientation to student
Teacher effort and demands	Clearer and more thorough explanations; more enthusiastic instruction; require more complete and accurate student answers
Questioning	Call on more often; allow more time to answer; prompt more
Feedback and evaluation	More praise; less criticism; provide more complete and lengthier feedback; more conceptual evaluations

evaluation. They're summarized in Table 2.1 (based on reviews by Good, 1987, and Good & Brophy, 2003; adapted from Eggen & Kauchak, 2004).

We see from Table 2.1 that teachers often treat students they perceive to be high achievers more favorably than those they perceive to be low achievers, and students are sensitive to these differences (Stipek, 2002). In one study, researchers concluded that, "After ten seconds of seeing and/or hearing a teacher, even very young students could detect whether the teacher talked about or to an excellent or a weak student and could determine the extent to which that student was loved by the teacher" (Babad, Bernieri, & Rosenthal, 1991, p. 230).

Expectations tend to be self-fulfilling. "Low expectations can serve as self-fulfilling prophecies. That is, the expression of low expectations by differential treatment can inadvertently lead children to confirm predictions about their abilities by exerting less effort and ultimately performing more poorly" (Weinstein, 1998, p. 83). Students "learn" that they have lower ability or are less worthy if they are rarely called on, left out of discussions, or have brief and superficial interactions with teachers. In contrast, high expectations communicate that the teacher believes students can learn and cares enough to make the effort to promote that learning. Over time, learning and motivation increase.

A Safe and Orderly Classroom

As students spend time in classrooms, they develop a sense about whether the classroom is a nurturing place to learn. **Classroom climate** refers to *teacher and classroom characteristics that promote students' feelings of safety and security, together with a sense of success, challenge, and understanding.*

In classrooms with a healthy climate, students feel safe, and they're treated as competent people. They understand the requirements of learning tasks, perceive them as challenging, and believe they will succeed if they make reasonable efforts (Pintrich & Schunk, 2002; Stipek, 2002).

To illustrate these ideas, let's look back at Javier's lesson. His students felt safe, as indicated both by their willingness to participate in his learning activities and by their lack of concern about how their questions and answers would be received. These feelings of openness and security are the ideal we strive for in all classrooms.

The need for safety and order can be explained in two ways. First, research on effective schools indicates that they are safe places where trust, order, cooperation, and high morale predominate (Marzano, 2003).

Second, an orderly environment is predictable, and students are able to function more effectively when they understand the learning structures and requirements of their classrooms (Connell & Wellborn, 1990).

Teachers set the tone for this essential factor by establishing and consistently enforcing rules that students perceive as fair. In addition, teachers model respect and courtesy and expect respect in return. Students who are criticized for venturing personal or creative thoughts about a topic are unlikely to take the risk a second time. Teachers also develop a sense of classroom community by setting a tone for a classroom environment in which students support each other, and learning is always the paramount goal.

Instructional Factors That Increase Students' Motivation to Learn

In addition to personal characteristics and a positive classroom climate, the ways teachers organize and conduct learning activities also influences students' motivation to learn. These factors include:

- Success
- Challenge
- Concrete and personalized examples
- Involvement in learning activities
- Feedback about learning progress

Let's look at them.

Success. Once a safe and orderly environment is established, positive expectations for success is one of the most important factors that exists in learner motivation (Wigfield & Eccles, 2000). Unfortunately, not all students are successful, but we can increase the likelihood of success for most students in several ways:

- Begin lessons with open-ended questions that assess learners' current understanding and invite success. (We examine open-ended questioning in detail in Chapter 5.)
- Develop lessons with questioning, and prompt students when they have difficulty answering. (We discuss questioning in detail in Chapter 3.)
- Provide practice with teacher support before putting students on their own.
- Conduct ongoing assessments and provide detailed feedback about learning progress.

Success, like most aspects of teaching and learning, isn't as simple as it appears, however. It must also be balanced with *challenge.*

Challenge. A long line of theory and research confirms the need not only for success but also for challenge. We saw earlier that presenting a challenge is one of the characteristics of intrinsically motivating activities (Lepper & Hodell, 1989; Ryan & Deci, 2000), and succeeding on challenging tasks has at least three motivating features. They include:

- Developing perceptions of *competence.* Research suggests that competence is a basic need for people (Ryan & Deci, 2000). Feeling competent is satisfying in itself because it leads to people's feelings that they're able to function effectively in their environments.
- Contributing to feelings of *control* and *autonomy,* additional basic needs for people (Baron, 1998; Kloosterman, 1997). Perceptions of control and autonomy lead people to believe that they can adapt to their environments, or, in some cases, even alter the environment.
- Creating a sense of *equilibrium.* People are in a state of equilibrium when they believe the world is orderly and predictable, and it makes sense to them. The drive for equilibrium, as with competence, control, and autonomy, is innate (Piaget, 1952, 1959).

Succeeding on challenging tasks increases perceptions of competence, control, autonomy, and equilibrium to a much greater extent than succeeding on trivial tasks.

Teachers capitalize on the motivating features of challenge by engaging students in cognitively demanding activities, such as encouraging them to identify relationships in the topics they study and the implications these relationships have for new learning. Limiting discussions to isolated, and often meaningless, facts has the opposite effect. When students complain about the difficulty of their tasks, rather than decreasing the challenge, effective teachers provide instructional support to ensure that students are able to meet it. The models in this book are intended to provide students with both a sense of challenge and the belief that they're able to meet the challenge.

Challenge is closely related to **curiosity motivation,** which is *motivation to understand experiences that can't be immediately explained with existing background knowledge,* such as problems and discrepant events. We saw earlier in the chapter that experiences that evoke curiosity are intrinsically motivating, and some research suggests that the part of the brain associated with reward and pleasure is more highly aroused when satisfying curiosity and meeting challenges than when succeeding on trivial tasks.

Concrete and Personalized Examples. Another way to increase students' intrinsic motivation is through the use of concrete and personalized examples. Concrete examples in general, and particularly concrete examples that are personalized, provide effective links to students' lives and background experiences (Schraw & Lehman, 2001). Let's look at one teacher's attempt to do this.

> Katrina Cardoza, who teaches sixth grade world history at Matthew Gilbert Middle School, begins a discussion of factors leading to World War I by displaying the following vignettes.
>
>> The students at Matthew Gilbert are very loyal to their school. "They don't talk the way we do," they comment when other schools are mentioned. They also say things like, "We go to the same church, and we like to hang out together on the weekends."

"We're Gilbertites," they say. "We don't want to be anybody else, and we don't want anyone telling us what to do."

Students at Mandarin Middle School have some similar thoughts. "I don't like the way they talk at Gilbert," some of them have been overheard saying. "They want to hang around with each other after school, and we want to go to the mall. I don't want anybody from there to tell us what to do.

We're Mandariners, and we want to stay that way."

Katrina used questioning to help the students arrive at the notion that both sets of students were loyal to their own schools, their language, and their school culture. She then used this information as an analogy to help the students understand the concept *nationalism.*

Creative teachers in other content areas also use concrete, personalized examples to improve student motivation.

Chris Emery, a science teacher, began a unit on genetics by saying, "Reanne, what color are your eyes?"

"Blue," Reanne responded.

"And, how about yours, Eddie?"

"Green."

"Interesting," Chris smiled. "When we're done with this unit, we'll be able to figure out why Reanne's are blue and Eddie's are green, and a whole bunch of other things related to the way we are."

Katrina and Chris both attempted to increase their students' interest through **personalization,** *the process of using intellectually and/or emotionally relevant examples to illustrate a topic* (Bruning, Schraw, Norby, & Ronning, 2004). A concept such as *nationalism* is distant from middle schoolers' lives, so it isn't likely to be intrinsically interesting. However, students often feel a strong sense of loyalty to their schools, so Katrina capitalized on this feeling to create an analogy between the school and the way people in Europe felt about their countries prior to World War I. Each of the examples on page 30 also used personalization to make the topics more meaningful for students.

The value of personalization can be explained in two ways. First, as we saw with Katrina's examples, personalized content is meaningful because it encourages students to connect new information to structures in long-term memory that already exist (Moreno & Mayer, 2000). Second, a survey of experienced teachers described personalization as widely applicable and one of the most effective ways to promote student interest in learning activities (Zahorik, 1996).

The use of examples is a major component of most of the models in this book, and we discuss different types of examples in detail in Chapter 5. The importance of examples for both learning and motivation is the reason we use them extensively to illustrate different topics in this text.

Involvement.   We emphasized the importance of involvement in our discussion of cognitive learning theory earlier in the chapter, and it is no less important for motivation. With respect to motivation, although personalization can initially attract student attention and interest, it may not sustain them. Involvement is one key to maintaining motivation.

Think about your own experiences at social situations, such as a lunch or a party. When you're talking and actively listening, you pay more attention to the conversation than you do when you're on its fringes. The same applies in classrooms. Conscious teacher efforts to promote active student involvement result in increased interest and motivation (Blumenfeld, 1992).

The importance of involvement for motivation can be explained in three ways. First, putting students in active roles is one way to personalize instruction, encouraging students to make personal links with content (Schraw & Lehman, 2001). Second, we said earlier that the need for control is innate in people, and involvement, versus passive listening, increases perceptions of competence and control (Bruning, Schraw, Norby, & Ronning, 2004; Ryan & Deci, 2000). Third, as we saw earlier in the chapter, participating actively is essential for meaningful learning because it encourages students to find links in the content they are learning.

All the models in this text strongly emphasize the importance of active student involvement, and provisions for promoting involvement exist within each of the models.

Feedback.   The need for feedback is a learning principle that can be explained with the principles of cognitive learning theory. Because learners construct their own understanding, they need continual feedback to determine the extent to which their ongoing constructions are valid. Feedback also has a motivational component, addressing people's intrinsic need to understand why they perform the way they do (Weiner, 1990, 1994b).

To be motivational, it is essential that feedback improves learning (Clifford, 1990). Feedback that involves social comparisons or focuses on grades rather than learning can actually detract from motivation (Crooks, 1988; Schunk, 1994). Feedback that focuses on grades instead of learning has a particularly detrimental affect on less able students who can end up as losers rather than competent learners. Effective feedback is so fundamental for both learning and motivation that we describe it as "an essential teaching strategy" in Chapter 3.

As you study each of the models in Chapters 5 through 10, you will encounter continual references back to the ideas in this chapter. These ideas are essential to learning and motivation and are integral parts of the models you'll study in the later chapters.

Summary

Learning: The Evolution from
Behaviorist to Cognitive Views

The first half of the twentieth century was dominated by behaviorism, a view of learning that focused on observable changes in behavior resulting from the influence of the environment.

About the middle of the century, views of learning changed because the behavioral view was unable to explain complex mental processes, such as language and problem solving. The result has been commonly called the "cognitive revolution." Since that time, cognitive learning theory has been an important influence on views of effective instruction.

Principles of Cognitive Learning Theory

Research on learning indicates that learners do not passively record what they see, hear, or read. Rather, they construct understanding of these experiences that makes sense to them. The understanding they construct depends on their existing knowledge, and social interaction strongly influences how valid this understanding becomes. Existing knowledge can be supplemented with concrete and real-world experiences, and learners must work extensively with the topics they study in order to develop thorough understanding.

Our Cognitive Architecture

Our mental structures provide the framework for the process of constructing understanding. These structures, sometimes called our *cognitive architecture* are composed of memory stores—sensory memory, working memory, and long-term memory—and cognitive processes—*attention, perception, encoding,* and *retrieval.* Metacognition, our control mechanism, monitors our thinking processes, and helps us make valid decisions.

Motivation and Learning

Teachers who believe that they can get students to learn regardless of circumstances, who model their own interest in the topics they teach, who are caring, and who have positive expectations for their students increase students' motivation to learn.

Motivation to learn also requires a safe and orderly learning environment and instruction that helps learners succeed on activities they perceive as challenging. Success on these activities can be increased with concrete and personalized examples, high levels of involvement, and detailed feedback about learning progress.

IMPORTANT CONCEPTS

Attention (p. 34)
Automaticity (p. 33)
Classroom climate (p. 41)
Cognitive processes (p. 31)
Curiosity motivation (p. 43)
Encoding (p. 34)
Extrinsic motivation (p. 36)
Information stores (p. 31)
Intrinsic motivation (p. 36)

Learning (behaviorism) (p. 26)
Learning (cognitive) (p. 26)
Long-term memory (p. 33)
Meaningfulness (p. 35)
Metacognition (p. 31)
Modeling (p. 38)
Motivation (p. 35)
Motivation to learn (p. 37)
Perception (p. 34)

Personal teaching efficacy (p. 38)
Personalization (p. 44)
Relatedness (p. 39)
Retrieval (p. 35)
Schema (p. 33)
Sensory memory (p. 32)
Teacher expectations (p. 40)
Working memory (p. 32)

EXERCISES

Read the following case studies and then answer the questions that follow.

Kevin Lageman is an eighth-grade English teacher at Ridgeview Middle School, where he teaches five sections of standard English.

We look in on his first period on Monday as he begins a unit on pronoun cases with one of his standard English classes.

It's 9:08 and, as students file into the room, Kevin greets them at the door and hurries them along. "Hurry everyone, two minutes until the bell rings. Anyone who's late gets a detention."

Kevin finishes taking roll as the last students slide into their seats, and he hangs the slip outside his door as the bell rings at 9:10.

"All right, listen everyone," Kevin begins as the bell stops ringing. ". . . Today, we're going to begin a study of pronoun cases. . . . Everybody turn to page 484 in your text."

He waits for a moment as students find the page.

"This is important," he continues, "because we want to be able to use standard English when we write, and this is one of the places where people get mixed up. . . . So, when we're finished with our study here, you'll all be able to use pronouns correctly in your writing."

He then displays the following on the overhead:

Pronouns use the nominative case when they're subjects and predicate nominatives.

Pronouns use the objective case when they're direct objects, indirect objects, or objects of prepositions.

"Let's review briefly," Kevin continues. "Give me a sentence that has both a direct and indirect object in it. . . . Anyone?"

"Mr. Lageman gives us too much homework," Leroy offers to the laughter of the class.

Kevin smiles and writes the sentence on the chalkboard, and then continues, "Okay, Leroy. Good sentence, even though it's incorrect. I don't give you *enough* work. . . . What's the subject in the sentence?"

". . ."

"Go ahead, Leroy."

"Ahh, . . . er, . . . *Mr. Lageman*."

"Yes, good. *Mr. Lageman* is the subject," Kevin replies as he underlines *Mr. Lageman* in the sentence.

"Now, what's the direct object? . . . Joanne?"

". . . *Homework*."

"All right, good. And what's the indirect object? . . . Anya?"

". . . *Us*."

"Excellent, everybody."

Kevin continues by reviewing predicate nominatives and objects of prepositions.

He then continues, "Now, let's look at a few more examples up here on the overhead."

He then displays ten sentences; the following are the first four.

1. Did you get the card from Kelly and (I, me)?
2. Will Antonio and (she, her) run the concession stand?

3. They treat (whoever, whomever) they hire very well.

4. I looked for someone (who, whom) could give me directions to the theater.

"Okay, look at the first one. Which is correct? . . . Omar?"

". . . *Me.*"

"Good, Omar. How about the second one? . . . Lonnie?"

". . . *Her.*"

"Not quite, Lonnie. This one is a little tricky, but it's the nominative case," Kevin responds.

Kevin then points up at the overhead and says, "How about the third one. . . . Cheny?"

"I don't know. . . . *whomever*, I guess."

"Excellent, Cheny. Indeed, that's correct."

Kevin then continues with the rest of the sentences, and assigns a page of similar exercises from their books as homework.

On Tuesday, Wednesday, and Thursday, Kevin covers the rules for pronoun–antecedent agreement (pronouns must agree with their antecedents in gender and number) and using indefinite pronouns as antecedents for personal pronouns—*anybody, either, each, one, someone*. He then has the students work examples as he had done before.

On Friday Kevin gives a test, which is composed of thirty sentences, ten of which deal with case, ten more with antecedents, and the final ten with indefinite pronouns. The following are some items from the test:

For each of the items below, mark A on your answer sheet if the pronoun case is correct in the sentence, and mark B if it is incorrect. If it is incorrect, supply the correct pronoun.

1. Be careful *who* you tell.

2. Will Renee and *I* be in the outfield?

3. My brother and *me* like waterskiing.

Suzanne Nelson, who teaches in the room next to Kevin, greets her students pleasantly, "Hurry up, everyone. We've got lots of work to do." Suzanne finishes taking roll as the bell stops ringing. The students are in their seats, and Suzanne steps to the front of the room and says, "We're making progress on the editorial piece that we're writing for the school paper. . . . I've read the essays you turned in on Friday, and your writing is getting better and better, but we have some things to work on today that will improve them even more. She then turns on two overheads, with several paragraphs displayed on each. On the left the following paragraphs appear:

Katrina and Simone were talking. "Did you get the information *from Kelly and me*?" Simone asked.

"No, I didn't," Katrina responded. "What was it about?"

"Kelly wanted to know if it's okay *that Molly and she* run the concession stand on Friday night at the game."

"Sure, that's fine with me," Katrina responded. "The teachers treat *whoever works there* very well, so everything will be fine. By the way, *to whom* do I give the list of people who are working that night."

On the right overhead the paragraphs looked like this:

Katrina and Simone were talking. "Did you get the information *from Kelly and I?*" Simone asked.

"No I didn't," Katrina responded. "What was it about?"

"Kelly wanted to know if it's okay *that Molly and her* run the concession stand on Friday night at the game."

"Sure, that's fine with me," Katrina responded. "The teachers treat *whomever works there* very well, so everything will be fine. By the way, *to who* do I give the list of people who are working that night."

Suzanne gives students a moment to read the paragraphs and then says, "Get together with your partner and make as many comparisons as you can about the two passages. . . . You've got two minutes."

After two minutes she calls the class back together and continues, "Okay, what did you notice about them? . . . Devon."

". . . *Me* over there" (pointing at the left screen) "and *I* over there" (pointing at the right screen), Devon offers.

"Okay," Suzanne smiles. "What else? . . . Tonya?"

"Both . . . have *Kelly.*"

"Okay, good. . . . What else? . . . Carlo?"

"*From.*"

"What do you mean, *from*?"

"Both have *from* in italics."

"All right, good observations everyone. . . . Now, . . . look at the one on the left again. What part of speech is the word *from*? . . . Andrew?"

". . . A . . . preposition."

"Yes, excellent, Andrew. It is a preposition. . . . So, let's take a look at this," and she then takes the paragraph off the right overhead and displays the following:

Pronouns use the nominative case when they're subjects and predicate nominatives.

Pronouns use the objective case when they're direct objects, indirect objects, or objects of prepositions.

She gives them a few seconds to read the rules, and she then continues, "I'd like you to work with your partner again and decide, based on these rules, which of the two versions up here is correct. Again, I'll give you two minutes."

At the end of the two minutes she continues, "So, which do you believe is correct, . . . 'from Kelly and me' or 'from Kelly and I'? . . . Jon?"

"I think . . . it should be 'from Kelly and I.'"

"And why do you think so."

". . . It sounds better."

"Listen to this and tell us which one sounds better. 'Kelly and me got some soft drinks,' or 'Kelly and I got some soft drinks.'"

". . . 'Kelly and I.'"

"Okay, good. . . . So, let's go back to 'from Kelly and me' or 'from Kelly and I.' What do you think? . . . Katrina?"

". . . Must be, . . . 'from Kelly and me,'" Katrina says hesitantly.

"Why do you think so?"

"Well, they're . . . not the subject, and *I* was used when it was the subject, . . . so, . . . must be *me*."

"Yes, . . . makes sense, doesn't it. . . . 'Kelly and I' are what part of the sentence . . . April?"

". . . The subject."

"Yes, good. Indeed they are. So, . . . let's go back to the other example. Which is correct?"

Suzanne continues the discussion until twenty minutes are left in the period. Students then begin revising their paragraphs based on information they learned in the lesson.

On Tuesday and Wednesday Suzanne continues the discussion with two additional passages, and on Thursday, she returns the students' writing assignments and completes the discussion of pronouns, their antecedents, and indefinite pronouns.

On Friday Suzanne assigns an additional passage to be written as a quiz. The students have to embed at least two examples each of pronoun cases, pronouns and antecedents, and indefinite pronouns in the paragraphs. In addition, she has students read each others' essays, checking for the content they've just been studying.

1. Was Kevin's lesson based more on behaviorism or more on cognitive learning theory? Explain specifically why. If you believe it was based on cognitive learning theory, identify as many of the principles of cognitive learning theory as you can that are illustrated in the case study.

2. Was Suzanne's lesson based more on behaviorism or more on cognitive learning theory? Explain specifically why. If you believe it was based on cognitive learning theory, identify as many of the principles of cognitive learning theory as you can that are illustrated in the case study.

3. Assess Kevin's lesson with respect to the discussion of motivation and learning presented in the chapter. In your assessment, include as many of the factors as apply to his lesson.

4. Assess Suzanne's lesson with respect to the discussion of motivation and learning presented in the chapter. In your assessment, include as many of the factors as apply to her lesson.

Feedback for these exercises begins on page 341.

DISCUSSION QUESTIONS

1. Identify at least two similarities and at least two differences between behaviorist and cognitive views of learning.

2. Which one of the cognitive learning principles is most important for classroom teachers? Which one of these principles is most often violated or ignored in classrooms?

3. If teachers lecture, do learners still construct their own understanding? Why or why not?

4. Which aspect or aspects of our cognitive architecture have the most important implications for teaching? Describe those implications.

5. If instruction is grounded in cognitive views of learning, is assessment a more or a less important aspect of the teaching–learning process than it would be if instruction was based on behaviorism?

6. Respond to the assertion, "My job as a teacher is to plan for promoting learning. Motivation is the students' responsibility."

7. Should teachers be held accountable for increasing the motivation of students who are alienated from school or who are disinterested in school? Why or why not?

3 Essential Teaching Strategies and the Teaching of Thinking

I. **Essential Teaching Strategies: The Foundation for Teacher Effectiveness**
  A. Teacher Characteristics
  B. Communication
  C. Organization
  D. Instructional Alignment
  E. Focus
  F. Feedback
  G. Monitoring
  H. Questioning
  I. Review and Closure

II. **Essential Teaching Strategies and Classroom Management: Creating Productive Learning Environments**
  A. Organization: A Key to Orderly Classrooms
  B. Classroom Order: Increasing Student Motivation

III. **Essential Teaching Strategies: The Influence of Our Cognitive Architecture**

IV. **Beyond Effective Teaching: Teaching for Thinking and Understanding**
  A. Thinking and Understanding
  B. Teaching Thinking: Increasing Learning and Motivation
  C. A Climate for Thinking
  D. Critical Thinking
  E. Dispositions for Thinking

In Chapter 1, we learned that research confirms the importance of teachers in promoting student learning. This research describes abilities that all teachers should have; it identifies the foundation for teacher expertise. Building on that foundation, effective teachers create lessons that promote learners' deep understanding of content and their ability to think critically.

We examine this research in this chapter, and discuss its implications for teaching practice. When you have completed your study of this chapter, you should be able to:

- Identify examples of teachers displaying essential teaching strategies in real-world contexts.
- Demonstrate essential teaching strategies in your own instruction.
- Identify characteristics of critical thinking.
- Promote critical thinking in your own teaching.

To begin our discussion, let's sit in on an American history class.

Teri Bowden is beginning a unit on the colonization of North America with her tenth-grade American history students. We join her class as she is standing at the door greeting the students at 9:57 as they file into class for her third period which begins at 10:00.

"Nice haircut Rafik. . . . Good morning José," she smiles as Rafik and José walk into the room.

"David, that goes in your locker. . . . Hurry up. You have 2 minutes," she directs as he starts through the door with a basketball in his hand.

"Take your seats quickly," Teri reminds them. "You have 5 minutes to answer the questions on the overhead."

As the bell stops ringing at 10:00, the students are peering at the overhead and hunching over their desks as Teri takes roll.

At 10:05 Teri asks, "How are you all doing?" Amidst "Fine," "Okay," and "Just about done," Teri says, "Okay, 1 more minute."

The students finish and pass their papers forward. Teri quickly goes over the exercises and says, "Get these out of your folders as you come in tomorrow morning."

"Now," she announces, "let's shift our thinking a little and begin to focus on the colonial period, which began in the 1600s. This is a very important part of American history, but what's most interesting about all of this is that what we're studying has ramifications for the entire world, even today. It's one of the most important ideas of the entire colonial period."

Damon smiles wryly and whispers to Charlene, "Bowden thinks everything is interesting."

Teri continues, "To get us started I want you to look at the two short passages that I'm going to display on the overhead. Read them carefully and look for any common features that they might have. So . . . our goal in this lesson is to look for patterns, and then we'll relate these patterns to the events we've been studying in American history." She then displays the following information:

In the mid-1600s the American colonists were encouraged to grow tobacco because it wasn't grown in England. The colonists wanted to sell it to France and other countries but were forbidden to do so. In return for the tobacco, the colonists were allowed to import textiles from England, but were forbidden from making their own. All of the materials were carried on British ships.

Early French colonists in the New World were avid fur trappers and traders. They got in trouble with the French monarchy, however, when they attempted to make fur garments and sell them to Spain, England, and other countries. They were told that the fur garments would be produced in and sent to them from Paris instead. The monarchy also told them that traps and weapons must be made in France and sent to them as well. Jean Forge complied with the monarchy's wishes but was fined when he hired a Dutch ship to carry some of the furs back to Nice.

"Now, let's take a look," Teri continues. "What do you see up here? . . . Ann?"

"Both of the examples deal with some type of colony."

"Okay, what else? . . . Rasheed?"

"Looks like there were some problems."

"What do you mean?"

"The colonies wanted to do something, but England and France wouldn't let them."

"Give us a specific example. . . . Aneesha?"

"The colonists produced something England and France wanted, such as tobacco and furs."

"Very observant, Aneesha," Teri smiles. "Go on, Pam?"

". . . They sent the stuff to England and France," Pam answers after a few seconds.

"And they couldn't send it anywhere else!" Steve jumps in.

"That's very good, both of you. Where do you suppose Steve got that idea? . . . Connie?"

". . . It says it right in the examples," Connie responds. "Like in the first one it says, 'The colonists wanted to sell it to France and other countries but were forbidden to do so.'"

"Excellent, everyone! That's good thinking, Connie. . . . Keep going. . . . Mary?"

". . ."

"What did they get in return in each case?"

"They got clothes from England . . . and from France . . . made out of fur, and traps and stuff," Mary answers after looking back and forth at the examples.

"And what did each get from other countries? Liz?"

". . . Nothing."

"They weren't allowed to," Bob adds.

"And what made you say that, Bob?"

"It says in the second example that they were told that their traps and weapons would be sent from France."

"Does this tell us for certain that they weren't allowed to import goods from other countries?"

". . . Not exactly," Jill adds. "We're sort of assuming it from the information, although it's really implied in the description."

"Very good, Jill. . . . Everyone, notice that Jill used the word *assume*. Actually, she made a conclusion, and the term we use for that kind of conclusion is *infer*. Here the information wasn't directly in the data; she had to go beyond the data to form her conclusion. That's an inference. Nice job," Teri nods.

"Now, let's go a bit farther. What other patterns do you see in the descriptions? Kim?"

". . ."

"How were the goods shipped, Kim?"

"On ships," Kim returns.

"Yes, good, Kim," Teri smiles. "What ships, or whose ships?"

". . . From England and France. It says that in the first example, and in the second one it says that Jean Forge got into trouble when he tried to hire a Dutch ship to carry some furs back to Nice."

"Now, anything else? . . . What do you think? Cherrie?"

". . . I think that they also couldn't make their own manufactured goods. It says in each case that when the colonists tried to make their own goods from the raw materials that they couldn't do it."

"They couldn't make any manufactured goods, not only those from the raw materials they provided," Kathy added.

"What made you say that?" Teri queried.

"The British colonists grew tobacco, but they weren't allowed to manufacture anything, not only something that you might make out of tobacco," Kathy answered.

"Yes, but you can't make anything out of tobacco," Gregg retorted.

"Oh, yes, you can," Kathy responded. "They could have made cigars and stuff."

"Those are both good points," Teri interjected. "Everyone, remember this," Teri noted, raising her voice. "This is important. Do you see how both Kathy and Gregg used information to support their arguments? Nice job!"

She then went on, "Do we have any other evidence that supports either Kathy's or Gregg's position, even though they're not really at odds?"

"I think so," Jack volunteered. "In the second case the French colonists were told not to manufacture traps and weapons, and they produced furs, so it wasn't only fur coats that were not allowed."

"That's excellent everyone! Very good analysis of the information we have here. Now let's look back and see what we've found. . . . We've studied the two examples, and now we want to take a broader look at the information in general. What kind of situation do we have here? . . . Toni?"

". . . Colonists related to a country produced only raw materials, no manufactured stuff . . ."

"Good. . . . Go on," Teri probes.

"And they can only be sold to the mother country," Toni continues.

"Who did the manufacturing and the shipping," Gregg adds.

"Excellent! Very clear description. . . . Now we know the features of this policy. Does anyone know what it's called?" Teri continues.

". . ."

"This is called *mercantilism.* It was a colonial economic policy designed to make money for the parent country by taking colonial raw materials in exchange for manufactured products." After a brief pause, she continues, "What other countries besides England and France have been guilty of mercantilism?"

The class then analyzes additional examples, such as Belgium and the Netherlands, and discusses their mercantile policies.

Teri then continues, "Let's look again at the question I asked, 'What other countries have been guilty of mercantilism?' What assumption is being made in that question?"

". . . It seems like you're suggesting that mercantilism is bad," Anthony offers tentatively.

"Good thinking," Teri smiles. "That's exactly what it implies. Now, mercantilism may very well have been bad . . . exploitation of colonialized lands and that kind of thing. However, the question I asked had in it an unstated assumption. Recognizing unstated assumptions is part of the thinking process, and we all need to be on the lookout for that kind of thing. . . . Again, that's good thinking, Anthony."

She then continues, "Now look at another case and see if it illustrates mercantilism. Remember, be ready to explain why or why not when you've made your decision." She then displays the following passage on the screen:

> Canada is a member of the British commonwealth. Canada is a large grain producer and exporter, deriving considerable income from selling grain to Great Britain, France,

Russia, and other countries. This trade has also enhanced the shipping business for Greece, Norway, and Liberia, which carry most of the products. Canada, however, doesn't rely on grain alone. It is now a major producer of clothing, high-tech equipment, and heavy-industry equipment.

"What do you think? Is this mercantilism? . . . Someone? Amy, we haven't heard from you," Teri continues.

". . . I would say no," Amy responds after a few seconds of studying the description.

"Okay, now tell us why."

". . . Well, there are several reasons," Amy continues. "Canada trades with several countries according to the information, uses a variety of ships to carry the goods, and produces a lot besides raw materials."

"Excellent analysis, Amy," Teri smiles. "Now that we're comfortable with that part, let's go a step farther and examine our thinking in this activity. What are some things you had to do in order to arrive at the conclusion?"

"First we had to observe, so we would eventually recognize the essential characteristics," Amelia responds.

"Good beginning! What else? . . . Serena?"

"We made comparisons."

"Good. . . . Jack?"

"We had to separate out the relevant from the irrelevant information," Jack replies.

"For example?" Terry probes.

". . . Well, whether it was guns, or traps, or clothing, or whatever, really didn't matter. The important point was that the colonists weren't allowed to manufacture anything."

"Excellent, Jack! Now, go on. . . . Patty?"

". . . We didn't see everything in the examples, so we had to infer some of it, and then you asked us for evidence to support our inference."

"Very good, Patty. Can you remember an example of where we did this?"

". . . Aneesha said that the colonies weren't allowed to get materials from other countries, and then said France told them the traps and weapons would be sent from there."

". . . Jill also said that it didn't tell us for sure, but that it was strongly implied and we inferred it from the information that we were given," Becky adds.

"We also generalized when we formed the definition of mercantilism," Lisa Jo puts in.

"Yes we did. Well done, Lisa Jo.

"Let's move on," Teri continues. "We now want to examine the impact of mercantilism on other events during the colonial period, and we want to think about mercantilism in other parts of the world, such as Africa. . . . So, for tomorrow, I want you to read this article that I copied from one of the news magazines recently. As you read the article, think about how the information in it relates to what we discussed today. Your warm-up activity at the beginning of the class will be questions related to the article."

She then continues, "You did a very nice job today. Your analysis of your own thinking is getting better and better. I'm proud of all of you."

To begin our discussion, let's look back at Teri's lesson and examine three essential features in it.

1. She displayed teaching abilities that all teachers—regardless of content area, grade level, or topic—should be able to demonstrate. We call these abilities *essential teaching strategies.*
2. Her objective for developing thinking and her content objectives were interdependent. Neither was "tacked on" to the other, and her instruction throughout the lesson was directed at both.
3. Her lesson focused on deep understanding of a particular topic—the role of mercantilism in colonization.

We examine each of these elements in detail in the following sections of the chapter. We begin with essential teaching strategies.

Essential Teaching Strategies: The Foundation for Teacher Effectiveness

Imagine that you're sitting unnoticed at the back of a classroom. This could be a veteran teacher's first-grade class working on math facts, a junior high life science class studying different types of worms taught by a first-year teacher, or a high school English class discussing one of Shakespeare's plays taught by a teacher with several years of experience.

Regardless of the teacher's personality or background, the grade level of the students, or the topic being studied, some teacher actions increase student learning more than others. We call these actions **essential teaching strategies,** and they are the *teacher attitudes and skills necessary to ensure that all students learn as much as possible.* They are derived from the teacher-effectiveness research described in Chapter 1, and they are analogous to basic skills, such as the abilities in reading, writing, and math that all learners must possess to function effectively in the world. We can think of essential teaching strategies as the basic skills of teaching.

We discuss these abilities separately for the sake of clarity, but they are interdependent, and none is as effective alone as it is in combination with the others. They are outlined in Figure 3.1 and discussed in the sections that follow.

Teacher Characteristics

Although teacher characteristics are admittedly not strategies, we begin with them to emphasize how important they are in teaching. Teachers set the emotional tone for the classroom, design and implement learning activities, and assess student learning. Their attitudes and beliefs are essential in this process.

In Chapter 2 we saw that teacher characteristics such as *personal teaching efficacy, modeling and enthusiasm, caring,* and *high expectations* promote learner motivation. They are also strongly linked to increased student achievement, which isn't surprising because motivation and learning are interdependent (Bruning et al., 2004; Noddings, 1999; Shuell, 1996).

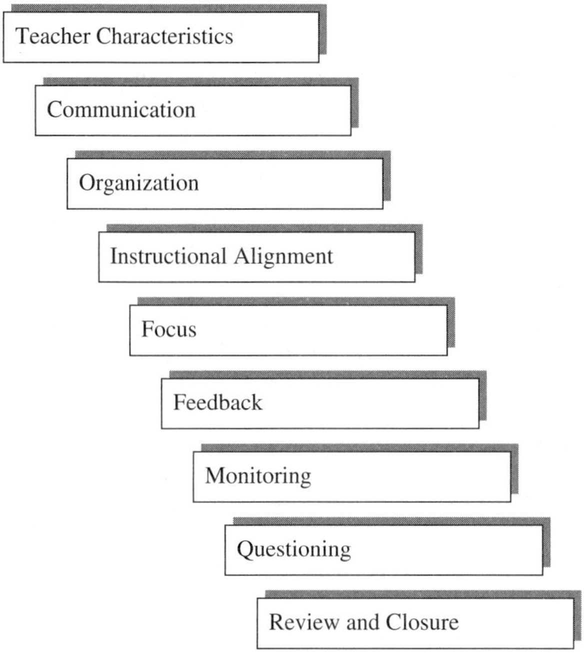

FIGURE 3.1   Essential Teaching Strategies

Teri displayed these characteristics in her work with her students. She identified clear lesson objectives, created examples (her vignettes illustrating mercantilism) designed to help students understand her topic, and guided students' involvement throughout the learning activity, all indicators of high personal teaching efficacy. She modeled her own interest in the topic, which is an indicator of enthusiasm; she demonstrated respect for students, which is an indicator of caring; and her questioning suggested that she expected all of her students to answer. These are the characteristics we hope to see in all teachers.

Communication

The importance of teachers being able to communicate clearly is intuitively sensible, and research documents a strong link between teachers' ability to communicate and student achievement, as well as student satisfaction with instruction (Snyder et al., 1991). Four elements of effective communication influence learning:

- Precise terminology
- Connected discourse
- Transition signals
- Emphasis

Precise Terminology.   **Precise terminology** is *teacher language that eliminates vague terms from presentations and answers to students' questions.* Although it's hard to eliminate all vague terms, with effort teachers can make their language precise, which in turn contributes to increased achievement.

If we look again at Teri's instruction, we see that she described her ideas clearly, and she avoided words such as *perhaps, maybe, might, and so on, probably,* and *usually.* These vague terms leave students with a sense of uncertainty, resulting in lowered achievement (Smith & Cotten, 1980).

Connected Discourse.   **Connected discourse** is *a type of teacher presentations that is clear, thematic, and leads to a point.* Teri's lesson is an example. The theme of the lesson was the concept *mercantilism,* and the entire lesson was developed around that theme. In contrast, let's look at another example.

> A teacher is beginning a lesson on the Civil War with a group of fifth graders. She tells the students that the goals of the lesson are to understand the dynamics of the war, to understand what caused the war, and to understand why the North won. Prior to the lesson she lists several terms on the chalkboard, including *Appomattox, amendment, free state, Underground Railroad, sectionalism, abolitionist,* and *secede.*
>
> After she states her goal, she begins by explaining the concept of sectionalism and shows the students different sections of the United States on a small map. She continues with a question-and-answer activity in which she asks students how they think it would feel to be a slave, then continues with a brief discussion of Abraham Lincoln, followed by an equally brief discussion of why the students think the North won the war, and finally provides some information on reconstruction.
>
> She then directs the students to write an essay about the Civil War using the vocabulary words on the board as a seatwork assignment. After they've completed it, she tells them to go home and write one or two paragraphs about the meaning of the word *indivisible* as a homework assignment (Ross, 1992).

This teacher discussed sectionalism, what it would feel like to be a slave, Abraham Lincoln, why the North won the war, and reconstruction, all in the same lesson. The lesson was not thematic and it didn't lead to a particular point. The discourse in her lesson was disconnected or "scrambled."

Two factors can detract from connected discourse: (1) The presentation can be sequenced inappropriately, or (2) extraneous information can be added to the discussion without clearly indicating how it relates to the topic. Both existed in the lesson on the Civil War, whereas neither was a problem in Teri's instruction.

Transition Signals.   A **transition signal** is *a verbal statement that communicates that one idea is ending and another is beginning,* and it is a third component of effective communication. As an illustration, let's look again at Teri's comment, "Now let's shift our thinking a little and begin to focus on the colonial period, which began in the 1600s." This comment prepared students to move from the warm-up exercise to the lesson for the day.

During any lesson, students are at different places mentally. Transition signals focus students' attention, increasing the likelihood that they will be concentrating on the appropriate topic at hand.

Emphasis.   **Emphasis,** a fourth aspect of clear classroom communication, is *the use of verbal statements, vocal inflection, or repetition to alert students to important information in a lesson* (Eggen & Kauchak, 2004). We know from the cognitive learning model in Chapter 2 that learners begin processing information by attending to it, and emphasis focuses this attention. Research confirms the role of emphasis in increasing achievement (Mayer, 1983). When Teri said, "Those are both good points. Everyone, remember this [raising her voice]. This is important. Do you see how both Kathy and Gregg used information to support their arguments? Nice job!" she was emphasizing the fact that providing evidence was important in the lesson. The use of emphasis increases the clarity of communication and helps students follow the theme of the lesson.

Repeating a point, another form of emphasis, also signals that an idea is important. For instance, a science teacher might say, "Remember when Juanita said that amphibians have a three-chambered heart? That tells about their position in the chain of evolution," or ask, "What did Juanita say about the structure of the heart of amphibians?" Each is a form of repetition, which serves to emphasize important ideas.

Language and Knowledge of Content.   Our discussion of clear language has two important implications for teachers. First, we should try to monitor our language to ensure that our presentations are as clear and logical as possible. Videotaping and reviewing lessons and developing lessons with questioning are simple and effective ways to improve on the clarity of our speech. Second, teachers who thoroughly understand the topics they teach use clearer language than those whose backgrounds are weaker (Carlsen, 1987; Cruickshank, 1985). If our grasp of a topic is uncertain, we should spend more time studying and preparing. Clear understanding is particularly important when using teaching models that emphasize teachers guiding learners rather than lecturing to them. Guiding students requires that teachers keep their learning objectives in mind, encourage student involvement, and ask appropriate questions at the right times. These are sophisticated strategies that require a deep and thorough understanding of the topics.

Organization

The importance of organization in teaching, as well as our lives in general, is intuitively sensible. We have all complained at one time or another about our lack of organization, and many of us have probably made conscious efforts to improve it. It affects both the way we live and the way we teach. Teachers who are organized have students who learn more than their less organized counterparts (Bennett, 1978; Rutter, Maughan, Mortimore, Ouston, & Smith, 1979).

The characteristics of effective organization are outlined in Table 3.1, and time is a key factor. Each characteristic allows teachers to maximize the time available for instruction. Beginning classes promptly, for example, having materials prepared in advance, using warm-up activities at the beginning of classes, and having students trained to perform routine tasks without being told all help teachers maximize their instructional time. Effective teachers use more of their available time for instruction than do less effective teachers.

Instructional Alignment

Instructional alignment describes *the congruence among objectives, learning activities, and assessments* (Bransford et al., 2000). This match is essential if teachers are to help students

TABLE 3.1   **Characteristics of Effective Organization**

Characteristic	Example
Starting on time	Teri's students were at their desks and working on her warm-up activity when the bell rang to begin the period.
Materials prepared in advance	Teri's materials were displayed on the overhead as her students walked in the door. The examples for her lesson were at her fingertips.
Established routines	The students knew how to pick up their papers from their folders without being told.

learn as much as possible. For example, Teri had clear and precise objectives; she wanted students to understand the concept of *mercantilism* while practicing critical thinking. Her instruction was directed toward those objectives, and her assignment for the next day, to read a news article and relate the information to mercantilism—which combined both instruction and assessment—was also directly related to her objectives.

Although the notion of instructional alignment seems simple, a surprising number of teachers have objectives and learning activities that are not consistent, and, in some cases, the instruction doesn't seem to be directed at any particular objective. As an example, let's think again about the teacher in the lesson on the Civil War. She described her objectives as wanting the students to understand the dynamics of the war, to understand what caused the war, and to understand why the North won. She had several terms listed on the board. She discussed sectionalism, what the students thought it would feel like to be a slave, Abraham Lincoln, why students thought the North won the war, and reconstruction. She assigned an essay using the terms on the board as a seatwork assignment, and she had the students write about the term *indivisible* as a homework assignment.

This is an extreme case of instruction that was out of alignment. The only part of the learning activity that related to her objective was the brief discussion of reasons why the North had won the war. She didn't refer to the terms on the board, yet her seatwork assignment focused on those terms. Then, her homework assignment dealt with the concept *indivisible,* to which no part of her instruction referred.

Instructional alignment is more sophisticated and subtle than it appears. On the surface, the teacher's instruction looked acceptable, perhaps even good. Her students were orderly and the teacher involved the students in a question-and-answer activity. The lack of alignment wasn't apparent. In fact, in a research study examining preservice, first-year, and veteran teachers' concepts of effective instruction, most of the preservice and first-year teachers missed the fact that the instruction in this lesson—which was videotaped—was not aligned, whereas veteran teachers quickly identified the alignment problem (Eggen & Austin, 2004).

Focus

In reviewing what we've discussed to this point, we see that we have examined teacher characteristics, clear communication, teacher organization, and the need for instruction to be aligned if student achievement is to be as high as possible. For these elements to be effective, students must be engaged or "with us" in the lesson. Lesson focus attracts and holds students' attention throughout the learning activity.

As we saw in our discussion of cognitive learning in Chapter 2, and earlier in this chapter in our discussion of emphasis, learning begins with attention, and attention must be maintained if learning is to continue. **Focus** is provided through *stimuli that maintain students' attention during learning activities.* The stimuli can be concrete objects, pictures, models, materials displayed on the overhead, and even information written on the chalkboard. The more concrete and attractive the materials, the better. The examples Teri displayed on the overhead served as her lesson's focus.

The simplest form of lesson focus is the chalkboard or other writing board, but it is often underused, particularly in elementary schools. Teachers commonly deliver their lessons verbally instead of using the board as a supplement; as a result, lessons lose focus, and students become inattentive. Some form of written lesson focus is particularly important for students with special needs or those who have trouble focusing their attention on verbal information.

Feedback

Feedback is *information about current behavior that can be used to improve future performance* (Eggen & Kauchak, 2004), and its importance is confirmed by both theory and research. From our discussion of learning in Chapter 2, we know that learners are active in their attempts to construct understanding of the topics they study. They can't be sure, however, that their evolving constructions are valid. Feedback gives them information they can use to assess the validity of their developing understanding.

Research confirms this theory. Regardless of topic, grade level, or task, students who receive detailed feedback about their learning progress achieve higher than those receiving less feedback (Good & Brophy, 2003; Rosenshine & Stevens, 1986).

Effective feedback has three essential characteristics, which are illustrated in Figure 3.2. These characteristics are equally important for both written and verbal feedback. Let's look at an example from the classroom.

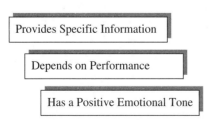

FIGURE 3.2 Characteristics of Effective Feedback

> A teacher is working with students on simplifying arithmetic expressions and displays the following expression on the board:
>
> 4 + 3(6 − 2) − 5
>
> The teacher asks, "What is the first step in simplifying the expression? . . . Leon?"
> "Add the four and the three."
> "Not quite, Leon. Can someone help Leon out?"

Although the feedback depended on Leon's performance, he only learned that his answer was incorrect; he received no specific, corrective information. By contrast, look at the following exchange:

> "What is the first step in simplifying the expression? . . . Emilio?"
> "Add the four and the three."
> "Look again, Emilio. If we first add the four and the three, we then would have seven times the numbers in the parentheses. What does the expression suggest?"
> ". . . That it's three times the numbers in parentheses."

In the second example, the teacher gave a specific response based on Emilio's answer (his performance) and provided information that helped him answer correctly. The feedback both helped Emilio understand why his first answer was incorrect and gave him the opportunity to answer correctly. Neither was true for Leon.

The emotional tone of feedback is also important. If students are to learn as much as possible, they must work in a safe classroom environment where they feel free to express themselves and describe their thinking. Feedback that includes criticism, sarcasm, or ridicule detracts from this safety, destroys motivation, and decreases learning (Lambert & McCombs, 1998; Stipek, 2002).

You may react to the fact that we didn't say that *immediate* is one of the characteristics of effective feedback. Immediate feedback *is* important when teachers are responding to students in a question-and-answer session. However, research indicates that feedback on written materials, such as quizzes or homework, is more effective if it is slightly delayed (Shuell, 1996). For example, feedback on a quiz is more effective the day after the quiz was taken than if it occurs the same day. Obviously, the delay shouldn't be too great. The next school day is ideal.

Monitoring

Monitoring is *the process of continually checking students' verbal and nonverbal behavior for evidence of learning progress.* It is important during all learning activities (and particularly during seatwork, when students may be making repeated errors). Alert teachers immediately recognize when students become inattentive and move near them or call on them to bring them back into lessons. Effective teachers also respond to nonverbal behaviors, such as puzzled looks on students' faces, and make statements (or asks questions) such as, "Would you like to have me repeat what I just said?" Less effective teachers seem not to notice the puzzled looks or inattention. Careful monitoring followed by appropriate teacher responses can strongly contribute to a climate of support while simultaneously demonstrating high expectations both for behavior and learning.

Questioning

In Chapter 2 we learned that the need for social interaction is one of the principles of cognitive learning theory. Questioning is the most effective strategy teachers have for promoting this interaction (Wang, Haertel, & Walberg, 1993). Expert teachers use questioning to help students see connections between the abstract ideas they're studying by relating them to real-world examples (Brown, 1994; Eggen & Kauchak, 2004). Questioning can also (1) help maintain attention, (2) involve shy and reluctant students, (3) provide emphasis through repetition, and (4) assess student understanding. Becoming skilled at questioning is difficult because it involves doing several things at once (Eggen & Kauchak, 2004), such as:

- Remembering the objectives of the lesson
- Monitoring students' verbal and nonverbal behaviors
- Maintaining the flow and development of the lesson
- Preparing the next question
- Deciding on who to call

With practice, however, teachers' can become skilled at questioning, and for expert teachers it essentially becomes automatic (Kauchak & Eggen, 2003; Kerman, 1979). Effective questioning has four characteristics:

- Frequency
- Equitable distribution
- Prompting
- Wait-time

Frequency.   **Questioning frequency** refers to *the number of questions teachers ask,* and research indicates that effective teachers ask a large number of questions (Morine-Dershimer, 1987). Questioning increases student involvement, which increases both motivation and achievement (Eggen & Kauchak, 2004; Lambert & McCombs, 1998), and effective questions promote student thinking, which leads to improved learning. Expert teachers develop entire lessons with questioning, and this is what Teri did with her students.

Equitable Distribution.   Merely asking a lot of questions isn't enough, however. If the same students are answering all of the questions, other students become inattentive and achievement decreases. Kerman (1979) used the term **equitable distribution** to describe *a questioning pattern in which all students in the class are called on as equally as possible.*

We saw earlier in the chapter that teachers sometimes treat students differently, based on the teachers' expectations. Because teachers expect more from higher achievers, teachers subconsciously call on those students more often. Further, most teacher questions are not directed toward particular students (McGreal, 1985). This means that students who want to volunteer, or even shout out answers, are allowed to do so, and those who don't are allowed to remain passive. When this occurs, less confident or aggressive students fall into a habit of not responding. They become inattentive and their achievement decreases (Good & Brophy, 2003).

The solution is to *call on all students as equally as possible and direct questions to students by name.* This promotes equitable distribution and prevents a vocal minority from dominating the activity. Equitable distribution communicates to students that the teacher expects them to be involved and able to answer. When this becomes a pattern, both achievement and motivation improve (McDougall & Granby, 1996).

To make the process work, however, the classroom must be managed to prevent student **callouts,** which are *answers given by students before the students have been recognized by the teacher.* Callouts usually come from higher-achieving or more aggressive students, and if calling out becomes a pattern, the less aggressive and lower-achieving students are often left out, equitable distribution is reduced, and overall achievement is lowered. Teri applied this research in her lesson. She directed her questions to specific students *by name,* and attempted to involve as many students as possible.

Equitable distribution is a simple idea but one that is difficult to put into practice. It requires careful monitoring of students and a great deal of teacher energy. Unfortunately, we don't often see it practiced in classrooms. However, its effects can be very powerful for both learning and motivation, and we strongly encourage you to persevere and pursue it rigorously.

Prompting.   Equitable distribution raises an important question. What do we do when the student called on doesn't respond or responds incorrectly? The answer is prompting. A **prompt** is *a teacher question or directive that elicits a student response after the student has failed to answer or has given an incorrect or incomplete answer.* As an illustration, let's look again at some dialogue from Teri's lesson.

> TERI: Excellent, everyone! That's good thinking, Connie. . . . Keep going. . . . Mary?
>
> MARY: . . .
>
> TERI: What did they get in return in each case?
>
> MARY: They got clothes from England . . . and from France . . . made out of fur, and traps and stuff [looking back and forth at the examples].

Let's look at one more example.

> TERI: Now, let's go a bit farther. What other patterns do you see in the descriptions? Kim?
>
> KIM: . . .

> **TERI:** How were the goods shipped, Kim?
>
> **KIM:** On ships.
>
> **TERI:** Yes, good, Kim. What ships, or whose ships?
>
> **KIM:** . . . From England and France. It says that in the first example, and in the second one it says that Jean Forge got into trouble when he tried to hire a Dutch ship to carry some furs back to Nice.

When Mary didn't respond, Teri asked another question that helped her provide an acceptable response. She did the same with Kim, and she then asked Kim to expand on her answer with an additional question. This is the essence of prompting.

As with equitable distribution, prompting contributes to a positive classroom climate. It communicates that the teacher expects students to answer and will provide assistance to ensure that they're able to do so. As a result, when students are called on again, they're likely to increase their efforts.

Wait-Time. Let's look once more at Teri's lesson. Although it's hard to directly observe in a written case study, after asking a student a question, Teri waited a few seconds for an answer, giving the student time to think. This *period of silence, both before and after a student responds,* is called **wait-time,** and research indicates that in most classrooms, it is very short, often less than 1 second (Rowe, 1986).

A more intuitively sensible label for wait-time might be "think time" because waiting gives the student a little time to think, ideally about 3 to 5 seconds. There are at least three benefits to this practice (Rowe, 1974, 1986):

- Students give longer and better responses.
- Voluntary participation increases, and fewer students fail to respond.
- Equitable distribution improves, and responses from cultural minorities increase as teachers become more responsive to students.

Wait-time must be implemented judiciously, however. For example, if students are involved in practice, such as multiplication facts, quick answers are desirable and wait-times should be short (Rosenshine & Stevens, 1986). Also, if a student appears uneasy, we may choose to intervene earlier. However, students need time to respond to questions asking them to compare, apply, analyze, or evaluate information. In general, increasing wait-time reduces student anxiety rather than increasing it because a climate of positive expectations and support is established. All students are expected to participate, they're given time to think about their responses, and they know that the teacher will help them if they're unable to answer.

Review and Closure

Review is *the process of summarizing previous work and forming a link between prior learning and the present topic.* **Closure** is *a form of review that occurs at the end of a lesson.*

Review can occur at any point in a learning activity, although it is most common at the beginning and end of lessons.

The value of review is well documented by research (Rosenshine & Stevens, 1986), and Dempster (1991) explains its effectiveness in this way: "reviews may do more than simply increase the amount learned; they may shift the learner's attention away from verbatim details of the material being studied to its deeper conceptual structure" (p. 71). This is especially important when we teach for understanding.

The notion of closure is intuitively sensible, and we often hear comments such as, "Let's try to get to closure on this," in everyday discussions. When a topic comes to closure, it is summarized, structured, and completed. As an example, let's look again at some dialogue from Teri's lesson.

> **TERI:** That's excellent everyone! Very good analysis of the information we have here. Now let's look back and see what we've found. . . . We've studied the two examples, and now we want to take a broader look at the information in general. What kind of situation do we have here? . . . Toni?
>
> **TONI:** . . . Colonists related to a country produced only raw materials, no manufactured stuff.
>
> **TERI:** Good. . . . Go on.
>
> **TONI:** And they can only be sold to the mother country.
>
> **GREGG:** Who did the manufacturing and the shipping.
>
> **TERI:** Excellent! Very clear description. . . . Now we know the features of this policy. Does anyone know what it's called?

At this point, Teri provided the term *mercantilism* because the students had identified the essential characteristics of the concept.

Coming to closure at the end of a lesson is important. This is the last information that students take away from the class, and if the ideas aren't clear, the students may develop (and remember) misconceptions that can be difficult to dispel.

Essential Teaching Strategies and Classroom Management: Creating Productive Learning Environments

From the 1960s until the present, national Gallup polls have identified classroom management as one of the most challenging problems teachers face. In 2002, 76 percent of those polled said discipline was a very or somewhat serious problem in U.S. schools (Rose & Gallup, 2002). It is the primary concern of beginning teachers, and disruptive students are an important source of stress for all teachers (Abel & Sewell, 1999). Nearly half of the teachers who leave the profession during the first 3 years do so because of problems with managing students (Curwin, 1992).

Commonly overlooked in discussions of classroom management is the role of effective instruction. Classroom management and effective instruction are, in fact, interdependent, and the combination of the two leads to **productive learning environments,** which are *classrooms that are orderly and focus on learning.* Research indicates that it is virtually impossible to maintain an orderly classroom in the absence of effective instruction and vice versa. This is one reason why the essential teaching strategies are so important, both for learning and for creating orderly classrooms. Let's look at this relationship in more detail.

Organization: A Key to Orderly Classrooms

We saw earlier in the chapter that *organization* is one of the essential teaching strategies, and it is also an important factor in classroom management. As an illustration, let's look again at Teri's class. First, her students had a task waiting for them when they walked in the room, which they completed while Teri took roll. This prevented "down time" at the beginning of the period, one of the times that management problems are most likely to occur. Second, she had well-established routines that made the environment predictable for students and allowed her to devote her energy to instruction instead of having to spend it maintaining order. Research indicates that expert teachers use daily routines as much as possible (Emmer et al., 2003; Evertson et al., 2003).

Classroom Order: Increasing Student Motivation

Orderly classrooms also increase student motivation. Brophy (1987a), in describing what he calls "essential preconditions for motivating students," concluded, "Nor is such motivation likely to develop in a chaotic classroom. Thus we assume that . . . the teacher uses classroom organization and management skills that successfully establish the classroom as an effective learning environment" (p. 208).

An orderly classroom doesn't mean that teachers lecture and students sit passively, however. We saw that Teri's class was orderly, but that a great deal of interaction took place throughout the lesson. Order implies that students are spending as much of their time as possible focused on learning; it doesn't mean that they sit quietly while a teacher does all the talking.

Essential Teaching Strategies: The Influence of Our Cognitive Architecture

In the previous section we described essential teaching strategies as the abilities that every teacher should possess—a foundation on which all other abilities are based. This implies that a first-year teacher should possess these abilities, which is a challenge.

To understand this challenge let's look again at the cognitive learning theory that we discussed in Chapter 2. There we saw that our cognitive architecture includes three memory stores: sensory memory, which receives stimuli from the environment; working memory, the conscious part of our cognitive system; and long-term memory, our permanent memory store (Mayer, 2002; Ormrod, 2004; Schunk, 2004).

An important aspect of our processing system is the fact that working memory is limited in capacity (Sweller et al., 1998). This limitation means that we are able to consciously process only a small amount of information at a time, and if we're faced with too much information, some will be lost or ignored in an effort to reduce the load. (This is where the term *cognitive overload* originated.)

This problem is common with students who haven't mastered basic operations in math or skills in reading, for example. When they are required to solve a word problem, too much of working memory's limited capacity is required to simply read the problem or perform the basic operations, leaving too little to find the solution. Similarly in reading, if students use too much working memory space to decode words, they don't have enough left to comprehend what they're reading.

The solution to this problem is **automaticity,** which refers to *mental operations that can be performed with little awareness or conscious effort* (Bloom, 1986; Case, 1978). Skills that are automatic take up virtually no working memory space. For example, remember when you learned to drive a car, particularly if it had a stick shift. Initially, the process was labored, and a great deal of conscious effort was spent on simply depressing the clutch, shifting, and releasing the clutch without killing the motor. In time, the process became nearly effortless, allowing conversation while smoothly shifting through the gears; the process of driving and shifting became "automatic."

So what does this have to do with essential teaching skills? Teaching is very complex and demanding. In a single learning activity, teachers are expected to maintain order, reengage inattentive students, maintain the pace and flow of the lesson, and help students clarify ideas they don't understand. Unless most of the essential teaching strategies are automatic, this is virtually impossible (Eggen, 2001). This is particularly true for questioning. Unless teachers' questioning strategies are nearly automatic, the models presented in Chapters 4 through 10 will be very difficult to use. As another example, if teachers are using much of their working memory to simply maintain order in their classrooms, using the models will also be difficult.

The limitations of working memory and the concept of *automaticity* help explain why we see so much lecture and seatwork in schools (Eggen, 2001). Lecture is simple; the teacher has to focus only on organizing and delivering content. Because students are passive, management problems are usually minimal. Seatwork is similar. The teacher only needs to monitor students for signs of disruption or confusion; demands on teachers' working memory and energy are low.

In contrast, actively involving students through questioning is much more complex and demanding. Teachers must organize the content, ask the right questions at the appropriate times, decide on who to call, and refocus the class when it has drifted away from the learning objective. All of this must be done while calling on all students equally, asking the question before identifying the student, watching for signs of confusion, and maintaining classroom order.

The solution is conceptually simple, but it isn't easy; essential teaching strategies must become automatic. They can be developed to automaticity if we are willing to make the effort and practice them. The outcomes can be very rewarding. Both student learning and motivation increase, and the sense of satisfaction that comes with truly guiding student learning can be tremendous.

Beyond Effective Teaching: Teaching for Thinking and Understanding

In Chapter 1, and earlier in this chapter, we said that effective teaching provides a foundation on which expertise is built, and that expert teachers go beyond this threshold to construct lessons that help students acquire a deep and thorough understanding of the topics they study. **Generative knowledge,** *"knowledge that can be used to interpret new situations, to solve problems, to think and reason, and to learn"* [italics added], is a term often used to describe this deep understanding (Resnick & Klopfer, 1989, p. 5).

Thinking and Understanding

Generative knowledge involves learning both content and the ability to think critically. "Learning is a consequence of thinking. Retention, understanding, and the active use of knowledge can be brought about only by learning experiences in which learners think about and think with what they are learning" (Perkins, 1992, p. 8). If deep understanding of content is a goal, emphasis on thinking must also be a goal. The models presented in Chapters 4 through 10 of this text are designed to capitalize on these two interdependent goals.

Concerns about student thinking have a long history. John Goodlad (1984), in one of the most comprehensive and widely publicized studies of American schools ever conducted, concluded:

> Only rarely did we find evidence to suggest instruction (in reading and math) likely to go much beyond merely possession of information to a level of understanding its implications and either applying it or exploring its possible applications. Nor did we see activities likely to arouse students' curiosity or to involve them in seeking a solution to some problem not already laid bare by teacher or textbook.
>
> And it appears that this preoccupation with the lower intellectual processes pervades social studies and science as well. An analysis of topics studied and materials used gives not an impression of students studying human adaptations and exploration, but of facts to be learned. (p. 236)

Another study found equally disquieting results:

> Many students are unable to give evidence of a more than superficial understanding of concepts and relationships that are fundamental to the subjects they have studied, or of an ability to apply the content knowledge they have acquired to real-world problems. The general picture of the thinking ability of U.S. students that is painted by these reports [national assessments of education progress, and studies from the National Commission on Excellence in Education] is a disturbing one. (Nickerson, 1988, p. 5)

This issue remains as important today as it was when these studies were conducted. In an era of accountability and high-stakes tests, the emphasis on thinking may be even further reduced. This is unfortunate for several reasons, one of the most important being the central role of thinking in motivation.

Teaching Thinking: Increasing Learning and Motivation

The need for teaching thinking is well documented. Without an emphasis on thinking, deep understanding of content is virtually impossible. The reverse is also true. In order to think effectively and productively in an area, a person must possess a great deal of generative knowledge about the area (Bruning et al., 2004; Resnick & Klopfer, 1989).

What receives much less emphasis, however, is the fact that objectives that increase critical thinking also increase learner motivation (Stipek, 2002). Teaching for thinking emphasizes learner autonomy and independent inquiry. Because of this emphasis, students' needs for control and competence are more likely to be met than when teachers lecture and students remain passive. Control and feelings of competence are essential for student motivation (Bruning et al., 2004; Pintrich & Schunk, 2002).

To see the motivational effects of teaching for thinking let's look again at Teri's instruction. She emphasized that students base their answers on their own thoughts as they interpreted information, not on what they had memorized or what they thought Teri wanted to hear. Being allowed the freedom to say what you think rather than what you believe someone expects to hear is intellectually liberating. This freedom, combined with learning to defend your position based on evidence, can lead to a personal sense of control and satisfaction. The combination can be very motivating.

A Climate for Thinking

As with other aspects of teaching, teaching for thinking requires supporting elements. To illustrate these elements, let's look again at Teri's lesson and the intellectual climate that she established with her students:

- She provided students with information and began the lesson in an open-ended and nonthreatening way.
- She promoted a spirit of cooperation rather than competition and avoided any comparisons of performance among students.
- She focused on improvement rather than displays of ability, as indicated by comments such as, "Very good analysis of the information we have here," "Very clear description," and "Your analysis of your own thinking is getting better and better. I'm proud of all of you."

Each of these factors created a climate in which the students felt safe. As a result, they were willing to risk offering their thoughts and ideas free from the fear of sarcasm or ridicule. This type of classroom climate is essential for both thinking and learner motivation (Maehr, 1992).

All of the models discussed in this text are grounded in this climate. Each requires an environment in which students feel safe and teachers facilitate learning with their questioning and other forms of support.

Critical Thinking

We have discussed the relationships between teaching for thinking, deep understanding of content, and learner motivation. Let's look now at what we mean by critical thinking. As with other aspects of human cognition, thinking is complex, and we realize that we may be oversimplifying the process. However, we offer this description of critical thinking as a foundation for your growth in this area.

In this text we define **critical thinking** as *the ability and disposition to make and assess conclusions based on evidence.* In some cases critical thinking is quite simple. For example, when we shop for a new vehicle we consider price, economy, reliability, and other factors, such as style. If one vehicle is advertised to get 29 miles per gallon whereas another gets only 24, we use that evidence as one factor in making a decision about which is a better buy. This is a form of critical thinking that is common in our shopping habits.

In other instances, critical thinking is more complex and sophisticated and can include abilities, such as:

- Confirming conclusions with facts
- Identifying unstated assumptions
- Recognizing overgeneralizations and undergeneralizations
- Identifying relevant and irrelevant information
- Identifying bias, stereotypes, clichés, and propaganda

To illustrate these dimensions, let's look again at some dialogue in Teri's lesson.

> STEVE: And they couldn't send it anywhere else!
>
> TERI: That's very good, both of you. Where do you suppose Steve got that idea? . . . Connie?
>
> CONNIE: . . . It says it right in the examples. Like in the first one it says, "The colonists wanted to sell it to France and other countries but were forbidden to do so."

Steve made a conclusion—colonies couldn't send their raw materials to any country other than their parent country—and Connie provided factual evidence from the examples that supported Steve's conclusion. Teri capitalized on this process at several points in the lesson.

Teri's lesson also provided opportunities to practice making conclusions based on evidence. For example,

> BOB: They weren't allowed to [get finished goods from other countries].
>
> TERI: And what made you say that, Bob?
>
> BOB: It says in the second example that they were told that their traps and weapons would be sent from France.

Teri's lesson focused on a deep understanding of the concept of *mercantilism* while simultaneously giving students practice in critical thinking—making conclusions based on evidence. We saw students practicing making and confirming conclusions with evidence in the preceding dialogue. Let's look now at some more dialogue where the students demonstrate more sophisticated thinking.

> JACK: We had to separate out the relevant from the irrelevant information.
>
> TERI: For example?
>
> JACK: . . . Well, whether it was guns, or traps, or clothing, or whatever, really didn't matter. The important point was that the colonists weren't allowed to manufacture anything.

Jack demonstrated critical thinking by identifying irrelevant information.

Now let's see how Teri helped her students recognize an unstated assumption.

> TERI: Let's look again at the question I asked "What other countries have been guilty of mercantilism?" What assumption is being made in that question?
>
> ANTHONY: . . . It seems like you're suggesting that mercantilism is bad.
>
> TERI: Good thinking. . . . That's exactly what it implies. Now, mercantilism may very well have been bad . . . exploitation of colonialized lands and that kind of thing. However, the question I asked had in it an unstated assumption. Recognizing unstated assumptions is part of the thinking process, and we all need to be on the lookout for that kind of thing. . . . Again, that's good thinking, Anthony.

Teri's lesson and the dialogue we have taken from it represent an ideal. Getting students to think the way hers did won't happen in every lesson, and it doesn't happen without teacher effort. However, knowing that it is possible gives us something to strive for, and it's an incentive to raise our expectations for our students. Seeing improvement in our students' thinking indicates progress and is a measure of success. It helps us move beyond the "preoccupation with the lower intellectual processes" that Goodlad (1984) saw so evident in most classrooms.

Dispositions for Thinking

We defined critical thinking as the ability and disposition to make and assess conclusions based on evidence. In this section we want to consider the idea of dispositions in more detail because they are arguably the most important aspect of thinking critically. The inclination to use evidence, for example, is limited if learners have to be continually reminded that evidence is required. Ultimately, our goals are for students to be predisposed or "inclined" to use evidence on their own. These inclinations develop over time if students have opportunities to practice them. The following simple example illustrates how such an inclination operates in everyday life.

> Terry and Tabatha are walking down the hall when they met Andrea coming the other way.
>
> "Hi Andrea," Terry and Tabatha say in unison.
>
> Andrea barely glances at the two girls and keeps walking.
>
> "Is she stuck up or what?" Terry grumbles.
>
> "We don't know that," Tabatha returns. "Maybe she isn't feeling well, or maybe something happened to her this morning."

Tabatha demonstrated the inclination to remain open-minded, and reserve judgment. Opportunities to promote and encourage these inclinations occur frequently in classrooms, and if teachers are aware of the possibilities, they can capitalize on them when they do occur. A number of attitudes and inclinations associated with critical thinking have been identified. They include:

- A desire to be informed and to look for evidence
- An attitude of open-mindedness and healthy skepticism
- The tendency to reserve judgment
- Respect for others' opinions
- Tolerance for ambiguity

Students learn these attitudes through teacher modeling and by directly experiencing them in classroom learning activities. As students acquire these inclinations and develop critical-thinking skills, their abilities to both learn and function effectively in the outside world increases. This is the essence of what it means to be educated.

Summary

Essential Teaching Strategies: The Foundation for Teacher Effectiveness

Teacher effectiveness describes patterns of teacher actions that result in increased student achievement. Essential teaching strategies, the abilities that all teachers should have, are based on teacher-effectiveness research. These strategies provide the foundation on which the models in this book are based.

Essential Teaching Strategies and Classroom Management: Creating Productive Learning Environments

Classroom management and effective instruction are interdependent; it is virtually impossible to teach effectively in a chaotic classroom, and it is very difficult to create an orderly classroom in the absence of effective teaching.

Organization is a key to effective classroom management, and orderly classrooms also increase student motivation to learn.

Essential Teaching Strategies: The Influence of Our Cognitive Architecture

People's working memories are limited. Because of this fact, to be employed effectively, the essential teaching strategies must be overlearned to the point of automaticity, meaning teachers can apply them with little conscious effort. Unless they are essentially automatic, too much of teachers' working memory space will be used in attempting to apply the strategies, which will likely result in teachers reverting back to rudimentary instruction, such as simple lecture.

Beyond Effective Teaching: Teaching for Thinking and Understanding

Expert teachers go beyond essential teaching strategies to promote deep understanding of the topics they teach, together with thinking. Much instruction in our schools focuses on knowledge and recall, and the ability of our students to think is a matter of ongoing concern. Fortunately, teaching for thinking also increases learner motivation.

Teaching thinking requires a classroom environment where learners feel free to offer their thoughts and ideas without fear of reprisal or embarrassment.

Critical thinking is the ability to make and defend conclusions based on evidence. It also includes an attitude of open-mindedness, tolerance for ambiguity, respect for others' opinions, the ability to separate relevant from irrelevant information and other positive attitudes and dispositions. Opportunities to practice critical-thinking abilities abound, both in classrooms and in everyday living.

IMPORTANT CONCEPTS

Automaticity (p. 70)
Callouts (p. 66)
Closure (p. 67)
Connected discourse (p. 60)
Critical thinking (p. 73)
Emphasis (p. 61)
Equitable distribution
    (p. 65)

Essential teaching strategies
    (p. 58)
Feedback (p. 63)
Focus (p. 63)
Generative knowledge (p. 71)
Instructional alignment (p. 61)
Monitoring (p. 64)
Precise terminology (p. 59)

Productive learning
    environments (p. 69)
Prompt (p. 66)
Questioning frequency (p. 65)
Review (p. 67)
Transition signal (p. 60)
Wait-time (p. 67)

EXERCISES

Read the following case study and answer the questions that follow:

1. Kathy Johnson is a fifth-grade teacher with twenty-seven students, about half of whom are classified as at-risk students, from mostly low- to middle-income families in an urban midwestern city. Four of her students have learning disabilities, and two are classified as behaviorally disordered. A veteran of 6 years, Kathy typically schedules her day as follows:

    8:15–9:15   Math
    9:15–10:45   Language Arts

10:45–11:00	Break
11:00–11:30	Social Studies
11:30–12:00	Lunch
12:00–1:25	Reading
1:25–1:35	Break
1:35–2:00	Science
2:00–2:45	Resource (art, music, physical education, computer)

2. In social studies Kathy has begun a unit on the northern and southern colonies prior to the Civil War.

3. As the students file into the room from their break, they see a large chart displayed at the front of the room that appears as follows:

	People	**Land and Climate**	**Economy**
Northern colonies	Small towns Religious Value education Cooperative	Timber covered Glacial remains Poor soil Short growing season Cold winters	Syrup Rum Lumber Shipbuilding Fishing Small farms
Southern colonies	Aristocratic Isolated Social class distinction	Fertile soil Hot weather Long growing season	Large farms Tobacco Cotton Unskilled workers Servants and slaves

4. Kathy is standing at the doorway as her students enter the room. She smiles and jokes with them as they pass by and reminds them of what they're about to do with comments such as, "Look carefully at the chart at the front of the room," and "See if you can find anything interesting about it and how the North and South were different?"

5. At 11:02 the students have their social studies books on their desks, Kathy has moved to the front of the room, and she begins, "We began talking about the northern and southern colonies yesterday. Let's see what we remember. . . . Where are they compared to where we live? . . . Lorenda?"

6. ". . . They're over here," Lorenda answers, motioning to the right with her hand.

7. "Yes, they're generally east of us," Kathy adds, as she walks quickly and points to the map at the side of the room identifying the general location of the colonies relative to the students' location with a wave of her hand.

8. "And about how long ago are we talking about, a few years or a long time? . . . Greg?"

9. ". . . A long time. Like when our great, great, great, great grandfathers and grandmothers might have lived."

10. "Yes, very good," Kathy smiles and nods. "We're talking about a time during the early and middle 1800s.

11. "We also talked about some important ideas, such as *Economy*," Kathy continues. "What do we mean by economy? . . . Carol?"

12. "... It's ... like ... the way they make their money, like when we said that the economy here is based on manufacturing, like making cars and parts for cars and stuff," Carol responds uncertainly.

13. "Very good description, Carol," Kathy nods. "You identified auto manufacturing as an important part of our economy, and that's a good example.

14. "Now, look here," Kathy directs, pointing to the column marked "Economy." "We see that the economy for the two groups of colonies is very different. Today, we want to see what some of these specific differences are and why the two economies are so different. So, remember as we go through the lesson that we're talking about the way the colonies made their money, and we're trying to figure out why they are so different. . . . Everybody ready?" Kathy surveys the class. "Good. Let's go."

15. She then begins, "What are some of the differences we see in the economies for the two regions? . . . Ann Marie?"

16. ". . ."

17. "What do you notice about the farms in the two colonies?"

18. ". . . The farms were much bigger in the southern colonies than they were in the northern colonies."

19. "Okay, good observation," Kathy nods energetically. "Now why might that have been the case? . . . Jim?"

20. ". . ."

21. ". . . Would you like me to repeat the question?" Kathy asks, knowing that Jim hasn't heard her.

22. "Yes," Jim responds quickly, with a look of relief. [Kathy repeats the question, and Jim responds by saying that, according to the chart, the soil was poor in the North but fertile in the South. Kathy then continues guiding the students' analysis of the information on the chart, in the process finding relationships between the geography, climate, and economy. When the students are unable to answer she rephrases her questions and provides cues to help them along. She then has them consider why the economy of their city might be the way it is. We return to her lesson now.]

23. "You have done very well, everyone," she smiles, pointing her finger in the air for emphasis. "Now, everyone, get with your partner, take 2 minutes and write two or three summary statements about what we've learned here today. . . . Quickly now, get started."

[The students start buzzing, pointing at the chart, and one of the two in each pair begin writing. In some cases they stop, crumple their papers, and begin again. As they work, Kathy walks among them offering encouragement and periodic suggestions.]

24. At the end of 2 minutes Kathy announces, "One more minute, and we're going to look at what you wrote."

25. After another minute she begins, "Okay, let's see what you've got. What did you and Linda write, David?"

26. ". . . We wrote that the weather and the land had a lot to do with the way the different colonies made their money."

27. "Excellent! That's a good one. How about someone else. . . . Danielle, how about you and Tony?"

[Kathy has several other pairs offer their summary statements, they further develop the statements as a whole group, and then Kathy collects the papers.]

28. At 11:28 she announces, "Almost lunch time. Please put away your papers."

29. The students quickly put their books, papers, and pencils away, glance around their desks for any waste paper, and are sitting quietly at 11:30.

Identify the essential teaching skill *best illustrated* by each of the following paragraphs or sets of paragraphs in the case study. (The paragraphs in the case study are numbered for your reference.) In each case, where appropriate, identify both the skill and the subskill. For example, if you select organization, also include "starting on time" or "preparing materials in advance" or "established routines" if it is appropriate to do so. Your answer would then be, for example, "organization—established routines." Explain your choice in each case.

1. 2–5

2. 5–13

3. 14

4. 15–18

5. 23–27

6. 5, 8, 11, 15, 19

7. 7, 13, 19

8. In paragraph 19 Kathy called on Jim, knowing that he wasn't listening (as we see in paragraphs 20 and 21). Is this [calling on a student who isn't paying attention] an effective teaching strategy? Why do you think so, or why do you think not?

9. Look at the type of questions Kathy asked in paragraphs 15 and 17. What kind of questions are these. Give at least three reasons why they're effective.

10. Of the following, which paragraph is the best example of Kathy asking a question that encouraged critical thinking?
    a. 5
    b. 11
    c. 15
    d. 19
    e. 23

    Explain how the question promoted critical thinking, including information from the case study that supports your choice.

    _____

    _____

    _____

Feedback for these exercises begins on page 341.

DISCUSSION QUESTIONS

1. According to research examining teachers' practices, most instruction is conducted at a knowledge/recall level. Why do you suppose this is the case?

2. Accountability and high-stakes testing are now facts of life for most teachers. Can teachers prepare students to meet standards and still promote critical thinking. Why or why not?

3. In the early 1980s and before, the emphasis was on "context-free" thinking skills instruction, or, in other words, critical thinking that deemphasized knowledge of specific content. What are some reasons the emphasis is now on the development of critical thinking combined with deep understanding of content?

4. What implications does an increased emphasis on thinking have for scope and sequence in curriculum design?

5. What implications does the limited capacity of people's working memories and the concept of automaticity have for teaching critical thinking?

6. When do you think teachers should begin focusing on critical thinking for students? Should it begin in kindergarten or some time later? Why?

7. The essential teaching strategies were described as a foundation for the learning of other teaching strategies. This implies that first-year teachers should be knowledgeable and proficient in all the essential teaching strategies. Is this realistic? Why or why not?

Group Interaction Models

The models in this chapter are all based on theory and research indicating that social interaction is an essential component of classroom learning. **Group Interaction Models** are *strategies that involve students working collaboratively to reach common goals.* These models have evolved as a result of efforts to increase learner involvement in classroom activities, develop their social interaction skills, provide students with leadership and decision-making experiences, and give them the chance to interact with peers from different cultural and socioeconomic backgrounds. When you have completed your study of the chapter, you should be able to:

- Explain how strategies within the Groupwork Model can be integrated with other models.
- Identify the characteristics of cooperative learning and how they differ from Competitive Learning Models.
- Plan, implement, and assess learning in lessons using the STAD, Jigsaw II, and Group Investigation Cooperative Learning Models.
- Describe how the Discussion Model can be used to encourage student learning.

To begin our discussion let's look at three teachers' classroom experiences with Group Interaction Models.

Isabelle Ortega walks around her fourth-grade classroom as groups of students take turns quizzing each other on the week's spelling words. Isabelle implemented the process when she noticed that her students' spelling grades were nearly bimodal; some of her students were doing well, but others were doing very poorly.

As an experiment, she had the students work in pairs and arranged the pairs so they were seated together. She begins by presenting new spelling words in the usual way, describing patterns in their spellings, discussing their origins, and explaining definitions. The students then work together, one student asking the other to spell a word. The first student confirms the spelling, they both write the definition, discuss it, and then move on to the next word. They practice for 15 minutes each day, and all students turn in their papers at the end of the practice session. As they work, Isabelle walks among the groups providing brief suggestions and answering questions. At the end of each week she gives the class a quiz on the words and definitions.

Jim Felton grins as he sees the assortment of cereal boxes on the front table in his classroom. He has finally found a topic that interests his middle school students. Jim's health class has been studying nutrition and the class has been discussing breakfasts. Some students claim that cereal provides a balanced meal; others argue that most are loaded with sugar, salt, and fat. Then the topic of school lunches came up. Some students defended the lunches, but the "brown baggers" claimed the meals were high in calories. Jim decided to do something to capitalize on this interest and energy.

He divided his students into teams, each focusing on a different aspect of nutrition. One group examines cereals, another soft drinks, and a third school lunches. Each group uses cereal boxes, magazine articles, the school dietitian, and the Internet as sources of information about their topic. The groups then present their findings, and the class discusses them.

Jesse Kantor watches as her biology students silently study a chapter on amphibians. The students each have study guides that help them focus on different aspects of amphibian anatomy. Some study the digestive system, others the circulatory, and still others the nervous system. The next day the "experts" on each system get together to pool their understanding and compare notes. The third day these "experts" take turns teaching their topics to other members of their group. This session is followed by a quiz that assesses all students' knowledge of each topic.

How are these teaching episodes similar? What characteristics do they share and how do these characteristics promote learning? What roles do teachers and students play in this process? We answer these questions in the sections that follow.

Group Interaction Models: An Overview

Five essential elements undergird all effective group interaction strategies (Johnson & Johnson, 1994):

- Face-to-face interaction
- Group goals

- Individual accountability
- Collaborative skills
- Group processing

Face-to-face interaction between students has at least three benefits. First, it encourages students to put their sometimes fuzzy thoughts into words. This is a cognitively demanding task (as anyone who has tried to write something will attest) that promotes clear thinking and learning. Second, it allows for the sharing of alternate perspectives, helping students view ideas in different ways. And third, it allows students to coconstruct knowledge, building on the ideas of others (Eggen & Kauchak, 2004).

Group goals refer to *incentives within a learning environment that help create a team spirit and encourage students to help each other.* A group goal focuses students' energy on an agreed-on and shared learning task, and individuals' efforts contribute to others' goal attainment (Slavin, 1995). This is similar to the reward that occurs on soccer or basketball teams where individuals of unequal ability work together for team goals. Though individual effort is important, the gauge of this effort is the team's performance. Contrast this orientation with what often occurs in classrooms.

> The teacher is in front of the class; he or she asks the students questions. Following each question a number of hands go up. Some students are anxiously stretching their hands in the hopes of being called. Others, of course, do not have their hands up and try not to have their eyes meet those of the teacher in hopes they will not be called. The teacher calls on Juan. Peter, who sits next to Juan, knows the right answer. As Juan begins to hesitate, Peter becomes glad and stretches his hand higher. Peter knows that if Juan misses, the teacher may call upon him. In fact, the only way in which Peter can obtain a reward in this situation is if Juan fails. It is only natural in this competitive class structure for students to begin to take pleasure in the failure of others. Their own rewards are contingent on the failure of others. (Kagan, 1986, p. 250)

Group interaction strategies help solve these problems by placing students in learning situations where group goals reward cooperation.

In support of this view, researchers found that successful groups had extensive interactions focusing on content, and group goals encouraged students to explain content to their teammates (Cohen, 1994). Group goals also encourage students to ask for and give help. Teachers can promote group goals by setting up grading systems that reward students for the whole group's performance, such as free time, certificates of achievement, bonus points for grades, or anything else that is important to students.

Individual accountability means that all students are responsible for meeting learning objectives as measured by quizzes, tests, or individual assignments. Without individual accountability, the most able students in the group may do all the work, with teammates being ignored or given a "free ride."

Collaborative skills are interaction abilities that students learn and utilize in groups. They include turn-taking, listening, learning to disagree constructively, giving feedback, reaching consensus, and involving every member in the group. They are some of the most important skills students learn in group activities, and they often have to be taught and developed (McDevitt & Ormrod, 2002).

Group processing encourages members to reflect on the effectiveness of their group. This makes the group more effective, and it helps individuals understand how their actions contribute to the workings of the group.

In this chapter we examine *groupwork, cooperative learning,* and *discussion.* Each strategy is designed to use group interaction to promote learning. They differ in the goals they are designed to reach and the amount of structure they provide teachers and students. We present these models at this point in the book, because they are often integrated with the other models presented in Chapters 5 through 10.

Let's look at the theoretical foundations of Group Interaction Models.

Group Interaction Models: Theoretical Foundations

Interest in the role of social interaction as an instructional tool came from an unlikely source, a Russian psychologist named Lev Vygotsky (1896–1934). As a boy, Vygotsky was instructed by private tutors who used Socratic dialogue, a question-and-answer process that challenges current ideas, to promote higher levels of understanding (Kozulin, 1990). These sessions, combined with his study of literature and experience as a teacher, convinced him of the importance of two major factors in human development: social interaction and language (Vygotsky, 1978, 1986). This perspective, called **sociocultural theory,** *emphasizes the essential role that social interaction and language, embedded within a cultural context, have on cognitive learning and development.* Vygotsky's sociocultural theory is based on three principles:

- Meaningful learning takes place within a social context.
- Knowledge is coconstructed as more knowledgeable others interact with and share their expertise with others.
- The culture that a person grows up in provides "cultural tools" or ideas that help make sense of the world.

Social interaction is central to understanding Vygotsky's theory. Students benefit from social interaction in at least three ways, by (1) sharing ideas, (2) appropriating understanding, and (3) articulating thinking.

Students sharing ideas is perhaps the most powerful outcome of social interaction. This sharing facilitates the process of knowledge construction and is sometimes described as occurring from the "outside in" (Brenner, 2001). Learners first think collaboratively, building on each others' understandings and negotiating meanings when ideas differ. After understanding is developed in a social environment, it is then internalized by individuals (Meter & Stevens, 2000).

Sharing ideas not only helps students learn *what* to think but also *how* to think and interact productively with others. For example, in a discussion about reintroducing wolves into northern forests, suppose a student spontaneously asks, "Yeah, but what if you were a rancher? Wouldn't you be upset if a wolf came and ate your cattle?" This is a form of perspective taking, and other students gradually may adopt and use it. Researchers call the spread of reasoning strategies such as this "snowballing" and consider it one of the most important outcomes of social interaction (Anderson et al., 2001).

The process of *appropriating understanding,* developing new meaning as a direct result of interaction (Leont'ev, 1981), is central to Vygotsky's theory. When students appropriate understanding, they borrow from and build on others' ideas.

Social interaction also facilitates learning by encouraging students to articulate their thinking, the process of trying to put ideas into words. As we said in the previous section, this is cognitively demanding but powerful for promoting learning (Bransford et al., 2000; Mason & Boscolo, 2000).

Teachers play an essential role in ensuring that student interaction results in learning (Webb, Farivar, & Mastergeorge, 2002). First, teachers structure small-group activities so that students stay on task. Second, while groups work, teachers carefully monitor interactions to ensure that ideas are being discussed and explained, and the focus is on understanding rather than merely getting the right answer. Finally, they hold students accountable for understanding, instead of merely completing the task, when they conduct or create assessments.

Teachers also benefit from group interaction because it provides them with access to students' developing thought processes. By listening to students as they interact in groups, teachers gain insights into the progress and pitfalls that students are encountering. Armed with this information, teachers can then remediate problems and build on developing student ideas.

Groupwork Strategies

Groupwork is *an instructional strategy in which students work together to supplement other models.* In contrast with Cooperative Learning and Discussion Models, groupwork isn't intended as a "stand-alone" model. Rather, it is designed to increase involvement when other models are used, and this is why we call it a *strategy* instead of a *model.* For example, Isabelle Ortega first used teacher-centered, whole-group instruction to introduce spelling words and then used groupwork as her students practiced. As you study Chapters 5 through 10 you'll see additional examples of teachers using groupwork within the context of other models.

Groupwork can be used to reach both lower-level learning objectives, such as basic math facts, historical names and dates, or chemical symbols and terms in science, and higher-level objectives, such as solving problems in math, identifying cause-and-effect relationships in social studies, designing experiments in science, or providing feedback on written work in language arts.

Planning Groupwork Activities

Because our goal when using groupwork is to have students work together to examine and discuss lesson content, the quality of the interaction is essential. What students talk about and how they talk about it determines what they learn (Gillies & Ashman, 1998; King,

1999). If, during groupwork, they talk about a football game, dance, or other social activity instead of the topic, they obviously learn less content. And if groupwork focuses on getting the right answer instead of understanding, learning also decreases.

Two factors influence the effectiveness of groupwork: (1) ensuring that students stay on task and (2) helping students work together productively.

Increasing On-Task Behavior.   Research indicates that merely placing students in groups doesn't ensure effective cooperation (Emmer & Gerwels, 1998). Though most students like talking with their peers, working together effectively doesn't automatically happen (Cohen, 1994). Students used to listening quietly to teachers often experience difficulties when faced with the freedom of groupwork. They need training and supervision.

One of the biggest problems is the tendency of students to drift off task during groupwork activities. Some students misinterpret the freedom of groupwork as an opportunity to play and visit with friends. If groups aren't well organized and supervised, a great deal of time can be wasted. Some suggestions for planning and organizing groupwork are outlined in Figure 4.1. Each of these suggestions is intended to increase the likelihood that students will stay on task and focus on learning (Gillies & Ashman, 1998; King, 1999).

Isabelle implemented each of these suggestions in her work with her fourth graders. She had the pairs sit near each other, the task was very clear, students wrote the words as they practiced (and turned in their papers), she limited the amount of practice time, and she monitored their work. Each of her actions was designed to help keep students on task.

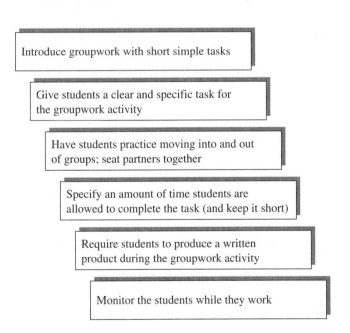

FIGURE 4.1   Planning Groupwork Activities to Increase On-Task Behavior

TABLE 4.1   Team-Building Activities

Activity	Description
Favorites	Team members interview each other about their favorites—food, music, hobby, sport, and so on
Biographies	Students interview each other and find out about each others' backgrounds
Occupations	Students talk about what they might want to be later on in life
Most interesting topics	Students interview each other about different class topics in which they are interested

Working Together Productively.   The inability of students to work effectively together can also be a problem when groupwork is used. Simple team-building exercises can address this problem (Slavin, 1995). The purpose of team-building exercises is to help students learn to accept, support, and trust each other; to develop a team identity; and to learn to work together effectively.

Having the students interview each other is one simple activity that can increase group rapport. Some potential interview topics are found in Table 4.1. If you introduce groupwork early in the year, interviewing can also help students initially get to know each other.

Other social interaction skill activities are also important, such as using quiet voices, making supporting statements, and listening while a teammate is talking. Teachers can model those behaviors and then have students practice them. In addition, teachers need a clear signal to capture students' attention when they get too noisy or when the teacher wants to reassemble the class.

Experts also advocate teaching students how to ask facilitating questions that promote thinking and learning (King, 1999). Examples include:

- Why is _____ important?
- What is _____ an example of?
- How is _____ similar to _____?
- How does _____ relate to _____?

Teaching students to ask questions such as these can improve the quality of group interaction and improve learning (King, 1999).

When you first divide students into groups you might want to have them identify the goals of the activity. Ask for feedback after several minutes and have different groups report to the whole group. This strategy focuses each groups' efforts and prevents confusion as the activity progresses.

Implementing Groupwork Activities

Groupwork exists in different forms, depending on the goals of the lesson, the size and composition of the group, and the learning task. The simplest arrangement consists of learning pairs. When seated next to each other, students working in pairs can be easily integrated into existing lessons. In this section we discuss four strategies:

- Think-pair-share
- Pairs check
- Combining pairs
- Teammates consult

Think-Pair-Share.   **Think-pair-share** is *a groupwork strategy in which individual students in learning pairs first answer a teacher-initiated question and then share it with a partner* (Kagan, 1994). This strategy is most effective when embedded in whole-group, teacher-led instruction. When using this strategy teachers ask a question as they normally would but then, instead of calling on a particular person, asks all students to think about the answer and discuss it with their partners. After a short period of time, the teacher asks students in each pair (or several of the pairs) to share their thoughts with the whole class. Three factors contribute to the effectiveness of this strategy:

- It elicits responses from everyone in the class and promotes involvement and active learning.
- Because each member of the pairs is expected to participate, it reduces "free rides," which are sometimes a problem in groupwork.
- It is easy to plan and implement and can help learners make the transition to more complex groupwork strategies.

Think-pair-share can also be adapted to a variety of different contexts and objectives. **Think-write-pair-share,** is *a variation in which students write down their answers before comparing them with a partner* (Kagan, 1994). It increases individual accountability and also encourages students to clarify their thoughts on paper before sharing with others.

Think-pair-square, a second variation, *substitutes a team discussion for the dyadic interaction* (Kagan, 1994). Instead of comparing their answers with one partner, students in think-pair-square discuss their responses in groups of four. This provides greater opportunities for students to hear different perspectives and to share their ideas with other students. It is especially useful in areas such as social studies and language arts where differing perspectives can enrich discussions.

Pairs Check.   **Pairs check** is *a strategy that involves student pairs in seatwork activities focusing on problems or questions with convergent answers* (answers that are clearly right or wrong, such as those for math problems, spelling words, grammar, or punctuation). The strategy is used following instruction in which a concept or skill has been taught and provides students with opportunities to practice the topic by alternating between the roles of "solver" and "checker." Pairs are given handouts containing the problems or questions. One member of the pairs works one or two problems, the second member checks the answers, and then the roles are reversed.

As students work, the teacher monitors the process and encourages students to discuss, when appropriate, the reasons the answers are correct or incorrect. If they don't, pairs check is little more than individual students checking answers at the back of the book. In addition, time is reserved at the end of the activity to allow whole-class discussion on general areas of disagreement or confusion.

Combining Pairs. **Combining pairs** is *a strategy in which learning pairs share their answers with other pairs.* It can be used in both interactive teaching and seatwork activities. It has the advantage of encouraging the active participation of pairs while simultaneously helping students develop social skills in larger groups.

In using this strategy during interactive teaching, the teacher identifies both the learning pairs as well as the groups of four (two learning pairs) and has them sit together so instruction can move from a small group to the whole class efficiently. Each group member is assigned a number from one to four, which identifies the students. The teacher asks the class a question with a convergent answer, such as the solution to a problem in math. The teacher asks each group to work on the solution and until everyone in the group knows the answer. The teacher then asks all the number ones (or twos or threes or fours) to raise their hands and calls on a student to explain the answer.

Similar arrangements are made with seatwork. Students are seated close to each other to facilitate communication. Students are given problems, and members of the pairs compare their answers. If they agree or can resolve disagreements, they continue. If they can't resolve disagreements, they confer with the other pair in their group, comparing and discussing their answers with the other pair. The teacher intervenes only when disagreements among the four students cannot be resolved.

Teammates Consult. **Teammates consult** is *a groupwork variation of combining pairs that requires discussion before students write down an answer* (Kagan, 1999). Students work in teams of four to complete worksheets or other assignments that have convergent answers. Rather than having students work independently before checking answers, teammates consult requires students to put their pens or pencils down until the group discusses each question, which is read by one member of the group. Once agreement is reached, students write down their answers then a second member of the group asks the next question. The need for dialogue before students write down their answers provides greater opportunities for cooperation and sharing.

Cooperative Learning Models

Having examined groupwork, we now want to turn to **cooperative learning,** *a group of teaching models that provide structured roles for students while emphasizing social interaction.* Research indicates that cooperative learning can be used to reach a variety of goals, including higher achievement, improved motivation, improved social skills, and better relations among students from diverse backgrounds (Emmer & Gerwels, 1998). In addition, it can be used to reach a variety of content goals ranging from automaticity with facts to higher-level goals such as problem solving and critical thinking.

In this section we examine three cooperative learning models: *Student Teams Achievement Divisions (STAD),* designed to teach facts, concepts, and skills; *Jigsaw II,* intended to teach organized bodies of knowledge; and *Group Investigation,* designed to help students learn to conduct research on specific topics.

STAD: Student Teams Achievement Divisions

Anya Lozano is beginning a unit on fractions with her fifth graders. She realizes that some of the content is review, so she gives a pretest to help her determine how much her students already know.

As she hands out the pretest, she says, "Class, this week we're starting a new unit in math on fractions and I'm passing out this pretest to help me find out how much you remember from last year." As she walks from aisle to aisle, she hears comments such as, "I hate fractions!" and "Not fractions again." Though students often don't care for math, she is surprised at how negative they are. She decides to talk to her friend, co-teacher, and mentor, Kay Reilly, at lunch.

"What do you do when the kids hate the stuff that you have to teach?" Anya asks as she rummages through her lunch bag trying to decide where to begin.

"Hate is a pretty strong word," Kay grins. "What could prompt those feelings in our fifth graders?"

"Fractions!" Anya responds. "When I gave them a pretest today, I was surprised at the faces and groans I got. Not all of them, granted, but more than usual. . . . I'm not looking forward to this unit."

"Well, be careful about jumping to conclusions, and think for a minute. What are kids usually telling us when they say they hate something?" Kay counters.

". . . Good question," Anya nods after thinking for a few seconds. ". . . Usually it's something like, 'I really dislike this stuff and I'm gonna make it miserable for you if you try and teach it to me.' "

"Oh, good, Anya. Very analytical and perceptive," Kay replies dryly. "But, seriously, usually when they say they hate something it means they don't understand it or they're afraid of it. They may have had a bad experience last year with fractions and are simply afraid of having the same thing happen again."

". . . Could be . . . actually, you're probably right," Anya acknowledges. "The ones who were complaining the loudest were the ones who are a little shaky in math anyway. Makes sense . . . but now what? What do I do now? Help help!"

"Well, here's what you might try. I've been doing it for awhile now, and it takes some work, but it's starting to pay off. . . . Have you got the pretests graded yet? . . . Good. Let me explain what I'm doing."

The next day Anya begins her math class in the same way she planned—by passing out squares of paper and having students divide the squares into halves, thirds, and fourths. Using the chalkboard, overhead, and the papers, she guides her students toward a concept of fractions, and the process of adding fractions with like denominators.

When students seemed to understood the concept and processes, Anya continues, "You've all been working hard and it looks like you remember a lot about fractions. Now to give you some practice with the ideas we've been discussing we're going to try something different. Rather than work on our practice sheets alone, like we usually do, we're going to work on them in groups. In a minute I'll tell you how we're going to do this and what group you're in."

She continues, "One of the first things I want you to do with your group is to get to know each other, then decide on a team name. Your team is important because you will work together for the whole unit. . . . Everyone look up here for a moment. I'm passing out this worksheet that I want everyone to do. It's important for everyone to do their own work and work hard on the worksheet because I'll be giving you a quiz in a week, and your team's score will depend on how well *all* the team members do—not only some. Any questions? . . . Hakeem?"

"But how do we know the teams are fair?" Hakeem asks. "Maybe some teams are smarter than others."

"Good question, Hakeem. We'll make sure the teams are fair in two ways. First, everyone took a pretest and I put people on the different teams on the basis of their scores. Second, the teams aren't competing with each other. You can all do well. All teams can win, and no team has to lose. That's the beauty of what we're going to do."

She goes on, "The way we all win is for team members to improve on their understanding. If we improve, we win, and if we all improve, we all win. I'll explain how this works after the first quiz. For now, let's get into our groups and get started. Listen carefully when I call your name. Team one, over here in this corner. Alysia, Manuel. . . ."

After students move to their groups, Anya spends the next half hour explaining to them how cooperative learning works and modeling for them effective small-group behaviors.

When Kay Reilly first explained cooperative learning to Anya she stressed the importance of teacher work and attention at this point. "Good cooperative learning groups don't simply happen, they need to be developed," Kay stressed. At first Anya was a little skeptical, but she listened anyway and as she listened she became convinced.

As Anya works with her students in these groups, she is grateful for Kay's advice. Some of the students argue; others have trouble sharing materials. But after some work in these areas Anya, finally has the groups working together.

As students talk in their groups, Anya circulates around the room to be sure all the groups are functioning as smoothly as possible. In some groups she has to stop some students from dominating the activity; in others, she has to clarify procedures and expectations. Once the groups are working satisfactorily, Anya quietly circulates among them thinking to herself, "Maybe this will work."

Each math class that week follows a similar format. Anya begins by introducing the concept or skill, then models different computational and problem-solving processes for the students, and finally has students work in their groups to practice. While they work, Anya continues to circulate around the room, monitoring their work and offering suggestions.

The fourth day of groupwork, she interrupts students to announce, "Class, can I have your attention for a minute? I just wanted to share with you an idea that the Eagle team is trying out. They weren't as confident about the topic today, so they started out by doing the first three problems together. When they thought they all understood what they were doing, they went back to doing them on their own and checking them with each other. This is an idea you might want to try out in your group. However you want to do these is fine with me. The important thing is that everyone should thoroughly understand how to do the problems when you're finished."

Anya checks students' papers each night to monitor her class's learning progress. She is pleasantly surprised by the work students are handing in—especially some of students who were low achievers. After five days of groupwork, Anya decides they are ready for the quiz. She gives the quiz and scores the papers over the weekend. She is pleased and somewhat surprised with the results. The general level of understanding on the quiz is high and, more importantly, she doesn't have the few scores that are well below those of the rest of the class. Most of the students seem to understand fractions!

Student Teams Achievement Divisions (STAD), developed by Robert Slavin (1986, 1995) is *a form of cooperative learning that uses multiability teams to teach facts, concepts, and skills.* It is one of the more popular cooperative learning strategies used in schools today.

STAD is commonly used with the Direct-Instruction Model, which we discuss in Chapter 9. Direct instruction follows four steps: *introduction, presentation, guided practice,* and *independent practice.* When STAD is used, the first three steps are identical to those in direct instruction, but independent practice isn't "independent"; rather it is done in cooperative learning groups. These groups function together for an extended period of time, providing opportunities for practice and feedback during a unit. Let's see how this works.

Planning Lessons with STAD.   Planning for the STAD Cooperative Learning Model is a four-step process as outlined in Figure 4.2 and discussed in the sections that follow.

Planning for Whole-Group Instruction.   When using STAD, the teacher plans to present the content that students will practice in groups. This can be accomplished through the Inductive Model, the Concept Attainment Model, or the Direct-Instruction Model, all of which focus on specific forms of content. (We discuss these models in Chapters 5, 6, and 9

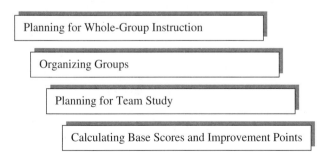

FIGURE 4.2   Planning Lessons with STAD

respectively). When you use any of these models, your planning will always include three essential steps:

- Identifying a topic
- Specifying clear learning objectives
- Preparing high-quality examples

Because you will use one of these models in planning for whole-group instruction, you will follow these steps in planning for lessons in which STAD is used.

Organizing Groups.   To effectively implement any kind of cooperative learning, teams must be organized in advance. The goal is to create teams that are of mixed ability, gender, and ethnicity (Slavin, 1995). Slavin suggests that four is an ideal number of members for a group, but groups of five members can also be used effectively. Teachers should assign the groups; when they don't, high and low achievers, boys and girls, and minorities and non-minorities tend to segregate themselves (Webb, Baxter, & Thompson, 1997).

One way to ensure that groups are similar in their range of abilities involves ranking the students, dividing them into quartiles, and assigning one student from each quartile to each group. Students can be ranked based on a pretest, as Anya did, or on grades or scores from previous units.

Forming groups based on the rankings are illustrated in Table 4.2 with a sample class of twenty-five students. An effective way of grouping students is to take the highest achievers from the first two quartiles and pair them with the lowest achievers from the third and fourth quartiles. For example, the first group would then include Natacha, Tolitha, Stephen, and Mary, and the second group would be Lucinda, Marvin, Howard, and David. The sixth group, having five members because of the number of people in the class, would then be Juan, Leroy, Gerald, Julia, and Cynthia.

TABLE 4.2   Grouping Students Based on Rankings

1	Natacha	14	Gerald
2	Lucinda	15	Henrietta
3	Vicki	16	Lawsekia
4	Jerome	17	Tolitha
5	Steve	18	Howard
6	Juan	19	Stephen
7	Tolitha	20	Cynthia
8	Marvin	21	Kevin
9	Enrico	22	Kathe
10	Sara	23	Ron
11	Eugene	24	David
12	Leroy	25	Mary
13	Julia		

After initially forming the groups, the teacher should check their makeup to ensure they're balanced by gender and ethnicity. For example, the first group has three girls and a boy, while the second has three boys and a girl. The teacher might arbitrarily switch two of the students to balance the groups with respect to gender.

Planning for Team Study.   The success of STAD learning teams depends on having high-quality materials to guide the interactions within groups. As teachers plan their lessons, they need to ask themselves, "What specific concepts or skills are students learning, and how can I design materials that will allow them to learn effectively in their groups?" This is where clearly specified learning objectives are important. They ensure that the group instruction and team study are aligned with the learning objectives.

A variety of team study materials can be used. In math, as in Anya's case, they might be problems to be solved. In language arts, they could be paragraphs to be punctuated or made grammatically correct. In geography, exercises might require students to identify cities closest to given longitude and latitude coordinates.

The team study materials should require convergent answers, which we described earlier as answers that are clearly right or wrong. If the content doesn't lend itself to convergent answers, STAD isn't the most effective model to use.

Calculating Base Scores and Improvement Points.   Equal opportunity for success is essential in STAD. **Equal opportunity for success** means that *all students, regardless of ability or background, can expect to be recognized for their efforts.* This element is particularly important in heterogeneous classes where background knowledge and skills vary widely. Equal opportunity for success is accomplished in STAD by awarding students *improvement points* if their score on a test or quiz is higher than their *base score.* A **base score** is *the student's average on past tests and quizzes, or a score determined by a previous year's or term's grade.*

Table 4.3 illustrates a sample calculation of base scores from previous grades. The teacher determines each student's base score prior to introducing the students to STAD.

Improvement points are awarded based on how students perform on a test or quiz compared to their base scores. A sample system for awarding improvement points is illustrated in Table 4.4.

TABLE 4.3   Calculating Base Scores from Grades

A	90
A–/B+	85
B	80
B–/C+	75
C	70
C–/D+	65
D	60
F	55

Adapted from Kagan, 1992; Slavin, 1995.

TABLE 4.4   **Sample System for Awarding Improvement Points**

Improvement Points	Score on Test or Quiz
0	Below base score
10	1 to 5 points above base score
20	6 to 10 points above base score
30	More than 10 points above base score, or Perfect paper (regardless of base score)

The system illustrated in Table 4.4 is arbitrary and can be adapted to meet the needs of specific classes. For example, you may choose to award some improvement points for any score that is no more than five points below the base score. However, you may require an improvement of twelve, fifteen, or even more in order to be awarded thirty improvement points. You can also change the system as student motivation and confidence increase. You may want to begin by rewarding virtually any effort, particularly with chronic low achievers, and then raise standards as students' achievement increases.

Before closing this section we want to emphasize one point. It is important that students can receive the maximum of thirty points if they get a perfect paper regardless of their base scores. This is important for high-achieving students. For example, if a student has a ninety-five average, it is impossible to improve by more than five points, so the student's incentive to improve would be reduced if the perfect-score provision didn't exist.

Implementing Lessons Using STAD.   Initially, implementing STAD lessons is much like implementing whole-group instruction that focuses on concepts or skills. The lesson is introduced, the content is explained, and students are involved in guided practice. Then team study takes the place of independent practice. However, STAD differs from the simple Direct-Instruction Model in that some instruction is often required to ensure a smooth transition from whole-group to team study. In addition, assessment, improvement points, and team recognition are an integral part of STAD. These phases and their learning and motivation functions are outlined in Table 4.5 and discussed in the sections that follow.

Phase 1: Instruction.   When using STAD, instruction is similar to typical whole-group instruction, focusing on specific concepts or skills. The teacher introduces the lesson; presents, explains, and models the skills or applications of concepts, principles, generalizations, and rules; and provides for guided practice. Anya's instruction illustrated these steps. She carefully explained and illustrated fractions with her manipulatives and had students practice under her guidance. When she felt students had an acceptable grasp of fractions and the procedures for adding them, she moved to team study.

Phase 2: Transition to Teams.   Obstacles to smoothly functioning cooperative lessons are often logistical. Research indicates that whole-group instruction is easier to manage than small-group work for at least two reasons (Good & Brophy, 2003). First, in whole-group work the teacher is able to "steer the lesson," speeding up and slowing down based on stu-

TABLE 4.5　Learning and Motivation Functions for the Phases of STAD

Phase	Learning and Motivation Function
Phase 1: Instruction Introduces and develops content	■ Attracts attention ■ Promotes schema production
Phase 2: Transition to teams Teacher explains how teams will function	■ Promotes sense of belonging ■ Creates feelings of safety and order
Phase 3: Team study Teacher monitors groups and supports groups' efforts	■ Develops automaticity ■ Promotes involvement
Phase 4: Assessment Individual students are formally assessed	■ Provides feedback ■ Develops perceptions of competence

dent progress; and second, interaction during whole-group work allows the teacher to monitor and deal with learning or management problems. These functions are harder to accomplish when students work in small groups.

When first introducing small-group work, the teacher needs to be carefully organized, anticipating logistical problems in advance. When first introducing team study, teachers should thoroughly explain how cooperative learning works and the specific procedures to be followed. Let's see how Anya helped her students make the transition to teams.

"Okay, everyone, I think we have a pretty good idea of what fractions mean and how we add them together when the denominators are the same. Now we're ready to practice. The way we're going to do that is by assigning each of you to a team, and each team will practice the new content. Because this is a little new, I'm going to show you how it works before I ask you to do it.

"In a few minutes I'm going to divide you into the groups that you'll be working with for this unit. But before that I want to show you how one group should work. Tanya, Mariko, Willy, can you come up here and sit at these desks? . . . Thanks! Class, this is what your group will look like—it will have four members, and for sake of this illustration, I will be the fourth member. After we divide into groups, I'll give each group four worksheets, just like I'm doing here."

Anya then takes a few seconds to pass out the materials to the group at the front of the room and takes one herself.

She continues, "Now, Tanya and Willy are a pair, and Mariko and I are a pair. Each person does the problem and checks with his or her partner. For example, Tanya does the first problem and then checks the answer with Willy, and Mariko and I do the same problem and we check with each other. If Tanya and Willy agree on the answer and believe that they both understand it, they move to the next problem. Mariko and I do the same. If Tanya and Willy disagree, they ask Mariko and me, and we do the same with them. We all discuss the problem until we're all sure we understand it. . . . Okay, let's go ahead."

The four of them then work the first problem and check with their partners. (Anya intentionally gets a wrong answer for sake of the illustration.)

"I didn't get that," she says loud enough for the class to hear. "Please explain that to me."

Anya then discusses different ways of providing helpful feedback to each other, and she also models appropriate and inappropriate ways of interacting with partners.

"What happens if we all disagree?" Leanne asks, after seeing the process modeled.

"Good question, Leanne. If all four of you have thoroughly discussed the problem and cannot come to an understanding, then you can ask me, . . . but remember," she emphasizes, "you can only ask me *after* all four of you have carefully discussed the problem."

Anya then assigns the rest of the class to their groups and has them begin.

Anya illustrated and modeled the process with one group before she had all the students begin team study. When first introducing students to cooperative learning, the initial directions need to be very detailed and explicit.

Teachers find it useful to place the following information on a poster, discuss it with the class, and leave it up for reference:

- Group memberships for different teams
- Location in the room for different teams
- Procedures for obtaining and turning in materials
- Time frames

Spending time on logistics at the beginning of cooperative learning lessons lays the foundation for smoothly functioning groups later on.

Phase 3: Team Study.   Team study provides opportunities for students to practice the new content and receive feedback from the other group members. As students work in their groups, you should monitor their work to ensure they are functioning smoothly, but be careful about intervening too soon. One of the goals of cooperative learning is to teach students to work together, and this process isn't always initially smooth. Early intervention may actually be counterproductive because students often need time and freedom to work through problems. However, if students aren't working together, one is dominating a group, or someone isn't participating, intervention is necessary. When to intervene is a matter of professional judgment.

What can be more helpful than individual interventions is calling attention to particularly productive groups. Let's see how Anya did this.

"Class, can I have your attention, please, just for a second? I know you're all working hard but I just wanted to share an idea with you. The Cheetah team came up with a great idea to work through their problems. They got a box of the blocks, the ones we used earlier, and every time one of the members is having trouble with one of the problems, they use the blocks to explain the answer, and I heard one of the group members say, 'Sure you can do this. Just try it again.' That is very helpful and supportive, and that's the way we want to treat our teammates."

Group interventions that focus on positive practice help students understand different roles in the groups and provide models for the other students.

Phase 4: Assessment.   Assessment serves at least two functions in the STAD Model. First, it provides both the teacher and students with feedback about learning progress, and second, it can provide incentives for work and effort. The key to the first function is a well-designed instrument that accurately assesses understanding of important concepts and skills. Again, clear learning objectives are essential because they identify what should be assessed.

Recognizing Achievement.   Assessment results can serve as motivators when they are integrated into a scoring system based on improvement points. Improvement scoring systems ensure that individuals compete only against their own past performance and not against each other. When students match past performance, they are given a small number of improvement points; when they exceed it, improvement points increase in proportion.

Team Scoring.   Team scoring is based on the improvement of individual team members. As an example, let's look again at the group composed of Natacha, Tolitha, Stephen, and Mary. Their averages and quiz scores are as follows:

Name	*Average*	*Quiz Score*
Natacha	95	96
Tolitha	88	90
Stephen	75	84
Mary	69	80

Based on the system discussed in the section on planning for improvement points, Natacha would receive ten improvement points and Tolitha would also get ten because their scores were in the range of one to five points higher than their base score (average). In comparison, Stephen would receive twenty improvement points because his quiz score was nine points above his base score, and Mary would receive thirty points because her score was more than ten points above her base. Mary, the lowest achiever in the group, actually got the most improvement points. This equal opportunity for success can be a powerful motivator when STAD is used.

Although the use of reinforcers, such as improvement points, is somewhat controversial, research indicates that the system has a positive effect on motivation (Slavin, 1995). The extent to which teachers use the system in their classes is a matter of professional judgment.

Team Awards.   Team scores are determined by averaging the improvement points for the team, and awards can then be given. The following is an example of one reward system.

Criterion *(Average Improvement)*	*Award*
10	Winners
15	Stars
20	All Stars
25	Major Leaguers

Team awards can exist in a variety of forms; teachers can decide on the exact form based on what will be motivating to their students. For example, Winners might be asked to stand and be recognized in class, Stars could get a certificate of achievement, All Stars a more elaborate certificate, and Major Leaguers a group photo on a hall of fame section of the bulletin board. Other options could include buttons to wear around school, letters to parents, special privileges, and leadership roles.

Students should be reminded that neither teams nor individuals are competing with each other; individuals only are competing with their past performances. If individuals improve, all teams can potentially become Major Leaguers. Teams can be changed periodically, such as every four or five weeks, to allow students to work with other classmates and to give students on low-scoring teams a chance for increased success.

Assessing Learning with STAD.   Assessment of STAD lessons occurs on two levels. The first relates to the content goals of the lesson and are similar to assessing understanding when other content-oriented models are used. As always, assessments should be aligned with learning objectives, instruction, and team study activities. For example, Anya had as her content objectives (1) identifying the numerator and denominator in a fraction and (2) adding fractions with like denominators. Assessment would measure individual students' attainment of these objectives.

Using Improvement Points in Grading.   As with all reinforcers, using improvement points in grading is controversial, but teachers often develop grading systems that reflect improvement. For instance, if students average fifteen or more improvement points on tests and quizzes, their grade might be raised from a B– to a B, or from a B to a B+. Many teachers believe that seeing improvement reflected in their grades is an added incentive for students; others believe that improvement points unduly penalize top students who may already be working at the upper limit of the grading system. Experts advise against basing final grades on improvement points because it provides a distorted picture of students' actual levels of achievement (Stiggins, 2001).

Assessing Groupwork and Cooperation.   At a second, more complex level, assessment of STAD activities attempts to answer questions such as, "Are students getting better at working together and learning to work together as a team?" The best source of information here comes from observing students as they work together in groups. Some questions that could be asked might include:

- Are all members contributing?
- Are some members dominating?

- Is the group interaction positive and supportive?
- Do boys and girls contribute equally?
- Are members from different racial and ethnic groups involved and being included?

By attending to these questions, teachers can help individuals and groups learn to cooperate and work together.

As teachers assess cooperation, they can provide feedback to the class, using smoothly functioning groups as models. This may be as simple as noting, "I really like the way this group is taking turns giving feedback," or it may involve role playing, where students publicly work out problems that individual groups are having. The goal is to help students become aware of their interactions in the groups and the effect these interactions are having on their own and others' learning.

Jigsaw II

Kevin Davis looks out his classroom window on a blustery spring Friday and lets out an audible "Hmmmm." So far the year has gone well for his world geography class but he isn't quite sure where to go from here. The next section of the text is Central America, and Kevin had problems with it last year. Maybe it was the timing—spring fever—and perhaps students were simply getting played out with their intellectual journey around the world. Or maybe, he thinks, it was the way he taught it last year— minilectures supplemented with small-group discussions. He tried this strategy on Thursday when he presented an overview of the new unit, but the students simply didn't seem excited about the content. Kevin knows he has to try something new, if only for his own professional sanity.

He spends part of that weekend going through notes and books from workshops and graduate classes that he has taken. One idea that keeps popping up is student involvement—how to get students actively involved in their own learning? As he thinks about this idea, he keeps flashing on cooperative learning. He tried learning teams in another class where students had to master, a number of important names and dates but he doesn't believe that would be appropriate here. What he really wants students to know is the "big picture" in terms of the Central American countries, not a lot of facts about each. He decides to try something different.

Monday morning he arrives early, sits down at his computer, and prepares several handouts. As he duplicates them, he finalizes plans for introducing the new activity and organizing the groups. He hopes he is ready.

"Class," Kevin begins as students settle in after the bell, "we're going to try something different for our next unit. I've decided to make each of you the experts on this content and have you teach each other."

He pauses to survey the class to gauge their initial reaction. From their puzzled looks at least they are curious. So far so good.

"To do this," he continues, "I've placed each of you in teams of four. I've tried to divide these teams so that all the teams are about equal. We'll be working in these teams for the next couple weeks. Your job on these teams is to do two things. First, each of you needs to become an expert on one part of each chapter. Can everyone take out their texts and turn to Chapter 17? That's on page 346. I'll show you what I'm talking about."

He pauses as students turned to the correct page and then goes on, "You'll notice in the introduction to the chapter on Costa Rica that it is divided into four sections—the physical geography of the country, its history, its culture, and its economy. We talked about these on Thursday. I'm going to ask each of you to become an expert in one of these areas and then teach that content to your other group members. To help you become experts, I've got a summary sheet for each of these topics to help you in your note taking. Let's see what one of these looks like." He walks over to the overhead and displays the transparency shown in Table 4.6 for the class.

"We'll call this our 'expert sheet'; each of you will have one of these when you read the chapter, and it will help you in your note taking. We'll take the rest of today and all of tomorrow to work on this. At the beginning of class on Wednesday, the experts on each topic will get together to review their notes and make sure everyone has the essential information. On Thursday the experts in each group will take turns teaching their topics to each other. So, for example, if Miguel has history, he'll teach the other members what he learned about the history of Costa Rica; then, let's say, if Yolanda has culture, she'll learn about history from Miguel and then teach him about the culture of Costa Rica. On Friday we'll take the first part of the class to review and put all this information together, and then we'll take a quiz on this chapter. The quiz will have an even number of questions on each of the topics, so you'll get some questions on the topic that you are an expert on and some on the others. That means you need to learn everything—not only your topic. We'll record team scores and keep a running tally from chapter to chapter. I'll talk more about this later. . . . Any questions? . . . Good.

"Then, let me quickly review our procedures. We'll break into groups in a minute. When you get into your groups, I've got an activity that will help you get to know each other a little better. Then you as a group decide who's going to be the

---

TABLE 4.6   Jigsaw II Expert Sheet

Physical Geography

1. Climate
   a. seasons
   b. temperatures
   c. rainfall
2. Topography
   a. mountains
   b. water
   c. land
      1) soil
   d. prominent features

expert in each of the four areas. If you don't get your first pick this time, you will the next. We'll rotate these around. . . .

"All right everyone, look up here for your group assignment. Note that the assignment also tells where in the room your group should meet. Let's go!"

After students quickly move into their groups, Kevin calls for their attention. He then has them do a team-building activity for 10 minutes. Finally, he announces, "I think you've done a good job with the activity, and we'll do more team building as we continue with the unit. . . . Now, I want the room quiet while each of you reads your section of the chapter and takes notes. We'll finish this on Tuesday and move into our expert groups on Wednesday. I'll be around to help you. Thursday is *expert teach day.* You'll each teach the other members of your group and learn from them about their topic. Make sure you take good notes to study from for the test on Friday. . . . Questions? . . . Good. . . . Look up at the board. I've written the schedule for the week there as a reminder. . . . Okay, let's go!"

Jigsaw II is *a form of cooperative learning in which individual students become experts on subsections of a topic and teach those subsections to others.* It differs from STAD in two ways. First, rather that focusing on specific concepts or skills, it is designed to teach **organized bodies of knowledge,** *topics that combine facts, concepts, generalizations, and the relationships among them.* Examples include the Industrial Revolution in social studies, structure and functions of different systems of the body in science, or a comparison of authors' works in language arts. Kevin's class focused on the geography of Central America, which is another organized body of knowledge.

Second, Jigsaw II uses a concept called **task specialization,** which *requires that different students assume specialized roles in reaching the objectives of a learning activity.* In the case of Jigsaw II, students become experts on a particular portion of a learning task and use their expertise to teach other students. Kevin had his students focus on different aspects of Central American countries. Then, when they worked as a team, each member contributed a different piece in the knowledge puzzle, thus the name *Jigsaw.* Jigsaw II is intended to foster interdependence in team members; students must depend on each other to learn the content.

As with STAD, Jigsaw II was developed by Robert Slavin (1986). It is an adaptation of the original Jigsaw strategy, developed by Aronson and his associates (1978). Because the original Jigsaw required customized materials, which required a great deal of teacher preparation time, and only the "experts" had access to the materials, which left students dependent on the "expert" presentations, its effectiveness was limited. Jigsaw II attempts to overcome these weaknesses.

Jigsaw II can be used to increase understanding of existing written materials such as student textbooks, but it can also be used to supplement other strategies (Kagan, 1994). For example, it could be used to provide background information on controversial issues in social studies, such as a discussion of nuclear energy. Some students might study the history, others the technology, and still others economic and ecological perspectives.

As another example, in a unit on poetry, different students might learn about rhyme, meter, symbolism, and authors' lives. Then, in analyses of different poems, each student, or group of students, would contribute their perspectives on the work.

Planning for Jigsaw II Lessons.   Planning for Jigsaw II lessons is similar to planning for STAD. Topics are identified, learning objectives are specified, materials are prepared, and students need to be assigned to teams. In addition, materials to assess learning progress must also be constructed.

However, because Jigsaw II relies on individual study, planning for whole-group instruction, as in STAD, is not required. The planning steps for Jigsaw II are summarized in Figure 4.3 and discussed in the sections that follow.

Identifying Topics and Specifying Learning Objectives.   As with the use of virtually any model, planning for lessons using Jigsaw II begins with identifying topics and specifying learning objectives. Any topic that involves an organized body of knowledge, as we discussed earlier in this section, is appropriate for use with the model. The learning objectives when Jigsaw II is used will be for students to understand the connections between ideas in a topic.

Designing Learning Materials.   The major tasks during this part of the planning process are the gathering of materials and the construction of expert sheets that guide students' study and teaching efforts. Resource materials can come from a number of sources: present texts, previously used texts, library books, encyclopedias, magazines, and nonprint sources, such as videotapes, videodiscs, and the Internet.

In addition to resource materials, teachers also need to design study sheets that help students focus on important information and issues. These can include questions, outlines, matrices, charts, or hierarchies. Kevin used outlines that divided key topics into subcategories. Well-organized expert sheets help guide student studying and result in effective expert presentations (Slavin, 1986).

Forming Student Teams.   In forming student teams, the same considerations that existed for STAD apply here. Groups should be balanced with respect to achievement, gender, and cultural background. Once groups are formed, it is important that members get to know each other and that group identity and cohesion develop. The same strategies described earlier for groupwork activities in general can be used here.

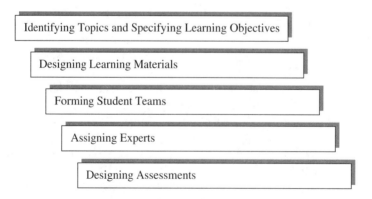

FIGURE 4.3   Planning Lessons with Jigsaw II

Assigning Experts.   Because each member of a team is required to develop expertise with respect to part of the topic, it is important that the expert teams also be mixed according to achievement, as in STAD. Kevin allowed students to select their topics and assured them that if they didn't get their first pick during the first round they would get it the next time.

Students will be more committed to a topic of their choice than to one that is assigned. However, if the lowest achievers for each group all happened to be responsible for one particular topic, the cultures of the countries, for example, the quality of learning for that segment of the topic might be reduced. In a mixed ability-group, by contrast, because all members of an expert group are responsible for understanding that aspect of the topic, the lower achievers in the group can learn from the higher achievers, and then the lower achievers would be in better positions to teach the other members of their teams.

Designing Assessments.   As we saw earlier in the chapter, individual accountability is an essential component of all Group Interaction Models. Also, hardworking individuals must be rewarded for their efforts. Effective assessments can help accomplish both.

In designing assessments, a table or planning matrix helps ensure that all topics receive equal weight on a quiz or test and that the items are at an appropriate level of difficulty. A sample assessment matrix for Kevin's class is shown in Figure 4.4.

Implementing Lessons Using Jigsaw II.   Jigsaw II is a four-phase strategy that begins with information gathering, proceeds through a process of disseminating information within groups, and culminates in assessment (Slavin, 1995). The specific phases with their learning and motivation functions are outlined in Table 4.7, and discussed in the sections that follow.

Phase 1: Information Gathering.   In the first phase of Jigsaw II, students are assigned topics with which they will develop expertise. Because Jigsaw II uses preexisting materials, such as chapters from books, the teacher's primary tasks are to be certain that the learning materials, such as textbooks, videotapes, and so forth, are available for students and the sheets guiding the experts' study are distributed and explained. The first time you use Jigsaw II, you may have to instruct the students on the use of the expert sheets to help them understand how they can be used to guide their study efforts.

Topic	Items		
	Knowledge	Comprehension	Application
Physical Geography			
History			
Culture			
Economy			

FIGURE 4.4   Planning for Assessment Matrix

TABLE 4.7   **Learning and Motivation Functions for the Phases of Jigsaw II**

Phase	Learning and Motivation Function
Phase 1: Information gathering Experts locate and study essential information	■ Develops background knowledge ■ Develops perceptions of competence
Phase 2: Expert meetings Experts compare notes and refine presentations	■ Acquires expertise ■ Increases self-efficacy
Phase 3: Team reports Experts teach content to team members	■ Promotes schema production ■ Increases involvement
Phase 4: Assessment Individual students are formally assessed	■ Provides feedback ■ Promotes encoding

Actual study time can be either in class or at home. When introducing Jigsaw II, it is helpful if the first few sessions are carried out as in-class activities. This provides you with opportunities to monitor student activity and offer suggestions to the groups.

Phase 2: Expert Meetings.   After students have had time to study their individual topics, "expert meetings" give students the chance to compare notes and clarify areas of misunderstanding. A discussion leader should be assigned to moderate the session and to ensure that everyone is actively involved. This role can be rotated so that everyone gets an opportunity to lead and participate. The expert sheets passed out earlier help provide structure for this discussion.

Phase 3: Team Reports.   During team report meetings, "experts" return to their groups and take turns teaching the group about their particular topics. This encourages them not only to share their knowledge but also to organize and summarize their information. Encouraging and helping students organize their information and offering suggestions for presentations can increases the learning in these sessions.

Phase 4: Assessment.   Assessing individual student performance serves to hold students accountable for the information from all groups and provides feedback to both students and the teacher about learning progress. The form that this assessment takes will vary with the content area, but teachers should assess all of the topics equally.

Assessing Student Understanding with Jigsaw II.   Assessing student understanding with Jigsaw II lessons occurs at three levels. First, we want to measure individual students' understanding of the content. Second, we want to assess the functioning of the groups and determine the extent to which students are growing in their ability to work together. And third, we want to know if students can investigate and organize topics and share this learning with others, that is, develop expertise.

Assessing Understanding of Content. With respect to assessing students' understanding of the topics, the objectives and evaluation matrices that were used during the planning process can help ensure that assessment instruments are consistent with learning objectives (see Figure 4.4). One of the challenges of assessing Jigsaw II activities is to construct instruments that challenge "experts" but don't overwhelm the other students. A combination of short-answer and essay questions, together with actual work samples, such as reports about different topics, can often be combined to form effective assessments. In Kevin's class, items focusing on the three elements of climate and four elements of topography would adequately sample the content.

Assessing Group Processes. In assessing group processes, we want to determine the extent to which students are functioning as productive members of a group. This includes speaking, listening, sharing ideas, and helping the group move in a positive direction. The same kinds of questions asked about STAD lessons apply here:

- Are all members contributing?
- Are some members dominating?
- Is the group interaction positive and supportive?
- Do boys and girls contribute equally?
- Are members from different racial and ethnic groups involved and being included?

To these questions about whether experts are explaining content clearly might be added. Again, this skill may need to be taught through modeling and role playing.

Assessing the Development of Expertise. Finally, we want to measure the extent to which students are growing as expert presenters and members of each team. Jigsaw II, which involves sophisticated learning skills such as note taking and organization, requires the even more sophisticated ability of teaching content to others. These skills must be taught and monitored. One way to teach the skills is through think-alouds in which the teacher models the skill while talking out loud. As students practice in their groups, you also should monitor their work and provide feedback.

Group Investigation

Kim Herron has been teaching junior high science for 3 years and is generally happy with her teaching. She believes that she provides students with a solid foundation for their work in high school and a general understanding of the role of science in their lives. But she isn't quite as happy with her progress in helping students "think." They seem all too happy to memorize the material she gives them, rather than thinking on their own. Kim decides that this year will be different.

The school science fair is coming up in 2 months. She has encouraged her students to participate and most will, but the quality of their projects is uneven. Kim can tell which students have received help from parents—which is fine—but what about the rest of the students? She decides to make Fridays in her class group project day, and the focal point for the projects will be the science fair to be held in May.

As she sits down to plan for these Fridays Kim asks herself, "Where do I start? What do they need to get started on their group projects?" After some gazing out the window, considerable doodling on her notepad, and occasional thumbing through old science methods texts and teachers' editions, she decides on a two-pronged attack. First, they will need some information about good science projects—what they did, how they were implemented, and how they were reported.

"That shouldn't be too difficult," she thinks "I've got some winners' projects from the past few years."

Then they will need some background knowledge on the topics they are studying. As she thinks about this, she jots down some possibilities and makes a note to work on them.

The next Friday, she begins her class by saying, "Okay, listen everybody. . . . We're going to try something different today and for the remainder of the Fridays until the science fair on May 7. We're going to use Friday's class to work on our science projects, and we're going to do this a little differently than we have in the past. First, I'll give you class time to work on the projects and I'll expect weekly progress reports on how you're doing. Second, I'd like you to do the projects in groups rather than individually. This will result in better-quality work, and I think you'll learn a lot from each other. To divide you into groups, I'm going to ask each of you to write your name and some topics you're interested in studying on a piece of paper. I'll pull this information together and assign you to groups by next Friday. These groups won't be unchangeable, but this process will allow us to get started."

The next Friday, she has listed the different groups on the bulletin board by topics and members. Students congregate around the board, chattering as they enter the room. Kim observes the excitement and hopes that it won't interfere with learning.

"Oh, well," she says to herself as the bell rings, "here goes."

As the class quiets down Kim walks to the front of the room, pauses briefly, and begins, "You've probably already seen your assignments as you came into the room. If you didn't, you can check up here (gesturing to the bulletin board) when we break into groups. For today, our first job will be to get to know the other members on our teams. To do that, I'd like each person to interview another team member, so when you first get into your groups, select a partner. Then, ask your partner why he or she is interested in the topic and what she or he knows about it." Kim wrote the interview information on the board and then continued, "Also, try to discover other interesting information about your partner with respect to science. Remember, the interview must focus on your topic and science in general. One person can interview another, then switch. Each person will make a short introduction of the person he or she interviews in your group. Take notes so you remember all the important points."

Kim pauses and then says, "Before we break into groups let's quickly review to make sure we know what each person's responsibility will be. What's the first thing you'll do in your groups? Alysha?"

"Find a partner."

"Good, Alysha. Then what? . . . Anyone? . . . Selena?"

"Interview your partner?"

"Fine. And what questions will you ask? . . . Antonia?"

"The ones on the board."

"Good. And what will you do with the interview information? Juan?"

"Report back to the group," Juan replies.

"Excellent, everyone!" Kim exclaims. "Now remember our goal here is to begin to get to know each other so we can work effectively in our teams.

"To avoid congestion, let's have Group 1 over here at the front of the room, Group 2 over here, Group 3 back there, Group 4 over there, Group 5 in the corner, Group 6 over here, and Group 7 up here. If you don't know what group you're in, check up here (pointing to the chart). All set? . . . It's 1:20. I expect you to be done by 1:40. Okay, let's go, move."

Kim watches as students get into their groups. Surprisingly, it goes smoother than she anticipated and the groups quickly settle into the rhythm of interviewing.

A hand goes up. "What do we do if there isn't an even number of students?"

"Good question, Jianna. Class, if there is an odd number in your group due to absence or some other reason, do your interviews in threes."

The class settles again into a low hum as Kim moves around the room. Most of the groups are working well and the others seem to need only a gentle reminder to stay on track.

At 1:30, Kim announces, "Everyone, you should be done with your interviews by now and should be sharing your findings with other members of the group. You've got 5 more minutes and then we'll move on to another activity."

At 1:35, Kim brings the class together again and announces, "Good job, everyone. We're now ready to begin our next task, . . . which is to try and understand what a good science project looks like. To help us, I've placed several award-winning projects around the room. I'd like the groups to rotate around the room, examining the projects to try to figure out why they won awards. Take notes and talk about your ideas in your group and then we'll come back together as a class to discuss our findings. Okay, questions? . . . Then let's move." The class spends the remainder of the period examining the projects and discussing the criteria for good projects.

Near the end of the period Kim concludes the class by saying, "We've made good progress in trying to understand what a good science project looks like. Our job next Friday will be to lay the foundation for one of the components we talked about today—background information. I'd like you all to be thinking about the kind of information you will need to enable you to ask meaningful questions and make interesting hypotheses for your investigations. I'll try to bring in some reference books for everyone to use, and each of you needs to bring in at least one book on the topic you are studying by Friday. You can get these either at the school library or a public library. Any questions? . . . Okay, then I'll see you on Monday and don't forget your books on Friday."

During the next week Kim works with the school librarian to build a collection of reference books on the different topics the students are studying. She also raids her own college textbook collection and asks her colleagues to do the same. By Friday, she has more than forty books on the different topics that students are investigating.

At the beginning of the period, she calls the class together and explains that their goals for the day are to look at the resources available to the groups and to begin a plan of action for their projects.

As students move into their groups, Kim again circulates around the room, talking to the groups and answering questions. She often sits down with a group and helps them structure the tasks so that members of the group can collaborate and help each other on the different tasks.

During the next few weeks, students work on their projects in their groups. A general topic, such as electricity or pollution, serves as the framework for each group, whereas the specific projects directed students' efforts during class. Some of the projects, such as the one on electricity, are actually done in school, whereas others, such as an investigation of factors affecting plant growth, are done at home.

During the fifth and sixth weeks students starts analyzing their results and writing reports. Kim helps students by again sharing exemplary reports with them and by working with students in their groups. Kim shows them how the computers in the back of the room could be used to describe and display data, and a number of groups use them to write up their projects.

For the next 2 weeks, students organize posterboard sessions where they present their results to other students. As students circulate from project to project, they evaluate each other's work with a form the class has discussed and prepared. At the end of each session, Kim takes 15 minutes of class time to discuss the different projects, pointing out strengths in each. Using this feedback, students in the groups refine their presentations. The unit culminates in the science fair where students present their projects to the whole school.

As Kim circulates up and down the aisles of the science fair, she is pleased with the comments she overhears from other people. The projects *are* of higher quality than in any previous year. But more important, Kim feels good about the confidence of the students' presentations. They aren't simply going through the motions, they really *do* understand the ideas contained in their projects.

Group Investigation is *a cooperative learning strategy that places students in groups to investigate an identified topic.* Like other cooperative learning models, it uses student interaction as a primary learning vehicle, but unlike the others, its focus is on the process of inquiry as groups investigate a specific topic.

The Group Investigation Model is grounded in the thinking of educational thinkers such as John Dewey (1916), who viewed the classroom as a microcosm of society; Herbert Thelen (1960), who stressed the importance of active inquiry in a social context; and Sharan and Sharan (1992), who emphasize social cohesion between different cultural and ethnic groups.

Teachers who use Group Investigation have at least three related learning objectives: (1) Students should acquire inquiry skills, that is, they should be able to investigate topics systematically and analytically; (2) students should acquire a deep understanding of a topic; and (3) they should learn to work cooperatively toward the solution of a problem. Learning to work cooperatively is a valuable life skill, and one students don't often practice in schools (Goodlad, 1984).

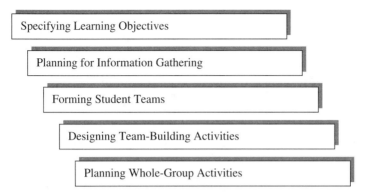

FIGURE 4.5   Planning Lessons for Group Investigation

Planning for Group Investigation Lessons.   Planning for Group Investigation involves five steps, which are outlined in Figure 4.5 and discussed in the sections that follow.

Specifying Learning Objectives.   In our discussions of STAD and Jigsaw II, we said that planning typically begins with a topic. This is less so for Group Investigation activities because the students are more involved in making the decision about what topic they will study.

Also, although developing a deep understanding of a topic is important for any model, if this is your primary learning objective, other models are more effective. Developing inquiry skills and learning to work cooperatively are the objectives emphasized most strongly in the Group Investigation Model, so your learning objectives should reflect this emphasis if you are using this model.

Planning for Information Gathering.   In order to solve problems and conduct inquiry, students obviously need access to information. Kim planned for information gathering by collecting used college science texts and working with the school librarian to be sure that school resources were available. Additional sources of information include:

- The Internet
- Videotapes, videodiscs, and CD-ROM discs
- Textbooks from other classes or levels
- Books from the public library
- Encyclopedias and other reference books
- Resource people (e.g., doctors, engineers, scientists)

To develop research skills, teachers may want to make this search part of the overall investigation. That is, instead of gathering the resources yourself, you may have students do it, so they learn how to access their own information.

Forming Student Teams.   In forming teams for Group Investigation, three factors should be considered. Perhaps the most obvious is interest, and this was the basis Kim used for forming her teams. Second, if possible, an equal number of high and low achievers should be included on each team, and third, the teams should be balanced with respect to gender and ethnicity. A benefit of all cooperative learning models is that they help students with varying backgrounds learn to work together. Group Investigation offers unique opportunities for promoting cooperation and teamwork because it is less structured than other models, and it requires higher levels of cooperation and trust. Forming teams whose members come from diverse backgrounds is a first step in reaching this objective.

Designing Team-Building Activities.   Group Investigation requires a greater degree of cooperation than does STAD or Jigsaw II, both of which have well-defined student roles. When Group Investigation is used, students must work together in making decisions about their interdependent roles. This makes team-building activities important.

Team-building activities can take a number of forms. In addition to the general team-building activities described in earlier sections of the chapter, teachers can use the content they're investigating as the focal point for student interviews. For example, Kim had her students interview each other about topics in which they were interested and why. This then served as a springboard for their work.

Planning Whole-Group Activities.   The final planning task is to design activities that introduce the class to the specific learning objectives for the Group Investigation. This is especially important when it is first used. Because Group Investigations are not highly structured, students must thoroughly understand the content focus and the procedures if investigations are to proceed smoothly.

This introduction/orientation is designed to have students understand the goal of the activity and the kinds of products expected. Kim, for example, shared and discussed examples of exemplary projects produced in previous years. In a sense, the process is like learning a concept primarily through the use of examples.

The introduction should also help students understand the procedures to follow in producing their product. An overview of the process on the first day, together with periodic reviews and additional reminders, help students gradually become comfortable with the procedures. Putting key steps on overheads, charts, or the board also helps.

Implementing Group Investigation Activities.   Implementing Group Investigation activities involves five phases, which are outlined in Table 4.8 and are discussed in the sections that follow.

Phase 1: Introduction.   The first phase of Group Investigation lessons involves organizing students into groups and having them identify a topic. The order of these two tasks will vary with the topic and students. In some cases, you may want to select topics first and then form groups based on student interest. This is what Kim did, and this is how she capitalized on the motivational benefits of intrinsic interest in her activity. An alternative is to form groups and let the students in each group democratically select the topic. This alternative provides students with experience in negotiating and compromising on a final choice. Regardless of

**TABLE 4.8   Learning and Motivation Functions for the Phases
of the Group Investigation Model**

Phase	Learning and Motivation Function
Phase 1: Introduction Groups are organized and topics are identified	■ Meets need for autonomy ■ Increases intrinsic interest
Phase 2: Group planning Students plan for investigation	■ Arouses curiosity motivation ■ Activates background knowledge
Phase 3: Implementing the investigation Students gather information	■ Begins schema production ■ Puts learners in active roles
Phase 4: Analyzing results and preparing reports Students analyze their data and prepare reports	■ Elaborates schemas ■ Puts students in active roles
Phase 5: Presenting reports Students report their findings	■ Increases perceptions of autonomy ■ Promotes perceptions of competence

the approach, students are given a substantial amount of control in making decisions about the process, and, as we saw in Chapter 2, the need for autonomy is basic in people.

Phase 2: Group Planning.   During Phase 2, students determine the scope of their investigations, assess resources, plan courses of action, and assign responsibilities to different members of the group. Many of their decisions will be driven by their curiosity about the topic, and during the process they will develop their background knowledge.

The difficulty of the group planning process will vary depending on the topic and scope of the investigation. If all members of the group are investigating the same topic, the primary task is deciding how to share background information. If pairs or groups of three are investigating subtopics related to the overall project, decisions must be made about coordinating their efforts, such as who will be responsible for gathering the different types of information, analyzing the data, combining the different subprojects within the overall project, and writing up the report. Dividing these tasks is not clear cut, and part of the learning process involves making decisions about how they will be handled.

In Kim's class, group planning took several forms. Groups had to decide on the portion of the overall project for which they would be responsible, how they would pool their resources, and how to collaborate on gathering data and reporting the results. These deliberations and negotiations serve to offer some of the learning opportunities that exist when the model is used.

Phase 3: Implementing the Investigation.   During Phase 3, the learners are most active as they gather information. The process of schema production begins as they begin to organize the information into a coherent whole.

This is usually the longest phase. Students need time to design data-gathering procedures, gather data, and carry out the investigation.

Keeping all groups working productively during this phase of the activity can be challenging because some projects take longer than others. Periodic progress reports help groups monitor their progress and help the teacher coordinate efforts among the groups.

Phase 4: Analyzing Results and Preparing Reports.   In Phase 4, the students actively elaborate on their schemas in the process of analyzing and evaluating the information they've gathered. Teachers can help in this process in at least three ways. One is to continually focus each group's attention on the question or problem they are investigating. In a lengthy investigation, students often lose track of the focus of their study. A second way to help students analyze results is to encourage them to talk about and share their findings with other group members. A third is to encourage students to experiment with different ways of displaying data. The construction of charts, diagrams, and tables helps students see relationships in their data. The students in Kim's class used the computer to help them display data.

The actual form the report takes is up to the teacher. Options include oral presentations, written reports, posterboards, and demonstrations. If oral presentations are used, they should be supplemented with a written report or some other product. The thinking that goes into writing a report helps students learn to present their findings clearly.

Phase 5: Presenting Reports.   Two objectives exist in Phase 5 of the process. The first is to disseminate information; the second is to help students learn to present information in clear and interesting ways. The format for these presentations can vary. Some options include:

- Whole-class presentations
- Presentations to segments of class
- Posterboard presentations
- Demonstrations
- Videotape presentation
- Learning stations or centers

The students' task in this phase of the activity is to go beyond the information itself, consider the audience, and create a presentation that is informative and interesting. This is a task that will be useful in later life and one that isn't often encountered in traditional classrooms. In the process, learners perceptions of autonomy and developing competence increase.

Assessing Group Investigation Activities.   Assessment of a Group Investigation activity should focus on each of the learning objectives addressed in the activity.

Assessing the Inquiry Process.   One objective for Group Investigation activities is for students to learn about the process of inquiry, its goals, procedures, and products. Students should be encouraged to reflect on the process and assess their own performance in each of the areas. A rating scale or checklist such as the one found in Figure 4.6 can be a valuable tool to guide self-assessment activities.

A rating scale such as this helps students reflect on the processes they used and encourages them to be analytical in their thinking. It can also stimulate discussion between group members by providing a concrete frame of reference.

	Needs Work	Fair	Good	Very Good	Excellent
Clearly stated problem	1	2	3	4	5
Clearly stated hypothesis(es)	1	2	3	4	5
Hypothesis connected to problem	1	2	3	4	5
Variables controlled	1	2	3	4	5
Data gathering appropriate to hypothesis	1	2	3	4	5
Data analyzed clearly	1	2	3	4	5
Conclusions logically connected to hypotheses and data	1	2	3	4	5
Inquiry evaluation instrument	1	2	3	4	5

FIGURE 4.6 **Rating Scale for Assessing the Inquiry Process**

Assessing Group Effectiveness. The efficiency of the group and the extent to which group members effectively work together is the second objective to be assessed. You can aid in this process by providing helpful feedback as the investigation progresses. You can also help by discussing the kinds of behaviors that help build effective groups. Rating scales can also help students learning to focus on these critical interaction skills. Figure 4.7 offers a sample.

	Rarely				Always
Group members listened to each other.	1	2	3	4	5
Group members shared information and ideas.	1	2	3	4	5
Group members helped each other clarify ideas.	1	2	3	4	5
Group members asked thought-provoking questions.	1	2	3	4	5
Group members gave each other feedback.	1	2	3	4	5

FIGURE 4.7 **Rating Scale for Assessing Group Effectiveness**

Rating scales can be used to help students understand how effective groups function, to provide feedback to different groups, or to make decisions about group composition and whether to intervene with some groups. They serve as a tangible reminder to both teachers and students that an important objective for Group Investigations is to learn to work together.

Assessing Understanding of Content. Understanding of content is the third aspect of Group Investigation that needs to be assessed. Teachers want to know if individual students understand their projects and the conceptual foundations on which they're based. The report itself, essay questions asking students to explain the project, oral presentations, and interviews can all help you assess this understanding.

The Discussion Model

The **Discussion Model** is *an instructional strategy designed to promote critical thinking and develop social skills.* Because it is less structured, it provides both teachers and students with more freedom and latitude to pursue ideas and opinions than most other models. Let's look at an example.

Martha Perez's American government class has been studying the election process at the national, state, and local levels and is preparing for a unit test the next week. Martha wants her class to use the information they have learned to think about some issues that will face them when they become voters.

She begins her Thursday's class by saying, "Please look up here. . . . We have some important elections coming up, both in our city and in our state. An idea that has gathered a lot of attention lately is term limits. Some people would like congressional representatives, such as senators and representatives, to be limited to two terms. The issue I'd like to consider today is [writing the following on the board]:

Should people in Congress be limited to two terms?

"To help us think about that question, I'd like us first to explore some of the advantages and disadvantages of this idea."

She now writes "Advantages and Disadvantages" on the board and asks each student to work with a partner to brainstorm as many of these as they can.

After a few minutes she continues, "Let's discuss your ideas. Can we focus on advantages first? What would be an advantage of limiting the terms of people in Congress? . . . Shaylynn?"

"Well, one advantage would be that more people could be in Congress so that we would get different ideas about how our government should be run."

"Okay, who else has an idea?" Martha responds, writing Shaylynn's ideas on the board. . . . "Rocio?"

"Do you think Governor Davis will be reelected?" Rocio asks. "He's not that popular."

"That's an interesting question, but can you tell us how it is related to the issue we're examining?" Martha asks supportively.

"It . . . I . . . guess it isn't," Rocio acknowledges.

"I believe it's an interesting question, and we might want to address it after we've examined the topic for today. . . . Now, who has another thought? . . . Kwan?" Martha asks directing the discussion back to the topic.

". . . How about not worrying about reelection all the time?"

"Say more, Kwan," Martha replies.

"Well, one of the problems we've been reading about is that politicians are always worried about being reelected and have to spend a large part of their time trying to raise money. . . ."

"How about special interest groups?" Antonio interjects. "We . . ."

"Antonio," Martha says, stopping him in midsentence, "what did we agree on in our discussions?"

"Whoops, . . . We agreed that we would wait until a person has finished what he's saying. . . . It just slipped out."

"Now, finish what you were saying," Martha says, turning back to Kwan.

". . . Anyway, to get reelected is what politicians are after. . . . Term limits would reduce this."

"Okay, good. . . . Now, go ahead, Antonio. Share your thinking with us," Martha says, going back to Antonio.

". . . Let's see. Where was I? . . . Okay. . . . We read about how special interest groups influence politics. If politicians weren't worried about special interest groups, then they could do the right thing and not worry about pleasing special interest groups."

The discussion continues, and Martha monitors the process to be certain that a small group of students don't dominate the discussion and that the students remain focused on the issue.

The Discussion Model involves students in content-oriented interactions as they attempt to resolve some issue, such as Martha's question about whether term limits should exist. Teachers using the Discussion Model want students to practice critical-thinking and social skills, and develop deeper insights into topics they are studying than typically occur in regular classroom activities.

Teachers facilitate the process, ensuring that the discussion remains focused on the issue and that the desired social skills are being practiced. For example, when Rocio brought up an unrelated idea, Martha directed the discussion back to the topic, and when Antonio interrupted Kwan, Martha intervened and reminded the students of the procedures they agreed on for their discussions. With the teacher's guidance, the students' critical-thinking skills and their social skills both develop as they experience concrete examples of the skills in action, as we saw with Rocio and Antonio.

Planning for Discussions

On the surface it may appear that discussions don't require the same amount of planning as would be needed with other models. This isn't true. Poorly planned discussions can become

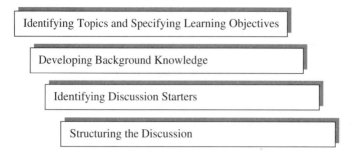

FIGURE 4.8   Planning for Discussions

essentially meaningless if teachers aren't clear about their learning objectives, haven't ensured that students have the necessary background knowledge to participate in a well-informed discussion, or haven't made provisions for ensuring wide participation.

Planning for discussions involves four steps, which are illustrated in Figure 4.8 and are discussed in the sections that follow.

Identifying Topics and Specifying Learning Objectives.   As with most other models, planning for discussions begins by identifying a topic. Topics that are most effective typically involve a controversy, such as the issue of term limits in Martha's class. Taking a stand on an issue can be motivating because it allows students to become personally involved in the topic. Teachers comment that students who are initially disinterested became excited and engaged when asked to take a personal position on a controversial topic. The discussion will often spill over into the hall and even class the next day.

Practicing critical-thinking skills is a primary objective when the Discussion Model is used. When students take and defend positions in discussions, they must use evidence to support their positions, which is the essence of critical thinking.

Developing social interaction skills is a second essential objective when discussion are used. In discussions students practice:

- Expressing ideas clearly
- Building on others' ideas by listening actively
- Taking turns
- Respecting others' opinions
- Recognizing that perceptions vary

Developing deeper insights into the topics they're studying is a third objective. Being able to defend a position requires that the student is well informed, and discussions provide students with practice in connecting ideas they have already learned and integrating them in new and different ways (Burbules & Bruce, 2001; Meter & Stevens, 2000). Research also indicates that discussing controversial issues increases students' knowledge about issues and encourages deeper understanding of different sides of an issue (Johnson & Johnson, 1994). As a result developing understanding and practicing critical thinking are interdependent in discussions (Sternberg, 1998).

Developing Background Knowledge.   The most essential factor that exists in determining the success of discussions is background knowledge, both students' and the teacher's.

Students' Background Knowledge.   To discuss a topic, students must knowledgeable about the topic; the lack of background knowledge is the most common reason discussions aren't successful. Attempting discussions when students lack background knowledge often result in expressing misinformed opinions and offering empty conjectures, which result in the discussion disintegrating into mindless "bull" sessions.

Because of this essential factor, discussions should be preceded by specific lessons targeting discussion topics, or the discussions should occur at the end of a unit of study. Martha, for example, held her discussion at the end of a unit examining American politics and the electoral process.

Teacher Background Knowledge.   Because students actually discuss the topic, and teachers merely guide the discussion, it might appear that teachers' knowledge of the topic is less important than when the learning activity is more teacher directed. This is a misconception. To guide a meaningful discussion, the teacher must be highly knowledgeable about the topic, including the controversies and issues related to it. This allows the teacher to ask a timely question if the discussion begins to wind down or get off track, or if students fail to identify some of the important factors related to the issue. Although the lack of student background knowledge is the most common reason discussions aren't successful, the lack of teacher background knowledge is also essential. Do not attempt to guide a discussion unless you're very well informed about the topic.

Identifying Discussion Starters.   Successful discussions must be focused on a single, specific—and ideally somewhat controversial—issue, such as Martha's question about term limits. Teachers accomplish this with a discussion starter. Some possible discussion starters in different content areas are found in Table 4.9.

To be effective, the discussion starter must link directly back to the topic or topics the class has been studying, such as Martha's question about term limits linking to their study of politics and the electoral process. This allows the students to use their background

TABLE 4.9   Potential Discussion Starters

Content Area		Issue or Question
Literature:	Shakespeare's *Julius Caesar*	Were Caesar's assassins justified in murdering him?
Science:	Genetics	Should scientists be allowed to use genetic engineering to change plants or animals?
Social Studies:	Political Science	Are gun control laws effective in reducing crime?
Health:	Drugs	Should there be a ban on tobacco products?

knowledge to develop informed opinions, and the discussion should then help them develop new insights into the topic.

Structuring the Discussion.   Teachers have at least two choices in structuring discussions. As a first choice, you may choose to conduct the discussion as a whole group for the entire lesson. This allows you to monitor the progress and direction of the discussion but results in less participation by a wide variety of students.

As a second option, you may have students discuss the issue in small groups. Small-group discussions provide increased opportunities for all students to participate, but you have less control over the interaction, so you can't be sure that the students are staying on task or practicing the critical-thinking and social skills that are at the core of discussions.

If small groups are used, you should always plan to have the class reconvened to discuss the groups' conclusions. Ending discussions with small-group work leaves students uncertain about what they've accomplished, and what they were supposed to have learned from the discussion. As a result, the practice is ineffective. Martha combined both small-group and whole-class discussions in her lesson.

Implementing Discussions

Implementing discussions occurs in three phases. The phases, together with their learning and motivation function are outlined in Table 4.10 and are discussed in the sections that follow.

Phase 1: Introduction.   A discussion begins when the teacher presents the discussion starter and frames the issue. This process is intended to attract the students' attention and activate the background knowledge they've acquired from earlier lessons. Martha's question about term limits was intended to serve this function. Having the students work in pairs to brainstorm advantages and disadvantages was also designed to activate and develop students' background knowledge.

Phase 2: Exploration.   During the exploration phase students examine the topic and form and defend positions. This phase is intended to promote involvement, clarify perceptions, and help students develop additional insights into the topic they're studying.

TABLE 4.10   Learning and Motivation Functions for the Phases of the Discussion Model

Phase	Learning and Motivation Function
Phase 1: Introduction The discussion starter and issue are presented	■ Attracts attention ■ Activates background knowledge
Phase 2: Exploration Students explore the topic, clarify thinking, and take a position	■ Promotes involvement ■ Clarifies perceptions
Phase 3: Closure Major points are summarized	■ Promotes schema production ■ Achieves equilibrium

Whether this occurs in small or large groups, teachers play two essential roles. One is to keep the discussion focused and moving. The other is to facilitate group interaction and help students develop their social interaction skills.

Successful discussions have both direction and momentum. Students need to feel that the discussion is heading somewhere and that the class is making progress toward an objective. Because discussions are student centered, the possibility of drift always exists. Teachers must monitor the progress of the discussion, refocusing it when necessary, and making sure that it doesn't become sidetracked into dead ends. As a brief example, let's look again at some of the dialogue from Martha's lesson.

> **MARTHA:** Let's discuss your ideas. Can we focus on advantages first? What would be an advantage of limiting the terms of people in Congress? . . . Shaylynn?
>
> **SHAYLYNN:** Well, one advantage would be that more people could be in Congress so that we would get different ideas about how our government should be run.
>
> **MARTHA:** Okay, who else has an idea? . . . Rocio?
>
> **ROCIO:** Do you think Governor Davis will be reelected? He's not that popular.
>
> **MARTHA:** That's an interesting question, but can you tell us how it is related to the issue we're examining?
>
> **ROCIO:** It . . . I . . . guess it isn't.

When Rocio offered a comment that wasn't relevant to the topic, Martha remained supportive but kept the discussion focused on the original question. Learning to stay focused on the topic is a valuable thinking skill.

Teachers also monitor the discussion to be sure that the students are practicing their social interaction skills. Let's look at some additional dialogue.

> **MARTHA:** Now, who has another thought? . . . Kwan?
>
> **KWAN:** . . . How about not worrying about reelection all the time?
>
> **MARTHA:** Say more, Kwan.
>
> **KWAN:** Well, one of the problems we've been reading about is that politicians are always worried about being reelected and have to spend a large part of their time trying to raise money. . . .
>
> **ANTONIO:** How about special interest groups? We . . .
>
> **MARTHA:** Antonio, what did we agree on in our discussions?
>
> **ANTONIO:** Whoops, . . . We agreed that we would wait until a person has finished what he's saying. . . . It just slipped out.

Antonio probably didn't intend to be rude; he interrupted Kwan without thinking about it. Martha's intervention reminded him of their agreed-on procedures, and hopefully it will serve to make him more sensitive in the future. It served as a concrete example that could help him improve his social interaction skills.

Other comments such as:

"Did you all see how Felicia built on Roberta's point?"

"So you disagree with Eric's point? You did that clearly. Any other opinions?"

"Good listening, Maria. I think you identified an important difference between those two ideas."

Make Felicia and Maria models for thinking and listening that other students can then imitate. By consciously targeting positive aspects of student interaction skills, teachers can help make students aware of their importance in effective discussions.

Obstacles to Effective Discussions.   Research has identified at least three obstacles to effective discussions (Cazden, 2001; Dillon, 1987). The most important of these is lack of background knowledge, which we discussed earlier. Others include too much teacher intervention and domination by a small group of students.

Teachers, used to being in charge of the class and fearful of off-task behavior, sometimes don't allow students to take ownership of discussions. Leading discussions in a democratic and noncoercive manner is sophisticated. It requires that the teacher be able to determine when and how often to intervene. Too much intervention can stifle the discussion, and too little can result in wasted time and limited learning.

Some authorities recommend that teachers stay out of discussions completely and allow them to develop naturally, but this isn't realistic (Dillon, 1987). Although the suggestion is well intentioned, discussions often flounder because of lack of direction. Teachers must intervene when necessary to keep the discussion focused and to ensure that a variety of students are participating. This leads us to the third obstacle.

Domination by a few students, which results in lack of participation by most of the class, is an important problem. Teachers can help prevent it by calling on a wide sample of students with directives and questions such as, "Let's hear another point of view from _____" and "We haven't heard from _____ yet. What do you think?" And, as we discussed earlier, participation can be increased by conducting part of the discussion in small groups.

Phase 3: Closure.   All effective lessons, regardless of the topic or the strategy being used, need closure. Closure helps students integrate and solidify their schemas and achieve a sense of equilibrium. This is especially true with discussions, where the direction of the lesson may be less clear or apparent than it is in more teacher-centered lessons.

Teachers can help students reach closure in at least two ways. They can ask for a summary of the major points made and write these on the board or overhead. They can also seek consensus on issues through a show of hands. In doing this, it is important to stress that personal opinion and dissent are valued. A simple comment, such as, "We found that different people believe different things. That's okay. What is important is that you know what you believe and why," can help students understand that the purpose of discussions is not necessarily conformity or agreement but the honest exchange of different ideas and opinions.

Assessing Learning in Discussions

As we said earlier in the chapter, the development of critical-thinking and social interaction skills, together with a deep understanding of a topic are the objectives for discussions. Assessing critical-thinking and social interaction skills is usually conducted during the course of the discussion, which is another reason why you need to carefully monitor the discussion and intervene when necessary. Let's look now at measuring content outcomes.

Measuring Content Outcomes. We want our students to leave discussions with a deep understanding of the content involved and an increased ability to analyze and evaluate ideas. Essay and short-answer items are often effective for measuring this outcome.

Essay Items. **Essay items** are *forms of measurement that require students to make extended written responses to questions or problems.* Essay questions are effective for two reasons. First, organizing, expressing, and defending ideas require critical thinking, and second, the essay format is often the only way these goals can be measured (Stiggins, 2001). Also, when students study for an essay versus a short-answer or multiple-choice exam, they are more likely to organize information in a meaningful way (Foos, 1992). For example, Martha might ask her students,

> Would term limits improve the political process in America? In your answer list, analyze, and evaluate the advantages and disadvantages of term limits.

In scoring this item, Martha would construct a scoring rubric that contained essential components (i.e., advantages and disadvantages as well as an evaluation of these) and the point total to be assigned to each. A scoring rubric such as this increases both validity and reliability and can be shared with students to help them become better essay writers (Stiggins, 2001).

Short-answer items are *forms of measurement that require students to make brief written responses to specific questions.* (The distinction between an essay item and a short-answer item is blurred but it isn't crucial.) As an example, Martha could assess her students' understanding of the pros and cons of term limitations with the following item:

> List and explain three advantages and three disadvantages of term limitations.

An item such as this clearly communicates expectations to students and is relatively simple to score. A drawback to this type of item, however, is that it fails to assess students' ability to analyze, integrate, and evaluate ideas.

Increasing Motivation with Group Interaction Models

Anyone who has worked in classrooms and interacted with young children and adolescents soon realizes that students are social beings motivated by the desire to interact with their peers. We consider ways teachers can capitalize on this desire in this section.

Interest in the motivating effects of social interaction goes back to the turn of the twentieth century, when researchers found that the performance of potentially boring tasks could be enhanced by doing them in groups (Pintrich & Schunk, 2002). More recent work in the area has focused on the social nature of learning as well as the role that social groups play in fulfilling basic human needs.

Group processes have also been linked to competence, affiliation, and power needs in students (Schmuck & Schmuck, 1997). When they are involved in learning groups, students are concerned about their competence. Each wants to appear knowledgeable, and this is especially important in small groups, which require risk taking and initiative. To accommodate their needs, teachers need to carefully structure group tasks so that all students have opportunities to contribute and succeed (Cohen, 1998).

Groups also satisfy students' needs for affiliation. Participating in groups can be motivating because it fulfills an important goal for students—the need to belong (Maslow, 1968). This need exists at all grade levels but is especially powerful during adolescence. Teachers can capitalize on this affiliation need by making working groups cohesive and supportive. Group-building exercises described earlier can be effective, as well as the teacher's emphasis on supportive interaction within groups.

Small groups also help fulfill students' need for control (Schmuck & Schmuck, 2001). This need can be negative or positive. For example, it can result in criticisms or other kinds of aggressive behaviors, but it can also promote leadership and individual contributions to the group. Teachers can direct student energies into constructive channels by creating multiple tasks within each group in which all can contribute and succeed (Cohen, 1994). For example, students can take turns being leader, recorder, facilitator, and summarizer. This exchange of roles not only gives students different ways to succeed but also teaches them different social interaction skills.

Summary

Group Interaction Models: An Overview

Five essential elements undergird all effective group interaction strategies. Face-to-face interaction encourages students to share their thoughts with others. Group goals focus students' interactions on agreed-on and shared learning tasks. Individual accountability makes every student responsible for learning lesson content. Collaborative skills not only develop during group interaction but also make the interactions more effective. These collaborative skills are developed through group processing, in which members reflect on the effectiveness of their groups.

Group Interaction Models: Theoretical Foundations

Group Interaction Models are based on the learning and development theories of Lev Vygotsky, a Russian psychologist. Vygotsky emphasized the importance of dialogue in the transmission of a culture's ideas. Social interaction encourages students to articulate their thinking, share their ideas with others, and transform their ideas based on comparisons with others. Social interaction also provides teachers with access to student thinking, allowing them to adjust what and how they teach.

Groupwork Strategies

Groupwork strategies are social interaction models designed to be integrated with other more inclusive, content-oriented models. Students are divided into small groups and encouraged to socially interact.

Cooperative Learning Models

Cooperative learning is a structured approach to learning that involves students working together to reach a common goal. Several cooperative learning strategies exist, and three of them were discussed in this chapter. Each is based on groups goals, individual accountability, and equal opportunity for success as guiding principles. Having students learn to work together effectively is an overriding goal for all cooperative learning strategies.

Student Teams Achievement Divisions (STAD) involves teams of four or five students working toward understanding facts, concepts, or skills. Closely related to the Direct Instruction Model, STAD uses team study in place of independent practice. Students compete with their past performances to earn improvement points that contribute to team awards.

Jigsaw II, designed to teach organized bodies of information, develops student experts, who in turn teach their teammates. Team members develop deep understanding of content as all team members share their expertise. Improvement points and team awards—as used with STAD—can also be used with Jigsaw II to promote success and provide recognition for team accomplishment.

With Group Investigation, the most complex and least structured model of the three, groups collaborate on inquiry problems. When Group Investigation is used, defining problems, gathering data, and analyzing and evaluating data are similar to processes used with the Problem-Based Learning Models found in Chapter 8. Group Investigation differs from these in its emphasis on groupwork, collaboration, negotiation, and making written and oral reports that summarize the group's work.

The Discussion Model

Discussion is a group interaction model designed to help students analyze and integrate ideas through interaction with peers. Discussions require sufficient student background knowledge to allow students to discuss ideas freely. In implementing discussions teachers need first to orient students to the topic, then allow them freedom to explore it, and finally to bring the lesson to closure through summaries and consensus seeking. Teachers evaluate discussions with extended short-answer and essay questions.

Increasing Motivation with Group Interaction Models

Group Interaction Models tap into students' need to interact with their peers. As opposed to behaviorist views of learning, social interaction models are more constructivist and cognitively oriented. These models also fulfill students' need for competence, affiliation, and power.

IMPORTANT CONCEPTS

Base score (p. 95)
Combining pairs (p. 90)
Cooperative learning (p. 90)
Discussion Model
    (p. 116)
Equal opportunity for success
    (p. 95)
Essay items (p. 123)
Group goals (p. 84)

Group Interaction Models
    (p. 82)
Group Investigation (p. 110)
Groupwork (p. 86)
Jigsaw II (p. 103)
Organized bodies of knowledge
    (p. 103)
Pairs check (p. 89)
Short-answer items (p. 123)

Sociocultural theory (p. 85)
Student Teams Achievement
    Divisions (STAD) (p. 93)
Task specialization (p. 103)
Teammates consult (p. 90)
Think-pair-share (p. 89)
Think-pair-square (p. 89)
Think-write-pair-share
    (p. 89)

EXERCISES

1. Examine the introductory cases at the beginning of the chapter involving Jim Felton and Jesse Kantor. Which type of model was each using? Defend your answer with specific information from the cases.

2. Analyze the following list of goals and decide whether they are most appropriate for STAD, Jigsaw II, or Group Investigation.
   a. A third-grade teacher wants her students to know their multiplication facts.
   b. A junior high school social studies teacher wants to teach his students how to analyze social issues. Because it is an election year, he selects voting and asks each group to design a research project around this topic.
   c. An English teacher is comparing Faulkner, Fitzgerald, and Hemingway and wants his students to understand similarities and differences among the writers.
   d. A junior high science teacher is studying pollution. She assigns students to groups and asks each group to investigate either air, water, or solid waste pollution in their geographic areas.
   e. A fourth-grade teacher wants to develop her students' ability to research a topic. She selects the topic of pets and asks each group to design and implement a project on this subject.
   f. A health teacher wants his students to know and understand the four major food groups.
   g. A social studies teacher wants her students to know the names of the states as well as their capitols.

3. Analyze the STAD lesson involving Anya Lozano and identify where each of the following components of cooperative learning were found:
   a. Group goals
   b. Individual accountability
   c. Collaborative skills
   d. Group processing

4. A math teacher is preparing to assign students from her basic algebra class to STAD learning groups. Averages of the students' past quiz scores are as follows:

Juan	97	Juanita	81
Bettina	94	Henry	80
Sheri	93	Lisa	79

Akeem	90	Joan	77
Kim	87	Pat	75
Heather	84	Alonza	72
Peter	83	May	70
Marcia	82	Ted	69

a. She wants to use teams of four. How might the teams be composed?

b. What factors other than past quiz scores might the teacher consider?

Feedback for these excercises begins on page 341.

DISCUSSION QUESTIONS

1. What content areas or models are most compatible with integration with Groupwork strategies? Least compatible? Why?

2. How are the following essential components of cooperative learning—group goals, individual accountability, and equal opportunity for success—contained in:
   - STAD?
   - Jigsaw II?
   - Group Investigation?

3. Identify at least three similarities among STAD, Jigsaw II, and Group Investigation. Identify at least two ways in which each differs from the other two.

4. Which of the three cooperative learning models presented—STAD, Jigsaw II, or Group Investigation—is easiest to implement? Most difficult? Why? From a student development perspective, what might this suggest about the order in which they're introduced.

5. Researchers have found that cooperative learning is an effective way of breaking down barriers between different ethnic and cultural groups. Which of the following elements is most important for reaching this goal? Explain your answer.
   - Group goals
   - Individual accountability
   - Equal opportunity for success

6. Which of the three cooperative learning models is most widely applicable to different grade levels and across different content areas? Why? Which is least applicable? Explain your answer.

7. How is the form that assessment takes in each of the three cooperative learning models similar? Different? How do these differences correspond to the different goals of each model?

8. In which areas of the curriculum are discussions most valuable? Least valuable? Why?

5

The Inductive Model

The Inductive Model, which is often described as *guided discovery,* is a straightforward but powerful strategy designed to help students acquire a deep and thorough understanding of well-defined topics. Teachers present students with examples that illustrate the content and then guide students' efforts to find patterns in the information. Grounded in the view that learners construct their own understanding of the world rather than record it in an already-organized form, the model requires teachers to be skilled in questioning and guiding student thinking. The model is effective for promoting student involvement and motivation within a safe and supportive learning environment. When you have completed your study of this chapter, you should be able to:

- Classify topics in the school curriculum as concepts, generalizations, principles, or academic rules.
- Plan and implement lessons using the Inductive Model.
- Adapt the Inductive Model for learners at different ages and with varying backgrounds.
- Assess student understanding of content taught using the Inductive Model.

To begin our discussion, let's look at three teachers, each using the Inductive Model.

Judy Nelson is beginning a study of longitude and latitude in social studies with her sixth graders. Knowing that some of them have limited backgrounds in this area, she plans as if they have virtually no experience with these ideas. In preparation, she buys a beach ball, finds an old tennis ball, and checks wall maps and globes in her classroom.

After conducting her beginning-of-class routines, Judy begins the lesson by having students identify where they live on the wall map and then saying, "Now suppose you made some new friends on your summer vacation and you want to describe for them exactly where you live. How might we do that?"

After getting suggestions, she notes that all are good ideas, but none is precise enough to pinpoint the exact location. Then she says, "Today, we are going to figure out a way to precisely identify where we live. When we're done, we'll be so good at this that we'll be able to pinpoint any city in the world. Keep this in mind as we work today. Okay, ready to go?"

Judy holds up the beach ball and globe and asks her students to compare the two, calling on individual students in each case.

After several comparisons, Judy asks them to identify north, south, east, and west on the beach ball. Then she draws a circle around the center of the ball as shown in Figure 5.1. "Now what can you tell us about this line? Let's begin. . . . Tara?"

"It's a circle."

"Good, Tara," Judy smiles. "What else? Andy?"

"It's in the middle of the ball."

"Fine, Andy. Now look at the tennis ball. How is it similar to and different from the beach ball? . . . Amy?" she asks, holding up the tennis ball, also with a line drawn around its center.

"It's . . . also in the middle of the ball."

Judy cuts the ball in half, leading the students to conclude that the center line divides the ball into two hemispheres, as illustrated in Figure 5.1.

Judy identifies the lines as "equators," draws additional lines parallel to the equator on the beach ball (see Figure 5.2a), and then says, "Now compare the lines to each other. Kathy?"

"They're all . . . even."

"What do you mean by even?" Judy encourages.

". . . They don't cross each other," Kathy explains, motioning with her hands.

"Excellent, Kathy," Judy smiles.

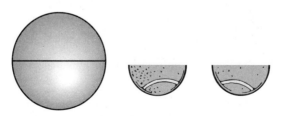

FIGURE 5.1 Beach Ball and Tennis Ball

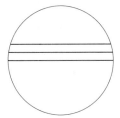 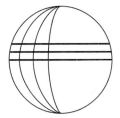

FIGURE 5.2A   Beach Ball with Lines of Latitude

FIGURE 5.2B   Beach Ball with Lines of Longitude and Latitude

She continues with her questioning, guiding students to additional comparisons, such as the fact that the lines all run east and west and get shorter as they move away from the equator.

Judy writes this information on the board as the students offer it, and she then introduces the term *latitude* to describe the lines they have been discussing.

Now Judy draws lines of longitude on the beach ball (see Figure 5.2b) and continues, "How do these lines compare to the lines of latitude? . . . Amarilis?"

". . . They go all around the ball."

"Yes, they do," Judy smiles. "What else? . . . Nicola?"

". . ."

"Let's look here. . . . What do all of the longitude lines do at this point?" Judy asks pointing the top of the ball toward Nicola.

"They all cross there."

"Good," Judy smiles. "So what do we know about the lengths of the longitude lines? . . . Johanna?"

"They get shorter up there," Johanna responds pointing to the north pole.

Judy pauses for a second, considering how to respond to Johanna's misconception.

"Okay, wrap this string around the ball," Judy suggests, handing Johanna a piece of string that she has on her desk.

Johanna measures the circumference of the ball through the poles with the string.

Judy has Elton repeat the process with another piece of string at a different point on the ball but still going through the poles.

"What do you notice about the pieces of string? . . . Johanna?"

"They're the same length."

"Excellent. . . . So, what do we know about lines of longitude? . . . Amber?"

"They're all the same length."

"Good, Amber," Judy smiles.

Then she has Andy and Karen measure the ball, simulating lines of latitude to demonstrate that the latitude lines get shorter near the poles.

"So, let's review for a minute," Judy directs. "How do lines of longitude compare to each other? . . . Leroy?"

"They're the same."

"And, how do we know?"

". . . The strings were the same," Leroy responds, motioning toward Johanna and Elton.

"And, how about lines of latitude? . . . Jackie?"

". . . They get shorter as we go up and down," Jackie responds pointing toward the top and bottom of the ball.

"Excellent thinking everyone," Judy waves enthusiastically.

Judy then continues by asking students to make some additional conclusions about latitude and longitude and relates both to the globe and her flat wall maps. Some of their conclusions include:

1. Longitude lines are farthest apart at the equator, whereas latitude lines are the same distance apart everywhere.
2. Lines of longitude are the same length; latitude lines get shorter north and south of the equator.
3. Lines of longitude intersect each other at the poles, and lines of latitude and longitude intersect each other.
4. Lines of longitude run north and south and measure distance east and west; lines of latitude run east and west and measure distance north and south.

We'll return to Judy's lesson later in the chapter.

Sue Grant is beginning a study of Charles's law with her chemistry students. She starts by stating, "We've been studying the kinetic theory of gases, and today we are going to examine another law describing the behavior of gases. This law was originally formed by a Frenchman named Jacques Charles, so the law was named after him. When we're finished today, you'll be able to solve problems using his law."

She continues by taking three identical balloons, inflating each with as equal an amount of air as possible, and holding them up for the class to observe.

"What do you notice about the balloons?" she asks and prompts students to conclude that they're the same size. Then, as students watch, she puts the first in a beaker of boiling water, the second in a beaker of water at room temperature, and the third in a beaker of ice, as shown in Figure 5.3. Now Sue displays three drawings for the students, as shown in Figure 5.4, and a graph, as shown in Figure 5.5.

Sue groups the students in pairs and says, "Now work with your partner, and make some careful comparisons. Compare the balloons, compare the drawings to the balloons, and compare both to the graph. Make as many conclusions as you can and be ready to support your conclusions with evidence. You have 5 minutes. Write your conclusions and evidence on your paper."

The classroom becomes a buzz of voices as students study the balloons, drawings, and graph. As they work, Sue walks among them, periodically making a comment or offering a few words of encouragement.

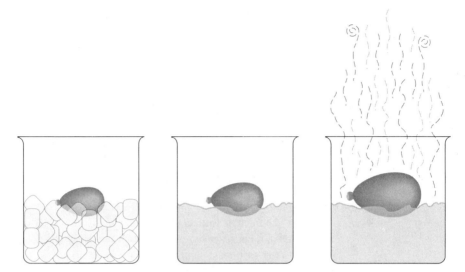

FIGURE 5.3   Beakers with Inflated Balloons

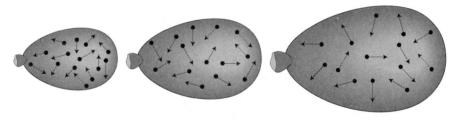

FIGURE 5.4   Models of Balloons at Different Temperatures

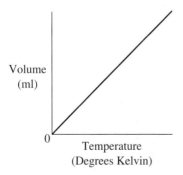

**FIGURE 5.5   Graph Relating
Temperature and Volume**

At the end of the 5 minutes, she begins, "Okay, what have we concluded? . . . Steve and Barbara?"

". . . We decided that the masses in each of the balloons were the same."

"Good," Sue nods. "And why did you say that?"

"The number of molecules—dots—in each balloon is the same."

"Good thinking, you two," Sue smiles.

She continues this process, calling on other pairs. Their conclusions and supporting evidence are summarized in Table 5.1.

"Look again at the graph," Sue now says. "We found that the volume is proportional to the temperature, but what temperature? . . . Greg?"

"I'm not sure what you mean."

"Look at the graph. Is the volume proportional to the Celsius temperature or the absolute temperature?"

"It looks like the absolute temperature."

"Yes, it does. That's what we see in the graph. Very good."

Then Sue writes $T_1 \propto V_1$ and $T_2 \propto V_2$ on the chalkboard. "What do the 1s and 2s mean? . . . Debbie?"

"The 1s mean, just . . . some temperature and some volume, and the 2s mean some other temperature and another volume."

"Good, so if we know they're proportional, what do we know about their ratios? . . . Mike?"

". . . They're equal."

"Excellent, so how can we write the relationship? . . . Tony?"

". . . It would be $\dfrac{T_1}{T_2} = \dfrac{V_1}{V_2}$"

"Outstanding, everyone. That's Charles's law, and that's what we're learning about today."

Sue continues, "We see from Charles's law how temperature affects volume. Let's think about how what we just learned relates to what we already know about

TABLE 5.1   Conclusions and Supporting Evidence

Conclusions	Supporting Evidence
The masses of air in the balloons are equal.	The number of dots in the three drawings is equal.
The molecular movement increases in the heated balloon.	The arrows in the third balloon are longest.
The volume of the heated balloon increased and the volume of the cooled balloon decreased.	The molecules are closest together in the first drawing and farthest apart in the third drawing.
Temperature and volume appear to be directly proportional.	The graph shows that the volume is proportional to the temperature.

mass and density. . . . As the temperature increases, what happens to the mass of the gas? Raul?"

"Nothing."

"Good. And how do you know?"

". . . The amount didn't change, only the volume."

"Excellent. And how about the density? . . . Jo?"

"It . . . gets less."

"Good. Explain that for us."

". . . The air is expanding, but the mass is the same, so it must be less dense."

"Good clear description, Jo," Sue nods, and she then gives the students the following problem:

You have a balloon filled with 1.5 liters of air in a freezer at –5° Celsius. You take the balloon out of the freezer and put it in the window where the temperature is 30° Celsius. What will the volume of the balloon be after it has warmed to 30°?

The students solve the problem, they discuss it, and Sue then gives them five more problems for homework.

We'll look at her homework assignment later in the chapter when we discuss the application phase of the model.

Jim Rooney, an English teacher at Lakeside Middle School, is trying to help his eighth graders better understand the rules for punctuating singular and plural possessive nouns.

He prepares a written passage about their school and the next day begins class by saying, "The objective for today's lesson is to identify some patterns in the way words are used in passages. When we're finished, these patterns should help us in our writing. . . . Okay, let's go." He then displays the following passage.

Lakeside is one of six **schools** in Jefferson county. We also have a high school, one other middle **school,** and three elementary **schools.** The schools are in Brooksville, the largest **city** in the **county.** The *city's* schools and the schools in three other **counties** hold an annual scholastic and athletic competition, and students in the *counties'* schools met this year in Brooksville. In all, students from five **cities** were involved, and the *cities'* students did very well.

The two **women** advisors of Brooksville's debate teams were particularly proud because the *women's* teams won both of their debates.

Four **girls** and three **boys** won both athletic and scholastic honors. The *girls'* accomplishments were noteworthy in math on the academic side and tennis on the athletic side. The *boys'* achievements were in writing and track. One boy set a record in the 100-meter dash; the *boy's* time was a new school record.

Many **children** from the elementary schools participated as well, and the *children's* accomplishments were equally impressive. Several of the children wrote short stories. One **child** wrote a story involving a **woman** and the *woman's* struggle to keep her farm in the face of hardship. The *child's* **story** and the *story's* plot were very sophisticated. Several *stories'* plots and characters were interesting and well developed. The **stories** were put in a display, and three of the **displays** were photographed for the local newspaper. The *displays'* contents included the stories as well as some background information on the authors.

Jim asks his students to look for patterns in the bold terms. The students make a number of observations, and with Jim's guidance they identify all the terms as either singular or plural nouns. He also guides them to conclude that plural nouns are formed by merely adding *s* if the noun ends in a consonant or in *y* preceded by a vowel, but that the *y* is removed and *ies* is added if the noun ending in *y* is preceded by a consonant. They also see that some nouns, such as woman and child, become plural by changing the form of the word.

Jim continues the lesson by turning to the italicized words in the passage, following a procedure similar to the one he used with the bold terms. He asks the students what the italicized terms have in common and leads the students to the rules for forming singular and plural possessive nouns based on their observations of the information.

The Inductive Model: An Overview

Let's begin our study of the Inductive Model by looking back at the episodes we've just read and identifying what they have in common.

- First, each topic was specific and well defined—longitude and latitude in Judy's lesson, the relationship between temperature and volume in Sue's, and the rules for forming singular and plural possessives in Jim's.
- Second, instead of displaying information for students and then explaining it, as would be typical in a lecture or demonstration, each teacher presented carefully chosen examples—Judy's beach ball, tennis ball, and maps; Sue's demonstration and drawings; and Jim's passage—and then guided the students as they formed their own understanding of the topic.
- Third, the teachers used a variety of teaching strategies to guide students from the examples to the conclusions. For instance, each used essential teaching strategies, such as careful organization, aligned instruction, and skilled questioning, extensively. Sue also incorporated groupwork in her lesson.
- Fourth, under the teachers' guidance, the students used basic cognitive skills, such as observing, comparing and contrasting, and finding relationships, to move from the examples to the conclusions.

The examples and the conclusions students reached in each lesson are summarized in Table 5.2.

Research indicates that providing students with data and helping them form abstractions increases achievement. A lesson using the Inductive Model "may take more or less

TABLE 5.2   Examples Leading to General Conclusions

Specific Examples	General Conclusions
Drawings of latitude and longitude on the beachball, and lines on maps.	Latitude lines are parallel, run east–west, and measure distance north and south of the equator. Longitude lines intersect at the poles, run north–south, and measure distance east and west of the prime meridian.
Demonstration with balloons and drawings of containers and molecules.	When pressure is constant, volume is directly proportional to absolute temperature. $$\frac{T_1}{V_2} = \frac{T_1}{V_2}$$
Passage containing illustrations of singular and plural possessive nouns.	To make singular nouns possessive we add apostrophe *s,* and to make plural nouns possessive we add an apostrophe (if the plural ends in *s*).

time than expository instruction, depending on the task, but tends to result in better long-term retention and transfer than expository instruction" (Mayer, 2002, p. 68). This doesn't imply in any way that the teacher is intentionally vague or withholding information from students. Clear objectives are as essential when using the Inductive Model as they are with any other instructional format. Instead of merely lecturing and telling students, however, the teacher guides them as they construct their own understanding.

This is sophisticated and demanding instruction. Teachers must be experts with questioning; they must monitor students for signs of inattention or misbehavior; and they must make on-the-spot decisions about what questions to ask and which students to call on. Most teachers can learn to deliver acceptable lectures, but it takes a highly skilled teacher to use the Inductive Model.

The students' roles in this process are to analyze the examples, identify the essential characteristics in them, and form general conclusions about the meaning of the characteristics. The social structure of the model and both the teachers' and students' roles in the process are grounded in the model's theoretical foundation.

The Inductive Model: Theoretical Foundations

As we saw in Chapter 2, four of the principles of cognitive learning theory include the following:

- Learning and development depend on learners' experiences.
- Learners are cognitively active in their attempts to make sense of those experiences.
- People construct the understanding that results from their efforts to make sense of their experiences.
- Constructing understanding strongly depends on social interaction.

The Inductive Model is designed to capitalize on these learning principles. It does so in the following three ways:

1. Lessons using the Inductive Model begin with and are built around examples. The examples become the experiences that learners use to construct their understanding of the topics they're studying.
2. Social interaction is used to analyze the examples. Examples, alone, won't necessarily result in valid construction of understanding because students may misperceive the information. Social interaction helps eliminate these potential problems.
3. The teacher guides students. "Real learning involves personal invention or construction, and the teacher's role in this process is a difficult one. On the one hand, the teacher must honor students' 'inventions,' or they will not share them. On the other hand, the teacher needs to guide students toward a more mature understanding" (Prawat, 1992, p. 11).

The teacher's guidance is essential. Without careful guidance, the students may not focus on the important features of the examples, their discussions may wander aimlessly, or they may even go off task. Research indicates that guided discovery, under the direction of a skilled teacher, is much more effective than lessons in which students explore on their own (Mayer, 2002). As we said earlier, this is demanding and sophisticated instruction.

Learning Objectives for the Inductive Model

The Inductive Model is designed to help students reach two types of learning objectives. The first is for students to acquire a deep and thorough understanding of specific and well-defined topics, such as longitude and latitude, Charles's law, or the rules for forming possessives, as we saw in the three lessons that introduced the chapter. The model is less appropriate for topics such as examining character development in a novel such as *Moby Dick;* writing a creative essay; or comparing the geography, climate, and economics of different countries of the world. None of these topics focus on specific and well-defined content.

Second, the model is designed to develop students' critical-thinking abilities. Each of the teachers provided students with examples—the balls with drawings on them in Judy's case; the demonstration, models, and graphs in Sue's; and the passage in Jim's. As students attempt to find patterns in this information, they—with the teacher's guidance—construct a thorough understanding of the topics and they learn to make and assess conclusions based on evidence.

The procedures Judy, Sue, and Jim used were similar, but the specific content they taught was different. Let's look at this content now, beginning with concepts.

Concepts: Categories with Common Characteristics

Concepts are *mental categories, sets, or classes with common characteristics.* For example, whenever Judy's students encounter parallel, imaginary lines on a map that run east and west but measure distance north to south, they know they are dealing with latitude. *Latitude* is a concept.

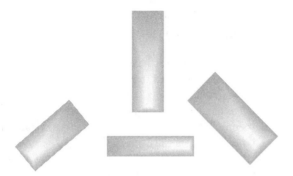

FIGURE 5.6   Rectangles

As another example, suppose children encounter the blocks that appear in Figure 5.6. Even though their sizes, dimensions, and orientations vary, they would be classified as rectangles because they all have opposite sides equal and parallel, with interior angles of 90°. *Rectangle* is also a concept.

The number of concepts taught in the school curriculum is nearly endless. Some are listed in Table 5.3. Similar lists could be generated for other areas, such as *major scale* and *tempo* in music, *perspective* and *balance* in art, or *aerobic exercise* and *isotonic exercise* in physical education. In addition, many other concepts exist that don't neatly fit into a particular content area, such as *honesty, bias, love,* and *internal conflict.*

Characteristics. A concept's **characteristics** are *its defining features.* For example, the characteristics of concept *latitude* in Judy's lesson were:

- Parallel lines
- Lines run east and west
- Lines measure distance north and south of the equator

Similarly, the concept *rectangle* has the characteristics:

- Opposite sides equal in length
- Opposite sides parallel
- All interior angles 90°

TABLE 5.3   Concepts in Different Content Areas

Language Arts	Social Studies	Science	Math
Infinitive	Culture	Monocot	Quadratic
Pronoun	Republican	Conifer	Pyramid
Plot	Liberal	Arthropod	Triangle
Hyperbole	Pork barrel	Work	Division
Indirect object	Community helper	Digestion	Equivalent fraction

Other characteristics, such as the size, color, or orientation, aren't essential. An important part of concept learning is the ability to discriminate between essential and nonessential characteristics.

Many concepts, such as *latitude* or *rectangle,* have well-defined characteristics, but others, such as *democracy* do not. In spite of the fact that our popular news frequently uses the term, most people are unable to define it in even a semiprecise way.

Even common concepts, such as car, can have "fuzzy boundaries" (Schwartz & Reisberg, 1991). For instance, some people describe sport utility vehicles as cars, but others don't. How about minivans? And, railroad "cars" also exist.

In cases like these, the concept is better represented with a **prototype,** *the best representative of its class,* or a series of **exemplars,** *the most highly typical members of its class* (Medin, Proffitt, & Schwartz, 2000). For instance, our country might be a prototype for the concept *democracy* and common passenger cars, such as Ford Taurus, Toyota Camry, or Chevy Lumina might be exemplars for the concept *car.*

When learners construct understanding of a concept they generalize from the characteristics if the characteristics are well defined, or from a prototype or set of exemplars if they are not. The teacher's role is to guide students so that they generalize appropriately and form valid understandings of the concept.

Concept Analysis: Making Concepts Meaningful.   We saw in Chapter 2 that topics should not be taught in isolation; rather, they should be connected to other related topics to make them as meaningful as possible. Concept analysis is a useful tool for this purpose. **Concept analysis** is *the process of describing a concept using its characteristics, related concepts, examples,* and *definition.* An analysis for the concept *adjective* is illustrated in Table 5.4.

From Table 5.4 we see that the concept analysis includes a **definition,** *a statement that includes the name of the concept, a superordinate concept, and the concept's characteristics.* The **superordinate concept** is *a larger category into which the concept fits.* The analysis also includes **subordinate concepts,** which are *subsets or examples of the concept,* and **coordinate concepts,** which are *other subsets of the superordinate concept.*

TABLE 5.4   Analysis of the Concept *Adjective*

Definition	An adjective is a part of speech that modifies a noun
Characteristics	Modifies noun
Examples	John and Karen drove his *old* car to the *football* game. The game was incredibly *exciting.* The *home* team won by a *bare* margin.
Superordinate concept	Part of speech
Subordinate concept	Participle Predicate adjective
Coordinate concept	Adverb

What Makes Concepts Easy or Hard to Learn?   Why do virtually all people, including small children, understand concepts such as *rectangle* and *triangle,* whereas few have a clear understanding of *democracy, justice,* or *bias*? And what can teachers do to help learners understand all concepts, regardless of their difficulty?

When a concept has a small number of concrete characteristics, concept learning is simplified (Tennyson & Cocchiarella, 1986). For example, *opposite sides equal, opposite sides parallel,* and *90° angles* are the characteristics of the concept *rectangle.* It has only three characteristics, and they're observable. We know that the concept is easy to learn because most students in kindergarten can identify rectangles. However, concepts such as *democracy, justice,* and *bias,* don't have well-defined characteristics, and people's prototypes, or sets of exemplars for them vary markedly. These concepts are much harder to learn, and consequently they're much harder to teach.

Regardless of their complexity, the key to learning concepts is experience with a carefully selected set of examples and nonexamples combined with a definition (Tennyson & Cocchiarella, 1986). We discuss the use of examples in more detail when we discuss planning lessons with the Inductive Model.

Relationships among Concepts: Principles, Generalizations, and Academic Rules

By generalizing from specific examples to describe broad categories, such as using the four examples in Figure 5.6 to construct the mental ideal of *rectangle,* concepts help us simplify our world; we remember the categories instead of each individual instance. The world would be totally bewildering, for instance, if we had to remember each individual insect among the billions that exist rather than understanding the broad class. Some practical aspects of our lives, such as pest control, would be literally impossible.

Generalizing can help us further simplify the world by describing relationships between concepts in general patterns. We then remember the pattern instead of the specific instances. As examples, look at the following statements.

- Like magnetic poles repel, and unlike poles attract.
- The greater the unbalanced force on an object, the greater its acceleration.
- People with high saturated fat diets have higher cholesterol levels than those with low saturated fat diets.
- Students from high socioeconomic (SES) backgrounds achieve higher grades than students from lower SES backgrounds.
- In words with two vowels, the first vowel makes a "long" sound, and the second vowel is silent.
- In rounding off a number, you round up if the last digit is 5 or more, and round down if it is 4 or less.

We see that all the statements relate concepts to each other in general patterns. For instance, the first statement relates *polarity* and *attraction,* the second relates *force* and *acceleration,* and a similar relationship can be identified for each of the others.

Differences exist, however. The first two statements are **principles,** which are *relationships among concepts accepted as valid for all known cases.* We accept the notion that all like poles repel, and all unlike poles attract, for example. The terms *principles* and *laws* are commonly used interchangeably. For instance, Sue Grant taught Charles's law, which could also be described as a principle. It describes a relationship between the concept *temperature* and the concept *volume,* which we accept as true. Principles are important in the school curriculum, particularly in the sciences. Much of the content in chemistry and physics involves examining principles and their applications.

The second two statements are **generalizations,** which are *general patterns with known exceptions.* For example, some people who have high saturated fat diets have lower cholesterol levels than others who consume less saturated fat, and many students from low SES backgrounds achieve higher grades than students from high SES backgrounds. Much of what we know about human behavior in general, and teaching and learning in particular, is in the form of generalizations. For instance, in general, teachers who call on their students as equally as possible increase achievement, but if they're disorganized, or if their objectives aren't clear, they won't increase learning. The same is true for much of the health-related information that we acquire from the media. For instance, the famous study suggesting that an aspirin every other day helps reduce the danger of heart attack is generally true, but many exceptions exist, particularly in cases where high cholesterol or smoking are involved.

Understanding the difference between principles and generalizations contributes to critical thinking. The validity of conclusions based on generalizations depends on the validity of the generalizations themselves. The ability to make and assess these conclusions are important critical-thinking skills.

The fifth and sixth statements in the list are **academic rules,** which are *relationships between concepts arbitrarily derived by people.* For instance, in the case of rounding, it would be equally valid to round up if the last digit were 6 or more, but it has been set at 5. Although arbitrary, rules are important for consistency, particularly in communication. For example, if we didn't have a rule to consistently communicate both singular and plural possessives—the objective in Jim Rooney's lesson—our writing would be confusing and communication would suffer. These relationships are outlined in Figure 5.7.

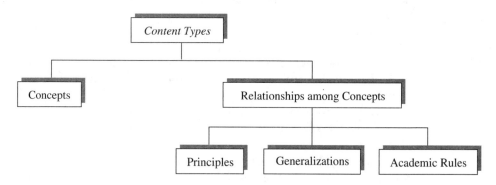

FIGURE 5.7   Types of Content Taught with the Inductive Model

Planning Lessons with the Inductive Model

The planning process for lessons using the Inductive Model involves three essential steps, which are illustrated in Figure 5.8 and discussed in the sections that follow.

Identifying Topics

Imagine that you're planning a lesson or unit. Where do you start? If you're typical, it's with a topic (Kauchak & Eggen, 2003). For example, the teachers in our opening episodes focused on longitude and latitude, Charles's law, and the rule for forming singular and plural possessives. Each was a topic, and each was the beginning point for the teacher's planning. Topics may come from textbooks, curriculum guides, or other sources, including teachers themselves. When the topics are concepts, principles, generalizations, or academic rules, the Inductive Model can be used effectively.

Specifying Learning Objectives

Having identified the topic, we must then decide what we want students to know about it. Effective teachers have clear and precise learning objectives in mind and teach directly toward them (Bransford et al., 2000). For example, Judy Nelson wanted her students to be able to do the following:

- State the characteristics of longitude and latitude.
- Identify the longitude and latitude of cities and other specified locations on a map.
- Identify a city or landmark nearest a given longitude and latitude.

These objectives were clear and precise, as were Sue's and Jim's, and this conceptual clarity provides focus during the lesson. Beginning teachers often specify their objectives in writing, and although veterans tend to not write them down, they are no less clear about that they want their students to understand or be able to do (Clark & Peterson, 1986).

Clear learning objectives—regardless of whether they're specifically stated in writing—are essential because they provide a framework for teachers' thinking in both planning and implementing lessons. During planning the objectives guide teachers as they select examples. If objectives aren't clear, teachers don't know what they're trying to

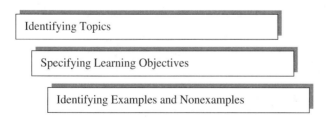

FIGURE 5.8   Planning Lessons with the Inductive Model

illustrate, and the likelihood of selecting the best possible examples is reduced. Clear and precise objectives also makes questioning much easier during lessons. When teachers know exactly what they want their students to understand, questioning that guides the students to the objectives is more focused and strategic.

Identifying Examples and Nonexamples

Once teachers have decided exactly what they want students to understand or be able to do, they create (or find) examples and nonexamples. Nonexamples are particularly important when teaching closely related concepts. For instance, if students are learning the concept *insect,* they should also be shown examples of spiders, which are arachnids, so they won't conclude that spiders are insects. By identifying differences between the two, such as eight legs for spiders instead of the six found on insects, learners are less likely to confuse the two. Research indicates that closely related concepts are most effectively taught together (Tennyson & Cocchiarella, 1986), such as in Judy's lesson on longitude and latitude. Examples of longitude served as nonexamples for latitude and vice versa.

Quality of Examples.   When teachers create examples, they want to use the most effective ones possible because they are the experiences from the outside world that the teacher brings into the classroom to help students construct their understanding. So, what constitutes a high-quality example? Ideally, it is one in which *all the information the students need to reach the learning objective is observable* (Eggen & Kauchak, 2004). For instance, in Judy's lesson the students *could see* that the lines of latitude didn't cross and that they got shorter closer to the poles. They could also see that the lines of longitude were the same length and intersected at the poles. The characteristics of the concept were observable in the examples. As another case, in teaching the concept *density,* filling a drink cup with cotton balls and then compressing the cotton would be a high-quality example because students could see that the mass (the amount of cotton) remains the same when compressed but that it takes up less space, so it is more dense.

When teaching principles, generalizations, or rules, a high-quality example is one in which the *relationship* between the concepts within these abstractions is observable. For instance, Sue Grant didn't illustrate differences in temperature or differences in volume alone; she illustrated the relationship between the two, both with her demonstration and with her models. The same was true in Jim Rooney's case. His examples illustrated the relationship between the spelling of words and the use of apostrophes.

We saw in Chapter 2 that learners' backgrounds often vary widely, and many students come to school without the necessary background knowledge to be successful. Using high-quality examples is the most effective tool teachers have for accommodating these differences. If the information learners need is observable in the examples, all students will have a chance to reach the teacher's learning objectives. Without high-quality examples, only those students with extensive background knowledge have a chance at success.

Variety of Examples.   How many examples are necessary? There is no clear answer to this question. Teachers need to use as many as necessary to illustrate the scope of the topic. For instance, if you were teaching the concept *adverb,* a minimum number would be at least one example each of an adverb modifying a verb, an adjective, and another adverb, plus adjectives as nonexamples. As another case, if you were teaching the concept *reptile,* you would need at least one example each of an alligator (or crocodile), snake, lizard, turtle, and a sea turtle (so the students don't conclude that sea turtles are some kind of fish), together with a frog (which is an amphibian) as a nonexample.

Context for Examples.   In Chapter 2 we saw that context is an important factor in learning. It helps students see how the topic relates to the real world. To further illustrate this idea, look at the following passage, which a teacher used to help his students understand the concept *adjective.*

> John and Karen drove his **old** car to the **football** game. They *soon* met their *very* **best** friends, Latoya and Michael, at the **large** gate near the entrance. The game was *incredibly* **exciting,** and, because the team's **running** game was in **high** gear, the **home** team won by a **bare** margin.

Let's examine the teacher's thinking in creating the examples. First, a variety of high-quality examples are included; in each case learners can see that the adjectives modify nouns.

Second, in typical contexts "running" is a verb, and "football" and "home" are nouns, but in the context of this passage they are adjectives. If examples weren't placed in a real-world context, such as when isolated, single words are used, students would be more likely to form misconceptions.

We can also see how the passage capitalizes on the concept analysis we outlined in Table 5.4. For instance, each of the examples represents a subordinate concept; "running" is a participle and "exciting" is a predicate adjective. Third, examples (e.g., soon, very, and incredibly) of the concept *adverb,* which is a coordinate concept, are used as nonexamples.

Context is important in other content areas as well. For instance, Sue Grant gave her students the following problem:

> You have a balloon filled with 1.5 liters of air in a freezer at –5° Celsius. You take the balloon out of the freezer and put it in the window where the temperature is 30° Celsius. What will the volume of the balloon be after it has warmed to 30°?

This was an attempt to put the content into a real-world context.

Types of Examples.   Having discussed the quality of and context for examples, let's look at some different types.

Concrete Materials.   Concrete materials are the "real thing." They are the most effective type of example and should be used wherever possible. For instance, an ideal example of the concept *arthropod* would be a live lobster (which could be purchased from a seafood store). The children could feel its hard, cold shell, and see its jointed legs and three body parts. The essential information the students need to understand the concept are observable in the example.

Demonstrations and hands-on activities are other forms of concrete examples. Sue Grant's balloons in three different conditions allowed her students to observe the relationship between temperature and volume. When students connect two wires to a battery and make a bulb light up, they are seeing a real complete circuit, not a simulation, model, role play, or other indirect method of illustrating the concept.

Pictures. When concrete materials are unavailable, pictures can be an acceptable compromise. Because we can't bring young and mature mountains into the classroom and it is often difficult to go to where we can observe them directly, for instance, pictures of the Rocky Mountains and Appalachian Mountains would be an effective way of illustrating these concepts. The key is to come as close as possible to reality. Detailed colored slides or photographs are better than black-and-white pictures, which in turn are better than outline drawings.

Models. Some content, particularly in science, is impossible to observe directly. In these cases, **models,** which are *representations that allow us to visualize what we can't observe directly,* are effective. The model of our cognitive architecture in Chapter 2, and Sue Grant's drawings, are both models. Our model helped us visualize the way we process information, and Sue's model helped her students to visualize the spacing, differences in speed, and random direction of the molecules under three different temperature conditions. The molecular motion was impossible to illustrate in any other way. Although models do not actually illustrate reality, they can help us identify essential characteristics of reality.

Vignettes. To begin this section, look at the following examples:

> Mary's dream had come true. John, a boy she had wanted to date for some time, had asked her to go to the movies. However, as she thought about her homework assignments for that night, she remembered the term paper that was due on Friday. She had been putting off work on the paper until the last moment, and now she didn't know what to do.

> Johnny knew if he cheated off Bill's paper, he'd do well on the test, but he also knew that he would feel guilty and dissatisfied.

> Although Lupe hated to leave her hometown friends and family, and even her room, which she had lived in since a child, she wanted to go to college in Boston, 500 miles away.

The examples are **vignettes,** which are *short case studies.* In each the character is faced with two choices either of which has both positive and negative consequences. They illustrate the concept *internal conflict.* The concept is difficult to describe, and a definition such as "to come into collision, clash, or be at variance within oneself" is abstract and would do little to clarify it for school-age learners. The vignettes, however, clearly illustrate the concept's characteristics. Vignettes and longer case studies are commonly used to illustrate abstract concepts in areas such as history, government, literature, and psychology where concrete materials, pictures, and models wouldn't be effective. As you've seen in this and earlier chapters, we make extensive use of vignettes and case studies in our writing.

Simulation and Role Play.   As with vignettes and case studies, simulation and role play can also be used when concepts are hard to illustrate in any other way. Both involve placing students in real-life situations. For instance, students hear a great deal about the concept *discrimination,* but most have had little experience with it. A simulation where some members of the class are discriminated against because of eye or hair color, height, or some other arbitrary characteristic provides a powerful illustration of an important concept. Social studies teachers also use simulations to illustrate our court system, the ways bills become laws, and the drudgery of assembly-line jobs.

Creating Examples: The Use of Technology.   Many of the topics we teach are difficult to represent, and this difficulty is what makes them hard to learn. In these cases technology provides an effective alternative (Forcier & Deci, 2002; Roblyer, 2003b). We might simply drop heavy and light objects, for example, to demonstrate that all objects fall at the same rate, regardless of weight, but it's virtually impossible to illustrate the actual acceleration of a falling object. Here, technology can be a powerful tool. For example, Figure 5.9 illustrates the

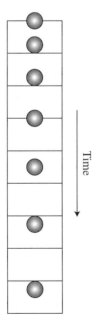

FIGURE 5.9   Illustration of Falling Object

position of a falling ball at uniform time intervals. We see that the distance between the images is greater and greater, indicating that the ball is falling faster and faster. This is an example of acceleration that is virtually impossible to represent without the use of technology.

Teachers can also use computer software to capitalize on the power of simulations. For instance, teachers might use software to simulate a frog dissection rather than cutting an actual frog. Although the simulation doesn't allow students the hands-on experience of working with a real frog, it is less expensive because it can be used over and over; it is more flexible because the frog can be "reassembled"; and it avoids sacrificing a frog for science (Roblyer, 2003a). As the quality of software improves, representations will become more sophisticated and the simulations will be more interactive, further increasing learner motivation and understanding.

The Internet also contains a virtually unlimited source of information for inductive lessons. Pictures, charts, graphs, models, and diagrams, all of which can be downloaded, can be used to represent topics that are hard to illustrate in other ways. And the convenience of downloading illustrations can save teachers time and energy.

Implementing Lessons Using the Inductive Model

You have identified your topic, carefully specified your objectives, and selected or created your examples. You're now ready to begin the lesson. Implementing a lesson using the Inductive Model combines five interrelated phases, together with an emphasis on thinking and strategies for increasing student motivation. The phases each have learning and motivation functions, which are illustrated in Table 5.5 and discussed in the sections that follow.

TABLE 5.5   Learning and Motivation Functions for the Phases of the Inductive Model

Phase	Learning and Motivation Function
Phase 1: Introduction The focus of the lesson is established	▪ Attracts attention ▪ Activates curiosity motivation
Phase 2: The open-ended phase Students make observations and comparisons that are used for further analysis	▪ Promotes involvement ▪ Ensures success
Phase 3: The convergent phase The lesson moves toward a single concept, principle, generalization, or rule	▪ Facilitates knowledge construction ▪ Aids schema production
Phase 4: Closure Student understanding is summarized and linked to previous understanding	▪ Achieves equilibrium ▪ Promotes encoding
Phase 5: Application Students apply their understanding in new contexts	▪ Facilitates transfer ▪ Links new learning to prior understanding

Phase 1: Lesson Introduction

Phase 1 is intended to attract students' attention and provide a conceptual framework for the lesson. It can begin in a variety of ways, for example, with a simple statement such as, "Today, I'm going to show you some examples. I want you to be good observers and try to see what kind of pattern exists in them." Or the lesson can begin as Judy did when she posed the problem of specifying for a new friend exactly where the students lived. In another case, Sue identified Charles's law by name and told the students that they would be able to solve problems with it when they finished the lesson. Jim began his lesson by simply elaborating on a review of the previous day's work. Each of these introductions provides a framework for the lesson to follow.

Phase 2: The Open-Ended Phase

The open-ended phase is intended to promote student involvement and ensure their success as the lesson develops. Teachers can start this phase in several ways:

- They can present an example and ask students to observe and describe it. This is what Judy did with her beach ball and what Sue did with her demonstration.
- They can present two or more examples and ask students what they have in common (search for patterns). This was Jim's approach.
- They can present an example and a nonexample and ask the students to contrast the two.
- They can even begin with a nonexample and have the students describe it. A teacher wanting the students to understand exoskeletons, for example, might begin by having students touch and squeeze themselves to demonstrate that their skeleton is internal.

Whichever option the teacher chooses, the lesson proceeds by having students respond to **open-ended questions,** which are *questions for which a variety of answers are acceptable.* Typically, open-ended questions begin with something similar to this: "What do you observe (notice) . . . ?" "How do these compare?" or "What do they have in common?" For example, Judy asked:

| "Now what can you tell us about this line?"

and later she asked,

| "Now compare the lines to each other. Kathy."

Open-ended questions have several advantages, both for students and for their teachers.

- Because a variety of responses are acceptable, the questions are safe, meaning shy or reluctant learners are virtually assured of success in answering them.
- Because the questions can be asked and answered quickly, it is easy for teachers to quickly call on several different students. Research indicates that increased numbers

of classroom questions promote students' involvement and increase achievement (Good & Brophy, 2003; Lambert & McCombs, 1998).

- The questions allow for brisk lesson pacing, which results in greater student attention than slower-paced lessons.
- Open-ended questions increase the participation of cultural minorities and students with limited English language proficiency (Langer, Bartolome, Vasquez, & Lucas, 1990).
- They are easy to prepare and ask. Teachers can ask students to describe or compare and then use students' responses as the basis for further questions. As a result, questioning is less demanding for teachers.
- Open-ended questions allow teachers to assess students' background knowledge. What the students "observe" in the examples reflects their perceptions of the examples, and these perceptions depend on their background knowledge.

This last point is important. As we've emphasized repeatedly, students construct new understanding based on their background knowledge, so assessing their existing understanding is essential. Asking open-ended questions is a simple, efficient way of getting this information.

Learning to ask open-ended questions requires some initial adjustment. Teachers not used to open-ended questioning tend to "hone in" on the idea they're after almost immediately. Loosening up a little, and asking several open-ended questions, can significantly increase student participation.

For instance, let's look again at the vignette that includes the examples of adjectives.

John and Karen drove his **old** car to the **football** game. They *soon* met their *very* **best** friends, Latoya and Michael, at the **large** gate near the entrance. The game was *incredibly* **exciting,** and, because the team's **running** game was in **high** gear, the **home** team won by a **bare** margin.

Teachers, knowing their objective is for students to understand adjectives, tend to ask questions such as, "What are the adjectives in the passage?" or "What do we know about John's car?" Nothing is wrong or technically undesirable about these questions, but fewer acceptable responses exist, and the opportunity to increase the involvement of lower achievers or shy and reticent students is reduced. A more effective beginning question in the open-ended phase would be, "What do you notice about the paragraph?" or "What do the terms in bold have in common?" These questions give students a chance to think about the sentences, describe their thoughts, and, perhaps most importantly, answer without fear of being wrong.

There is no rule that tells you how many open-ended questions to ask. With practice, teachers become comfortable with the process and use their judgment about when to move on. The students' behavior can help teachers decide. If they appear eager to continue describing or comparing the examples, you may continue a bit longer; if they appear antsy or eager to move on, you might move more quickly to Phase 3.

Phase 3: The Convergent Phase

The open-ended phase is designed to increase student involvement and motivation, and to ensure success. However, you have a specific learning objective that you want the students to reach. To do so, you narrow the range of student responses and assist them in identifying the essential characteristics if you're teaching a concept, or identifying the relationship if you're teaching a generalization, principle, or academic rule. Because the students' responses converge on a specific learning objective, this is called the *convergent phase,* and this is the phase in which knowledge construction and schema development primarily take place.

Let's look at some dialogue from Judy's lesson to see how she made the transition from the open-ended to the convergent phase.

> **JUDY:** How do these lines compare to the lines of latitude? . . . Amarilis?
>
> **AMARILIS:** . . . They go all around the ball.
>
> **JUDY:** Yes, they do. What else? . . . Nicola?
>
> **NICOLA:** . . .
>
> **JUDY:** Let's look here. . . . What do all of the longitude lines do at this point? [pointing the top of the ball toward Nicola]
>
> **NICOLA:** They all cross there.
>
> **JUDY:** Good. So, what do we know about the lengths of the longitude lines? . . . Johanna?

Judy began the convergent phase with the question, "What do all of the longitude lines do at this point?" which was intended to prompt Nicola and lead the students to recognize that they all crossed at the poles. It was convergent because a single answer was expected.

Lessons don't always proceed as planned, however, and we saw that in the preceding dialogue. In spite of the fact that she asked an open-ended question, Judy still had to prompt Nicola, so she began the convergent phase a little sooner than expected. Then, when she asked Johanna the question about the lengths of the longitude lines, Johanna demonstrated a misconception, thinking that the lines of longitude are shorter at the poles. Let's look at some more dialogue.

> **JOHANNA:** They get shorter up there.
>
> **JUDY:** Okay, wrap this string around the ball [handing Johanna a piece of string that she has on her desk and having Elton repeat the process with another piece of string at a different point on the ball but still going through the poles].
>
> **JUDY:** What do you notice about the pieces of string? . . . Johanna?
>
> **JOHANNA:** They're the same length.
>
> **JUDY:** Excellent. . . . So, what do we know about lines of longitude? . . . Amber?
>
> **AMBER:** They're all the same length.
>
> **JUDY:** Good, Amber.

When Johanna was unable to provide the correct answer, Judy might simply have told her that the lines were the same length and moved on. This would have taken less time and would seem to be more efficient. However, this would have been less meaningful to Johanna than actually seeing that the strings were the same length, and simply telling her would probably have done little to change her misconception. Explanations alone are often ineffective for helping learners develop a deep understanding of the topics they study (Eggen & Kauchak, 2004). All students bring a considerable amount of background knowledge with them to the learning situation, and this knowledge influences new learning. Merely "telling" students often has little influence in changing previous conceptions. Learners require high-quality examples combined with a great deal of discussion to help them change their thinking and "reconstruct" misconceptions. This is what Judy did in her work with her class in general and Johanna in particular.

Phase 4: Closure

Closure occurs when students embed their understanding in a complex schema, encode it into long-term memory, and achieve a sense of equilibrium. Language is important in the process of encoding. For instance, Judy's closure occurred when her students were able to summarize the characteristics of longitude and latitude in words. Sue reached closure when students were able to state Charles's law and relate it to the balloons, and Jim reached closure when his students could state the rule for punctuating singular and plural possessive nouns.

Although a formal statement of closure is usually important, certain exceptions exist. For example, suppose the concept *above* is being taught to a group of young children. It could be defined as "a position in space where one object is at higher altitude than another." Obviously, young students would be unlikely to generate such a statement even with considerable prompting. In this case, the teacher would move directly to the application phase in lieu of a formal statement of closure.

Phase 4 also provides opportunities to help students develop their abilities to recognize irrelevant information, which is an important thinking skill. For instance, in Jim's case the content of the sentences was irrelevant to the rule. With any topic, it is quite easy to assess the examples for nonessential information, which in turn sensitizes students to this important thinking skill.

Phase 5: Application

Although being able to state a definition of a concept or describe a principle, generalization, or rule reflects understanding at one level, to make the topic meaningful and ensure transfer, students must be able to apply it outside the classroom. Judy's students, for example, were asked to find the longitude and latitude of different locations around the world, Sue had her students solve problems with Charles's law, and Jim asked his to correctly punctuate singular and plural possessive nouns in their writing. During the application phase, teachers reinforce learning by providing opportunities for students to relate the topic to the real world.

The application phase typically includes a seatwork or homework assignment. However, in spite of careful development of the concept, principle, generalization, or rule, application is a transition that often requires additional help from the teacher.

Let's return to Judy's lesson now to see how she handled this part of the learning activity.

> "Okay, everyone. Suppose now that you were trying to tell someone exactly how to locate Denver, Colorado," Judy says. "How would we do that? . . . Connie?"
>
> ". . . We would find the longitude and latitude."
>
> "Good, Connie. Everyone, do that with your maps," Judy directs. [All the students have maps in front of them.]
>
> Judy walks among the students to check their progress and make brief suggestions.
>
> After about a minute she begins again, "What did you find? . . . Kim?"
>
> ". . . It's about 40°."
>
> "North or south?" Judy asks.
>
> "North," Kim answers after thinking for a few seconds.
>
> "How do you know?" Judy continues.
>
> ". . . Because it's north of the equator."
>
> "Yes. Excellent, Kim." [Judy then continues by discussing Denver's longitude.]

Carefully monitoring and discussing students' initial efforts at application reinforces learning by helping the students bridge the gap between the teacher-led learning activity and independent practice.

When you're satisfied that most students can apply the information on their own, you can give an assignment that requires further application. While most of the students work independently, you can help those who haven't fully grasped the idea or who aren't yet ready for application on their own.

Application: The Role of Context. The application phase is most effective when students are required to apply their understanding in a real-world context. Judy capitalized on the importance of context with her initial problem of trying to specify exactly where the students lived. Jim used paragraphs that related to the students' experiences as the context for applying his rule. This strategy is more effective than having the students apply the rule to isolated sentences.

As another example, we saw that Sue Grant gave her students a real-world problem in the application phase at the end of her lesson. Now, for homework she gives the following problem.

> You have a balloon filled with 1,000 milliliters (the same volume as a liter bottle that commonly is filled with water) of air at room temperature, 72° Fahrenheit. Suppose that you put it in the freezer, which is 10° Fahrenheit. What will its volume be? What assumptions are we making when we solve this problem?

This problem, situated in a common household context, measures whether students realized that they have to first convert to Celsius and then to absolute temperature. Her problem was easy to write but effective in its ability to make Charles's law meaningful in a variety of contexts.

Application: Linking New and Old Learning.   The application phase also helps students link new learning with prior understanding. For example, Sue's students connected Charles's law to their earlier understanding of mass, volume, and density; Jim's linked possessives to earlier understanding of singular and plural nouns; and Judy's related their understanding of latitude and longitude to earlier knowledge about the Earth. If these links don't occur naturally during the lesson, the teacher should formally link the information with a review.

To see how Sue accomplished this, let's look again at some dialogue near the end of her lesson.

SUE: We see from Charles's law how temperature affects volume. Let's think about how what we just learned relates to what we already know about mass and density. . . . As the temperature increases, what happens to the mass of the gas? Raul?

RAUL: Nothing.

SUE: Good. And how do you know?

RAUL: . . . The amount didn't change, only the volume.

SUE: Excellent. And how about the density? . . . Jo?

JO: It . . . gets less.

SUE: Good. Explain that for us.

JO: . . . The air is expanding, but the mass is the same, so it must be less dense.

SUE: Good clear description, Jo.

Through social interaction, Sue helped students link their understanding of Charles's law to their earlier understanding of mass and density.

Implementing Lessons Using the Inductive Model: Emphasis on Thinking and Understanding

In both planning and implementing lessons using the Inductive Model, the explicit focus is on content learning objectives. However, the development of higher-order and critical thinking is an integral part of the process. For example, in each of our lessons we saw teachers promote thinking in their students in the following ways:

- Each emphasized comparing (and contrasting). This is a basic thinking skill.
- In each case, students were required to find patterns and generalize from the patterns— by identifying the characteristics of longitude and latitude in Judy's lesson, and stating Charles's law and the rule for punctuating possessives in Sue's and Jim's lessons, respectively.

- The students were required to apply the information they learned in a realistic context.
- The students were asked to explain their thinking and provide evidence for their conclusions.

Providing evidence for conclusions is the essence of critical thinking. To illustrate, let's look again at some dialogue from Judy's lesson.

> JUDY: How do lines of longitude compare to each other? . . . Leroy?
>
> LEROY: They're the same [length].
>
> JUDY: And, how do we know?
>
> LEROY: . . . The strings were the same.

When Leroy was asked "how do we know?" he was required to provide evidence for his conclusion that the lengths of the longitude lines are equal.

To further illustrate this process, let's also look at some dialogue from Sue's lesson.

> SUE: Okay, what have we concluded? . . . Steve and Barbara?
>
> BARBARA: . . . We decided that the masses in each of the balloons were the same.
>
> SUE: Good. And why did you say that?
>
> BARBARA: The number of molecules—dots—in each balloon is the same.
>
> SUE: Good thinking, you two.

As with Judy's questioning, when Sue asked, "And why did you say that?" she was asking students to provide evidence for their conclusion.

At least two aspects of this process are important: First, promoting a deep understanding of the content and critical thinking were interdependent and woven together; students' understanding of the topic became deeper as they practiced critical thinking. This is the essence of the idea that learning results from thinking (Perkins, 1992) that we saw in Chapter 3.

Second, having students practice critical thinking didn't significantly increase the length of the lessons. Teachers, in responding to the pressures of standards and high-stakes testing, might think to themselves, "I don't have time to get the kids ready for the tests and teach thinking at the same time." Our response is that it takes little extra time, and they will be more ready for the tests because their understanding of the topics is more thorough.

With some practice teachers recognize opportunities to ask questions such as, "How do you know?" "Why?" and "What would happen if . . . ?" each of which is excellent for promoting thinking. As they practice, capitalizing on these opportunities gets easier and easier, ultimately to where asking open-ended questions is essentially automatic. The payoff is a higher level of student thinking and deeper understanding of the content with little additional effort or extra class time.

Implementing Lessons Using the Inductive Model: Increasing Student Motivation

In addition to promoting deep understanding of content and developing student thinking, the Inductive Model can be effective for increasing student motivation. Because high levels of involvement, assured success, and a sense of the unknown are features of lessons when the Inductive Model is used, they contribute to learner motivation. Let's look at these features in more detail.

Learner Involvement and Success.   In Chapter 2 we saw that involvement is a major factor that increases peoples' intrinsic interest in an activity. For example, if you're involved in a conversation with two other people, and you're actively participating, your interest remains high, but if the other two are doing most of the talking, your interest quickly wanes. The same is true for students in learning activities. The greater their involvement, the greater their interest (Blumenfeld, 1992).

We saw earlier that promoting involvement is an important function of the open-ended phase of the model. First, because they're easy to ask, open-ended questions allow teachers to call on a number of students quickly. Second, because success is virtually assured, students are more willing to attempt to answer, so they're more willing to be involved. Research indicates that involvement also increases learners' perceptions of control and autonomy, both of which increase learner motivation (Bruning et al., 2004).

A Sense of the Unknown.   In Chapter 2 we also saw that people are intrinsically motivated by activities and experiences that evoke curiosity, challenge, and a sense of the unknown (Pintrich & Schunk, 2002; Stipek, 2002). The structure of the Inductive Model capitalizes on these features. Because, instead of having the teacher present and explain information, the process involves students' attempting to find patterns in the examples the teacher provides, a sense of curiosity and challenge can be induced in the students. As learners identify the patterns and (with the teacher's guidance) reach an agreed-on conclusion, their perceptions of competence are also increased, and research indicates that the need for competence is innate (Ryan & Deci, 2000). The combination of these factors—increased interest through involvement, increased perceptions of control and competence, and assurance of success afforded by open-ended questions—can significantly increase student motivation.

Adapting the Inductive Model to Varying Teaching Contexts

To this point we have discussed and illustrated the planning and implementation of lessons using the Inductive Model. Applying the model in different content areas and with students of different ages and experiential backgrounds, however, requires flexibility. Let's consider some of these factors.

Accommodating Individual Differences

Adapting the Inductive Model for use with students at different levels of development and experience depends on two factors: the background of the students and the examples that you choose. For instance, Sue's students had experience with concepts such as *mass, volume, temperature,* and *pressure,* as indicated by their ability to use them in their conclusions and supporting observations. Had they lacked an understanding of the concepts, Sue would have had to back up, provide examples of each, and discuss the examples as she would in any other lesson. (As we saw earlier, because the Inductive Model begins open endedly, informal assessment of the students' backgrounds is built into the process.) Also, the students were able to deal with the abstraction involved in Sue's models of molecular motion and the information in the graph she presented. Her illustrations were more abstract than would have been effective with younger students. In comparison, because she was dealing with younger students who had little experience with longitude and latitude, Judy used a concrete beginning—the beach ball with the lines on it. Abstract illustrations would have been less effective because of the students' developmental levels and lack of background knowledge. In general, the younger the students or the less experience they have had with a topic, the greater the need for concrete, high-quality examples. High-quality examples are the ideal for everyone; with young children and learners lacking experience, they are essential.

Creativity in Teaching

We have all heard about creative teachers. Creativity often amounts to teachers' abilities to find or prepare eye-catching, attractive, or clever examples. Children's television programs, such as *Sesame Street* and *Barney,* illustrate this process. For instance, a muppet who runs off into the distance and announces, "Now I'm far," then comes closer and says, "Now I'm near," is simply cleverly and creatively illustrating the concepts *far* and *near.*

Judy was creative in using the beach ball for her examples of longitude and latitude. They were reasonably eye-catching and very clear. Sue's balloons attracted students' attention and posed a problem to solve. Both teachers were able to creatively use everyday examples to illustrate abstract ideas.

Spontaneous Inductive Lessons

Describing Inductive Model lessons as spontaneous means that you're able to generate examples on the spot and guide your students toward an unplanned idea that appears during a lesson. As your expertise with the model develops, your ability to guide your students will require less conscious effort, and you will be able to recognize opportunities to use mini-inductive lessons in the context of larger topics. Let's look at some examples.

In the middle of a class discussion, one of Sandy Clark's students raises her hand and says, "I don't get this 'division by zero is undefined.' I just don't understand what they mean by 'undefined.'"

Sandy pauses, thinks a moment, and says, "okay, look," and she writes the number 12 on the board. "Now I'm going to give you each a number to divide into 12, and when I call your name, you give me the answer. Roy, divide by 2; Maria, 0.03; Karen, 0.01; Jeff, 0.002; Duk, 0.0004; Raheem, 0.000006; John, 0.000000002; Donna, 0.0000000000003."

"We'll go ahead and make a table," and she then writes the following on the board as the students give their answers.

Divided by	Answer
2.0	6
0.03	400
0.01	1,200
0.002	6,000
0.0004	30,000
0.000006	2,000,000
0.000000002	6,000,000,000
0.0000000000003	40,000,000,000,000

"So let's look at the patterns we have here," Sandy directs. "What do you notice about the left column? . . . Terry?"

"The numbers are getting smaller and smaller."

"Good. So imagine now that we kept going with those numbers. Eventually we would be approaching what? . . . Leah?"

"I'm not following you."

"Imagine that we have many more numbers in the left column," Sandy goes on, "and they continued to get smaller and smaller. Eventually, they would be nearly what?"

". . . Zero."

"Yes, exactly," she smiles at Leah.

"Now look at the right column. What pattern do you see there? . . . Rene?"

"They're getting bigger and bigger."

"Now imagine that the numbers in the left column got incredibly small, so small that we can hardly imagine. What would happen to the numbers on the right?"

"They would be huge," Brent volunteers.

"And ultimately if we actually got to zero, what would happen to those on the right? . . . They would sort of what?" Sandy gestures openly as if illustrating an explosion with her arms.

". . . They would sort of explode?" Dennis responds with uncertainty in his voice.

"Yes, exactly," Sandy smiles. "That's what is meant by 'undefined.'"

Three points about this lesson are important. First, Sandy had the insight to be able to generate her examples on the spot. This required both a clear understanding of her subject matter and what it would take to effectively illustrate the topic for her students. This illustrates both her *knowledge of content* and *pedagogical content knowledge,* topics that we studied in Chapter 1.

Second, helping students understand that "division by zero is undefined" took less than 10 minutes. This is what we mean by mini-inductive lessons in the context of larger discussions. Third, and perhaps most importantly, Sandy could have simply tried to verbally explain division by zero, and it would have taken less time. However, it is unlikely that an abstract explanation would have been meaningful to her students. In contrast, Sandy cleverly and creatively helped her students understand a very abstract idea with a simple illustration that she created on the spot. This is the essence of spontaneous teaching.

Research indicates that in-depth study of fewer topics results in much more learning than superficial coverage of many, and that students need time and opportunities to think about the topics they're studying (Bransford et al., 2000; Bruning et al., 2004). This admittedly presents a dilemma for teachers who are required to "cover" a certain number of topics and meet a variety of standards. Using the Inductive Model with its emphasis on high-quality examples and interaction is one way to help develop this depth of understanding.

Length of Lessons

In working with teachers, we're often asked, "How long should an inductive lesson be?" The answer is the same for all lessons: It should be as long as it takes students to reach the learning objective. In some cases, it may be rather long; for example, it took Judy Nelson's students about 30 minutes to develop an understanding of latitude and longitude, and they spent the rest of the class period practicing identifying the longitude and latitude of various locations around the world. In comparison, Sandy Clark's "spontaneous" lesson took less than 10 minutes. In some cases a lesson may take more than a single class period.

Assessing Student Learning

Research indicates that effective learning environments are assessment centered (Bransford et al., 2000; Stiggins, 2001). This means that assessing student understanding is an integral part of the entire teaching–learning process; it is not something "tacked on" after a series of topics have been taught.

Content outcomes of a lesson using the Inductive Model can be assessed in a variety of ways, ranging from standard paper-and-pencil tests to performance measures and portfolios.

Aligning Assessments and Objectives

Regardless of the type of measure, teachers must be sure that their objectives, learning activities, and assessments are aligned. Maintaining this alignment can be challenging. It's easy to fall into the trap of thinking you're measuring one level of understanding when in reality you're measuring another. For example, consider the following item designed to measure students' understanding of the concept *arthropod*.

Circle all of the following that are arthropods.

    a. alligator
    b. shrimp
    c. oyster
    d. dragonfly

In order to respond correctly, students must know the characteristics of each of the animals or how it appears. If they don't, they could understand the concept and still respond incorrectly. This invalidates the item. Although it's intended to measure students' understanding of the concept, it more nearly measures students' knowledge of the individual animals. As a result, the assessment is not aligned with the learning objective.

Pictures would be a more effective alternative. If pictures are used (assuming characteristics are displayed in detail), students could respond to the item without knowing the names of the animals, and those with less experience would be less disadvantaged compared to the rest of the class.

Better yet, though more demanding, would be for the teacher to display two real examples (or detailed models), such as a grasshopper and a clam, and have the students explain in writing why the grasshopper is an arthropod and the clam is not. This requires the students to apply their understanding of the concept, and it also provides the teacher with insights into students' thinking.

As another example, suppose Sue wanted to measure her students' understanding of Charles's law and presented the following problem:

$$T_1 \ 50°C, T_2 \ 40°C, V_1 \ 100 \text{ ml. Find } V_2.$$

The problem presented in this way measures little more than recall of the procedure. In situations such as this, students commonly memorize formulas, plug in numbers, and find answers that have little meaning for them. Research indicates that students study more in response to the way they're assessed than in the way they're taught (Crooks, 1988), so if the measurement focuses on knowledge and recall, students will attempt to memorize procedures rather than understand topics in depth. If understanding is the objective, the assessment is out of alignment. The following is a better problem:

It's July 15 and extremely hot outside. You have three closed containers, each filled with 250 milliliters of air in your kitchen, which is 23° Celsius. (Imagine that the containers are made of an elastic that can expand and contract without changing the pressure.) You put container A in the freezing compartment of your refrigerator, B in the other part of the refrigerator, and C outside your house.

1. Which of the following best describes the volume of each container after they have been in these conditions for an hour?
   a. Because the mass of air for each doesn't change, each container will have 250 milliliters of air in it.
   b. All three containers will have more than 250 milliliters of air in them.
   c. A will have less than 250 milliliters of air, the volume of B will not change, and C will have more than 250 milliliters of air.
   d. A and B will have less than 250 milliliters of air, and C will have more than 250 milliliters of air.
   e. We don't have enough information to make conclusions about the volume of the air in each case.
2. If the freezing compartment of your refrigerator is –6° Celsius, what will be the volume of air in the container placed there (when the air reaches that temperature)?

Notice that the first item is qualitative. This measures a different kind of understanding than does the quantitative problem. Both are valuable. Qualitative assessments require students to explain and justify their thinking, which makes their quantitative answers more meaningful.

In both Judy's and Jim's cases, simple performance measures would be effective. For instance, Jim could have his students write paragraphs—just as he did in the application phase of the lesson—to determine the extent to which his students could correctly punctuate singular and plural possessive nouns in their writing. Judy could simply have her students find the longitude and latitude of several locations and also find cities and landmarks when given the coordinates. She could personalize the process by having students find the longitude and latitude of the city they came from if they lived somewhere else, the city their grandparents live in, or a city they visited. Judy might also extend the thinking of her students with an item such as the following:

> Look at the map displayed on the overhead and find Chicago. Which of the following is the best predictor of Chicago's longitude and latitude?
>
> **a.** 40° N. latitude, 90° E. longitude
> **b.** 40° S. latitude, 90° W. longitude
> **c.** 40° N. longitude, 60° E. latitude
> **d.** 40° S. longitude, 60° W. latitude
> **e.** 40° N. latitude, 90° W. longitude

Explain the reasons for your choice.

An item such as this one assumes that the latitude and longitude of Chicago have never been discussed in class. The item would require that students:

- Know that latitude measures distance north and south of the equator.
- Know that longitude measures distance east and west of the prime meridian.
- Recognize that Chicago is north of the equator.
- Recognize that Chicago is west of the prime meridian.

As another example, consider the following item (again based on an unmarked map).

> Look at Lisbon, Portugal, on the map. Its longitude is approximately 10° W. Now look at Madrid, Spain. Based on our understanding of longitude and the location of Lisbon, which of the following is the best prediction of Madrid's longitude?
>
> **a.** 4° W.
> **b.** 4° E.
> **c.** 14° W.
> **d.** 6° E.

This item would require that students recognize that Madrid is east of Lisbon but still west of the prime meridian. It is easy to write but requires that students both apply previous understanding to a new problem and predict an outcome. Items such as these measure both deep understanding of the content and students' abilities to think critically.

Using Assessment to Increase Learning

Teachers sometimes think that assessment is used primarily as a process for assigning grades. It can, however, be a powerful way to promote learning and motivation. Two factors are required, however. First, the assessment items or tasks must measure more than knowledge and recall of information, and second, detailed feedback and discussion of the items are essential. Time spent in providing feedback can be some of the most productive learning time we have because students' interest in their performance is high. Because of this interest, explanations and discussions of quiz items often result in more learning than occurs in the initial learning activity, when the students have less at stake.

Summary

The Inductive Model: An Overview

The Inductive Model is a powerful approach to instruction that uses examples to teach well-defined content. With the teacher's guidance, students find relationships in the examples that lead to general conclusions and applications. Based on constructivist views of learning, the Inductive Model emphasizes learners' active involvement and the construction of their own understanding of specific topics.

The Inductive Model: Theoretical Foundations

The Inductive Model is based on basic principles of cognitive learning theory. Through examples, teachers provide experiences that learners can use to construct new understandings. Through interactive questioning, teachers not only provide for active involvement but also provide opportunities for students to articulate and share their developing ideas.

Learning Objectives for the Inductive Model

The Inductive Model is used to teach concepts, categories with common characteristics; principles, relationships between concepts accepted as true; generalizations, relationships between concepts that have exceptions; and academic rules, relationships between concepts arbitrarily derived by people. At the same time, the model is designed to help students develop their critical-thinking abilities.

Planning Lessons with the Inductive Model

During planning, teachers identify topics, create precise learning objectives, and find or prepare high-quality examples. Examples can include concrete materials, pictures, models, case studies, or simulations and role plays. High-quality examples include all the information students need to understand the topic, and they are the most effective tool teachers have for accommodating background differences among students.

Implementing Lessons Using the Inductive Model

Lessons using the Inductive Model begin with a short introduction followed by an open-ended phase in which students are encouraged to make observations and comparisons among examples. The open-ended phase is followed by students' gradually moving toward the objective with the teacher's guidance. Lessons are completed when the students are able to define a concept or state the relationship in a principle, generalization, or academic rule, and apply the topic to a new, and ideally real-world, situation.

Promoting deep understanding of topics and developing critical-thinking abilities are interdependent and accomplished primarily through teacher questioning. Questions such as, "Why?" "How do we know?" and "What would happen if?" promote both thinking and understanding. With effort and practice teachers' abilities to use them become virtually automatic.

The Inductive Model capitalizes on the intrinsically motivating effects of student involvement and a sense of the unknown. The open-ended phase of the model, with it's emphasis on open-ended questions is uniquely capable of promoting high levels of student involvement, which increases both student interest and perceptions of control and autonomy.

Because lessons begin with an attempt to find patterns that haven't been explicitly stated by the teacher, a sense of curiosity and challenge is induced. When the challenge is met, learners' perceptions of competence are increased.

Adapting the Inductive Model to Varying Teaching Contexts

The Inductive Model easily accommodates background differences in students and varying lengths of lessons. Teachers can be creative in the ways they prepare and use examples, and as their expertise increases they can learn to use the model spontaneously. The model, because of its emphasis on involvement and success, can be effective in introducing students to groupwork and cooperative learning.

Assessing Student Learning

Effective assessments are consistent with teachers' objectives. Both paper-and-pencil and performance assessments can be used to measure student understanding. Assessments that capitalize on applications in real-world contexts and include detailed feedback are among the most powerful tools we have for increasing learning.

IMPORTANT CONCEPTS

Academic rule (p. 142)
Characteristics (p. 134)
Concepts (p. 138)
Concept analysis (p. 140)
Coordinate concept (p. 140)

Definition (p. 140)
Exemplars (p. 140)
Generalization (p. 142)
Model (p. 146)
Open-ended questions (p. 149)

Principle (p. 142)
Prototype (p. 140)
Subordinate concept (p. 140)
Superordinate concept (p. 140)
Vignette (p. 146)

EXERCISES

1. Explain how each of the lessons at the beginning of this chapter was based on cognitive views of learning. (Think back to your study of cognitive learning in Chapter 2.)

2. Identify an instance in her lesson where Judy Nelson was attempting to establish positive expectations for her class.

3. Examine each of the following statements and classify each as a generalization, principle, or academic rule.
   a. People immigrate for economic reasons.
   b. Subjects and verbs in sentences agree with each other in number.
   c. A diet high in saturated fat raises a person's cholesterol level.
   d. Like magnetic poles repel and unlike poles attract.

4. Identify the concepts being related in each of the statements in Item 3.

5. For each of the statements in Item 3, describe one or more examples that could be used to effectively illustrate the concept, principle, generalization, or academic rule.

6. Do a concept analysis of the concept *rectangle.*

7. Classify each of the following according to type of example: concrete materials, pictures, models, case studies, or simulation and role play.
   a. Jim Rooney's passage
   b. Judy Nelson's beach ball with lines drawn on it
   c. Judy Nelson's maps
   d. Sue Grant's balloons
   e. Sue Grant's drawings of the balloons and molecules

8. Consider a teacher wanting to teach the following principle: "Less dense materials float on more dense materials if they don't mix." The lesson is introduced by displaying two vials of the same volume, one containing water and the other containing cooking oil, and placing them on a balance. The mass of the water is measurably greater than that of the cooking oil. The water and oil are then poured together into a third vial and the oil floats. Answer the following questions based on the information.
   a. How many examples did the teacher use?
   b. What kinds of examples were they (concrete materials, pictures, etc.)?
   c. What specific observations would the teacher have to prompt the students to make?
   d. What might the teacher do in Phase 5 of this lesson for application of the principle?

Feedback for these exercises begin on page 341.

DISCUSSION QUESTIONS

1. Consider the motivational features of Judy Nelson's, Sue Grant's, and Jim Rooney's lessons. In what ways were each motivating? How could student motivation be increased in each case?

2. Teachers obviously do not have time to develop an inductive lesson for every concept, principle, generalization, or academic rule existing in curriculum materials. How do they decide what concepts and relationships to select?

3. Are some concepts and relationships among them more conducive than others to being taught using the Inductive Model? If so, what characteristics do they have in common?

4. Are there instances when verbal examples would be sufficient for teaching a concept, generalization, principle, or rule? If so, what would these instances be?

5. What are the major advantages of inductive teaching? The major disadvantages?

6. We have briefly discussed options for using the Inductive Model with different age groups. What other factors would have to be considered in using the model with younger students? With advanced high school students?

7. A lesson using the Inductive Model can begin with little or no introduction to the content being taught. What are the advantages and disadvantages of beginning in this way?

The Concept
Attainment Model

T he Concept Attainment Model is an inductive teaching strategy designed to help students of all ages reinforce their understanding of concepts and practice hypothesis testing. Developed from concept-learning research (Klausmeier, 1992; Tennyson & Cocchiarella, 1986), the model uses positive and negative examples to illustrate concepts as simple as *square* and *dog* or as sophisticated as *oxymoron* and *socialism.*

The Concept Attainment Model is also useful for giving students experience with the scientific method and particularly with hypothesis testing, experiences that are often hard to provide in content areas other than science. When you have completed your study of this chapter, you should be able to:

- Identify topics appropriately taught with the Concept Attainment Model.
- Prepare a list of examples that effectively illustrate a concept and promote hypothesis testing.
- Implement lessons using the Concept Attainment Model.
- Adapt the Concept Attainment Model for learners of different developmental levels.
- Assess student understanding of content objectives taught with the Concept Attainment Model.

To begin our discussion, let's look at two teachers using the Concept Attainment Model with their students.

Karl Haynes, a fifth-grade teacher, begins a science lesson by calling students' attention to a bag he holds in his hand. "Today, we're going to do something a little different than what we've been doing. I have an idea in mind, and your job is to figure out what it is. To help you I'm going to show you some things that *are* examples of the idea, and I'm also going to show you some things that *are not* examples of the idea. Then, based on the things that are examples and the others that are not, you'll need to figure out what the idea is. This will give us all some practice in being good thinkers. If you're not quite sure of what we're doing, you will catch on once we get started. Okay, ready? . . . Here we go."

Karl reaches into the bag, pulls out an apple that has been cut in half and puts it on the table in front of a cardboard sign on which is printed the word *Examples.* He also takes a rock out of the bag and places it in front of a sign that reads *Nonexamples.*

"Now," he continues, "the apple *is* an example of the idea I have in mind, and the rock *is not* an example of the idea. . . .What do you think the idea might be?"

"We eat apples," Rasheed volunteers.

"Good," Karl smiles, "so the idea might be . . . ?"

When Rasheed doesn't respond, Karl prompts him with, "Things . . . we . . . ?"

". . . Eat?" Rasheed continues hesitantly.

With that, Karl writes the word *HYPOTHESES* on the board, underlines it, and asks, "What do we mean by the term *hypotheses*? . . . Anyone?"

". . . It's, like, . . . kind of a guess," Mike volunteers after a few seconds.

"Yes," Karl nods to Mike. "For our purposes that's okay. Our *hypotheses* will be our educated guesses as to what the idea might be." He then writes *things we eat* under the word *HYPOTHESES.*

"What else might be a possibility?" Karl continues. ". . . Sharonda?"

"It could also be things that are alive, or . . . were."

"Fine," Karl replies writing the words *living things* on the board. "Any others? . . . Tenille?"

"Well, this is sort of like Sharonda's, . . . but it's a little different. How . . . about *things that grow on plants*?"

"Okay. . . . Does everyone see how living things and things that grow on plants are different? . . . No? Karen, explain that for us."

". . . Well, there are some living things that don't grow on plants. . . . Like animals."

"Excellent thinking, Karen. Do we have any other ideas?"

After pausing for a few seconds he continues, "Well then, let's look at a few more examples." He then takes out a sliced tomato and puts it under the *Examples* sign and places a carrot that had been sliced in half under the *Nonexamples* sign.

He continues, "What does this new information tell us? Let's first look at the hypotheses we have. Are they still all acceptable? . . . Serena?"

". . . It can't be *things to eat,*" Serena responds.

"Explain why Serena," Karl encourages.

". . . Well, we eat carrots, . . . and *carrot* is not an example."

"Good, Serena," Karl smiles. "Very good, clear explanation. The added information we have requires that we eliminate that hypothesis."

"Now, let's look at the rest of the hypotheses. . . . How about *things that grow on plants*? . . . Sherry?"

". . . Things that grow on plants is out."

"Why? . . . Explain," Karl smiles.

". . . A carrot grows from a plant."

"And?" Karl probes.

"And . . . it's not an example," Sherry adds quickly after Karl's prompt.

"Excellent, Sherry. Good thinking and good explanation.

"Now, how about *living things*?"

"Also out," Jaime volunteers.

"Go on."

". . . Carrot is living and it's not an example," Jaime explains, beginning to see how the process is intended to work.

"Yes! That's fine," Karl waves enthusiastically. "You are really catching on to this."

"How about things that we eat that grow above the ground?" Renita offers.

"Are you suggesting another hypothesis?" Karl asks.

". . . I . . . think so."

"Very good. I should have pointed that out in the beginning. We can always add hypotheses as long as the data support them. . . . Now, how will we know if the data do indeed support them? . . . Anyone?"

". . ."

"This is a little tough to describe, so I'll try and help you. A hypothesis is supported if *all* the examples fit it, *and* if *none* of the nonexamples fit the hypothesis."

"For example," he goes on, "do both an apple and a tomato grow above the ground?"

"Yes," the class says in unison.

"Do either a rock or a carrot grow above the ground?"

"Part of the carrot does," Heidi notes.

"Good thinking," Karl nods. "What is your reaction to Heidi's point, Renita?"

"I meant the part that we eat."

"Okay, is that alright with you, Heidi?"

Heidi shakes her head. " . . . I think we should say, 'plant parts we eat that are aboveground'."

"Excellent, Heidi. We can also modify hypotheses so that they better fit our data. This is the kind of thinking that we're after. Very well done!

"Now, . . . is the hypothesis, *plant parts we eat that are aboveground,* acceptable? . . . Remember, all the examples *must* fit the hypothesis, and *none* of the nonexamples *can* fit the hypothesis."

Among nods, "Yeses," and "Okays," Karl continues. Shawn offers the hypothesis *things we eat with seeds in them,* and Marsha offers *red foods,* to the giggles of the class.

Karl then asks in a form of admonishment, "Are apples and tomatoes both red, and are either the rock or the carrot red?"

"No," the students respond.

"Good. . . . Now, I want us to have fun with this, of course, but remember that the only thing that determines whether a hypothesis is acceptable is whether the data support it. . . . And do the data support *red foods*?"

The students nod, a bit sheepishly.

"Good. Now, I know you didn't mean any harm, but keep that in mind."

Karl then adds an avocado to the *Examples* list, a piece of celery to the *Nonexamples* list, and they again analyze the hypotheses as they did before.

Karl continues by adding and analyzing hypotheses with a peach, a squash, and an orange as positive examples, and a head of lettuce, artichoke, and potato as negative examples.

The students continue the process with Karl's guidance, narrowing their hypotheses to *things with seeds in them* and finally modifying the hypothesis to *seeds in the edible part of the plant*.

Karl then asks, "Does anyone know what we call foods that have seeds in the edible part of the plant, like the ones we have here?"

After hesitating a few seconds and hearing no response, he says, "We call these foods *fruits*," and he then writes the word *fruit* on the board.

Karl continues, "Excellent everyone. Now, we need a good clear definition of *fruit*. Someone give it a try. . . . Go ahead, Goeff."

"Okay, . . . Fruits are . . . things we eat that have seeds in them."

"Seeds in what part?"

". . . In the part we eat."

"Good, Goeff. I'll revise this a tiny bit to smooth it out a little, but we essentially have it."

Karl then writes on the board, *Fruits are edible parts of plants that we eat with seeds in them.*

"So what are the essential characteristics of the concept that we're learning? . . . Tanya? What does something have to be to be called a fruit?"

"Um. It has to grow on a plant, and we have to eat it?"

"Good, Tanya," Karl responds, listing these under *Essential Characteristics* on the board. "And there's one more, Sharon."

". . . They have to have seeds in them."

"Good, Sharon," Karl replies, listing this third characteristic on the board. "Now, let's link this idea to other things that we know."

Karl then draws the diagram opposite on the board.

"So, what other parts of a plant do we eat, besides the fruit? Think about this and look at our negative examples. Maybe one of our negative examples will give you a clue."

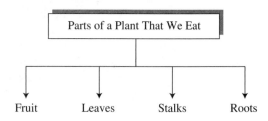

The lesson continues with the class differentiating fruits from roots and leafy parts of plants. Karl then has the class take out a piece of paper to categorize additional examples as either positive or negative examples of the concept *fruit.*

Let's look now at another teacher using the model to help high school students reinforce their understanding of the concept *metaphor.*

Tanya Adin, a ninth-grade English teacher, begins her sixth period class on Friday by saying, "I know that you're all anxious to start the weekend, so to break the routine we're going to do something a little different today. It will both help us review some of the ideas we have dealt with in the past, and it will give us some practice in being good critical thinkers.

"Now, this is what we're going to do. . . . I have a list of sentences on this overhead," she continues, pointing to the overhead. "Some illustrate a concept I have in mind, and others *do not* illustrate the concept. The ones that do I've marked with a *Y,* which stands for *yes,* meaning they *do* illustrate the concept, and the others are marked with an *N,* meaning *no,* they *do not* illustrate the concept. You need to figure out what the concept is based on the yeses—the examples—and the noes—the sentences that are not examples.

"Let's try it," she continues. "I'll show you an example and a nonexample to start with. Remember, all the examples—yeses—must illustrate the concept, and none of the nonexamples—can illustrate the concept."

Tanya then uncovers the first two sentences on the transparency.

1. John's Camaro is a lemon. (Y)
2. Hurricane Andrew did a great deal of damage in Florida. (N)

The students look at the examples for a few seconds, and Carlos then offers, "Cars. It might be something about cars."

"Okay, good," Tanya nods. "The example is about cars and the nonexample has nothing in it about cars, so *something about cars* could be the concept. . . . Any other possibilities?"

". . . I think *linking verbs,*" Antonio adds.

"You mean you think *linking verbs* is the concept?"

"Yeah, there's a linking verb in the first sentence, but there isn't one in the second one."

"Very good, Antonio. Good thinking. . . . Now, this is what we're after. We see both a description of a car and a linking verb in the *yes* example, but we don't see either of them in the *no* example, so *cars* and *linking verbs* are both possibilities for the concept.

". . . Now let's go on. Are there any other possibilities?"

"How about *present tense?*" Nancy wonders.

"Good thinking, Nancy. Class, is *present tense* acceptable?"

". . ."

Seeing the uncertainty on the students faces, Tanya continues, "Does the *yes* example illustrate present tense?"

The students agree, and Tanya goes on, "Is there anything about present tense in the *no* example?"

"No," Bruce says quickly, beginning to see how the process works.

"Good," Tanya smiles. "Now, let's go on."

Tanya then briefly explains that they are *hypothesizing* the possibilities that they have listed, so each was a *hypothesis.* She then notes that she will refer to the items on the list as hypotheses from that point on.

Tanya uncovers two more sentences on the overhead, so her list now appears as follows:

1. John's Camaro is a lemon. (Y)
2. Hurricane Andrew did a great deal of damage in Florida. (N)
3. Mrs. Augilar's Lexus is a gem. (Y)
4. My grandmother's hat is a garden of daisies. (Y)

"I know," Adam says eagerly after looking at the list for a few seconds. "It's *possessives.* Each of the yeses has a possessive in it."

"What does everyone else think?" Tanya queries. "Can we accept Adam's hypothesis?" emphasizing the word *hypothesis* as she asks the question.

"How about number two?" Rachael wonders.

". . . It's a no," Karla points out.

". . . Oh, yes," Rachael nods, recognizing Karla's point.

"Good, . . . any others?" Tanya continues. "Okay, let's look at our hypotheses so far. . . . How about *cars*? Is it still okay? . . . Heidi?"

". . . I . . . don't think so."

"Explain why for everyone."

". . . Well, . . . number four has nothing about a car in it."

"And?"

". . . It's a *yes* example," Heidi says after realizing what Tanya is after.

"Very good, Heidi," Tanya nods, and she then continues, "How about *present tense*? Is it still acceptable? . . . Lisa?"

". . . I . . . think so."

"Please explain," Tanya encourages.

". . . All of the *yes* examples are in the present tense."

"And?" Tanya probes.

". . . The *no* is in the past tense."

"Very good," Tanya nods and smiles.

Tanya has the students analyze *linking verbs* in the same way, and then goes on, "Now, is there anything else we can add?"

". . . How about *metaphors*?" Ramona offers.

"Okay. . . . Is metaphor an acceptable hypothesis?" Tanya asks over her shoulder as she adds *metaphor* to the list she is writing on the board.

The students look at the examples uncertainly, and in response Tanya continues, "Is each positive example a metaphor?"

Tanya smiles as some of the students nod that they are, and she goes on, "Any other hypotheses?"

"... How about *figures of speech*?" Frank suggests.

"Good! ... *Figures of speech* okay?"

"... Yes," several students say simultaneously getting comfortable with the process.

"Any others?"

After waiting a few seconds, Tanya says, "Okay, let's look at another example," and she uncovers one, so her list now appears as follows:

1. John's Camaro is a lemon. (Y)
2. Hurricane Andrew did a great deal of damage in Florida. (N)
3. Mrs. Augilar's Lexus is a gem. (Y)
4. My grandmother's hat is a garden of daisies. (Y)
5. My bedroom is green. (N)

"Anything else we can add to our list of hypotheses?" which now appears as follows:

~~cars~~
linking verbs
present tense
possessives
metaphor
figures of speech

Hearing nothing, she continues, "Okay, let's look at them. How about *linking verbs*? Is it still okay? . . . Amanda?"

"... No."

"Why not?"

"... There's a linking verb in the last one, ... and it's a *no*."

"Very good thinking, and a good complete explanation," Tanya responds, gesturing at the board. "So, how about *present tense*?"

"Also out," Shannon volunteers quickly. "... The nonexample is in the present tense."

"Excellent. ... How about *possessives*?"

"Out," Danielle offers.

"Explain why."

"There's no possessive in the last sentence."

"Wait. It's a *no*," David interjects.

"Go on, David," Tanya encourages.

"... It's a nonexample, ... and it doesn't have a possessive in it, ... so *possessive* is still okay," David says slowly as he describes his thoughts.

"Do you agree with that, Danielle?"

"... I guess ... I see now," she responds after looking at the examples again.

"Excellent. . . . Now, how about *metaphor*?"

The students conclude that *metaphor* is still acceptable, since number five is *not* a metaphor and it also is *not* an example, and they go through similar reasoning with *figures of speech.*

Tanya then adds the following example to her list.

6. Autumn leaves are the skin of trees, wrinkled with age. (Y)

The students decide that *possessives* must be rejected because the sentence does not illustrate possessives, and it is a positive example, and they further conclude that *metaphor* and *figures of speech* are still acceptable.

Tanya then adds a seventh example.

7. I had a million pages of homework last night. (N)

After some discussion the students conclude that *metaphor* is acceptable, but that *figures of speech* is not unacceptable, since number seven is a figure of speech— a hyperbole—and it is a nonexample.

"Now," Tanya interjects, "let's stop for a moment and take a look at what we've been doing. Let's look back at the process. Let's try and describe it. . . . Go ahead, someone."

". . . Well, we've been trying to guess what the concept is that you have in mind," Alandrea volunteers after several seconds.

"Actually, you haven't been guessing, and I want to emphasize that," Tanya responds, gesturing to the board. "You made your decisions based on information. In this case the information is in the form of the examples I've given you, but the thought processes apply to nearly everything you do. For example, why did you decide that *figures of speech* wasn't an acceptable hypothesis?"

". . . That sentence—*I had a million pages of homework last night*—is a figure of speech and you told us it was a nonexample," Sydney offers.

"Exactly. You made the decision to reject *figures of speech* based on the data, not on a whim.

"The same thing applies in life in general," Tanya goes on. "For example, your dad decides to fix you cooked oatmeal for breakfast instead of another cereal because it says on the box that oatmeal has no partially hydrogenated vegetable oil in it, whereas the other cereal does. Just as you used information in this exercise to direct your thinking, your dad used information about partially hydrogenated vegetable oil in the cereals to reject the other one on that basis.

"So we're learning a fundamental process here that helps us live better as a result of thinking more clearly. Keep the oatmeal example in mind, and we'll remind ourselves of it and others as we do lessons like these."

Tanya then goes back to the theme of the lesson, displaying the following examples, one at a time, asking students to consider whether *metaphor* is still an acceptable hypothesis after each one.

8. At night you are the moonlight floating through my window, lifting the curtains. (Y)

9. So far my life has been like an unmarked chalkboard. (N)

10. He touched her cheek as the sun touches a rose. (N)

11. The blank sheet of paper reclined on my desk and stared at me with its blank eyes, waiting for me to tease it with my pencil. (N)

12. The guns cracked and the bullets squealed as the battle raged for hours. (N)

After displaying and analyzing the last example, Tanya asks, "Now, what do you think? Did we prove that the concept is *metaphor*?"

"Yes," several students say simultaneously, and others nod in agreement.

"It looks promising doesn't it," Tanya smiles, "but suppose, for instance, that sometime later we found a sentence that we were told was an example, but it wasn't a metaphor. Then what?"

". . . I guess we'd have to cross off *metaphor*," Wendy offers uncertainly.

"Yes, that's exactly right," Tanya replies. "A hypothesis is acceptable as long as *all* the data—examples of the concept in our case—support it, but we have to reject a hypothesis if *only one* item of data do not support it. . . . So, technically, you never actually prove a hypothesis. You can only gather more and more data that support it.

"You'll understand the process of analyzing hypotheses better and better as we do more of these," Tanya assures the students seeing uncertain looks on some of their faces. "For now let's make sure we have a clear idea of what a metaphor is," Tanya continues. "Look at the positive examples. What do they have in common? . . . Camilla?"

". . . They all use figurative language."

"What do you mean by that, Camilla?" Tanya probes.

"Well, like a car isn't really a lemon or a gem. It's just a vivid way to describe it."

"Good," Tanya replies, writing *figurative language* on the board under *metaphor.* "What else? . . . Jaron?"

"They all say that something is like something else," Jaron replies.

Seeing that some students' looks suggest Jaron's response isn't clear, Tanya continues, "Explain further, Jaron, using one of our examples."

"Um, like grandmother's hat really isn't a garden of daisies. It just has lots of flowers on it."

"Okay, so we can say that something stands for something else, suggesting a likeness or analogy," listing that characteristic on the board. "Do we know any other figures of speech? Think for a moment. Have we studied any other figures of speech?" she asks as she writes the term on the board. " . . . Collin?"

Tanya then asks individual students to give additional examples of metaphors to reinforce the concept, discussing each as they are offered. She has them compare the concepts *metaphor, simile, personification,* and *hyperbole,* and she then closes the lesson.

The Concept Attainment Model: An Overview

Let's begin our study of the Concept Attainment Model by looking back at the two lessons and identifying their key elements.

- First, both lessons focused on a concept—*fruits* in Karl's case and *metaphors* in Tanya's—rather than a principle, generalization, academic rule, or other form of content.
- Second, the teachers began by explaining the procedure that the students would follow in the activity.
- Third, they began each lesson with an example and a nonexample of the concept—an apple and a rock for Karl and the first two sentences for Tanya.
- Fourth, the activity focused on the process of making and analyzing hypotheses, which resulted in the elimination of some, modification of others, and finally the isolation of a single hypothesis.
- The hypothesis that was isolated became the content focus of the lesson. The teachers then helped the students analyze the concepts' characteristics and link them to related concepts.

The Concept Attainment Model: Theoretical Foundations

As we saw in Chapter 5, **concepts** are *mental structures that categorize sets of objects, events, or ideas,* and they represent a major portion of the school curriculum (Klausmeier, 1992). We also saw that concepts help us simplify our world by allowing us to think in terms of categories instead of specific objects, and we saw the example of pest control being impossible if we had to think of insects individually rather than as a class.

Experts offer different theories in an attempt to explain how people form concepts. In this section, we consider three.

The first, and historically the oldest, suggests that people form concepts based on their essential **characteristics** (sometimes called attributes or features), *the concept's defining elements,* embedded in examples of the concept. This theory can explain how we learn concepts such as *square, triangle,* or *perimeter* because they have well-defined characteristics (Medin et al., 2000). For instance, "equal sides" and "equal angles" are the essential characteristics of the concept *square.* Learners identify examples of squares based on a rule stating that squares are plane, closed figures with these attributes. Other characteristics, such as size, color, or orientation aren't essential, so learners disregard them in making their classifications.

Early researchers (e.g., Bruner, Goodenow, & Austin, 1956) suggested that learners acquire concepts by identifying the essential characteristics of a concept and classifying examples accordingly. Concepts are differentiated from one another on the basis of the rules for each (Bourne, 1982), so this is a *rule-driven* theory of concept learning.

Many concepts don't have well-defined characteristics, however, so creating rules to help differentiate them is difficult (Ashcraft, 2002). For instance, what are the characteristics of the concepts *Democrat* or *Republican*? Despite frequent exposure to the terms in our popular news, most people are unable to define the concepts in even a somewhat precise way. Even common concepts, such as *car,* can have "fuzzy boundaries" (Schwartz & Reisberg, 1991). For instance, some people describe sport utility vehicles as cars, but others don't. How should minivans be classified? And railroad "cars" also exist.

This leads to the second theory. It asserts that concepts such as *Democrat, Republican,* and even *car* are represented in memory by a **prototype,** which is *the best representative of its category* (Hampton, 1995; Medin et al., 2000). For example, Abraham Lincoln, George W. Bush, Justice Clarence Thomas, and others might be prototypes for the concept *Republican,* and many choices also exist for *Democrat.* Similarly, a common passenger car, such as a Ford Taurus or Toyota Camry, might be a prototype for *car.*

Prototypes aren't necessarily physical examples, such as a person or object. Rather, they may be a mental composite, constructed from examples that individuals experience (Reisberg, 1997; Ross & Spalding, 1994). For instance, a person who has encountered a number of different dogs might construct a prototype that doesn't look exactly like any particular breed.

A closely related third theory suggests that, instead of a single prototype, learners analyze and store **exemplars,** which are *highly typical examples of a class* (Medin et al., 2000). For instance, a person having experience with dogs may store images of golden retrievers, cocker spaniels, collies, dachshunds, and German shepherds in memory as *exemplars* (Sadoski & Paivio, 2001). This is why positive and negative examples are used with the Concept Attainment Model.

Each theory can explain different aspects of concept learning. For instance, concepts such as *square* or *odd number* are likely encoded in terms of characteristics. Others, such as *car* are probably represented as prototypes, and still others, such as *dog* or *bird* may be encoded as exemplars.

Regardless of their complexity, and as we saw in Chapter 5, the key to concept learning is a carefully selected set of examples and nonexamples together with a definition (Tennyson & Cocchiarella, 1986). This is also true for the Inductive Model. Let's briefly compare the two.

The Concept Attainment and Inductive Models: Similarities and Differences

The Concept Attainment and Inductive Models are closely related, but differences exist both with respect to the content objectives they are intended to help students meet and in their emphasis on critical thinking.

Content Objectives

The Concept Attainment and Inductive Models are similar in that they are both designed to help students understand concepts, so if concept learning is your objective, either model could be effective. However, because the Concept Attainment Model focuses exclusively on concepts, the Inductive Model is a better choice if understanding principles, generalizations, or academic rules is your objective.

Also, whereas the Inductive Model can be used to teach a topic essentially from "scratch," the Concept Attainment Model requires that the students have some background knowledge related to the topic. For example, Tanya's students had some experience with metaphors and other figures of speech or they wouldn't have been able to suggest either as hypotheses. For this reason the Concept Attainment Model is effective for review or enriching a concept by helping students see relationships between it and closely related concepts. We saw this at the end of Tanya's lesson, where her students examined differences among the concepts *metaphor, simile, personification,* and *hyperbole.*

However, as we saw in Karl's lesson, students don't necessarily have to know the *label* for the concept. His students identified the essential characteristic of the concept *fruit,* and he then supplied the label.

Critical-Thinking Objectives

Although developing critical thinking is an aspect of all the models in this book, it is a primary objective when using the Concept Attainment Model. In fact, the model is uniquely designed to provide students with practice in the **scientific method,** which is *a pattern of thinking that emphasizes forming conclusions based on observation, developing hypotheses, and testing the hypotheses with additional observations.* A common description of the scientific method is outlined in Figure 6.1.

The scientific method is described at the beginning of many science texts, but students get very little experience with the actual process. And virtually no experiences exist in content areas other than science. The Concept Attainment Model can be used to provide students with experience using the scientific method in virtually any content area and with any topic.

Both Karl and Tanya provided their students with practice using the scientific method because much of the emphasis in both lessons was on the students' analyses of the hypotheses and why they were accepted, modified, or rejected. The kinds of conclusions students

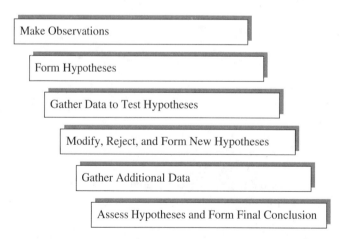

FIGURE 6.1   The Scientific Method

practice making, such as, "The nonexample is in the present tense," as an explanation for why the hypothesis *present tense* had to be rejected, are as important as understanding the concepts themselves.

If developing a deep understanding of a concept, principle, generalization, or rule is your primary objective, the Inductive Model is the better alternative. If developing critical thinking and providing practice with the scientific method are important objectives, the Concept Attainment Model is a good choice. And because research indicates that varying the way we teach is more effective than teaching the same way all the time (Shuell, 1996), the Concept Attainment Model is an effective way to vary your instruction.

Planning Lessons Using the Concept Attainment Model

The planning process for lessons using the Concept Attainment Model involves four essential steps. They are outlined in Figure 6.2 and discussed in the sections that follow.

Identifying Topics

Research indicates that teachers begin the planning process by identifying a topic they believe is important for students to understand (Morine-Dershimer & Vallance, 1976; Peterson, Marx, & Clark, 1978). This was an appropriate beginning point with the Inductive Model, and it's equally appropriate for Concept Attainment.

As we saw earlier, the students' background experiences are factors to consider in selecting topics for Concept Attainment lessons. To be effective, students ideally need some familiarity with the topic itself and other topics related to it.

Specifying Learning Objectives

As we saw earlier in the chapter, objectives for the Concept Attainment Model include helping students develop concepts and the relationships among them, and giving them practice with critical thinking by forming and testing hypotheses.

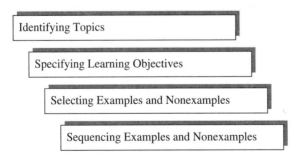

Identifying Topics

Specifying Learning Objectives

Selecting Examples and Nonexamples

Sequencing Examples and Nonexamples

FIGURE 6.2   Planning Lessons with the Concept Attainment Model

In Chapter 5 we emphasized that teachers must know exactly what they are trying to accomplish when using the Inductive Model. Being clear about learning objectives is no less important for Concept Attainment lessons. As you plan, you need to be clear about the essential characteristics of the concept because these characteristics must be observable in the examples. Because Karl was teaching fifth graders, he had identified *seed contained in the edible part of the plant* as the key feature of the concept *fruit.* A biology teacher would attach more sophisticated attributes to the concept, such as the fruit being an enlarged and ripened ovary and the stage after flowering and pollination.

The same was true in Tanya's case. In her planning, she had specified "a nonliteral comparison that avoids the words *like* and *as*" as the characteristics of the concept *metaphor,* and she had these characteristics clearly in mind as she planned and conducted her lesson.

Both teachers were also clear in their intent to have the students practice critical thinking in the form of hypothesis testing. Had this not been an important objective for them, they would probably have chosen a different model.

Selecting Examples and Nonexamples

Because Concept Attainment lessons are developed around examples and nonexamples, their selection is a crucial part of the planning process. We begin with examples.

Selecting Examples.   The principles involved in selecting examples to teach a concept are the same regardless of the model being used. As we saw with the Inductive Model, selecting examples that best illustrate the characteristics of the concept is essential. Karl chose effective examples when he used the apple, tomato, avacado, squash, peach, and orange because in each case the students *could see* the essential characteristic—the seeds in the edible part of the plant—in the examples. The same was true in Tanya's case. The students *could see* a nonliteral comparison in each of the positive examples.

The teachers were both strategic in their choices of positive examples. Karl, for example, used a tomato and squash as examples—fruits commonly thought of as vegetables. Using them as examples helped the students to broaden their understanding of the concept *fruit.*

Examples are chosen so that *all* of the positive examples contain the essential characteristics and *none* of the nonexamples do. To further illustrate this process, consider the characteristics of the concept *proper noun* and then analyze the following examples based on those characteristics:

1. Mary
2. New York
3. John
4. Los Angeles
5. United States
6. George Washington

Two aspects of this list are problematic. First, the examples should have included the idea that a proper noun names a specific person, place, or *thing.* There are no specific *things* in the list. To ensure that the concept is complete, we would need to add positive examples such as *German shepherd, Honda,* and *Old Testament.*

Second, the examples aren't presented in context. For instance, the examples could be presented as follows:

1. Mary is one of the most common names that girls are given, and John is one of the most common for boys.
2. New York is the largest city in the United States, and Los Angeles is the second largest.
3. George Washington is often called the father of our country.
4. The German shepherd is one of the smartest working dogs that exist.
5. One of the first Japanese cars to be sold in this country was the Honda.
6. The Old Testament is strongly related to the Koran in many ways.

We emphasized putting examples in context in our discussion of the Inductive Model, saying that it makes them more meaningful. It is equally true for Concept Attainment lessons.

Selecting Nonexamples.   Nonexamples should help students differentiate the concept from closely related concepts. For instance, Tanya used the following sentences (in addition to the simple statements, "Hurricane Andrew did a great deal of damage in Florida" and "My bedroom is green") as nonexamples in her lesson on metaphors.

- I had a million pages of homework last night (hyperbole).
- So far my life has been like an unmarked chalkboard (a simile using the word *like*).
- He touched her cheek as the sun touches a rose (a simile using the word *as*).
- The blank sheet of paper reclined on my desk and stared at me with its blank eyes, waiting for me to tease it with my pencil (personification).
- The guns cracked and the bullets squealed as the battle raged for hours (onomatopoeia).

From this list we see that the negative examples served to differentiate *metaphor* from other figures of speech. Each of the nonexamples—examples of *hyperbole, simile, personification,* and *onomatopoeia*—illustrated a concept coordinate to the concept *metaphor.* Thinking of concepts that are coordinate to the concept being taught is a useful planning strategy as the list of examples and nonexamples is being prepared. By analyzing differences between the positive and negative examples (nonexamples), students can construct a valid concept that will not be confused with closely related concepts.

Sequencing Examples and Nonexamples

The final planning task is to sequence the examples and nonexamples. Because practicing hypothesis testing is an important objective when the Concept Attainment Model is used, examples should be arranged so students are given practice with this process. The shortest route to a concept, with the most obvious examples presented first, won't give students this opportunity, and it may be less motivating for them because their sense of challenge is reduced. (As we saw in Chapter 2, challenge is one of the characteristics of intrinsically

FIGURE 6.3   Karl's and Tanya's Sequences of Examples

Karl's Sequence	Tanya's Sequence
1. Apple (Y)	1. John's Camaro is a lemon. (Y)
2. Rock (N)	2. Hurricane Andrew did a great deal of damage in Florida. (N)
3. Tomato (Y)	3. Mrs. Augilar's Lexus is a gem. (Y)
4. Carrot (N)	4. My grandmother's hat is a garden of daisies. (Y)
5. Avocado (Y)	5. My bedroom is green. (N)
6. Celery (N)	6. Autumn leaves are the skin of trees, wrinkled with age. (Y)
7. Peach (Y)	7. I had a million pages of homework last night. (N)
8. Squash (Y)	8. At night you are the moonlight floating through my window, lifting the curtains. (Y)
9. Orange (Y)	9. So far my life has been like an unmarked chalkboard. (N)
10. Lettuce (N)	10. He touched her cheek as the sun touches a rose. (N)
11. Artichoke (N)	11. The blank sheet of paper reclined on my desk and stared at me with its blank eyes, waiting for me to tease it with my pencil. (N)
12. Potato (N)	12. The guns cracked and the bullets squealed as the battle raged for hours. (N)

motivating activities.) Tanya, for example, purposely sequenced her examples so students could initially offer *cars, possessives, present tense,* and *linking verbs* as valid hypotheses, all of which ultimately had to be rejected. This gave students considerable practice in analyzing hypotheses.

Notice also in sequencing examples that teachers don't have to alternate examples and nonexamples. They may choose to present two or even three positive examples in a row, which might be followed by two or more nonexamples. This is a matter of teacher judgment. Karl's and Tanya's sequences, for instance, appear as shown in Figure 6.3.

To further illustrate this point, let's look at a simpler example. Suppose the concept is *numbers with perfect square roots.* Consider the sequences illustrated in Figure 6.4.

In Sequence A the pattern is quickly established. Many students would probably hypothesize the concept after two positive examples. In contrast, the concept is less obvi-

FIGURE 6.4   Two Sequences of Examples for Numbers with Perfect Square Roots

Sequence A		Sequence B	
4	Yes	1	Yes
5	No	1/2	No
9	Yes	81	Yes
15	No	7	No
16	Yes	64	Yes
2	No	12	No
25	Yes	9	Yes

ous in Sequence B, providing the students with more practice in hypothesis testing. In preparing sequences of examples, such as Sequence B, teachers are not trying to hide information from the students or trick them. Instead, they want to maximize challenge and students' opportunities to practice hypothesis testing.

For any set of examples a number of sequences can be designed. The organization depends on the teacher's judgment, the objectives for the lesson, and the backgrounds of the students.

Implementing Lessons Using the Concept Attainment Model

Because Concept Attainment lessons are quite different from traditional instruction, the procedures may initially be confusing. Lessons often need some introduction so that students become comfortable with the process. Let's look at it a bit further.

Introducing Students to Concept Attainment

Both Karl and Tanya addressed this issue by providing specific directions for the activity and by initially prompting students to form hypotheses based on the examples. To illustrate, let's look again at some dialogue from Karl's lesson.

> **KARL:** Now, the apple *is* an example of the idea I have in mind, and the rock *is not* an example of the idea . . . What do you think the idea might be?
>
> **RASHEED:** We eat apples.
>
> **KARL:** Good. So the idea might be . . . ?
>
> **RASHEED:** . . .
>
> **KARL:** Things . . . we . . . ?
>
> **RASHEED:** . . . Eat?

Here we see that Karl nearly put the words in Rasheed's mouth as Rasheed attempted to state the first hypothesis of the activity. This is sometimes necessary, particularly with younger students, until they begin to understand the process.

To avoid overloading learners' working memories by requiring that they simultaneously learn the procedure and cope with a demanding concept, you may want to introduce Concept Attainment with a familiar idea the first time or two you use the model. Topics such as *living things, wooden objects, objects in the room that are round,* or even *students with red hair* are all simple and concrete and help students familiarize themselves with the procedure.

Using a simple topic also gives students practice with initially forming and testing hypotheses. This can be challenging, especially for younger students. As we saw in Karl's and Tanya's lessons, students are often required to do some reversals in their thinking as they process the information. For example, after Tanya had presented her fifth sentence the students had to reason as follows:

> The fifth sentence does *not* illustrate a possessive, and it is *not* an example; therefore, *possessives* is still an acceptable hypothesis.

This kind of reasoning is difficult, and students won't initially be good at it. It develops with practice, and when students do improve, it's satisfying and can be motivating because they've met the challenge. This is the reason having the students put their thinking into words is so important, and why using familiar topics to introduce them to the model can be helpful.

We also saw in both lessons that the teachers had to initially prompt students to fully explain why they accepted or rejected hypotheses. In practice, teachers may have to do even more prompting than was illustrated in the episodes. We intentionally abbreviated them because of length.

We turn now to the specific phases of the Concept Attainment Model.

Phases in Concept Attainment Lessons

The Concept Attainment Model occurs in five phases. The activity begins when the teacher presents examples (and nonexamples) and continues until the students have isolated a single hypothesis and applied this hypotheses to new examples. The phases are outlined in Table 6.1 and described in the sections that follow.

Phase 1: Presenting Examples.   After the activity has been introduced and explained, the lesson begins when teachers present students with an example and a nonexample as

TABLE 6.1   Learning and Motivation Functions for the Phases of the Concept Attainment Model

Phase	Learning and Motivation Function
Phase 1: Presenting examples Students are presented with examples and nonexamples	■ Attracts attention ■ Arouses curiosity motivation
Phase 2: Generating hypotheses Students hypothesize possible names of concepts based on the examples	■ Promotes involvement ■ Activates background knowledge
Phase 3: The analysis cycle Hypotheses are generated and analyzed with additional examples	■ Promotes perceptions of competence ■ Presents challenge
Phase 4: Closure A single hypothesis is isolated and defined	■ Promotes encoding ■ Promotes success
Phase 5: Application Additional examples are analyzed based on the definition	■ Facilitates transfer ■ Aids schema production

Karl and Tanya did in their lessons. Karl began with an apple as an example and a rock as a nonexample. Using a nonexample that was so "distant" from the example was designed to allow the students to form as many hypotheses as possible. He could have chosen a nonexample more closely related to the concept, such as *milk* or another food, but this would have reduced the emphasis on hypothesis testing.

Phase 2: Generating Hypotheses. After presenting the initial examples in Phase 1, the teacher asks students to hypothesize possible concept names. In Karl's lesson, for example, students initially hypothesized *things we eat, living things,* and *things that grow on plants,* whereas Tanya's students generated *cars, linking verbs,* and *present tense* as hypotheses. These hypotheses become the focus of the lesson.

The hypotheses the students offer will vary in specificity. For example, consider possible hypotheses for the following examples. Some might include:

closed figures
four-sided figures
squares
figures with equal sides and equal angles
figures with straight lines

We see that *square,* for example, is a more specific hypothesis than any of the others. This isn't a problem because the more general hypotheses will be eliminated or modified as new examples are presented and the hypotheses are analyzed.

Phase 3: The Analysis Cycle. Phase 3 of the lesson exists in a repeating cycle. The cycle includes presenting examples (and nonexamples) and analysis of the hypotheses based on the new examples. The analysis can include generating new hypotheses and accepting, rejecting, or modifying existing hypotheses. The process is then repeated by adding additional examples and/or nonexamples, and again analyzing the hypotheses. The cycle repeats until one hypothesis is isolated.

To illustrate the analysis cycle, let's look again at Tanya's lesson. She had initially presented

1. John's Camaro is a lemon. (Y)
2. Hurricane Andrew did a great deal of damage in Florida. (N)

as examples in Phase 1, and the students had generated *cars, linking verbs,* and *present tense* as hypotheses in Phase 2. She then presented

3. Mrs. Augilar's Lexus is a gem. (Y)
4. My grandmother's hat is a garden of daisies. (Y)

as additional examples in the beginning of Phase 3.

She then guided the students as they analyzed the hypotheses. To illustrate the analysis, let's look at some dialogue.

> **ADAM:** I know. . . . It's *possessives.* Each of the yeses has a possessive in it. [new hypothesis generated]
>
> **TANYA:** What does everyone else think? Can we accept Adam's hypothesis?
>
> **RACHAEL:** How about number two?
>
> **KARLA:** . . . It's a no. [explaining why the hypothesis is still acceptable]
>
> **RACHAEL:** . . . Oh, yes. [hypothesis accepted]
>
> **TANYA:** Good, . . . any others? . . . Okay, let's look at our hypotheses so far. . . . How about *cars*? Is it still okay? . . . Heidi?
>
> **HEIDI:** . . . I . . . don't think so.
>
> **TANYA:** Explain why for everyone.
>
> **HEIDI:** . . . Well, . . . number four has nothing about a car in it. [hypothesis rejected]
>
> **TANYA:** And? [encouraging Heidi to put her thinking into words]
>
> **HEIDI:** . . . It's a *yes* example.

She then had the class analyze *linking verbs* and *present tense* as they had done with *possessives* and *cars,* the class added *metaphors* as a hypothesis and they analyzed it as they had done with the others. The cycle was then repeated as Tanya added

5. My bedroom is green. (N)

as a nonexample, and the class analyzed the hypotheses based on the additional data (the nonexample). The cycle was then continually repeated until the class isolated *metaphors* as the concept.

It is important during the analysis of hypotheses that the teacher refrain from passing judgment. It would be inappropriate at this point to say, "You've got it!" or "That's it!" if a student hypothesizes the concept the teacher has in mind. For example, in Tanya's lesson, Ramona offered *metaphors* as a hypothesis after Tanya had displayed three examples and one nonexample. Tanya then added *metaphor* to the list with no more or less reaction than she gave to other hypotheses. If Tanya had acknowledged that *metaphors* was the concept she had in mind, the lesson would be reduced to a simple guessing game between teachers and students rather than an intellectual process where the students learn to make conclusions based on data. Reacting as Tanya did in response to Ramona's hypothesis puts the responsibility for identifying and verifying the concept on students. This is consistent with emphasis on constructivist learning activities in which students are given primary responsibility for learning (Eggen & Kauchak, 2004).

We want to emphasize two additional aspects of both Karl's and Tanya's lessons. First, they listed the hypotheses on the board as they were offered. This seemingly minor factor is important for two reasons: It reduces demands on working memory, allowing students to use their working memory spaces for hypothesis testing and not for remembering; and it provides a record of the class's thinking, preventing students from offering hypotheses that have been discussed and previously rejected.

Second, they asked the students to explain *why* they accepted or rejected the hypothesis. Putting their reasoning into words helps students develop their own thinking, and other students benefit from hearing their reasoning articulated. If one student decides that a hypothesis must be rejected, for instance, others may not understand why, or may disagree. Explaining helps students share their understanding, making their logic visible and allowing other students to use and build on their ideas (Eggen & Kauchak, 2004).

Finally, we also want to note again that during the analysis cycle hypotheses can be revised instead of being totally rejected. For instance, in Karl's lesson Heidi wasn't satisfied with the hypothesis *things we eat that grow above the ground,* based on the argument that part of a carrot grows above the ground and *carrot* had been given as a nonexample. So, the hypothesis was revised to *plant parts we eat that are aboveground.* In this instance, the students had a concrete experience that was consistent with the philosophy of hypothesis testing.

At this point you might wonder, "What do I do if I get to the end of my list of examples and students haven't isolated the specific term for the concept I had in mind?" If your set of examples and nonexamples is complete, students may have isolated the essential characteristics but come up with a term that is a synonym for the concept you targeted. In that case, you can retain both and, when all the others have been eliminated, note that the two are synonymous, explaining how your term differs from the one offered by students.

The second possibility exists: "What do I do if the students eliminate all the hypotheses but one before all the examples are used?" Here the answer is simple. Simply allow the lesson to come to closure, and use the remainder of the examples as part of the application phase.

Phase 4: Closure.   Once students have isolated one hypothesis, the lesson can proceed to *closure.* In this phase, the teacher asks students to identify the essential characteristics of the concept, state a definition, and link it to closely related coordinate concepts. As we saw in Chapter 5, the definition reinforces the students' understanding by including a superordinate concept and the concept's characteristics. Karl, for example, helped his students form the definition, "Fruits are *edible parts of plants* (superordinate concept) that we eat with seeds in them. (*Seeds in the edible part* is the essential characteristic of the concept.) He then proceeded to link *fruit* to other coordinate concepts, such as leafy parts of plants and roots. Tanya did the same with *metaphor.* After defining it, she linked it to a superordinate concept (figures of speech) and closely related coordinate concepts (simile, personification, and hyperbole).

One way to ensure that the concept is connected to related ideas is through concept mapping. **Concept mapping** is *a strategy that helps learners construct visual relationships among concepts* (Mayer, 2002). Concept mapping capitalizes on the effects of organization, imagery, and the dual-processing capabilities of working memory to make relationships between concepts meaningful (Robinson, Katayama, Dubois, & Devaney, 1998).

Concept mapping benefits both students and teachers (Hall, Hall, & Saling, 1999). Creating concept maps puts students in active roles by encouraging them to visually represent

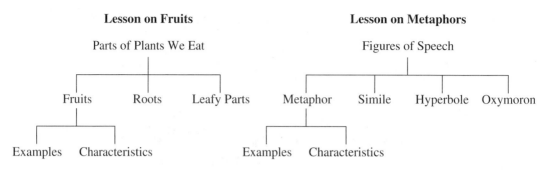

FIGURE 6.5   Concept Maps for Two Lessons

relationships among concepts. For example, Karl and Tanya used simplified concept maps to show how the concepts students were learning related to other, closely linked concepts. Examples of these maps are found in Figure 6.5. Our goal in Concept Attainment activities is to not only teach the target concept but also to help students understand how it relates to other important ones.

Phase 5: Application.   The application phase of Concept Attainment lessons is designed to increase students' understanding of the concept and help them generalize to new examples. In this phase students classify additional teacher-generated examples as positive or negative, and/or they generate additional examples of their own. In Karl's lesson the students categorized additional examples as either positive or negative examples of the concept *fruit,* and Tanya asked her students to supply additional examples of *metaphors.*

This phase is important for both students and the teacher. It provides students with opportunities to test their understanding with additional examples, and it gives the teacher feedback about their developing understanding.

Using the Concept Attainment Model to Increase Motivation and Self-Regulation

As we saw in Chapter 2, motivation and achievement are interdependent; anything teachers can do to promote motivation contributes to learning. Concept Attainment activities can be motivating because they are intellectual puzzles in which the students use clues (examples and nonexamples) to identify the idea (concept) the teacher has in mind. This can increase learners' **intrinsic motivation,** which is *motivation to engage in an activity for its own sake* (Pintrich & Schunk, 2002). The puzzlelike features of Concept Attainment lessons can induce curiosity and a sense of challenge, both identified by researchers as characteristics of intrinsically motivating ideas (Lepper & Hodell, 1989). Further, as we said earlier in the chapter, the activities can be used to add variety to classroom activities, which also increases student motivation (Stipek, 2002).

Increasing Motivation with Student Groupwork

Concept Attainment lessons can also capitalize on the motivating effects of students working together. For example, Tanya conducted her lesson as a whole-class activity; she could as easily have had the students work in pairs or groups of three to create a list of hypotheses after she presented her first two examples. Allowing students to work in groups increases student involvement, which can increase motivation (Eggen & Kauchak, 2004; Stipek, 2002).

Organizing students into groups is easy; groups could be seated together, and each group could be encouraged to analyze examples and share their thinking. The groups could then report their hypotheses to the whole class; the hypotheses then could be compiled into an overall list.

After Tanya presented her second pair of examples, the groups could be asked to decide which hypotheses were acceptable and which ones had to be rejected. To increase accountability and on-task behavior, they could also be directed to *write* the reason they accepted or rejected the hypothesis in each case. This would capitalize on critical thinking, give students practice in working together, and it would require little extra teacher effort.

Developing Self-Regulation

Concept Attainment activities can also be used to increase students' metacognition and self-regulation. As we saw in Chapter 2, **metacognition** is *awareness of and control over our mental processes,* and attention is one of those processes. Developing metacognitive abilities in students is important because it can contribute to learner self-regulation. **Self-regulation** is *an individual's conscious use of mental strategies designed to improve thinking and learning.* Self-regulated learners take responsibility for their own learning progress and adapt their learning strategies to meet task demands (Bruning et al., 2004). Concept Attainment learning activities can develop student self-regulation because so much emphasis on critical thinking exists in them.

Tanya attempted to help her students develop their metacognitive abilities when she compared the process of hypothesis testing in her lesson to the simple decision-making process involved in selecting oatmeal rather than another cereal. This simple example was a first step in helping students become aware of making conclusions and decisions based on information instead of whim, emotion, belief, or something potentially destructive, such as stereotyping. In addition, encouraging students to think about their own thinking helped them recognize that the processes they were involved in had utility beyond the classroom. Developing metacognitive abilities and self-regulation would take much more than the one example we saw in Tanya's lesson, of course, but if provided with ongoing experiences, these abilities will gradually develop. The same applies to the construction of all forms of knowledge and skill.

Modifications of Concept Attainment Activities

Although Concept Attainment learning activities exist in five interrelated phases, the procedure need not be rigid and inflexible. It can, in fact, be adapted to a variety of goals and learning situations. In this section we describe several modifications that can be used to make the model more adaptable to specific teaching goals and situations.

Developmental Considerations

To implement Concept Attainment activities most effectively, we must consider the developmental level of the students. In general, the younger the students the more concrete the examples need to be (Eggen & Kauchak, 2004). Karl's lesson, for example, would be more appropriate for young children than Tanya's, because *nonliteral comparison,* a characteristic of the concept *metaphor,* is much more abstract than *seeds in the edible part of the plant,* the key characteristic of the concept *fruit.*

Increasing the emphasis on positive examples and using fewer nonexamples is a second developmental adaptation that makes the model more effective with young children; they have difficulty dealing with the notion that something *is not* an example (Berk, 2003, 2004). The practice of inferring categories and doing rudimentary analysis of hypotheses is excellent for young children, however, and with modification they can become skilled with the strategy. Teachers of young children have found the model effective as a form of review and to add variety to classroom activities. As they become more experienced, learners become adept at generating their own sequences of examples and "playing the game" with each other.

Concept Attainment II

To this point we have discussed basic procedures in implementing Concept Attainment lessons and modifications that can be made for young children. The procedure can be further modified, however, to increase the emphasis on thinking. Let's look at these modifications.

Concept Attainment II (CA II) is a modification in the basic procedure designed to increase the emphasis on hypothesis testing and critical thinking. It begins in the same way as the basic procedure (which we'll call CA I for reference); the students are presented with a positive and a negative example, and they hypothesize concept names, which are listed on the board, overhead, or chart paper. Then, instead of presenting subsequent examples one at a time, as is done with CA I, the teacher displays all of the additional examples. The students are then encouraged to scan the list for examples that might substantiate or refute the hypotheses on the list. They choose an example and indicate whether they think it is positive or negative. They also state which hypotheses would have to be rejected if their classification is correct. The teacher then verifies the classification. If the classification is correct, the appropriate changes are made in the list of hypotheses; if it is incorrect, the hypotheses are reanalyzed in light of the new information. The students then select additional examples and continue the process until one hypothesis is isolated.

For example, a Concept Attainment II lesson might begin like this. The teacher, wanting to teach the concept *carnivores,* might provide pictures of the following animals.

Examples
dog—yes   cat
car—no   beaver

tree	tiger
cow	hamster
chair	mouse

Students might respond to this information with the following hypotheses, which would be listed.

Examples		*Hypotheses*
dog—yes	cat	living things
car—no	beaver	animals
tree	tiger	domestic animals
cow	hamster	mammals
chair	mouse	carnivores

An important objective in using Concept Attainment II is for the students to develop efficiency in their hypothesis testing. Efficiency is achieved if an example can be used to test all or several of the hypotheses. For example, one way to test all of these hypotheses is with *cat.* If cat is a nonexample, all the hypotheses would be rejected. However, in the case of *carnivore,* cat is a positive example, so none of the hypotheses can be rejected. Even though this example didn't result in the elimination of hypotheses, it provided excellent practice with the process. Teachers can assist in the development of students' thinking by making the logic behind different choices clear.

Students might then decide to choose *beaver* as the next example. If beaver is an example, all the hypotheses except *carnivores* and *domestic animals* are acceptable, but if beaver is a nonexample, *carnivore* and *domestic animals* would be the only acceptable hypotheses. The teacher would verify beaver as a nonexample because beaver is not a *carnivore.* Therefore, *living things, animals,* and *mammals* would have to be rejected. *Domestic animals* and *carnivores* would be retained as viable hypotheses because beaver was a nonexample, and dog and cat have been classified as positive examples. Now look at the list and see if you can determine an effective way for students to investigate the hypothesis *domestic animal.*

Examples		*Hypotheses*
dog—yes	cat—yes	domestic animals
car—no	beaver—no	carnivores
tree	tiger	
cow	hamster	
chair	mouse	

Consider the choices *cow* and *tiger.* The two choices provide slightly different information, and the difference is enough to make one a more effective choice. First, if tiger is a *yes, domestic animal* must be rejected because a tiger is not a domestic animal. If tiger is a *no,* it merely says that the category cannot be rejected, but it actually isn't supported either. The data are neutral with respect to the hypothesis because tiger may be a *no* for reasons other than the fact that it's not a domestic animal. Remember that when students select examples and examine hypotheses, they don't know what the concept is; they must infer it from the information provided.

Now, consider *cow* as a test of the hypothesis *domestic animal*. If cow is a *no, domestic animal* is rejected because cow is a domestic animal, and succinct information about the inference is obtained. However, if cow is *yes,* not only is the category not rejected, but it is directly supported (again because cow is a domestic animal). The choice of *cow* provides more information about the hypothesis than does the choice of *tiger,* so *cow* is the more efficient choice. The reverse would be true if we had wanted to test the hypothesis *carnivore.* In that case, tiger would be a more efficient choice.

Through practice with Concept Attainment II activities, students become efficient at gathering data, obtaining maximum information with each example. A primary goal with this strategy is acquiring experience with the logic of science. In a sense, students are designing their own investigation or experiment.

Concept Attainment III

A second modification, Concept Attainment III (CA III), is designed to extend the process of hypothesis testing even further. The basic strategy and thinking processes are essentially the same for CA II and CA III, but the procedure is slightly different. With CA II, after seeing the first two examples, the students hypothesize concept names, and the remaining examples are displayed. With CA III, after seeing the first two examples identified and labeled, students hypothesize concept names (as with CA II), but then *they* must supply their own examples to test the hypotheses. For example, consider the following activity designed to teach the concept *vegetables with edible roots.* The teacher begins by showing the class:

> carrot—yes
> corn—no

Some possible hypotheses might be:

> Orange-colored vegetables
> Vegetables with edible roots
> Vegetables rich in vitamin A
> Vegetables that are eaten raw

The responsibility for providing examples to test these hypotheses now rests with the students. The students could test the hypotheses by selecting additional examples of vegetables. An efficient choice might be *radish.* If radish is a *yes, orange-colored vegetables* and *vegetables rich in vitamin A* are eliminated, but if *radish* is a *no, vegetables with edible roots* and *vegetables that are eaten raw* are eliminated. In this lesson, *radish* is a *yes,* which leaves *vegetables with edible roots* and *vegetables that are eaten raw* as possible concepts. The students' task would now be to examine these remaining hypotheses further. One choice now might be *potato.* Potato as a *yes* would further support *vegetables with edible roots* but would force rejection of *vegetables that are eaten raw.* Because of the concept being taught, *potato* would be a *yes,* causing the latter hypothesis to be rejected and lending further support to the hypothesis *vegetables with edible roots.* Students would continue to test the hypothesis and, in so doing, would be both reinforcing and enlarging their notion of the concept.

In planning for a CA III activity the teacher should have additional examples available for use if the students' examples do not provide a complete picture of the concept. If their use is not necessary during the lesson, they could be used to assess the students' understanding.

One additional advantage of CA III is the opportunity it affords learners to gather data. From the perspective of practicing with the scientific method, CA III is more authentic than the other two formats because students more actively investigate a concept they don't fully understand. Because students are not limited to the examples the teacher provides, they can use more of their own background knowledge and initiative in investigating hypotheses. This increases their control of the learning activity, which has been identified by researchers as a factor increasing learners' intrinsic motivation (Lepper & Hodell, 1989). As with other variations of the model, critical thinking is best developed with practice in which students are encouraged to share and explain the thinking processes they use in arriving at their answers.

Assessing Student Learning in Concept Attainment Activities

Two major outcomes result from Concept Attainment activities. One is a deeper understanding of concepts, usually those with which students have had some experience, and the other is increased critical-thinking abilities. In this section we address the assessment of both.

Assessing Understanding of Concepts

Students' attainment of a concept can be measured in four primary ways. We can ask them to:

1. Identify or supply examples of the concept not previously encountered.
2. Identify the concept's characteristics.
3. Define the concept.
4. Relate the concept to other concepts.

A simple and effective way of measuring concept attainment is by asking students to identify or provide additional examples of the concept. This type of measurement item is relatively easy to prepare, and—unlike stating a definition or characteristics—if the teacher uses unique examples, it can determine whether the students have constructed a valid understanding of the concept. For instance, consider the following item designed to measure the concept *direct object.*

Read the following passage and underline all the direct objects in it.

Damon and Kerri were out riding their bikes. As they rode Kerri spotted a funny-looking animal in the bushes.

"Let's catch it," she suggested.

"No way," Damon responded. "I'm not chasing any strange animal. It might bite me."

"C'mon, chicken," she retorted. "I'll bet it's harmless."

"Ohh, all right. But, if it jumps you, I'm out of here."

The kids then chased the animal. Unfortunately for Kerri, but fortunately for Damon, they had no luck in catching it.

The effectiveness of this item is increased by the fact that the examples of direct objects were presented in the context of sentences within a paragraph; presenting examples this way increases the likelihood that students will be able to transfer their knowledge to new settings.

A variation of this format is to ask students to provide their own examples of the concept rather than identifying examples generated by the teacher. In this case, the students would be asked to write their own passage containing a specified number of examples.

A second way to assess students' understanding is to ask students to identify characteristics of the concept. For example, an item for the concept *mammal* might look like this:

Circle all the following that are characteristic of mammals:

    a. Naked skin
    b. Lays eggs
    c. Four-chambered heart
    d. Scaly skin
    e. Regulated body temperature
    f. Nurses young

The disadvantage of this type of measurement is that the item generally measures little more than recall of knowledge because the characteristics will have already been identified during the activity.

A third alternative for measuring concept learning is to ask students to provide a definition of the concept or to identify the correct definition from a list of alternatives. The disadvantage of this type of measurement item is that it, like items used to measure students' knowledge of characteristics, typically involves recall of information.

Students' understanding of concepts can also be measured by having students relate them to other concepts. Here the teacher asks the students to identify coordinate, superordinate, or subordinate concepts, or a combination of them. The following is an example.

If *figure of speech* is superordinate to the concept *metaphor,* which of the following are coordinate to the concept *metaphor*?

    a. Simile
    b. Personification
    c. Alliteration
    d. Trope

    e. Meter

    f. Iambic pentameter

This item tests students' understanding of the relationship between *metaphor* and other concepts that are also figures of speech. Similar items can be designed to measure superordinate and subordinate relationships. Use of items such as these assumes that the teacher has discussed these relationships in class.

As this discussion suggests, there is no one best way to measure students' understanding of concepts. Each provides the teacher with a different dimension of students' understanding, and the best strategy is to use a combination of them to gain a comprehensive picture of student understanding.

Assessing Students' Critical-Thinking Abilities

When using the Concept Attainment Model, assessing learners' critical-thinking abilities is sometimes as important as assessing their understanding of the concept itself. This type of assessment is difficult using a paper-and-pencil format, but it can be done. For example, consider the following item:

You have been given the following examples:

Yes	*No*
36	5
81	111

The following hypotheses have been listed:
    Two-digit numbers
    Composite (not prime) numbers
    Perfect squares
    Multiples of 3

1. Which of the hypotheses are acceptable? Explain.

_____

_____

_____

2. You are given two more examples, so your list now appears as follows:

Yes	*No*
36	5
81	111
49	45

Which hypotheses are now acceptable, and which ones must be rejected? Explain why in each case.

_____

_____

_____

_____

_____

As we see from these items, the ability to assess hypotheses requires that students understand the concepts *two-digit numbers, composite numbers, perfect squares,* and *multiples of 3.* Thinking critically doesn't exist in the absence of knowledge, and assessing critical thinking cannot be done without simultaneously assessing learners' understanding of content.

Summary

The Concept Attainment Model: An Overview

The Concept Attainment Model is a strategy designed to teach concepts and promote critical thinking. As with the Inductive Model, it requires a classroom environment in which learners feel free to share their thinking without fear of embarrassment.

The Concept Attainment Model: Theoretical Foundations

The Concept Attainment Model is based on cognitive views of learning. It emphasizes placing learners in active roles, depends on their background knowledge, and uses examples to develop understanding. In addition, it provides learners with experience in the logical processes of science.

Concept Attainment activities are based on three different theories of concept learning. One theory emphasizes exemplars and suggests that people focus on examples and store these in long-term memory. A second theory emphasizes essential characteristics and suggests that learners focus on these as they attempt to form a concept. A third theory suggests that learners form idealized prototypes from the examples they encounter. In all three theories, examples form an essential link between the student and the learning environment.

Planning Lessons Using the Concept Attainment Model

Whereas the Inductive Model is designed to teach concepts, principles, generalizations, and academic rules, the Concept Attainment Model focuses exclusively on concepts. In addition, it is designed to provide learners with extensive experience in the processes of generating and testing hypotheses, and it emphasizes the scientific method, which can be used in all content areas.

As with the Inductive Model, teachers plan for Concept Attainment activities by identifying a specific concept and creating or finding positive and negative examples. In addition, the teacher carefully sequences the examples to maximize the amount of practice learners get with hypothesis testing.

Implementing Lessons Using the Concept Attainment Model

Because learners are likely to be unfamiliar with the Concept Attainment procedure, using a familiar topic to introduce the strategy is recommended. Lessons begin with the teacher's presentation of a positive and negative example. Students then generate hypotheses, which is followed by more examples, analysis of hypotheses using the additional examples, and continued hypothesis testing until a single hypothesis has been isolated. The lesson comes to closure when the concept is defined, characteristics are identified, and the concept is linked to related concepts.

Modifications of Concept Attainment Activities

Concept Attainment activities can be used with young children by making the topics and examples concrete and decreasing the emphasis on nonexamples.

Concept Attainment II is a modification in which learners strategically select examples from a list provided by the teacher to test hypotheses. Concept Attainment III is a further modification in which learners generate their own examples to test their hypotheses.

Assessing Student Learning in Concept Attainment Activities

In using the Concept Attainment Model, teachers assess learners' understanding of concepts as well as their abilities to think critically. Teachers can assess concept understanding by having students classify or produce additional examples; identify essential characteristics; or relate the concept to superordinate, coordinate, or subordinate concepts.

Teachers can assess critical thinking by having learners analyze hypotheses in light of additional concepts. Assessing thinking always involves simultaneous assessment of content understanding.

IMPORTANT CONCEPTS

Characteristics (p. 176)   Exemplars (p. 177)   Prototype (p. 177)
Concept mapping (p. 187)   Intrinsic motivation (p. 188)   Scientific method (p. 178)
Concepts (p. 176)   Metacognition (p. 189)   Self-regulation (p. 189)

EXERCISES

1. Examine the following learning objectives. Identify which are appropriately taught with the Concept Attainment Model. For those that are inappropriate, explain why.
   a. An English teacher wants her students to understand *gerund.*
   b. An elementary teacher wants his students to understand *soft.*
   c. A science teacher wants her students to know why two coffee cans released at the top of an inclined plane roll down the plane at different speeds.
   d. A science teacher wants his students to understand *miscible fluids* (fluids that are capable of being mixed).
   e. A literature teacher wants her students to know the time period in which Poe did his writing.

2. For each of the content goals identified in Item 1 as appropriate for Concept Attainment, prepare and sequence a list of examples that would help students attain the concept.

3. Select a topic of your choice and design a sequence of examples that will maximize the students' practice with thinking skills.

4. Read the following case study illustrating a Concept Attainment activity and answer the questions using information from the scenario.

Michele Scarritt wants her sixth-grade students to practice their abilities to test hypotheses, and in order to provide practice with the process, she focuses on the concept *canine*. She has done a number of Concept Attainment activities with her students, so they are familiar and comfortable with the process, viewing it as a "thinking game."

She cuts pictures of various animals and plants from magazines and pastes them on posterboard.

"Today we are going to do another Concept Attainment activity, and I've thought up a really good one for you," she says in her introduction to the class. "You're going to have to really think about this one, so I'm curious to see how you'll do."

"You can't stump us, Mrs. Scarritt," the students retort. "We get 'em all."

"We'll see," Michele continues smiling. "Here we go. . . ."

She shows a picture of a German shepherd as a *yes* example and an oak tree as a *no* example.

1. "I know what you're thinking of," Mary volunteers. "It's an *animal*."
2. "It could be *pet*," Tabatha adds.
3. "I think it's *mammal*," Phyllis puts in.
4. "Let's take a quick look at those hypotheses," Michelle adds, writing them on the board. "We want to be sure we're all in the same place. Phyllis, where did you get *mammal?*"
5. ". . . A German shepherd's a dog, and dogs are mammals."
6. "Okay," Michele nods, "and I think we can all see where Mary and Tabatha got *pet* and *animal*. Let's go on and look at some more data." She shows a collie (*yes*) and a magnolia tree (*no*).
7. "I think it's *dogs*," Judy adds.
8. "Okay, let's put that on the board. Now let's go a bit further," Michele says. She shows a beagle (*yes*) and a Siamese cat (*no*).
9. "It can't be *pet*," Kathy says quickly, "because Siamese cat is a *no* and it's a pet."
10. "It can't be *animal* or *mammal* either," Mike notes, "because a cat is both an animal and a mammal."
11. "Let's continue," Michele requests. She then shows a fox (*yes*) and a leopard (*no*).
12. "It can't be just *dog*," Don asserts. "Maybe it's *dog family*."
13. "I'll show you another picture," Michele says. Then she shows a picture of a wolf (*yes*).
14. "It must be *dog family*," Denny stated. "All the yeses support the idea of dog family."
15. Michele then adds, "What do we call *dog family?*" After hearing no response she says, "Animals in the dog family are called *canines*."
16. Then Michele suggests, "Let's look at these pictures again (the yeses) and see what they have in common."
17. "They all have four legs," Sharon notes.
18. "They bark," Ann adds.
19. "They have sharp, prominent teeth," Jimmy says.
20. "They all have hair," Jane suggests.

> The lesson continues as Michele helps the class form a definition for *canine* and links the concept to other animals. Then she shows them some additional pictures and asks them to classify them as *canine* or not.

Using information from the anecdote, respond to the following questions.

    a. Identify all the positive examples of the concept.

    b. Identify all the characteristics of the concept that were presented in the lesson.

    c. Identify all the statements in the lesson that were statements of hypothesizing.

    d. Explain how Michele's sequence of examples promoted the development of students' thinking abilities in the activity?

    e. What could Michele have done to further enrich the concept the children attained?

    f. What did Michele do that did not quite follow the Concept Attainment procedure?

    g. Where in the lesson did Michele make students' thinking processes explicit?

Feedback for these exercises begins on page 341.

DISCUSSION QUESTIONS

    1. What would a Concept Attainment activity be like if only positive examples were used? Only negative? What is the optimal mix of positive and negative examples?

    2. What are the advantages of using coordinate concepts as negative examples in Concept Attainment activities? Disadvantages? What can be done to minimize these disadvantages?

    3. The amount of time that a teacher waits after asking a question has been found to be an important determinant influencing the quality of student answers (Rowe, 1974). How important is wait-time in a Concept Attainment activity? When should it occur?

    4. In implementing Concept Attainment activities in classrooms with diverse learners, students who do not typically participate sometimes become quite involved. What might be a reason for this?

    5. In what areas of the curriculum is it hardest to provide effective examples for Concept Attainment activities? Easiest? Why do you think so?

    6. In what order should CA I, CA II, and CA III activities be introduced to students? What can be done to help students understand similarities and differences among the different strategies?

    7. In comparing CA I, CA II, and CA III, which is easiest to implement in the classroom? Hardest? Which requires the most planning?

    8. How could the critical thinking developed in CA II and CA III be assessed?

The Integrative Model

The Integrative Model is designed to help students develop a deep understanding of organized bodies of knowledge while simultaneously developing critical-thinking skills. It is closely related to the Inductive Model, differing primarily in the type of content it is designed to help students learn. Whereas the Inductive Model is designed to help students understand concepts and the relationships between them (using principles, generalizations, and academic rules), the Integrative Model is designed to teach these forms of content organized into general bodies of knowledge.

The historical foundations of the Integrative Model are based on the work of Hilda Taba (1965, 1966, 1967), and we gratefully acknowledge her contributions to our work. When you have completed your study of this chapter, you should be able to:

- Describe the characteristics of organized bodies of knowledge.
- Identify topics that are organized bodies of knowledge.
- Plan and implement lessons using the Integrative Model.
- Adapt the Integrative Model for learners of different ages and with varying backgrounds.
- Assess learner understanding of topics taught with the Integrative Model.

To begin our discussion, let's look at two teachers, each using the Integrative Model to help students understand organized bodies of knowledge while simultaneously practicing critical thinking.

Kim Soo is involved in a science unit on amphibians with her fourth graders. To this point the class has read about amphibians and Kim has used a CD-ROM to show a variety of amphibians. As a class project, groups of students have found pictures of different frogs and toads and the foods they eat. They bring the pictures to class and, with Kim's help, organize them in a matrix. Kim supplied some additional information for the matrix and the result is shown in Figure 7.1. Kim laminates the matrix so she can use it again later and prepares to guide students' analysis of the information in it.

After directing the class to study the chart for a moment, she begins by saying, "First, let's look at the words at the top of the chart," and pointing to *Characteristics* she continues, "this is kind of a big one. What do you think it means?"

". . . It's . . . kind of the way they look," Andrea responds uncertainly.

"Sure," Kim nods. "It's a way of describing them. The way they look, their color, the way they're built."

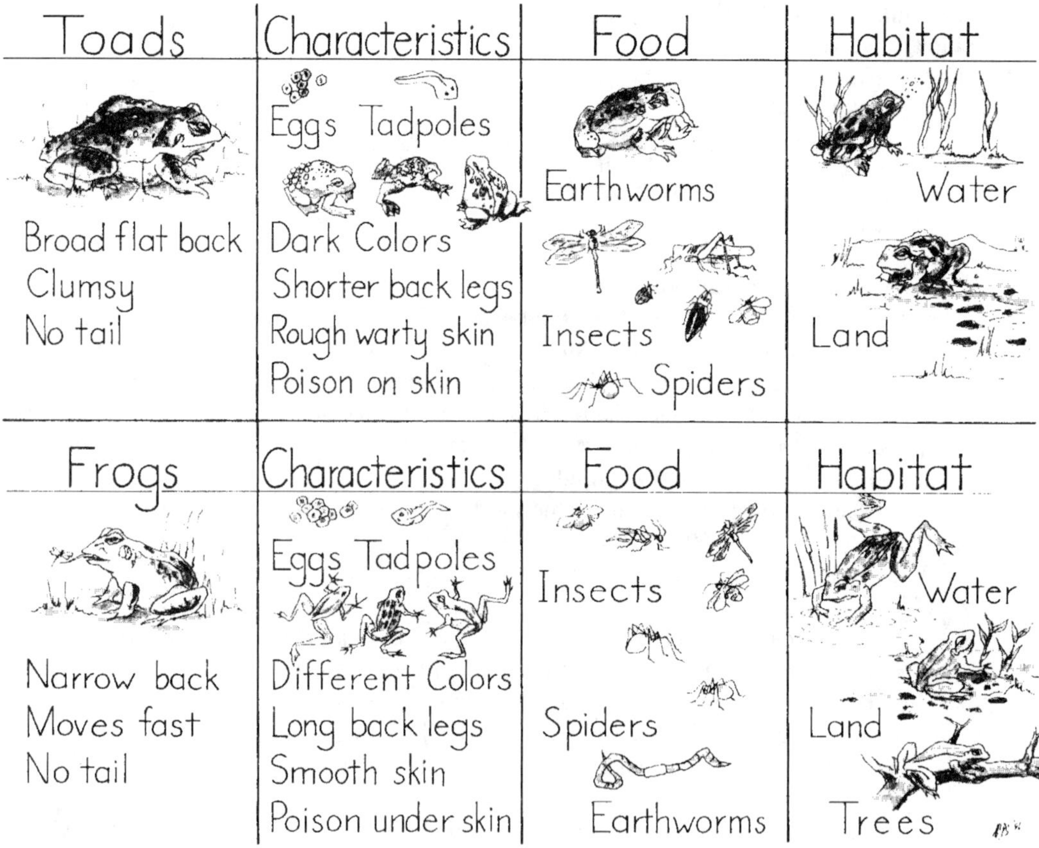

Toads	Characteristics	Food	Habitat
Broad flat back Clumsy No tail	Eggs Tadpoles Dark Colors Shorter back legs Rough warty skin Poison on skin	Earthworms Insects Spiders	Water Land
Frogs	Characteristics	Food	Habitat
Narrow back Moves fast No tail	Eggs Tadpoles Different Colors Long back legs Smooth skin Poison under skin	Insects Spiders Earthworms	Water Land Trees

FIGURE 7.1   Matrix Comparing Frogs and Toads

Kim also has students describe what *habitat* means to them and she then continues, "Let's start with 'food' because we're all familiar with food. Look carefully at the part that tells what toads eat. What do you notice here? . . . Serena?"

"They . . . eat earthworms," Serena responds.

"And what else? . . . Dominique?"

"Spiders," Dominique answers.

"Also grasshoppers," David volunteers.

"Yes, very good, everyone," Kim smiles. "Now look at the frogs. Let's do the same with them. What can you tell me about what they eat? . . . Judy?"

". . . They eat insects," Judy replies.

"Also earthworms," Bill adds.

"Now, let's go a bit further," Kim encourages. "Look at both the frogs and the toads. How would you compare what they eat? Is there any kind of pattern there?"

"They both eat insects," Tim notices.

"Leroy?"

"They both eat earthworms too," Leroy offers.

". . . The food is . . . almost the same," Kristy adds tentatively.

"Why do you suppose that the food seems to be the same? . . . Fernando?" Kim continues smiling, acknowledging Kristy's answer.

". . . The frog and toad live in about the same places," Fernando responds after several seconds of studying the chart.

"How did you decide that?" Kim probes.

". . . It says on the chart that frogs live on land, in the water, and in trees, and it says for toads that they live on land and in the water," Fernando responds pointing to the chart.

"Yes, excellent, Fernando," Kim nods. "Remember how we have talked about justifying our thinking in some of our work in math. This is exactly the same thing. Fernando provided evidence for his conclusion based on the chart that their environments are about the same by pointing out where they live. This is the kind of thinking we're after."

"Also, the frog and toad are a lot alike," Sonya adds, turning back to the chart.

"What do you see that tells you that, Sonya?"

"They look . . . about the same," Sonya replies.

"Also, both start from eggs and then get to be tadpoles. See where there are eggs and tadpoles on the chart," Lakesha adds.

"Very good everyone!" Kim exclaims. "That is particularly good, Lakesha. You provided evidence for your comment without being asked for it. That's the kind of thinking we want to do."

"Now here's a tough one," Kim continues. "Suppose that frogs and toads were quite different rather than being very similar. What kinds of conclusions might we make about them then? . . . Donna?"

". . . Maybe the food that they would eat would be different," Donna shrugs.

"Can you give us an example of where that would be the case, Donna?" Kim queries.

". . ."

"Think about some animals that we know about. What do they eat?"

". . . Dogs eat dog food and stuff."

"Sure. There's an example," Kim smiles. "Dogs are different from frogs and toads, and we see that they eat different kinds of foods."

"Wait," Emmitt waves. "Dogs and cats are different, but they eat the same kinds of foods."

"Excellent thought, Emmitt," Kim nods. . . . "Now think about Emmitt's point everyone. Do you have some other thoughts?"

". . . Dogs and cats *are* different, but a cat is more like a dog than a toad," Tabatha adds to the laughter of some of the other students.

"Some of you are laughing," Kim smiles, "but consider what Tabatha said. What do you think?"

". . . I think she's right," Sylvia adds. "Cows and horses are different, but they eat the same food."

"Okay," Kim waves. "I think you've all come up with some good thoughts. . . . Now, let's think some more about all this. Look again at the toad and frog in the first column of the chart. In what ways are they different? . . . Fred?"

". . . It says the toad is clumsy, but it doesn't say anything about the frog."

". . . Suppose the toad wasn't clumsy," Kim continues nodding to Fred. "How might that affect the food toads eat or where they live? . . . Anyone?"

". . ."

"Look over at the 'Food' column and the 'Habitat' column."

". . . Maybe toads could live in trees if they weren't clumsy," Marcy suggests.

"That's an interesting thought," Kim nods. "Why do you think so?"

". . . They couldn't be clumsy and get up there. . . . If they were clumsy, they might fall out," Andre suggests after studying the chart for several seconds.

"Sounds sensible. What does anyone else think?"

The rest of the class nods and murmurs, and Kim goes on, "How about food?"

"That would be different too," Kathy says quickly.

"Why do you think so, Kathy?" Kim probes.

". . . Well, maybe not?"

"Why not?"

"The frog and toad eat the same food."

"What does that have to do with it?"

". . . If the frog wasn't clumsy, and the toad was, . . . and they eat the same food, . . . it doesn't matter."

"What doesn't matter?"

". . . Whether the toad is clumsy?"

"What do you think of Kathy's suggestions, anyone?"

The class discusses Kathy's ideas for a few more minutes and finally concludes that what she said made sense.

Kim then continues, "Now, let's summarize what we've found here, and let's think about animals in general. . . . I want you to try and extend beyond the toad and frog, and I'll help you if you need it.

"For instance," she goes on, "what can we say about the characteristics of animals that look a lot alike?"

". . . They're, like . . . mostly the same," Adella responds.

"So, how should we write that? Help me out," Kim urges as she moves to the board.

". . ."

"I'll get us started." She writes, 'Animals that look alike . . . ' on the board.

". . . Will have the same characteristics," Ladonna offers.

"Okay," Kim replies, and she then writes, "Animals that look alike have similar characteristics" on the board.

"What else?" she urges.

"They also eat the same kind of food," Tonya offers.

"Good. So, . . . tell me what to write."

"Animals that look alike . . ."

"And have the same characteristics," Nancy interjects.

"And have the same characteristics," Tonya repeats, "eat the same kind of food."

Kim then writes the statement on the board, and asks the students for any additional summarizing statements. They developed a list of statements as follows:

- Animals that look alike have similar characteristics.
- Animals that look alike and have similar characteristics eat the same kind of food.
- Animals that are similar live in similar habitats.

Finally, Kim asks the students if they can think of some examples that fit their statements, and they discuss deer and elk, different kinds of birds, and predators, such as lions and leopards. They also discuss exceptions, such as the fact that deer and elk both live in the mountains, but some deer live on the plains as well, and Kim then closes the lesson.

Let's look now at another teacher, Tony Horton, using the Integrative Model in his eighth-grade American history class. As you read the second lesson, compare what Tony is doing with what Kim did.

Tony is beginning a unit on immigration with his class. He asks the students what *immigrant* means and then asks them to suggest some representative immigrant groups from the late nineteenth century until the 1960s, saying that they would look at immigration from the late 1960s to the present later in the unit. Students suggest that they study a group from Europe and another from the Far East. Tony also encourages them to consider one or more groups closer to the United States as well, and at his suggestion they settled on Puerto Rico.

Just as he begins, Juan interjects, "What about Cuba? I have some relatives in Florida who came from Cuba."

"Sounds good to me," Tony nods. "What do the rest of you think?"

The class agrees that it is a good idea, and Tony comments, "I really like your idea, Juan. Also, everyone, we will extend what we're doing to consider Hispanic Americans in the Southwest, and many other immigrant groups particularly in California."

Tony draws a matrix on the board as shown in Figure 7.2. Tony then organizes the class into pairs and each pair is directed to gather information about different aspects of the four immigrant groups, such as their reasons for coming, characteristics, and assimilation. The pairs work for 3 days gathering the information, turn in their notes, and Tony compiles the information together with some of his own into the matrix that appears in Figure 7.3.

The next day Tony begins by saying, "All right everyone, slide your desks next to your partners and we're going to analyze the information that we've put together in our chart." He passes out copies of the chart to each of the pairs.

He continues, "Now, here's your assignment. I want you to look in each column of the chart and try to find patterns. For instance, when you look at the immigrants' reasons for coming, compare the groups to see what they have in common. Then describe the similarities in writing.

"Let's look at a sample. Everyone take a look at the first column for a minute and see if you find some things that the four groups have in common, or something that two or three of the groups have in common."

After about half a minute, Aurelia volunteers hesitantly, "It looks like the Italians, Chinese, and Puerto Ricans all had population problems, but that didn't seem to be the case for the Cubans."

"Excellent, Aurelia. That's exactly what we're trying to do," Tony smiles, and he writes "Population problems for the Italians, Chinese, and Puerto Ricans; not for the Cubans," on the board.

He then continues, "Now, I want you to work with your partner and find as many patterns as you have evidence for in each of the columns. I want you to work as follows: . . . First write your own response . . . find your own patterns and write them down. . . . Then share them with your partner. . . . Discuss them with each other and be ready to share them with the class. You have 10 minutes."

"Do we turn these in, Mr. Horton?" James asks.

	Reasons for Coming	Characteristics	Assimilation
I T			
C H			
P R			
C			

FIGURE 7.2   Matrix Organized for Data Gathering

FIGURE 7.3   **Matrix Containing Gathered Information**

	Reasons for Coming	**Characteristics**	**Assimilation**
I T A L I A N S	Small farms couldn't support families Large estates controlled land Population increases Poor land, little irrigation, wooden plows Few factories, little industry Heavy taxes Stories of wealth in America	Many from low-income backgrounds Religious; Catholic Large families Tight family structure Many from farm occupations Most could not read or write English English language learned quickly by second generation	First generation did not mix Church schools Second generation moved away from home "Little Italy" in New York City Second generation "Americanized"
C H I N E S E	Large population Land controlled by warlords High taxes Crop failures Famine Promise of high wages in America	Many brought to United States initially as laborers Religious; Confucianism Most could not read or write English Retained many former customs Tight family structure Slow to learn English language	Men as job hunters initially lived together "China Towns" established in major cities Major influx from 1868 to 1890 Little social association with others Large population in western United States Eager to preserve customs
P U E R T O R I C A N S	Large population increases Few factories Little land Close to the United States Descriptions of "good life" in America Became U.S. citizens in 1917	Many had low-income backgrounds Religious; Catholic Large families Most could not read or write English English language learned quickly by second generation Tight family structure	Major influx in 1940s and 1950s "Spanish Harlem" in New York Many stayed in northeastern United States Initially church, then public schools Second generation "Americanized"
C U B A N S	Batista overthrown Castro into power Promises of opportunity to return to Cuba	Many had upper-income backgrounds Religious; Catholic Tight family structure Many could not read or write English Politically powerful in South Florida Economically powerful in South Florida English language learned quickly by second generation	Major influx in 1960s Large population in South Florida Adapted quickly to American politics Adapted quickly to American business practices

"Absolutely," Tony nods. "Now get to work quickly and quietly."

The room becomes a buzz of voices as the students begin studying the chart and writing information on their papers. At the end of the 10 minutes, Tony says, "Okay, let's take a look. What do you have there?"

"Wait, we're not done," several protest.

"All right. Five more minutes."

At the end of the 5 minutes Tony says, "Now, here we go. What are some of the comparisons you made?"

Each of the pairs report some of the comparisons that they found, and Tony records them on the board. When they are finished, they have the following lists.

Reasons for Coming	*Characteristics*	*Assimilation*
Poor agriculture except for Cubans	Tended to come from lower classes except for Cubans	First generation stayed to themselves
Large populations except for Cubans	Most didn't speak English	Chinese assimilated less rapidly than did the others
Promises of a better life in America	All were religious	Initially stayed where they landed
Political problems in Cuba	All except Chinese learned English quickly	

"That's well done," Tony nods, pointing to the lists. "Good work. . . . Now, let's look a little more closely at the information. Why do you suppose that the Italians, Chinese, and Puerto Ricans tended to come from the lower socioeconomic classes, whereas the Cubans did not? . . . Anyone?"

". . . I think it's because of why they came," Antonio offers. "The Italians, Chinese, and Puerto Ricans came so they could have a better life, but the Cubans were escaping from Castro."

"They wanted a better life too," Kevin interjects.

"Well, that's true, but the reasons were different. The others wanted to make a better living, and in Cuba it was politics mostly."

"Good thoughts everyone," Tony goes on. "Is there anything that we can say in general about the reasons immigrants move from one country to another?"

". . . I think they think that they will have a better life in the new country," LaQuana puts in. "It might be to make more money, or it might be for political reasons, but they all think they'll be better off in the new country than they are in the old one."

"Does everyone agree with that?" Tony asks, turning to the rest of the class.

Seeing several nods, Tony writes on the board, "Immigrants immigrate in search of a better life."

He then continues, "Let's look again at some of the comparisons we've made. We wrote that the Chinese assimilated less rapidly than did the other groups. Why do you suppose that was the case?"

". . . Their culture was like . . . more different than the others," Christine volunteers hesitantly.

"What evidence do we have on our chart that tells us they were more different culturally?"

". . . Their religion maybe. The Italians, Puerto Ricans, and Cubans were mostly Catholic, which a lot of people in the United States are, but the Chinese were Confus . . . Confushist . . . whatever that religion is," Christine continues.

"Also, it says in the chart that the Chinese were slow to learn English, and it says for each of the others that English was learned quickly by the second generation," Estella adds.

"And why might that have been?"

"Their language is different. There are letters for each of the languages in the chart, and the Italians, Puerto Ricans, and Cubans use the same letters as English, but the Chinese letters are really different."

"Suppose they weren't different, meaning they used the same letters as we do. How do you suppose that would have affected how fast they assimilated?"

". . . It would have speeded it up," Dean offers.

"What do you think, Gayle? You've been sort of quiet," Tony encourages.

". . . It might have speeded it up, but it still would have been slower than for the others."

"Why do you think so?"

"Well, the religion for one thing."

"And they kept their customs," Shelli adds.

Tony continues with the process of having students explain their comparisons and hypothesize outcomes until the information in the chart has been covered.

He then says, "Now, let's try and make some summary generalizations about the information we have here, and then we'll see if we think it applies to immigrant groups today."

With Tony's guidance the students offers some generalizations, which he writes on the board. The list appeared as follows:

- Immigrants immigrate in search of a better life.
- Immigrants usually immigrate to make a better living. (Tony adds, "Usually for economic reasons.")
- Some immigrants immigrate for political reasons.
- Immigrants usually hear stories of how good it will be in the new country.
- If immigrants immigrate for economic reasons, they're usually in the lower economic classes in their native country.
- Immigrants assimilate more easily if their language and customs are similar to the language and customs of the new country.
- Immigrants tend to first settle where they first land in the new country.

"Now let's take a look at our list and see if we think everything we've said is valid. How do they all look?"

". . . I don't think that 'economic reasons' is right," Troy says after several seconds.

"Go on, Troy. Why don't you think so?"

". . . It looks to me like both the Italians and Chinese also had political problems, sort of like the Cubans. The Puerto Ricans are the only ones that didn't have political problems."

"What evidence do you have for that?"

Troy points to information on the chart, such as "heavy taxes" from government for the Italians and "warlords" and "high taxes" for the Chinese.

Tony acknowledges his point, asks the rest of the class if they think the generalization should be revised, does so in response to their comments, and then analyzes each of the other generalizations in the same way.

Finally, he says, "Now, we're going to keep this list on the board, . . . and when we study immigrants further, we'll see if our generalizations are still valid. We'll ask ourselves, did we overgeneralize, or maybe even undergeneralize? Did we stereotype any immigrant groups? Then, we'll look back at some of the early colonialization, such as the Jamestown and Plymouth colonies. Can the people that came then even be legitimately called immigrants? We'll start there tomorrow."

The Integrative Model: An Overview

Let's look again at the teaching episodes and identify their similarities and differences.

The lessons were similar in the following ways:

- The topics the teachers taught were organized bodies of knowledge, topics that combine facts, concepts, generalizations, and the relationships among them (Kauchak & Eggen, 2003).
- The teachers began their lessons by displaying information that the students and teacher had gathered and compiled in a matrix.
- The students, under the guidance of the teachers, analyzed the information in the matrix; they increased their understanding of the topic and practiced critical thinking at the same time.

Because of the topics, ages of the students, and the teachers' learning objectives, some differences existed in the lessons:

- Kim began her lesson by having students first describe the information in a specific cell of the matrix, whereas Tony Horton had students make comparisons as the first part of the activity.
- Kim did her entire lesson with a whole group, whereas Tony had the students initially work in pairs and report their findings. The class then analyzed the findings as a whole group.
- Kim had the students first make observations, which were followed—essentially in order—by making comparisons, forming explanations, hypothesizing and generalizing. Tony had his students practice the same processes, but they didn't follow a sequence in the same way Kim's did.

The similarities and differences are summarized in Table 7.1.

TABLE 7.1   Comparison of the Two Lessons

Similarities	Differences
Both teachers taught an organized body of information.	Kim's students began by describing information in a single cell. Tony's students began by making comparisons and looking for patterns.
The teachers displayed information in a matrix for the students.	
In both classes, the students' analysis was based on the information in the matrix rather than on information they recalled from reading or lecture.	Kim conducted her lesson as a whole-group activity. Tony's students began working in pairs followed by a whole-group discussion.
The teachers guided the students' analyses with directed questions.	Kim guided her students through the model's phases in order. Tony did not follow a specific sequence.
Both lessons focused simultaneously on deep understanding of content and higher-order and critical thinking.	
Both lessons included all phases of the model.	

The Integrative Model: Theoretical Foundations

In Chapter 2 we saw that people construct understanding of the experiences they have, and learning can be defined as changes in the way understanding is organized in memory. The *forms of understanding that exist in memory* are called **schemas** (Slavin, 2003). Concepts are simple schemas, and when learners link concepts to facts, other concepts, principles, generalizations, and academic rules their schemas become much more complex. A simple schema for the concept *work,* which you first saw in Chapter 2, is shown in Figure 7.4.

Because people construct their own understanding, the schemas learners construct are individual and may or may not be valid. For example, many students equate work with effort, such as believing that they're doing work if they hold up a chair while standing still. In this case they've constructed a schema, but it isn't valid. Only when they realize that work requires a combination of force and movement have they constructed a valid schema for the concept.

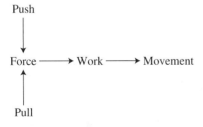

FIGURE 7.4   Simple Schema for the Concept *Work*

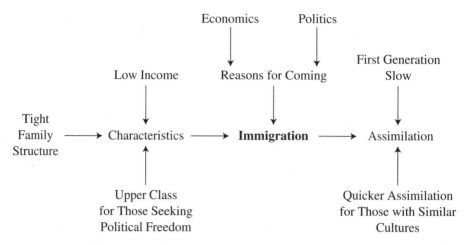

Economics   Politics

Low Income   Reasons for Coming   First Generation
                                            Slow

Tight
Family ——→ Characteristics ——→ **Immigration** ——→ Assimilation
Structure

Upper Class   Quicker Assimilation
for Those Seeking   for Those with Similar
Political Freedom   Cultures

FIGURE 7.5   Schema for Immigration

A more complex schema for the topic of immigration, constructed by one of Tony's students, appears in Figure 7.5.

In this figure we see that the student has linked the concept *immigration* to generalizations about reasons immigrants came to the United States, their characteristics, and the way they assimilated into U.S. culture. The schema also includes facts, such as the major influx of Cubans occurring in the 1960s.

The development of schemas is important for one primary reason. We also saw in Chapter 2 that the understanding learners construct depends on what they already know. Seeing that learners organize knowledge in memory in the form of schemas helps us better understand why. For instance, more than 7 million people immigrated to the United States in the 1970s, and another 7 million came during the 1980s (Kent, Pollard, Haaga, & Mather, 2001). The student's schema helps him understand that economics is likely the reason that most of the people came. Without the existing schema, the information would be an isolated series of facts and not meaningful to the individual. The schema also helps us understand facts that exist today, such as why so many people from Mexico come to the United States (even at the risk of being illegal aliens). The more complex and interconnected a schema is, the more places learners have to connect new knowledge and understanding.

We saw how schema production occurred in Tony's lesson. To see another example of schema production, let's look at some dialogue from Kim's lesson.

KIM: Why do you suppose that the food seems to be the same?

FERNANDO: . . . The frog and toad live in about the same places.

KIM: How did you decide that?

FERNANDO: . . . It says on the chart that frogs live on land, in the water, and in trees, and it says for toads that they live on land and in the water.

> **KIM:** Yes, excellent, Fernando. . . .
>
> **SONYA:** Also, the frog and toad are a lot alike.
>
> **KIM:** What do you see that tells you that, Sonya?
>
> **SONYA:** They look . . . about the same.
>
> **LAKESHA:** Also, both start from eggs and then get to be tadpoles. See where there are eggs and tadpoles on the chart.

Here we see that, with Kim's guidance, the students linked the food frogs and toads eat to where they live. Their resulting schemas would help them understand why deer, antelope, and other grass eaters appear similar and live in similar habitats; their existing understanding would aid new understanding.

Both Kim's and Tony's lessons focused on the development of complex schemas. This is what the Integrative Model is designed to do.

Learning Objectives for the Integrative Model

The Integrative Model is designed to help students reach two interdependent goals. The first is to construct a deep and thorough understanding of *organized bodies of knowledge,* and the second is to develop critical-thinking abilities. Let's look at them.

Organized Bodies of Knowledge: Relationships among Facts, Concepts, and Generalizations

In our overview of the Integrative Model we said that Kim and Tony taught **organized bodies of knowledge,** *topics that combine facts, concepts, generalizations, and the relationships among them* (Kauchak & Eggen, 2003). To put these ideas into context, let's look back at the lessons in Chapters 5 and 6. In Chapter 5, Judy Nelson taught *longitude* and *latitude* (concepts), *Charles's law* was Sue Grant's topic, and Jim Rooney wanted his students to understand the rules for forming singular and plural possessive nouns. The concepts *fruit* and *metaphor* were the topics in Chapter 6.

Each topic was specific and well defined. The concept *latitude,* for example, has clear characteristics—parallel imaginary lines that measure distances north and south of the equator, and Charles's law describes a specific relationship—as temperature increases, volume increases when pressure is constant. The same is true for the other topics.

By comparison, the topics that Kim and Tony taught were not as specific and well defined. For instance, Kim's lesson included several facts, the kinds of foods frogs and toads eat, for example; concepts, such as *habitat;* and generalizations, for example, *animals with similar characteristics tend to eat the same kinds of foods.*

Tony's lesson was similar. There were facts, such as the major influx of Cubans occurring in the 1960s, and there is a place in New York City called "Little Italy" among several others; concepts—*socioeconomic status, assimilation,* and *Confucianism;* and generalizations, such as *the Chinese were eager to preserve their customs,* and *second-generation Italians quickly learned English.*

The learning objectives in the lessons was not to teach these specific facts, concepts, or generalizations themselves; rather it was for students to find and understand relationships among them, form explanations for those relationships, and consider additional possibilities (hypotheses).

Much of the content we teach in schools exists in the form of organized bodies of knowledge. For example, geography teachers compare the characteristics of different countries, such as the climate, culture, and economy of Brazil, Argentina, and Venezuela. English teachers compare the works of Faulkner, Fitzgerald, and Hemingway. Life science teachers compare different body systems and their functions. Teachers of young children compare food, clothing, and recreation for different seasons of the year. Each of these topics combines facts, concepts, and generalizations into organized bodies of knowledge just as Kim and Tony did in their lessons. Additional examples of topics that are organized bodies of knowledge include:

- Life science—a comparison of different animal phyla and the characteristics of each
- Health—an analysis of well-balanced and poorly balanced meals
- Art—a consideration of prominent artists in different historical periods
- Music—a comparison of baroque, romantic, and classical music
- Early elementary—a discussion of different community helpers
- History—a comparison of settlements in the northern and southern colonies

Each topic combines facts, concepts, and generalizations, and the teacher would want students to understand relationships among them.

Developing Critical Thinking

Developing critical thinking is a second learning objective when the Integrative Model is used. Developing critical thinking requires practice in finding patterns, forming explanations, hypothesizing, generalizing, and documenting the findings with evidence. Throughout this book we have emphasized that "Learning is a consequence of thinking" (Perkins, 1992, p. 8), which suggests that content objectives and objectives for thinking are interdependent. Learners practice thinking critically as they construct deep understanding of the topics they study. Teachers help make this practice conscious and systematic.

The interdependence of these objectives is essential. As we saw in Chapter 3, only about 5 percent of class time is typically spent on higher-order thinking (Goodlad, 1984), and additional research indicates that fewer than 1 percent of all teacher questions require student responses beyond factual information or the demonstration of a routine procedure (Boyer, 1983). Kim's and Tony's lessons were in direct contrast with the patterns identified by these studies.

Although they are atypical for many teachers, the abilities Kim and Tony demonstrated can be developed with practice. First, it takes some adjustment in thinking (away from teaching as *telling* and toward teaching as *guiding*), and second, it requires that students are provided with information, such as Kim's and Tony's matrices. As with the use of examples in Inductive Model lessons, the information becomes the experiences students use to construct their understanding. Let's look now at how we can plan to make this happen.

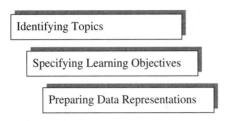

FIGURE 7.6   Planning with the Integrative Model

Planning Lessons with the Integrative Model

Planning for lessons using the Integrative Model is similar to that for using either the Inductive Model or the Concept Attainment Model. The steps are outlined in Figure 7.6.

Identifying Topics

As we saw in Chapters 5 and 6, research indicates that planning most commonly begins with a topic (Kauchak & Eggen, 2003). The topics Kim and Tony taught were *Frogs and Toads* and *Immigrants.* Topics may come from textbooks, curriculum guides, and other sources, including the interests of students or teachers themselves. When topics are organized bodies of knowledge, the Integrative Model can be used effectively.

Specifying Learning Objectives

Having identified the topic, teachers must decide exactly what they want students to understand about the topic. This decision specifies the content objective.

Content Objectives.   Specifying content objectives when using the Integrative Model requires more thought than lessons involving the Inductive or Concept Attainment Models because organized bodies of knowledge are less precisely defined than specific concepts, generalizations, principles, or rules. For example, the characteristics of longitude and latitude are clear, so Judy Nelson's objective (in Chapter 5) was for the students to identify and apply these characteristics. However, knowing that he wanted his students to understand relationships among the *reasons for coming, characteristics,* and *assimilation* of the four immigrant groups wouldn't have been precise enough to help Tony guide his students' analysis. He needed to anticipate some of the generalizations that were summarized in his lesson, such as the relationships between *immigration* and *economics, characteristics of immigrants* and *their reasons for coming,* and *characteristics of immigrants* and *their rates of assimilation.* As they practice, students often identify other generalizations incidentally, which is desirable, but identifying potential generalizations, explanations, and possible hypotheses in advance makes lessons flow more briskly and smoothly.

Planning for Critical Thinking.   Planning for critical thinking is primarily a matter of awareness. The steps involved in implementing the model include having students find patterns, form explanations, and hypothesize, all on the basis of evidence. As students use these processes they develop critical-thinking skills. If teachers are aware of critical thinking as an objective, with practice they increasingly recognize opportunities to promote it. We examine this topic further when we discuss implementing the model.

Preparing Data Representations

Having identified the topic and objectives, teachers must now prepare information that the students will analyze. As we saw in Kim's and Tony's lessons, the data are typically organized in a matrix. We will examine matrices first, and later in the chapter we will discuss how alternate forms of information displays can be used with the Integrative Model.

In each of the examples we've discussed, the topic involved a comparison of two or more elements—toads and frogs in Kim's lesson and the four immigrant groups in Tony's. The number of elements to be compared depends on the developmental level of the students and the teacher's objective.

Each of the other topics that we outlined in the previous section also involved comparisons. However, the comparisons don't have to include closely related concepts, such as *toads* and *frogs,* or *different immigrant groups.* For example, a teacher might have the students compare arthropods to mammals to demonstrate—among other things—that animals with external skeletons are smaller than animals with internal skeletons.

Decisions about the elements to be compared and the dimensions on which the comparisons will be made can be the teacher's, the students', or any combination of the two. For example, Kim alone made the decision to study toads and frogs and to include their appearance, *food, characteristics,* and *habitat,* as the dimensions to be examined. Tony decided to include *reasons for coming, characteristics,* and *assimilation* as the dimensions on which the immigrant groups would be compared, and he and the students collaborated on the choice of immigrant groups. Although Kim and Tony left none of the decisions to the students alone, doing so is perfectly acceptable if it is consistent with the teacher's objectives.

Gathering Data.   Once the dimensions for the matrix have been identified, the next step is to gather the actual data. The data serve the same function as do examples when the Inductive Model is used; the data become the background knowledge students use to construct their understanding of the topic. In gathering data you have at least three options.

- Assign individuals or groups of two or more students to gather the data that will appear in each of the cells of the matrix. A teacher would choose this option if learning to do research and/or organizing information is part of the objective.
- Have students gather some of the data, and add some additional data yourself. This is the option Kim and Tony chose.
- Prepare the entire matrix yourself. This approach saves time and ensures that the content in the matrix leads to desired content objectives. The disadvantage of this option is that students aren't involved in the data-gathering process, and they may be less interested in the topic as a result.

The process of gathering and organizing data may appear time consuming, and, initially, it may be if you do all the preparation yourself. However, if students help gather the initial information, your preparation time is reduced, and, once it is gathered, you can store the information in your computer and quickly modify it the next time you teach the topic. So, although initial preparation is demanding, once the matrix is prepared, additional preparation is minimal. Let's look now at effective ways of displaying the data.

Effective Data Displays. Although data can be displayed in different ways, some are more effective than others. Two guidelines are important. First, *display the information in as factual a form as possible.* This provides students with increased opportunities to analyze the data and practice critical thinking. If this is impossible, next best is a series of relatively narrow generalizations or a mixture of narrow generalizations and facts. Least desirable is a series of broad generalizations. For example, let's consider Tony's lesson again, and compare the matrix he used to the one displayed in Table 7.2.

Because the information in Table 7.2 is already in the form of broad generalizations, the opportunity for students to analyze data and form generalizations themselves is reduced. To be consistent with the principle, "Learning is a consequence of thinking," students must have the opportunity to think about the topics they're studying. Reducing this opportunity decreases the likelihood that they will develop the deep understanding that is so important to learning.

A second guideline is to *provide sufficient information* so that students can use data from one part of the matrix as evidence for a conclusion about another part. For example, Kim asked the students to *explain* why the frog and the toad would eat the same food, and she called on Fernando. He responded by saying that the animals live in essentially the same places. When asked to provide evidence for his response, he was able to point to the section of the chart that showed the habitat for each. If that section hadn't existed, Fernando wouldn't have been able to use the matrix to provide the evidence for his conclusion.

TABLE 7.2 Matrix Containing Broad Generalizations

Reasons for Coming	Characteristics	Assimilation
Italians Economic problems Political problems Overpopulation	Lower socioeconomic class Religious	Relatively rapid assimilation
Chinese Overpopulation Economic opportunity Political problems	Lower socioeconomic class Religious	Relatively slow assimilation
Puerto Ricans Overpopulation Economic opportunity	Religious Lower socioeconomic class	Relatively rapid assimilation
Cubans Political problems	Higher socioeconomic class	Relatively rapid assimilation

We saw the same kind of processing in Tony's lesson. For instance, we saw the following dialogue in his lesson.

> **TONY:**   Let's look again at some of the comparisons we've made. We wrote that the Chinese assimilated less rapidly than did the other groups. Why do you suppose that was the case?
>
> **CHRISTINE:**   . . . Their culture was like . . . more different than the others.
>
> **TONY:**   What evidence do we have on our chart that tells us they were more different culturally?
>
> **CHRISTINE:**   . . . Their religion maybe. The Italians, Puerto Ricans, and Cubans were mostly Catholic, which a lot of people in the United States are, but the Chinese were Confus . . . Confushist . . . whatever that religion is.
>
> **ESTELLA:**   Also, it says in the chart that the Chinese learned English slower than the others.

If the information about the immigrant groups' religions or the rate at which they learned English had not been included in the matrix, the students wouldn't have been able to provide evidence based on data they could observe.

Including enough information in the chart so students are able to make links and verify their responses through observation is important. We illustrate this process in greater detail when we discuss implementing Integrative Model lessons.

Capitalizing on Technology with the Integrative Model

Technology is an additional tool that teachers can use to prepare and store data. One of the most effective ways to employ technology is with the use of **databases,** which are *computer programs that allow users to store, organize, and manipulate information, including both text and numerical data* (Roblyer, 2003a). For example, a social studies teacher might have his students create a presidential database that would include personal information, such as date and place of birth, state of residence, family background, height and weight, religion, interests, political party, occupation prior to election, highest academic degree earned, and age at death and cause of death. It could also include other information, such as world events during the presidency and significant accomplishments according to historians. Students could then see if patterns exist in factors such as occupations, family backgrounds, or states of residence. As another example, a life science teacher might have her students create a database about trees, which could include the type, color, and width of leaves; length of stem; region of the country in which the tree is found; and common uses for the wood.

As a third example look at the database related to our solar system that appears in Table 7.3. It includes information such as the diameter of the planets, their distance from the sun, average temperature, length of year and day, gravity compared to Earth's, and other characteristics. A database such as this is rich with opportunities for analysis. (You will be asked to examine the information in this database again when you complete the exercises at the end of the chapter.)

TABLE 7.3 **Matrix with Information about the Solar System***

Name	Origin of Name	Diameter (in miles)	Distance from Sun (in miles)	Length of Year (orbit)	Length of Day (rotation)	Gravity Compared w/Earth's
Sun	Sol, Roman god of the Sun	865,000				
Mercury	Mercury, messenger of the Roman gods	3,030	35,900,000	88 Earth days	59 Earth days counterclockwise	0.38
Venus	Venus, Roman goddess of love and beauty	7,500	67,200,000	225 Earth days	243 Earth days counterclockwise	0.88
Earth	Terra Mater, Roman earth mother	7.900	98,000,000	365¼ days	24 hours counterclockwise	1
Mars	Mars, Roman god of war	4,200	141,500,000	687 Earth days	24½ hours counterclockwise	0.38
Jupiter	Jupiter, Roman king of all gods	88,700	483,400,000	12 Earth years	10 hours counterclockwise	2.34
Saturn	Saturn, Roman god of agriculture	75,000	914,000,000	30 Earth years	11 hours counterclockwise	0.92
Uranus	Uranus, Roman god, father of Saturn, grandfather of Jupiter	31,566	1,782,400,000	84 Earth years	24 hours counterclockwise	0.79
Neptune	Neptune, Roman god of the sea	30,200	2,792,900,000	165 Earth years	17 hours counterclockwise	1.12
Pluto	Pluto, Greek god of the lower world	1,423	3,665,000,000	248 Earth years	6½ days counterclockwise	0.43

(continued)

TABLE 7.3 *Continued*

Name	Moons	Average Surface Temperature (F)	Other Interesting Characteristics
Sun		10,000°	The sun is a star, Earth's star; a gigantic ball of glowing gases; more than 1 million Earths could fit inside the sun; sun's gravity keeps the nine planets in orbit; sun gives planets light and heat.
Mercury	0	300° below zero to 800° above zero	No atmosphere; no water; many craters.
Venus	0	900° average	Atmosphere mostly carbon dioxide and poisonous sulfuric acid; no water; brightest planet; hottest planet; desert; huge lightning flashes; thick cloud cover; enormous winds.
Earth	1	57° average	Atmosphere contains about 78% nitrogen, 21% oxygen, 1% other gases; water covers about 70% of surface; has plant life, animal life, and people.
Mars	2	67° below zero average	Atmosphere—thin carbon dioxide; no water; white ice caps at poles; salmon sky; frequent dust storms; red, rocky surface (the Red Planet); appears to have no life; home of Earthlings' first space colony(?).
Jupiter	16 or more	162° below zero average	Atmosphere has hydrogen, helium, ammonia; no water; bands of color; Great Red Spot (hurricanes); faint horizontal ring; huge lightning bolts.
Saturn	21 or more	208° below zero average	Atmosphere has hydrogen and helium; no water; has at least four rings tilted from horizontal position; mostly big ball of gas; clouds; some bands of color in shades of yellow. Mostly gas. Small solid core.
Uranus	15 or more	355° below zero average	Atmosphere of hydrogen and helium; no water; greenish color; has at least nine vertical rings. Would float on water.
Neptune	2 or more	266° below zero average	Atmosphere of hydrogen and helium; no water; bands of color in shades of blue.
Pluto	1	460° below zero average	No oxygen; no water; extremely cold and dark; orbiting closer to the sun than Neptune from 1979 to 1999.

*Matrix adapted by permission of Dr. June Main.

In fact, each of the matrices that we've illustrated in this chapter are types of databases. Being able to easily store and manipulate the data is an important advantage that computer-derived databases have over the traditional matrix. Also, as information is entered into the computer, it is stored with similar information (Morrison & Lowther, 2002). For instance, as information from the Mars probe is made available, it is automatically stored with other information about Mars, no matter how many different ways the information is organized or sorted. And once databases are initially constructed, your preparation time for later lessons is significantly reduced.

Scope of Lessons

We saw in the examples that Kim and Tony essentially covered all the information in the matrix in their lessons. This need not be the case, and often it won't be. You may create data displays that will organize information for a 2- or 3-day lesson or even a unit. You would then guide the students' analysis on one portion of the chart the first day, a second portion the next day, and so on. The scope of the lesson depends on your objectives and the amount of information you include in the chart.

Implementing Lessons Using the Integrative Model

You have identified your topic, specified your learning objectives, gathered data and organized it in a matrix, and now you're ready to begin the lesson. Implementing a lesson using the Integrative Model combines four closely related phases together with emphasis on thinking and strategies for increasing student motivation. The phases each have learning and motivation functions, which are illustrated in Table 7.4 and discussed in the sections that follow.

Though they are listed in order, and teachers will usually start with Phase 1, *the phases are not hierarchical and they don't imply a rigid sequence.* For example, you may

TABLE 7.4 Learning and Motivation Functions for the Phases of the Integrative Model

Phase	Learning and Motivation Function
Phase 1: The open-ended phase Learners describe, compare, and search for patterns	■ Promotes involvement ■ Ensures success
Phase 2: The causal phase Learners explain similarities and differences	■ Begins schema production ■ Develops perceptions of competence
Phase 3: The hypothetical phase Learners hypothesize outcomes for different conditions	■ Advances schema production ■ Facilitates transfer
Phase 4: Closure and application Learners generalize to form broad relationships	■ Achieves equilibrium ■ Promotes encoding

move directly from a comparison in Phase 1 to a hypothesis in Phase 3, and then return to another comparison. Students' abilities to hypothesize in Phase 3 don't always require that they have first formed explanations in Phase 2. The order you follow should depend on your learning objectives and the students' responses.

This flexibility was illustrated in Kim's and Tony's lessons. Kim went through the phases pretty much in order, whereas Tony varied the sequence. Let's look at the phases in more detail now.

Phase 1: The Open-Ended Phase

Phase 1 is the beginning point for students' analysis. It begins when the students describe, compare, and search for patterns in the data. Looking again at Kim's and Tony's lessons, we see that Phase 1 can begin in one of two ways:

- You simply direct students' attention to a cell in the matrix and ask them to observe and describe the information. This is what Kim did.
- You ask students to look for similarities and differences in two or more of the cells. This was Tony's approach.

Kim's students were younger than Tony's, and focusing on a single cell better matched their developmental level.

Both beginnings are open ended, and they capitalize on the advantages that also exist in the beginning of a lesson using the Inductive Model. Because Phase 1 is open ended, it breaks the ice for the students, ensures success, promotes involvement, and allows the teacher to quickly and easily involve a number of students by asking a large number of questions, which we have repeatedly seen is a factor that increases achievement (Eggen & Kauchak, 2004; Lambert & McCombs, 1998).

The point on the matrix where students begin the analysis is a matter of judgment. Most commonly, it begins with the top left cell, primarily because we're in the habit of reading beginning with the upper left. You don't have to begin there, however; any point can be productive.

The time you spend on a single cell (or column) is also a matter of judgment. You most likely wouldn't ask for a single observation or comparison and move on, but you don't want to overdwell on a single portion of the chart to the point of reducing the momentum of the lesson.

After describing information in the first cell or making comparisons in the first column, you move to a second, a third, and so on until all the information in the matrix has been examined.

In looking again at Kim's and Tony's lessons, we see a smooth process that promoted high levels of success and interaction. They first asked the students to make observations (in Kim's case) or comparisons (in Tony's). Teachers sometimes feel that they should have to work harder at the initial question, but this isn't the case. Simple, straightforward questions that involve students are effective. To illustrate, let's look again at some of the dialogue from Kim's lesson.

KIM: Let's start with *"food"* because we're all familiar with food. Look carefully at the part that tells what toads eat. What do you notice here? . . . Serena?

SERENA: They . . . eat earthworms.

KIM: And what else? . . . Dominique?

DOMINIQUE: Spiders.

DAVID: Also grasshoppers.

KIM: Yes, very good, everyone. . . . Now look at the frogs. Let's do the same with them. What can you tell me about what they eat? . . . Judy?

JUDY: . . . They eat insects.

BILL: Also earthworms.

Kim began the lesson in a comfortable, open-ended way with the students, which ensured success and built lesson momentum.

In comparison, Tony started his lesson by having the students work in groups, beginning by saying, "Now, here's your assignment. I want you to look in each column of the chart and try to find patterns," and then got them started with an example when he said, "Let's look at a sample. Everyone take a look at the first column for a minute and see if you find some things that the four groups have in common, or something that two or three of the groups have in common." Though Kim asked for descriptions and Tony called for comparisons, both lessons were open ended in the beginning.

As we saw in our discussion of the Inductive Model, becoming more open ended requires some adjustment for many teachers because it isn't a natural inclination and few have been taught that way. However, once the adjustment has been made, you will find it a desirable alternative to the traditional one-question, specific-answer dialogue that is typical of most classrooms.

Recording Information. As students conduct their analyses, you will typically write their observations or comparisons on the board, overhead, or chart paper. This provides reference points for the students' further analyses. Tony recorded both the comparisons the students made in groups and the summarizing generalizations, whereas Kim recorded only the summary statements. Both teachers made a record of the information, however. Without a public record, students will lose some of the most important points in the analysis, and the understanding that results will be less thorough. The process of recording information typically continues in Phases 2, 3, and 4.

Phase 2: The Causal Phase

The causal phase begins when the students attempt to explain the similarities and differences they identified in Phase 1, that is, they look for causal relationships. This is the point where the students are immersed in critical thinking, and, with practice, their analyses can become quite sophisticated. Although the questioning in Phase 2 is more demanding than it was in the first phase, if you persevere, you will become skilled to the point where your questioning is essentially automatic.

In Phase 1 of Kim's lesson we saw that making comparisons was a natural outgrowth of observing and describing. Moving from comparing to explaining has a similar relationship. To illustrate this process let's look again at some dialogue from Kim's lesson.

KIM: Look at both the frogs and the toads. How would you compare what they eat? Is there any kind of pattern there?

TIM: They both eat insects.

KIM: Leroy?

LEROY: They both eat earthworms too.

KRISTY: . . . The food is . . . almost the same.

KIM: Why do you suppose that the food seems to be the same? . . . Fernando?

FERNANDO: . . . The frog and toad live in about the same places.

Asking students to explain why a certain similarity (or difference) exists marks the shift from Phase 1 to Phase 2. The shift is smooth, but the students' thinking is significantly advanced. In Phase 1, students are merely asked to make an observation or identify a similarity or difference, whereas in Phase 2 they are asked to explain why it exists. This is a higher level of reasoning.

The transition to Phase 2 in Tony's lesson was more formal, primarily because he had his students work in pairs during Phase 1. Let's look again at some of the dialogue:

TONY: Good work. . . . Now, let's look a little more closely at the information. Why do you suppose that the Italians, Chinese, and Puerto Ricans tended to come from the lower socioeconomic classes, whereas the Cubans did not? . . . Anyone?

ANTONIO: . . . I think it's because of why they came. . . . The Italians, Chinese, and Puerto Ricans came so they could have a better life, but the Cubans were escaping from Castro.

KEVIN: They wanted a better life too.

ANTONIO: Well, that's true, but the reasons were different. The others wanted to make a better living, and in Cuba it was politics mostly.

This type of analysis is what we're looking for in students, and this is where schema production begins. For example, when Fernando offered the frog and toad living in the same places as an explanation for why their food was the same, he created a link between food and habitat. The process was similar in Tony's lesson. In the preceding dialogue, we see that Antonio and Kevin identified relationships between reasons people immigrate and socioeconomic class and politics.

The creation of relationships among the parts of an organized body of knowledge is the essence of schema production. As a lesson progresses and new links are created, students' schemas become more complex and meaningful, which leads to deep understanding of the topic.

Being able to identify these causal relationships is also motivating for students. As we saw in Chapter 2, genuine accomplishment leads to feelings of competence, which is an innate need according to motivation theory. These feelings are further enhanced when students are praised for their accomplishments. The combination of the learning and motivation function in Phase 2 makes it the most essential phase of the model.

Not every comparison is automatically "explainable," however. Let's examine this issue.

Explainable Comparisons.   Although Phases 1 and 2 are closely related and the move from one to the other should be smooth and comfortable, teacher judgment is required to effectively manage the transition. For example, consider Kim's lesson again. Suppose she said, "Look at the frog and toad in the left column. How would you compare them?" (a question in Phase 1), and a student responded, "The toad has rough skin with bumps on it and the frog's skin is smooth." This type of comparison is essentially "unexplainable." The difference is characteristic of their physiologies, and no data exist in the chart that could be used to help form the explanation. Asking students to explain "why" the toad's skin is bumpy and the frog's smooth is somewhat analogous to asking, "Why does gravity make objects fall to the earth?" It is one of the characteristics of gravity that we merely describe; it doesn't have a readily available explanation.

As a contrasting example, Tony's students noted in their comparisons that the Chinese seemed to assimilate less rapidly than did the other immigrant groups. This is a highly "explainable" comparison. The students explained the slower assimilation for the Chinese by suggesting that differences in culture was a cause, and they could find information in the matrix to support the explanation.

The teacher's task in guiding students' analysis is to recognize comparisons that can be appropriately explained and ask students to provide the explanation, while at the same time leaving "unexplainable" ones as simple comparisons.

As with other aspects of the Integrative Model, recognizing explainable comparisons is not difficult and only requires some practice. The exercises at the end of the chapter offer some practice with this process.

Promoting Critical Thinking: Documenting Assertions.   In Chapter 3 we said that critical thinking involves making and assessing conclusions *based on evidence*. Phase 2 of the Integrative Model provides an excellent opportunity for students to practice this ability. To illustrate, let's look again at some dialogue from Kim's lesson.

KIM: Why do you suppose that the food seems to be the same? . . . Fernando? (A question in Phase 2.)

FERNANDO: . . . The frog and toad live in about the same places.

KIM: How did you decide that?

FERNANDO: . . . It says on the chart that frogs live on land, in the water, and in trees, and it says for toads that they live on land and in the water.

KIM: Yes, excellent, Fernando. . . . Remember how we have talked about justifying our thinking in some of our work in math. This is exactly the same thing. Fernando provided evidence for his conclusion based on the chart that their environments are about the same by pointing out where they live. This is the kind of thinking we're after.

Kim's question, "How did you decide that?" asked Fernando for evidence when he concluded that the animals' environments were about the same. You can ask students for evidence with questions such as:

- How do you know?
- Why do you say that?
- What evidence do we have for that conclusion?

The exact wording of the question isn't important as long as it asks students to provide evidence for their conclusions.

Although asking students for evidence is rare in classrooms (Boyer, 1983; Goodlad, 1984), it isn't difficult once teachers get used to it, and students quickly "warm to the task" and begin to provide evidence without being prompted by their teachers. To illustrate, let's look again at Tony's lesson.

TONY: Let's look again at some of the comparisons we've made. We wrote that the Chinese assimilated less rapidly than did the other groups. Why do you suppose that was the case?

CHRISTINE: . . . Their culture was like . . . more different than the others.

TONY: What evidence do we have on our chart that tells us they were more different culturally?

CHRISTINE: . . . Their religion maybe. The Italians, Puerto Ricans, and Cubans were mostly Catholic, which a lot of people in the United States are, but the Chinese were Confus . . . Confushist . . . whatever that religion is.

ESTELLA: Also, it says in the chart that the Chinese learned English slower than the others.

Here we see that Estella, without prompting from Tony, offered additional information as evidence to support the conclusion that cultural differences explained the slower assimilation of the Chinese.

Once students get used to providing evidence, teachers can begin to promote sophisticated critical-thinking discussions, such as examining the quality of evidence. For instance, Tony could ask the class to examine Estella's comment with questions such as,

- Is learning English less quickly really evidence for cultural differences?
- Why is it, or why is it not, "good" evidence?
- What would be better evidence of cultural differences?

When questions such as these are discussed and analyzed, students obtain valuable critical-thinking experience.

Phase 3: The Hypothetical Phase

Phase 3 marks an additional advance in students' abilities to analyze information, and it evolves directly from Phase 2. Let's look again at Tony's lesson.

> ESTELLA: . . . it says in the chart that the Chinese learned English slower than the others. [evidence for a response in Phase 1]
>
> TONY: And why might that have been? [a question marking the transition to Phase 2]
>
> ESTELLA: Their language is different. There are letters for each of the languages in the chart, and the Italians, Puerto Ricans, and Cubans use the same letters as English, but the Chinese letters are really different. [an explanation—a response in Phase 2]
>
> TONY: Suppose they weren't different, meaning they used the same letters as we do. How do you suppose that would have affected how fast they assimilated?

The preceding question called for a hypothesis. Tony's question asked students to consider the outcome if conditions were changed—a hypothetical situation in which the Chinese used the same letters as the Italians, Puerto Ricans, and Cubans. This process advances schema production and facilitates transfer.

Though the dialogue we just read illustrates how Phase 3 evolves naturally from Phase 2, this isn't a requirement. To illustrate, let's look again at Kim's lesson.

> KIM: Look again at the toad and frog in the first column of the chart. In what ways are they different? (a question in Phase 1)
>
> FRED: . . . It says the toad is clumsy, but it doesn't say anything about the frog. (a response in Phase 1)
>
> KIM: . . . Suppose the toad wasn't clumsy. . . . How might that affect the food toads eat or where they live? . . . Anyone?

Here Kim asked a question calling for a hypothesis (Phase 3) that followed directly from a comparison (Phase 1). The fact that Kim didn't ask the students to explain "why" the toad is clumsy, which would have been a question in Phase 2, is a matter of teacher judgment. It is part of decision making that makes teaching an art. Kim might have felt that the toad's clumsiness was an "unexplainable" comparison, or she might have had another reason for choosing not to ask for an explanation. As with Phases 1 and 2, the process of hypothesizing continues until opportunities for analysis have been exhausted.

During the hypothetical phase, schema production is further advanced because suggested relationships for different conditions are offered. When students suggest the relationships, additional links in their schemas are created, and their schemas become more complex and interconnected. This is the ideal in schema production.

As students see that they're able to offer hypothetical relationships, their *beliefs about their capabilities of accomplishing these tasks,* their **self-efficacy,** increases. As we saw in Chapter 2, the most important factor in increasing learners' self-efficacy is success on challenging tasks. Responding to hypothetical questions is challenging, and being able to respond successfully can be very motivating.

Phase 4: Closure and Application

During the closure and application phase, students generalize to form broad relationships, which summarizes the content, promotes encoding, and helps students achieve a sense of equilibrium. To illustrate this process, let's look again at Kim's lesson.

> **KIM:** Now, let's summarize what we've found here, and let's think about animals in general. . . . I want you to try and extend beyond the toad and frog, and I'll help you if you need it. . . . For instance, what can we say about the characteristics of animals that look a lot alike?
>
> **ADELLA:** . . . They're like . . . mostly the same.
>
> **KIM:** So, how should we write that? Help me out. . . . I'll get us started. [She then wrote, "Animals that look alike . . . " on the chalkboard.]
>
> **LADONNA:** . . . Will have the same characteristics.
>
> **KIM:** Okay. . . . What else? [after writing, "Animals that look alike have similar characteristics," on the chalkboard]
>
> **TONYA:** They also eat the same kind of food.
>
> **KIM:** Good. So, . . . tell me what to write. Animals that look alike. . . .
>
> **NANCY:** And have the same characteristics.
>
> **TONYA:** And have the same characteristics eat the same kind of food.

Kim then wrote the statement on the board and asked the students for additional summarizing statements, which resulted in the following list:

- Animals that look alike have similar characteristics.
- Animals that look alike and have similar characteristics eat the same kind of food.
- Animals that are similar live in similar habitats.

Kim then asked the students for additional examples, such as deer and elk, different kinds of birds, and predators, such as lions and leopards, plus some exceptions to the patterns, and she then closed the lesson.

We can see from this dialogue that students aren't automatically good at making summarizing statements, and you may initially have to prompt extensively, as Kim did in her lesson. With practice, however, students' abilities to summarize quickly develop.

In comparison, Tony Horton's students were older than Kim's, and they had more experience with summarizing information, so Tony didn't have to prompt and guide as much as Kim did.

Using the Integrative Model to Increase Student Motivation

As we discussed each of the phases, we saw how the Integrative Model capitalizes on the motivating effects of involvement, success, challenge, and perceptions of increasing competence. In addition, the model can capitalize on the motivational benefits of cooperation and personalization. For example, Tony had the students work together to gather information that was included in the chart, and research indicates that "students often perform better in groups than when working alone" (Pintrich & Schunk, 2002, p. 184). In addition, when students see the products of their efforts displayed on the chart, they have a greater personal stake in the information, which can increase their intrinsic interest in the topic. For this reason, and particularly with older students, making them responsible for gathering at least some of the information to be placed in the chart is effective for increasing motivation.

Tony further capitalized on the motivational benefits of cooperation when he said, "Now, I want you to work with your partner and find as many patterns as you have evidence for in each of the columns. I want you to work as follows: . . . First write your own response . . . find your own patterns and write them down. . . . Then share them with your partner. . . . Discuss them with each other and be ready to share them with the class. You have 10 minutes." This was an application of "think-pair-share," and other forms of cooperative activities can be used effectively with the model as well.

Modifications of the Integrative Model

As with all the models we discuss in this book, modifications can often increase both the usability and effectiveness of the Integrative Model. In this section we discuss three:

- Using the Integrative Model with young children
- Increasing efficiency by using existing materials
- Developing matrices during class discussions

Using the Integrative Model with Young Children

Modifying the Integrative Model for use with young children primarily involves presenting the information in a visual form. Tony's matrix—in a lesson designed for eighth graders—had the information presented in words. Kim used both words and pictures in her lesson with fourth graders. A primary teacher, or a teacher whose students lack language skills might choose to present the information exclusively in pictures. As an example, consider the information in Figure 7.7.

FIGURE 7.7   Matrix Containing Information about Winter and Summer

Let's examine some dialogue between Gina Davis, a first-grade teacher, and her students discussing the information in the matrix.

> **GINA:**   How are the foods we eat in the summer different from the foods we eat in the winter? . . . Alexandria. (Phase 1)
>
> **ALEXANDRIA:**   Foods with ice in summer.
>
> **KATRINA:**   Hot drinks in winter.
>
> **GINA:**   Why do you think we have hot drinks in the winter? . . . Irvin. (Phase 2)
>
> **IRVIN:**   It's cold outside.
>
> **GINA:**   How do we know it's cold outside? (Asks for evidence)
>
> **IRVIN:**   . . .
>
> **GINA:**   Do you see anything on the chart that tells us that it's cold outside in the winter?
>
> **IRVIN:**   They're wearing coats. (Pointing to the chart)

FIGURE 7.7   Continued

GINA: What else? . . . Monica?

MONICA: No leaves on the trees.

GINA: Suppose we lived in the South, where it's warm all year around. How might the foods we eat in winter be different from what we see on the chart? . . . Kaleb? (Phase 3)

KALEB: Our drinks might not be as hot.

GINA: What have we learned here about our foods? . . . Rudy? (Phase 4)

RUDY: We eat different foods.

GINA: How are they different? . . . Katrina

KATRINA: We eat warm foods when it's cold outside.

GINA: And why do we do that?

KATRINA: Hot foods help keep us warm.

Special things to do and clothing were analyzed and summarized in the same way. As students develop their skills, teachers are able to move away from traditional teacher-student-teacher-student interaction and toward a more teacher-student-student-student discussion, which we illustrated at different points in Kim's and Tony's lessons.

In some cases teachers may choose to develop a matrix together with actual objects or people. For example, a teacher wanting to develop a lesson on community helpers could ask an actual firefighter and a member of the police to come into the class as guests. After these guests visit the classroom, the teacher and students could list information they had learned, which could be used as the basis for the analysis.

Children's Language Abilities.   Language ability is another factor to consider when using the Integrative Model with young children (Kuhn, 1999) because comparisons, causal relationships, and hypothesis are described verbally. An acceptable modification would then be to emphasize Phase 1 more strongly than the other phases because it focuses on observation and comparison. However, as they acquire experience, even young children learn to form explanations and respond to hypothetical questions. Much of the value in using the model is the opportunity it provides for experiences that promote the development of language ability and thinking skills.

Increasing Efficiency by Using Existing Materials

Anyone familiar with classrooms knows that teaching is enormously complex and demanding. Anything that can be done to help reduce the time spent planning new lessons—and still help students meet their learning objectives—is beneficial.

One way to reduce planning time is to use existing materials, which often are organized in ways that allow the phases of the Integrative Model to be applied directly to them. To use this time-saving measure, you must be able to recognize existing materials that can be used to help you reach your objectives. Virtually any chart, graph, or map that contains raw data, and these often appear in textbooks, can be used for analysis with the Integrative Model. Let's look at some examples.

TABLE 7.5   Table of Ionic Radii*

IA	IIA	IIIA	VIA	VIIA
Li^+	Be^{2+}		O^{2-}	F^-
0.60	0.31		1.40	1.36
Na^+	Mg^{2+}	Al^{3+}	S^{2-}	Cl^-
0.95	0.65	0.50	1.84	1.81
K^+	Ca^{2+}	Ga^{3+}	Se^{2-}	Br^-
1.33	0.99	0.62	1.98	1.95
Rb^+	Sr^{2+}	In^{3+}	Te^{2-}	I^-
1.48	1.13	0.81	2.21	2.16
Cs^+	Ba^{2+}	Ti^{3+}		
1.69	1.35	0.95		

*Radii given in angstrom units.

Table 7.5 contains information in a chart taken from a typical chemistry book. A chart such as this is found in the text, and the teacher would need to do nothing more than direct students to the page on which it appears, or scan it into a computer file, make an overhead, and display it.

Then, the teacher could guide the students' analysis based on the chart. Let's see how Trish Gillespie, a chemistry teacher, uses the chart with her students:

Phase 1

TRISH: What kind of pattern do you see in the Group IA ions? . . . Vernon?

VERNON: They get bigger as we move down the column.

CARLOS: They also all have a valence of plus one.

TRISH: How about the other groups? . . . Andrea?

ANDREA: They all get bigger as they move down the columns.

TRISH: How would you compare the radii in each column to each other? . . . Amelia?

AMELIA: They get smaller for the positive ions and then get bigger for the negative ions.

TRISH: What do you mean?

AMELIA: Magnesium (Mg) is smaller than sodium (Na), and aluminum is smaller yet, but sulfur and chlorine are bigger.

Phase 2

TRISH: Why do you suppose magnesium is smaller than sodium? . . . Josh?

JOSH: Magnesium loses two electrons, so its ionic radius will decrease more than sodium's, which loses only one electron.

TRISH: Then, why isn't the ionic radius for chlorine bigger than the radius for sulfur? . . . Brandie?

BRANDIE: Chlorine only adds one electron, so its ionic radius won't increase as much as sulfur's will.

Phase 3

TRISH: Suppose somehow that sulfur was involved in a reaction in which it actually lost electrons rather than gained them. How would its ionic radius be affected? . . . Hajar?

HAJAR: It's ionic radius would maybe be smaller than aluminum's rather than larger.

TRISH: Can we be sure?

HAJAR: No; it may not follow that pattern. We would need more information to be sure.

Phase 4

TRISH: What kinds of generalizations can we make about ionic radii? . . . Mistee?

MISTEE: As elements lose electrons, their ionic radii get smaller and the more electrons they lose the smaller the radii get.

ELLIS: Ionic radii with positive valences tend to be smaller than those with negative valences in the same row.

We have abbreviated this interaction for the sake of clarity; it wouldn't go as smoothly as it appears here, and teachers would likely have to provide a considerable amount of support in the form of prompting to help students recognize the patterns. However, because most of

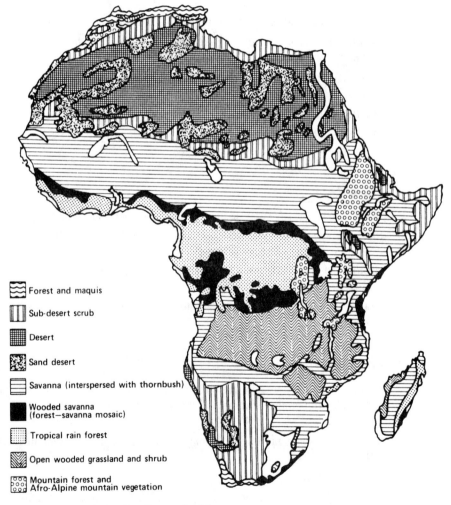

Forest and maquis

Sub-desert scrub

Desert

Sand desert

Savanna (interspersed with thornbush)

Wooded savanna
(forest—savanna mosaic)

Tropical rain forest

Open wooded grassland and shrub

Mountain forest and
Afro-Alpine mountain vegetation

FIGURE 7.8A Vegetation Zones of Africa

the information needed to make the conclusions is available in the chart, students only need some guidance to get them started.

We also see from the dialogue that the chart—which already exists in the text—can be used for a great deal of critical thinking. In fact, a number of patterns, explanations, hypotheses, and generalizations could be added to those previously described. In this case, using the Integrative Model requires *no additional preparation*. The teacher only needs to recognize opportunities to capitalize on already existing data.

As another example, consider the maps in Figures 7.8a and 7.8b. Now look at some interaction based on the maps between Judy Holmquist, a geography teacher, and her students.

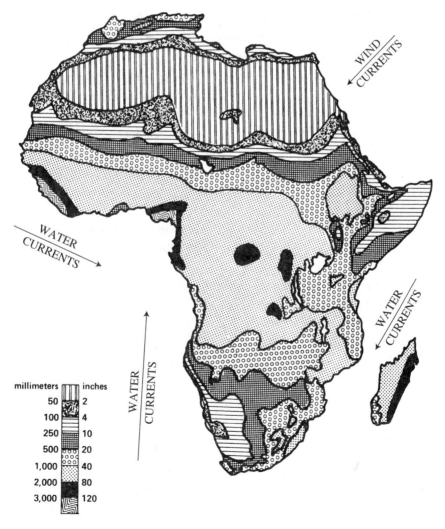

FIGURE 7.8B   Average Annual Precipitation in Africa

Phase 1

JUDY: Look at the northern parts of the two maps. How do they compare? . . . Karen?

KAREN: The northern part of the first one is mostly desert.

JUDY: And the second one?

KAREN: Very little rain, 2 inches a year.

JUDY: How about other parts of the map? . . . Ola?

OLA: There is tropical rainforest around the area near the equator, and there is a lot of rain in that area.

Phase 2

JUDY: Why is much of the northern part of the continent desert? . . . Stephan?

STEPHAN: It gets very little rain.

JUDY: Why do you think the rainfall is so sparse?

STEPHAN: Maybe it has to do with the direction of the wind. The prevailing winds come from huge land areas, so they don't have much rain in them.

JUDY: What else might impact the amount of rain a region gets? What do you see on the map? . . . Lynn?

LYNN: Maybe the direction of the ocean currents has something to do with it.

Phase 3

JUDY: Suppose the winds over northern Africa came primarily from the west. How would the climate of that part of the continent be affected? . . . Mike?

MIKE: Maybe it wouldn't be a desert.

JUDY: Can you look at any part of the map for some evidence that supports that idea?

MIKE: We see that the winds are from the west over the central portion of the continent.

Phase 4

JUDY: What kinds of summary statements can we make based on the map? . . . Katrina?

KATRINA: The ocean currents and wind direction have an important impact on the amount of rain a region gets.

This dialogue only gives us a sample of the possibilities. Much more analysis of the maps could be done, and the process could be expanded by adding a map showing physiographic regions on the continent. The students could then consider altitude, latitude, wind direction, and ocean currents as factors impacting climate.

This can all be done with little preparation; teachers only need to be clear about their objectives and seize on opportunities such as these. As they get used to the process, teachers will recognize more and more opportunities for using the charts, maps, and other instructional aids in their textbooks as a basis for promoting analysis by the students.

Developing Matrices during Class Discussions

Teachers can also use information gathered in class discussions to capture data essentially "on the spot," which can then be used to further analyze the topic being studied. Let's look at Vicki Barnhart, an English teacher, who is involving her students in a discussion of *Romeo and Juliet.*

> **VICKI:** Let's think about some of the things we've found from the play. Let's just list anything you can think of based on your reading. . . . Nicole?
>
> **NICOLE:** The Montagues and Capulets were feuding.
>
> **DAVID:** Escalus, the prince, threatened the Montagues and Capulets with death if they didn't stop feuding.
>
> **LISA:** Some of the people seemed to be sort of hung up on sex.
>
> **VICKI:** Why do you say that? Can you give us an example?
>
> **LISA:** Sampson and Gregory were always fantasizing about women.
>
> **KIRSTEN:** And the nurse and Mercutio seemed to be focused on sex.
>
> **VICKI:** Okay, what else? . . . Lee?
>
> **LEE:** Tybalt killed Mercutio, and then Romeo killed Tybalt.
>
> **BETTY:** Romeo and Juliet killed themselves.
>
> **VICKI:** Let's focus on the characters a little more. What kind of a young man was Romeo? . . .
>
> **MARVIN:** Well, he was actually a kid.
>
> **RITA:** And he was sort of innocent and naïve.

As the students made their comments, Vicki listed them on pieces of chart paper, which she rolled up and stored after the discussion. She also prompted them for additional information, similar to her question, "What kind of a young man was Romeo?" and she added some information of her own about the themes of the play. She then stored the chart paper telling the students that they would return to the information after they had read some additional plays. She then repeated the process with *Hamlet* and *Julius Caesar.*

After the students had read and reported on all three plays, the teacher displayed all the information and began a more extensive analysis of the plays by comparing them to each other. The information appears in Table 7.6.

In this case Vicki used the information students gathered from their reading as the matrix, which reduced her preparation time, and provided a visual record of the plays, which made the students' analysis more effective.

TABLE 7.6   Matrix Comparing Shakespearean Tragedies

Plot	Key Characters	Themes
Romeo and Juliet		
Montagues and Capulets feud	Romeo:	Symbolism of "star-crossed lovers"
Escalus, the prince, threatens Montagues and Capulets with death	romantic love struck	Love amidst hate
Sampson and Gregory fantasize about women	guileless	Innocence amid mature bawdry
The nurse and Mercutio focus on sex	young	Conflicted loyalty to self and family
Romeo and Juliet fall in love	unthinking	
Tybalt kills Mercutio	innocent	
Romeo kills Tybalt	Juliet:	
Juliet takes a potion	romantic	
Romeo kills himself	love struck	
Juliet kills herself	guileless	
Montagues and Capulets end feud	young	
	innocent	
Hamlet		
King Hamlet dies	Hamlet:	Ingenuousness and deceit
Claudius marries Gertrude	sentimental dreamer	Moral ambiguity
Hamlet regrets and resents Claudius's and Gertrude's marriage	witty sensitive	The search for natural justice
Hamlet seeks revenge on Claudius	loyal	Loyalty and revenge
Hamlet mistreats Ophelia	weak	Private and public conflict
Laertes wounds Hamlet in a duel	intelligent	
Hamlet wounds Laertes in a duel	romantic	Internal conflict
Hamlet kills Claudius	indecisive	Courage and cowardliness
Gertrude dies of poison meant for Hamlet	ambitious	
Laertes dies	Claudius:	Purging of evil
Hamlet dies	strong	Restoration of morality
	hypocritical	
	skillfully political	
	deceitful	
	adroit	
Julius Caesar		
Caesar defeats Pompey	Caesar:	Power
Caesar becomes a dictator	great soldier	Ambition
Caesar pardons Brutus	great politician	Jealousy
Caesar pardons Cassius	brilliant scholar	Revenge
Romans fear Caesar's growing power and ambition	arrogant	Idealism
Conspiracy against Caesar develops	ambitious	
Cassius influences Brutus	Brutus:	
Brutus feels he must stop Caesar	quiet	
Brutus kills Caesar	idealistic	
Antony incites citizens	Caesar's friend	
Rome is in chaos	feared Caesar's ambition	
The armies of Brutus and Cassius engage the armies of Antony and Octavius	Cassius: thin	
Cassius is stabbed by his servant and dies	quick-tempered	
Brutus falls on sword and dies	practical	
	grudge against Caesar	

This type of analysis does not have to be the focus of an entire lesson. For example, the illustration with the chemistry chart could be embedded within a unit on atomic structure, and the entire sequence may take only a few minutes. The same could be the case with maps.

As we see, charts, existing charts, and maps can be effectively used as the basis for lessons using the Integrative Model, and graphs and tables can also be sources of data. Also, we see that the Integrative Model is applicable at most grade levels and in many content areas. We hope this discussion has increased your awareness of the possibilities.

Assessing Integrative Model Activities

Measuring student understanding of organized bodies of knowledge is more complex than measuring understanding of single concepts, principles, generalizations, or academic rules. As a result, the assessment process is more demanding when the Integrative Model is used than it would be for lessons involving either the Inductive or Concept Attainment Models. The following are some possibilities. This isn't an exhaustive list; it is designed primarily to stimulate your thinking about the process.

Measuring Content Outcomes

To illustrate measuring content objectives, let's see how Kim might measure her students' understanding of the generalizations they derived in her lesson. Look at the following item.

> Think about the conclusion made about the frog and the toad and their habits. Based on that conclusion, which of the following pairs of animals would likely have the most similar habits?
> a. A deer and a bear
> b. A deer and an elk
> c. A deer and a rabbit
> d. A rabbit and a bear

This item is designed to measure students' abilities to apply the generalization, "Animals with similar characteristics have similar habits," to animals other than toads and frogs.

The item has the potential weakness, however, of measuring students' knowledge of the animals, rather than their understanding of the generalization. For example, if students don't know what an elk is or where it lives, the item would be invalid. To eliminate this possibility the teacher might prepare an item such as the following:

> Look at each of the following descriptions of animals. Then, based on the descriptions, decide which two will have the most similar habits.
>
> > The lemu is a swift-running, four-legged animal. He stands about 4 feet high and weighs more than 200 pounds. He has long legs, hooves, and big horns on his head. The lemu has fairly sharp teeth in the front of his mouth and large, flat ones in the back.

The habax is a muscular, four-legged animal. She has a bulky, strong body covered with thick fur. Her teeth are sharp and two of them are a bit longer than the others. The habax is about 3 feet high and weighs about 280 pounds.

The cradle is a short animal with a long tail. He has four short legs that are attached to the sides of his body. The cradle can move swiftly for a short distance. He can see in almost all directions with his eyes on the top of his head. His teeth are sharp and stick out a little bit even when his mouth is closed.

The viben is a beautiful animal. She stands tall and gracefully on her four slim legs. Her small hooves allow her to move swiftly if necessary. She is about 5 feet tall at the shoulder and weighs more than 300 pounds. She is covered with short, light brown hair all over her body.

In this item the characteristics of the animals are described and students would make their interpretation on the basis of these descriptions, so the need to be familiar with some existing animal is eliminated. Also note that any reference to food or where they live is avoided in the descriptions. If they were included, the validity of the measurement would be reduced because the item is designed to determine students' understanding of the relationship between characteristics and habits, such as where they live and what they eat.

Measuring Critical Thinking

Student thinking can be measured at several levels. At the first level, students can be referred to the chart used in the lesson and asked to form conclusions not developed in class. For instance, referring again to Kim's lesson, consider the following item.

Look again at the chart involving frogs and toads. Based on the chart, which of the following would be the best conclusion?

  a. You would be more likely to be harmed by a frog than by a toad because a frog is poisonous and a toad is not.
  b. A frog would be more likely to survive in a strange place because his habitat is more varied than that of a toad.
  c. A toad would win a race with a frog because he can run faster.
  d. Toads get bigger than frogs because the food they eat is different.

In this item each of the choices but (b) is directly contradicted by information in the chart. An item such as this would be an effective beginning point for helping students learn to critically assess information.

The process can also be advanced by changing the level of sophistication. For example, consider the following item.

Look again at the information in the chart. Based on this information which is the best conclusion?

  a. A frog is more adaptable than is a toad.
  b. A toad's diet is more varied than that of a frog.
  c. A toad would probably win a race with a frog.
  d. You would be in more danger holding a frog than you would be holding a toad.

In this item, the data in the chart support choice (a) more than any of the other choices, but more interpretation is required by students than with the previous item.

As we saw from the illustrations, the first level of measuring critical thinking involves asking students to extend their thinking using familiar data, as was the case with the frogs and the toads. At succeeding levels, the teacher could prepare items similar to the illustrations presented in this section, but students would have less experience with the content. In these cases, students would be presented with a chart not covered in a lesson and would then be asked to form or identify conclusions based on the information.

Now let's look at some sample items based on Tony's matrix with information in it about immigrant groups.

> Look again at the chart. Of the following, the conclusion most supported by the data in the chart is:
>
> a. The Chinese came primarily because of adventure, whereas the Puerto Ricans came because of undesirable conditions at home.
> b. Although the Chinese and Italians came because of agricultural problems at home, the Puerto Ricans came primarily because of population pressures.
> c. All four groups came partially because America seemed to offer more opportunities than their homelands.
> d. All four groups came because of industrial problems in their homelands.

As a final example, consider an item designed to measure students' abilities to identify irrelevant information.

> Look at the chart. Based on the information in it, which of the following is least relevant to the issue of assimilation?
>
> a. The Italians were Catholics, whereas the Chinese were Confucians.
> b. The Italians learned English more quickly than did the Chinese.
> c. The Chinese were found mostly in the western United States.
> d. The second generation of Italians tended to intermarry with other Americans.

Each sample item so far has been written in a multiple-choice format. Short essay formats can also be used. For instance, consider the following item designed to measure students' abilities to assess hypotheses.

> Let's think about some immigrant groups. Consider immigrants to the United States coming from Pakistan, Greece, and Kenya. Based on the information in the chart, which of the three would be likely to assimilate most rapidly, and which would be likely to assimilate least rapidly? Defend your answer based on the information in the chart and your understanding of the immigrant groups.

This item measures several outcomes:

- The students' knowledge of the immigrant groups and their cultures
- Students' abilities to apply generalizations about assimilation to new immigrant groups

- Students' abilities to make and defend an argument with evidence
- The ability to communicate clearly

All these are appropriate outcomes if the teacher has helped students develop these skills and abilities, and if the assessment is consistent with the teacher's learning objectives.

Measuring critical thinking requires careful planning and judgment by the teacher. For instance, if items are based on a chart used in the lesson and the information related to the item has been discussed, it measures knowledge and not thinking. This is appropriate if the teacher's objective is to measure knowledge but not if the objective is to measure critical thinking. It is important that teachers are clear about what they are trying to accomplish.

One solution is to develop items based on content not covered in the lesson. This also requires caution to be sure that all the information needed to form the conclusions is included in the chart and that students understand the chart's content. Otherwise, the item measures students' knowledge of the content or their reading comprehension.

Writing items, such as those presented in this section, is initially demanding and it takes some practice. However, once the items are written, they can be revised when necessary and used over and over. Gradually, teachers can develop an excellent pool of items that not only will measure deep understanding of the content and critical-thinking ability but also can be used to increase learning.

Using Assessment to Increase Learning

We've said repeatedly that effective assessments can be an important tool for increasing learning. This is true for all the models in this book, and because of its complexity, it is particularly true for the Integrative Model. For instance, look again at the item with the hypothetical animals—the lemu, habax, crandle, and viben. A discussion of the item during feedback after a quiz could include not only an examination of the evidence about those that would have the most similar habitats but also a consideration of what those habitats would be. The discussion could also consider the type of food the animals are likely to eat and other instincts, such as how they would protect themselves. Feedback with respect to the item's answer is always essential, but in addition, the item can be used to extend students' understanding. This further demonstrates that assessment is an integral part of the entire teaching–learning process (Bransford et al., 2000).

Summary

The Integrative Model: An Overview

The Integrative Model is designed to help students understand organized bodies of knowledge, topics that combine facts, concepts, generalizations, and the relationships among them. Lessons involve the analysis of data usually presented in a matrix. The data that appear in the matrix can be gathered by the students, the teacher, or both. With the teacher's guidance, the students develop a deep understanding of the content while simultaneously developing their thinking skills.

The Integrative Model: Theoretical Foundations

The Integrative Model is grounded in schema theory, the view that people record information in memory in organized networks of understanding. Teachers using the model attempt to guide students' schema development as they analyze organized bodies of knowledge.

Learning Objectives for the Integrative Model

The Integrative Model is designed to teach organized bodies of knowledge, which are combinations of facts, concepts, generalizations, and the relationships among them.

While developing understanding of organized bodies of knowledge, learners involved in Integrative Model lessons practice critical thinking, specifically finding patterns, generalizing, forming conclusions and hypotheses, and justifying their thinking in each case.

Planning Lessons with the Integrative Model

Planning for lessons using the Integrative Model includes identifying topics, specifying clear learning objectives, and then preparing displays of data to help learners reach the objectives. The data displays commonly exist in the form of matrices, but they can include graphs, maps, and charts in pictorial form.

Implementing Lessons Using the Integrative Model

Integrative Model lessons involve four phases. In the Open-Ended Phase, learners observe, compare, and search for patterns. In the second, the Causal Phase, they offer explanations for the similarities and differences they find. In the third, the Hypothetical Phase, they consider possibilities for different conditions, and in the final phase, Closure and Application, form broad generalizations based on their analysis of the data.

As often as possible, they are asked to justify their thinking by offering data taken from the display of data to defend their conclusions.

Using the Integrative Model to Increase Student Motivation

The Integrative Model capitalizes on the motivating effects of involvement, success, challenge, and, as students abilities to form and document explanations and hypotheses increase, their perceptions of increasing competence and self-efficacy also increase.

In addition, the model is compatible with cooperative activities, which can capitalize on the motivating benefits of cooperation.

Modifications of the Integrative Model

The Integrative Model can be made more effective with young children by designing data displays in pictorial form. Organizing information in this way also increases its effectiveness with students lacking experience with the topic or non-native English speakers.

Charts, graphs, and maps from textbooks also serve as ready-made data displays that can be used for analysis with the Integrative Model, and data to be analyzed can be gathered during class discussions.

Assessing Integrative Model Activities

Learners understanding of the topic and their abilities to think critically can be simultaneously measured by having them make and assess conclusions about information from matrices they've already studied or with unique data displays.

As with all instruction, assessment should be an integral part of the teaching–learning process. When assessments are frequent and thorough and students are provided with detailed feedback about their performance, assessment can be a powerful tool for increasing learning.

IMPORTANT CONCEPTS

Database (p. 218)
Organized bodies of knowledge
  (p. 213)

Schemas (p. 211)
Self-efficacy (p. 228)

EXERCISES

Look at the following dialogue, which is based on the matrix in Table 7.6 containing information about Shakespeare's *Romeo and Juliet, Hamlet,* and *Julius Caesar.* Classify each teacher question as Phase 1, Phase 2, Phase 3, Phase 4, or JT—a question that asks students to justify their thinking.

1. _____ **T:** Look at the "Events" for the three plays. What similarities do you see in the events?
   S: People die or are killed in each of the plays.

2. _____ **T:** What else?
   S: There are conflicts or fighting in each.

3. _____ **T:** For instance?
   S: For *Romeo and Juliet* it says that the Montagues and Capulets were feuding, and it says that Hamlet was seeking revenge on Claudius, and in *Julius Caesar* it says that the armies of Brutus and Cassius fought with the armies of Antony and Octavius.

4. _____ **T:** We know that each of the three plays are tragedies. Suppose one or more of them were comedies instead. Do you think the patterns in the events would be different, and if so, how?
   S: I wouldn't expect to see so much conflict and death.

5. _____ **T:** What makes you say that?
   S: Conflict and death aren't all that happy, so they don't fit with comedies.

6. _____ T: Let's look at the second column. What similarities or differences do you see there?

S: The characters in _Hamlet_ and _Julius Caesar_ appear to be less likable than the characters in _Romeo and Juliet._

7. _____ T: What makes you say that?

S: It says for both Romeo and Juliet that they are innocent and guileless, but in _Hamlet_ it says that Claudius is deceitful and hypocritical and in _Julius Caesar_ it says that Caesar is arrogant and that Cassius is quick-tempered.

8. _____ T: Look at the themes for _Julius Caesar._ We see ambition, jealousy, and revenge as themes, which appear somewhat negative, but we also see idealism as well. Why do you suppose idealism appears as a theme?

S: Brutus was idealistic. He did what he did because he thought it was in the best interests of Rome and the people.

9. _____ T: Let's describe some general patterns in Shakespeare's tragedies if we can.

S: The themes are complex and they vary a lot.

10. _____ T: What else?

S: The characters aren't all good or all bad; they have some characteristics of both.

S: There's a great deal of conflict between people in the plays.

S: The characters all have conflicts within themselves too.

11. _____ T: Can you give us an example of what you mean?

S: Hamlet is described as sentimental and sensitive, and at the same time he's ambitious.

S: Brutus is caught between his feeling of loyalty to Caesar and his fear of Caesar's ambition.

12. Look again at the matrix containing the information about the solar system (Table 7.3). Write a minimum of one question for each of the phases, and provide what would be an acceptable answer to the questions.

Feedback for these exercises begins on page 341.

DISCUSSION QUESTIONS

1. We said that the Inductive Model is designed to teach concepts, generalizations, principles, and academic rules, and the Integrative Model is designed to teach organized bodies of knowledge. Prepare a list of topics that you have taught or you have seen taught in schools and identify which of the two models is more appropriate for each of the topics. Are there topics that are inappropriate for either model? What characteristics of those topics makes them inappropriate?

2. Phase 4 in the Integrative Model is similar to closure for the Inductive and Concept Attainment Models. Explain how it is similar. In what way or ways is it different?

3. We discussed prompting and repetition as questioning skills used with the Inductive Model. How might they be employed with the Integrative Model?

4. The Integrative Model is commonly described as an "inductive" model. What does this mean? How would the procedure for a "deductive" model be different from the procedure for an inductive model?

5. Consider using the Integrative Model in content areas such as art, music, physical education, and technology. Discuss how lessons could be designed to promote critical thinking in those areas.

6. How might data be gathered and displayed in ways other than using matrices, charts, maps, or other written materials? Provide an example in a content area of your choice.

8 Problem-Based Learning Models

In this chapter we examine **problem-based learning models,** *teaching models designed to develop problem-solving skills and self-directed learning.* As the name implies, a specific problem is the focal point for problem-based lessons, during which students design and implement investigations and solutions (Krajcik, Blumenfeld, Marx, & Soloway, 1994). In this chapter we examine problem solving and inquiry, two models in this group. When you have completed your study of this chapter, you should be able to:

- Identify the characteristics of problem-based learning.
- Design problem-solving lessons that include all the characteristics of problem-based learning.
- Design case-based instruction lessons.
- Plan and implement inquiry lessons, including each of the elements of the inquiry process.
- Prepare assessments that validly measure learners' understanding of the problem-based process.

Let's look now at three examples of teachers using problem-based models with their students.

> Candy Armstrong, a third-grade teacher, is beginning a unit on plants in science. As she gives an overview of the unit she holds up several packets of seeds, explaining that the class can plant these to study plant growth. One student raises her hand and asks, "Why don't seeds grow in those packets?" "Good question," Candy replies. "I wonder how we can find that out."
>
> She then divides the students into groups to investigate factors that influence seed germination. Each group is given packets of different kinds of seeds along with

pots, potting soil, fertilizer, and water. Each group is responsible for designing an experiment to answer the germination question, carrying it out, and reporting the results to the class.

Laura Hunter, a middle school math teacher, has had her class studying area in math. One day Laura announces that their classroom is getting new carpeting and enlists the class's assistance in figuring out how much carpet they will need. The task is made more complex by the fact that the classroom is irregularly shaped, with alcoves, corners that aren't square, and areas where linoleum is used. Laura hands out meter sticks and other equipment needed to complete the task and, after the class measures the room, she separates the students into groups and asks each to devise a strategy for finding the amount of carpeting they'll need.

A high school health class has been studying how different diseases are spread. One day, Maria Novelo, their teacher, places the following on an overhead:

Your Mission:

Protect the Islanders from the Muscle- and Mind-Killers

The client is a health officer at a military base on a Pacific island. He knows that many of the people who have lived on the island for a long time suffer from neurological diseases. Many lose control of their muscles and become rigid and paralyzed. Others lose their memories.

What causes this? What action should he take to protect the people?

Your mission is to determine the cause of these problems and report on your findings.

Students use their computers and the Internet to gather data about this problem.

How are these episodes similar? What characteristics do they share, and how do these characteristics contribute to learning? What specific roles do students and teachers play in problem-based learning? We attempt to answer these questions in this chapter as we examine problem solving and inquiry.

Problem-Based Learning: An Overview

Problem-based learning models share three characteristics. First, they begin with a problem or question that serves as the focal point for the students' investigations (Duffy & Cunningham, 1996; Grabinger, 1996). In Candy's lesson the student's question, "Why don't seeds grow in those packets?" provided a focus for the student's inquiry. Laura used the carpet problem to frame her student's investigation, and Maria used the question about neurological diseases as the framework for her lesson.

Second, students assume primary responsibility for investigating the problem (Slavin, Madden, Dolan, & Wasik, 1994), and third, the teacher facilitates the process by guiding the students' efforts and providing support when necessary (Stepien & Gallagher, 1993). As opposed to more content-oriented approaches, such as the Inductive Model or Integrative Model, learning to design and complete investigations is the focus in problem-based learning lessons.

Teachers typically have three goals when they conduct problem-based lessons. First, they want students to learn to systematically investigate a question or problem. Second they want to encourage **self-directed learning,** which is *students' abilities to take control of their learning progress.* Self-directed learning is grounded in metacognition, which we saw in Chapter 2 is the awareness of and control over our learning strategies. Hmelo and Lin (1998) developed a model of self-directed learning, which is shown in Figure 8.1.

When operating within this model students first assess what they know about the problem they are facing. Then, based on this assessment they decide what additional information they need and develop plans to address these deficiencies. As they gather new information, they use it to solve the problem. If the information is sufficient, the problem is solved. If it is not, students devise new learning strategies. The teacher assists in the process by asking questions such as:

What do you already know?
What additional information do you need?
Where can you find this information?

A third, less prominent goal is content acquisition. Much of the content that students learn in problem-based lessons is implicit and incidental to the problem-solving process.

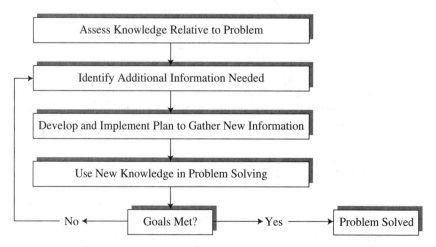

FIGURE 8.1   Model of Self-Directed Learning

Because of this, problem-based strategies are less effective for teaching content than more content-focused models, such as the Inductive Model (Chapter 5), the Integrative Model (Chapter 7), the Direct-Instruction Model (Chapter 9), and the Lecture-Discussion Model (Chapter 10) (Bruning et al., 2004). However, there is some evidence that information gained through problem-based learning is retained longer and transfers better (Duffy & Cunningham, 1996; Sternberg, 1998).

Problem-Based Learning: Theoretical Foundations

Problem-based learning is based on two conceptual and theoretical foundations. One of these is the work of the educational philosopher John Dewey, who emphasized the importance of learning through experience. The second is sociocultural learning theory, a cognitive view of learning that emphasizes student participation in authentic learning activities. Let's examine them.

John Dewey's Pragmatism

John Dewey (1859–1952) is probably the most influential educational philosopher in America. His views about teaching and learning and the place of schools in society had a major impact on educational thinking in the early part of the twentieth century and are still influencing teaching and learning today.

Dewey basically believed that children are socially active learners who learn by exploring their environments (Dewey, 1902, 1916). Schools should take advantage of this natural curiosity by bringing the outside world into the classroom, making it available and accessible for study, which is the reason the term *pragmatism* is associated with Dewey's work (Kauchak & Eggen, 2005).

In studying the natural world, students should be involved in active inquiry (Dewey, 1916), which has the following characteristics:

- Learners are involved in a real-world experience that interests them.
- Within this experience, learners encounter a problem that stimulates thinking.
- In solving the problem, learners acquire information.
- Learners form tentative solutions to the problem.
- Learners test these solutions. The application helps the learners validate their knowledge.

Dewey believed that the knowledge, instead of being inert as that acquired from books and lectures, becomes useful when it is applied to the solution of problems. Dewey's work continues to influence education in the United States and is one framework for—in addition to problem-based learning—strategies such as teaching thematic units and interdisciplinary teaching (Jacobsen, 2003).

Sociocultural Theory

Sociocultural theory is *a cognitive view of learning that emphasizes student participation in communities of learning* (Vygotsky, 1978, 1986). Vygotsky stressed the importance of social interaction in learning, asserting that we learn by exchanging and comparing our ideas with those of others. As learners share ideas, they are active participants in the learning process.

Central to sociocultural theory is the concept of **cognitive apprenticeship,** *an approach to instruction in which students work with an expert to learn both how to perform cognitive tasks and why they perform certain tasks in certain ways* (Lave, 1988, 1990). Complex learning tasks are mastered by students working with someone who is already good at the task. For example, think about the way we learn tasks, such as driving, cooking, or changing a tire. First, we watch someone who is skilled perform the task and then we try to perform it ourselves under the expert's direction. In addition, experts describe their thinking out loud (think-alouds) as they model the process, and they guide the learner (apprentice) through the process with questioning. This is the essence of cognitive apprenticeships.

Students work together to solve problems in learning communities. Social interaction is an essential component of the process, and the students are involved in cognitive apprenticeships as the teacher guides their efforts. This is the foundation of both problem solving and inquiry. Let's turn to them now.

The Problem-Solving Model

Laura Hunter, the middle school math teacher that we saw at the beginning of the chapter begins her problem-solving lesson by explaining that their classroom needs new carpeting and enlisting the assistance of students in finding how much they need. She structures her lesson by displaying the Problem-Solving Model shown in Figure 8.2.

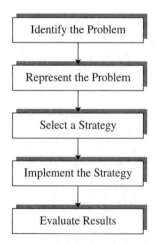

FIGURE 8.2   Problem-Solving Model

"According to our model" Laura continues, "What do we have to do first? Kara?"

"Identify the problem?" Kara answers hesitantly.

"That's right, Kara, the first thing we do is identify the problem. Do we know what our problem is? Janelle?"

"To find out how much carpet we need," Janelle replies.

"Good, Janelle, and, class, what kind of problem is this? When we try to find out how much carpet we need what are we trying to do? . . . Alicia?"

"Umm . . . area?"

"Excellent, Alicia, we're trying to find the area of the room. What problem did we talk about yesterday that is similar to this one? Think! Antonio?"

"Umm. . . . It's kind of like the playground problem where we had to find how many rubber tiles we needed to cover the jungle gym area."

"Does everyone remember that problem? And what were two ways that we used to solve that problem. What was one way, Shalynne?"

"We counted the squares in the box."

"Okay, first we counted the tiles in the box. Then what did we do? What was an easier way to find the area, Lynn?"

"Well, like we measured the outside, uh, the perimeter, and then we multiplied and that told us how many squares that equaled."

"Good, Lynn. We multiplied the length times the width and that gave us the area. So, what do we have to do with our carpet problem? . . . Any idea? I'll give you a hint. Do we have any squares to count?" Pausing for a few moments Laura scans the room to see if the class is with her. Then she continues.

"Not really, so what do we have to do next? Look up here" [pointing to the overhead]. "It says 'Represent the problem.' How did we represent our problem yesterday? What did we have to do Tamara?"

"We drew a picture of it on graph paper."

"Good, Tamara. Class, do you think that might work here?"

Responding to the students' nods, Laura then divides the class into groups to measure different parts of the room. As the different groups complete their task, they report back to Laura who records the information for the next day.

At the beginning of class the next day, Laura passes out a diagram of the room with the dimensions her students have given her. After she does this she turns on the overhead and begins, "Class, we're still working on the carpet problem. We decided it was an area problem and we measured the room to get this diagram. What's our next step? . . . Geno?"

"I think it's select a strategy."

"Good, Geno. I'd like us to get into our regular groups, and each group is responsible for not only selecting a strategy but also carrying out the strategy. That means use it to find the area. I'll be around to answer questions.

"Any questions? . . . Let's do that now."

Laura's class then separates into groups of four, and each group uses the diagram and calculations to work on the problem.

As students attempt to solve the problem, they come up with two basic strategies. One is to find the area of the whole room and subtract the linoleum and odd-shaped corners; the other is to find the area of an interior rectangle in the middle of the carpeted area and then add extra, irregularly shaped carpeted areas. As the groups complete their tasks, Laura reconvenes the class.

"Okay, let's look back up here at our diagram," Laura directs after the class again reassembles. "In the select-your-strategies part, there were several different strategies that I saw as I was walking around. Raise your hand and tell me what one of the strategies was. . . . Yashoda."

"We measured everything first, and then we subtracted where the linoleum was. We figured out . . . we multiplied the perimeter. And then we subtracted the places where the linoleum was."

"Okay, when you multiplied the perimeter, what did you get?"

"1,440 square feet."

"Okay, that's called the . . . ?"

"Area," several students respond.

"Okay, raise your hand if your team tried that strategy," Laura directs.

Students from several groups raise their hands.

"Raise your hand if you tried a different strategy."

Several more students raise their hands.

"Matt, explain what your team did," Laura directs.

"We had a different strategy. We took the middle . . . we squared it off, like covering up this," Matt responds, pointing to the diagram, "and then we multiplied the two sides, then we got the area of the middle part of the carpet, and then we put the other pieces together. . . . We added these others."

"Okay, I'm going to put 'found inside measurements and added other areas.' Is that okay?" Laura asks.

"Uh-huh," Matt answers.

Laura then asks each group to put their findings on the board and her class discusses differences and discrepancies between the different groups' answers.

"Well, are you comfortable with the fact that some groups got slightly different answers?"

Several students say "No," whereas a few said, "Yes."

"If you were the person purchasing the carpet, would you be comfortable with that? . . ." Waiting for an answer, Laura pauses.

"If you were the person *estimating,* would you be comfortable with that?" Laura continues.

Most of the class say they wouldn't be comfortable if they were the person purchasing the carpet, but offer that they would be if they were merely estimating.

"If we were going to redo this tomorrow, what could we do to be more accurate? . . . Talk to your team for 2 minutes," Laura then directs.

The students talk to their teammates and offer some suggestions, such as remeasuring the room, rechecking to see if the strategy made sense, and even asking the janitor about the dimensions of the room. (Adapted from Eggen & Kauchak, 2004)

A **problem** exists when we're in *a state that differs from a desired end state and there is some uncertainty about reaching the end state* (Bransford & Stein, 1984). In other words, "a problem occurs when the problem solver has a goal but lacks an obvious way to reach the goal" (Mayer & Wittrock, 1996). For Laura's students the goal was finding the carpeted area of their classroom, and a way to reach the goal wasn't obvious. Defining a problem in this broad way is beneficial because it recognizes how pervasive problem solving is in our daily lives, and it allows people to apply the model outlined in Figure 8.2 to a variety of problems (Bruning et al., 2004).

Planning for Problem-Solving Lessons

Problem-solving lessons have both short- and long-term learning objectives. In the short term, the teacher wants students to solve the problem successfully and understand the content, such as finding the area of irregularly shaped geometric figures in Laura's lesson.

The long-term objectives are for students to understand the process of problem solving and develop as self-directed learners. They develop these abilities by acquiring experience with problem solving.

The planning process for lessons using the Problem-Solving Model involves three steps, which are illustrated in Figure 8.3 and discussed in the sections that follow.

Identifying Problems and Learning Objectives. The first step in planning for problem solving is obviously identifying the problem the students are to examine and the learning objectives associated with the problem. As we saw in Chapter 2, using concrete and personalized examples can increase motivation, and Laura capitalized on these factors by using the students' classroom as the focus for the problem.

When selecting problems, teachers must also consider the students' prior knowledge. If, for example, Laura's students didn't understand area and perimeter and the differences between the two, they wouldn't have been able to develop strategies to attack the problem.

Solving the specific problem and learning problem-solving skills will always be the learning objectives when the Problem-Solving Model is used. As a result, planning learning objectives requires fewer decisions when this model is used than would be required for a more content-focused model, such as the Inductive or Integrative Models.

Accessing Materials. If problem-solving lessons are to go smoothly, students must both understand what they're trying to accomplish, and they must have access to the materials needed to solve the problem. For instance, Laura attempted to help the students understand

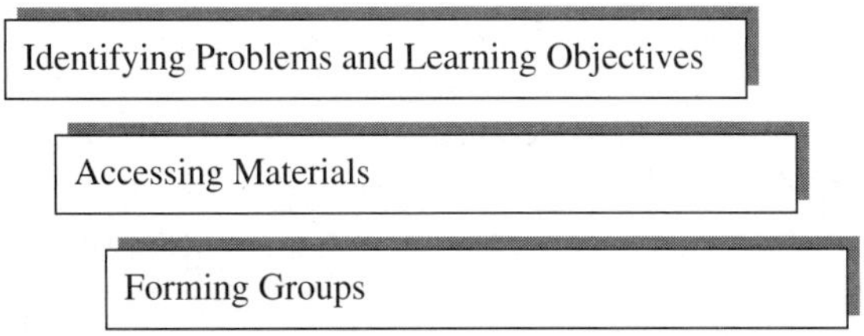

Identifying Problems and Learning Objectives

Accessing Materials

Forming Groups

FIGURE 8.3   Planning Lessons with the Problem-Solving Model

the steps in problem solving by displaying information on the overhead, which provided focus and structure for the lesson.

Laura also provided the meter sticks and other equipment needed to investigate the problem. This seems simple and obvious, but many lessons lose momentum because students must share equipment, so they have time on their hands, during which they can go off task and even become disruptive.

Forming Groups. We discussed grouping and the characteristics of effective groups in Chapter 4. In problem-solving activities, as with any form of cooperative learning, groups should be mixed with respect to ability, gender, and ethnicity. Then, as part of the cognitive apprenticeship process, the teacher carefully monitors the groups to ensure as much as possible that all members of the group are involved and taking a responsible part in the activity. Pairs or groups of three are generally the most effective. In larger groups two or three people often do most of the work while others merely watch passively. However, small groups require more equipment, so you must judge the size of the groups you assign.

Implementing Problem-Solving Lessons

Effective problem-solving lessons exist on two levels, which correspond to the major learning objectives of this model. The first is for students to solve a specific problem. This process is guided with the process of cognitive apprenticeship. At the second level, we want our students to understand the process of problem solving and become self-directed learners. To accomplish these goals, the Problem-Solving Model occurs in five phases, which are summarized with their learning and motivation functions in Table 8.1.

Phase 1: Identify the Problem. The process begins with the students identifying the problem, which is intended to attract attention and present the students with a challenge. At first glance, this appears straightforward, but, in fact, it is one of the most difficult aspects of problem solving. This results from several factors, such as lack of background knowledge, lack of experience in defining problems, and the tendency to rush to a problem too soon (Bruning et al., 2004).

An additional issue is the fact that most of students' experiences are with **well-defined problems,** which are *problems with only one correct solution and a certain method for finding the solution* (Bruning et al., 2004), whereas most of what we encounter in the real world are **ill-defined problems,** which are *problems with more than one acceptable solution, an ambiguous goal, and no generally agreed-on strategy for reaching a solution* (Dunkle, Schraw, & Bendixon, 1995; Mayer & Wittrock, 1996).

Further, problem solving is personal and contextual (Mayer & Wittrock, 1996). For example, finding the amount of carpeting necessary for the room is well defined for experienced problem solvers; they simply determine the total area of the floor and subtract the areas covered by linoleum. Only one answer exists, and the solution is straightforward. For Laura's students, however, the problem was ill defined. Their understanding of the goal wasn't clear, some of them were uncertain about the difference between area and perimeter, and they used different strategies to reach the goal. Evidence of their uncertainty is indicated in their answers, which varied widely.

TABLE 8.1 Learning and Motivation Functions for the Phases
of the Problem-Solving Model

Phase	Learning and Motivation Function
Phase 1: Identify the problem The teacher and students collaborate to identify the problem	■ Attracts attention ■ Capitalizes on the motivating effects of curiosity and challenge
Phase 2: Represent the problem Students use drawings and analogies to think about the problem	■ Activates background knowledge ■ Reduces the load on working memory
Phase 3: Select a strategy Students select the best strategy for solving the problem	■ Develops metacognition ■ Begins schema production
Phase 4: Implement the strategy The strategy is implemented using data from the problem	■ Promotes involvement ■ Promotes perceptions of competence
Phase 5: Evaluate results Students analyze results to see if their solution makes sense	■ Facilitates transfer ■ Advances schema production

The only realistic solution is to provide students with a great deal of practice in problem solving. We saw in Chapter 2 that learning and development depend on learners experiences, and this principle is nowhere more evident than in problem solving. The more experiences students have with problem solving, the better they get at it.

Phase 2: Represent the Problem. Phase 2 is intended to activate students' background knowledge, and, as they use drawings or analogies to represent the problem, the load on their working memories is reduced. Teaching students how to represent problems provides them with a tool to bridge the conceptual gap between defining a problem and selecting a strategy. Students can be overwhelmed in this phase, and strategies such as drawing a sketch or listing what is known and what is unknown can often help. Laura did this when she had her students measure the room and report their findings. This not only provided students with firsthand experience with the problem but also resulted in a diagram prepared by Laura that they could use when they selected a strategy.

Phase 3: Select a Strategy. In this phase, students are assisted in choosing an appropriate strategy to solve the problem. A common difficulty at this point is the tendency for students to select the first strategy that comes to mind without thinking about alternatives. This may or may not give them the correct answer, but, more importantly, it can lead to a superficial understanding of the problem, which can reduce the likelihood of transfer to other problem solutions.

Teachers can encourage students to be more reflective at this stage of problem solving by having them practice with **heuristics,** which are *general, widely applicable problem-solving strategies* (Mayer, 1996). Two of the most widely applicable heuristics are means–end analysis and drawing analogies. When we use means–end analysis, we identify our ultimate goal and then work backward in substeps. For example, Laura could have used this strategy by encouraging her students to identify the ultimate goal (finding the area of the carpeted part of the room) and then working backward to subgoals, such as finding the area of the whole room, finding the area of the portions without carpet, and then subtracting the two.

Drawing analogies is a second valuable heuristic. When using it, we ask questions such as, "What is this problem like?" or "What other problems have we solved that are similar?" Laura did this when she compared the classroom problem to finding the area of the playground. By thinking of the problem in terms of squares, Laura activated students' background knowledge and provided a concrete frame of reference from which to think.

Phase 4: Implement the Strategy.   If the previous steps are effectively completed, implementing the strategy is a natural extension of them. Although this stage should flow smoothly from the other three, sometimes it doesn't, and then you can provide scaffolding with questions that guide the students through the process. Sometimes students get so close to a problem, they fail to see the logical next step, and it may take no more than encouraging the students to step away from the immediate problem, think about what they're doing, and then look back at their data.

Phase 5: Evaluate Results.   In this, the final phase, teachers ask students to judge the validity of their solutions. A major issue in this phase is the tendency of students to accept the answers they've found, even if they don't make sense. This occurred in Laura's class when several students were satisfied with discrepant answers.

Let's look at another example.

> One boy, quite a good student, was working on the problem, "If you have six jugs, and you want to put two thirds of a pint of lemonade into each jug, how much lemonade will you need?" His answer was eighteen pints. I [Holt] said, "How much in each jug?" "Two thirds of a pint." I said, "Is that more or less than a pint?" "Less." I said, "How many jugs are there?" "Six." I said, "But that doesn't make any sense." He shrugged his shoulders and said, "Well, that's the way the system worked out." (Holt, 1964, p. 18)

This kind of thinking is common. Without considerable prompting and support from teachers, students rarely step back and ask themselves if a solution is sensible in the real world.

Resolving this dilemma might involve a series of teacher questions that require the students to think about their answers. Some possible questions in the case of the lemonade problem could be:

Will we have more or less than six pints of lemonade altogether?
[Less]

How do we know we will have less than six pints?
[We have six jugs and we put less than a pint in each one.]

If the students answer "more" in response to the first question, we need to return to the problem and ask questions, such as, "How many jugs to we have altogether?" and "Are we putting more or less than a pint in each jug?" With enough practice responding to questions such as these, students will gradually develop the inclination to consider whether their answers makes sense. Arguably, this is the most important phase of the entire problem-solving process.

This concludes our discussion of implementing the Problem-Solving Model. In the next section we examine inquiry, a second problem-based learning model.

Inquiry

Inquiry is both a teaching strategy and a way of examining how the world works. Inquiry involves asking questions and making systematic attempts to answer them. The processes involved in the Inquiry Model may seem, at first glance, somewhat remote, but, in fact, they are very much a part of our everyday lives. For example, conclusions suggesting that smoking, high cholesterol foods, and lack of exercise are detrimental to health are all results of inquiry processes. These conclusions originate in studies that ask questions such as, "Why does one group of people have a higher incidence of heart disease than another?" The research studies cited throughout this text are all based on inquiry, which attempted to answer questions such as, "Why do students in one kind of classroom learn more than those in another?"

Involving students in inquiry is an effective way to help them learn to think critically, develop as self-directed learners, and acquire a deep understanding of specific topics. The Inquiry Model is designed to give students practice with critical thinking while focusing on questions about how the world operates.

The Inquiry Model is similar to the Problem-Solving Model in that both are types of problem-based learning. It differs in its approach. Instead of focusing on the solution to a specific problem, such as the carpeted area of their classroom in Laura Hunter's lesson, it asks a question and then gathers information in an attempt to answer it. Let's look at an example from a life-skills class.

Karen Hill, a life-skills teacher, is beginning a unit on baking. As she discusses baking procedures at the beginning of a lesson on bread making, she begins kneading some dough at the front of the room, while she provides an overview of the bread-making process.

Part way through her explanation, José raises his hand and asks, "Why do you have to knead it so long?"

"That's a good question, José. Why do you think so? . . . Anyone?"

". . . Maybe it's to mix the ingredients together well," Jill offers.

Ed adds, "Yeah. If the stuff isn't mixed well enough, it might affect the way the yeast works. If you don't knead the dough enough, it won't rise."

Seizing on the chance to expand her objectives for the lesson, Karen writes the students' ideas on the board, and then says, "What Jill and Ed have offered is a tentative answer to José's question. When people offer tentative answers to questions or tentative solutions to problems, we call them *hypotheses*. They suggested that thorough mixing affects the yeast, which affects how well the bread will rise.

"Now," she continues, "does anybody have an idea of how we could check to see if this idea is correct?"

"... We could take a batch of dough and separate it into about ... maybe ... three parts ... and then knead them for different amounts of time," Chris suggests tentatively after thinking for several seconds.

"Excellent thinking, Chris," Karen smiles. "What do you say, everyone? ... Should we try it?"

Amid, "Sure," "Okay," "Why not?" and a number of nods at a unique idea, Karen continues, "How long should we knead each? Our book recommends about 10 minutes."

"... How about 5 minutes for one, 10 for the second one, and 15 for the third," Naomi suggests.

"Then we'll bake them all the same way," Natasha adds.

"To be sure that we're getting a good test of the *hypothesis*," Karen continues, "what else do we need to take into account?"

"... Well, we'd have to use the same dough," Jeremy suggests, "and we'd have to have the same amount of dough wouldn't we?"

"And we'd have to knead them the same way," Andrea adds, beginning to see the point in the activity. "If people's kneading was different, it could affect the mixing, and that's what we're trying to test isn't it?"

"Very good thinking, Andrea," Karen nods. "Anything else, anyone?"

"... I think one more thing," Mandy adds. "You said that the ovens in here are different. We need to bake them all in the same oven, won't we, or won't that throw us off?"

"That's excellent thinking, everyone. ... Now, let's think back for a minute. ... We talked about having the same dough, kneading them all the same way, and baking them all in the same oven. ... Why do we want to do that?"

"... Well, if we ... like ... had different dough, and they came out different ... we wouldn't know if it was the amount of time we kneaded them or if it was the dough, would we?" Talitha offers uncertainly.

"Excellent thinking, Talitha. What we're doing is keeping each of those constant, and the only thing we're changing is the amount of time we knead each piece of dough. When we keep them the same, we say that we've controlled those variables. ... So let's review for a minute and write down the variables we're controlling. ... Someone?"

"... Type of dough," Adam offers.

"Good, ... what else?"

"The way we do the kneading."

"Excellent. ... What else?"

"The oven."

"Good, everyone. That's excellent thinking."

Her students then follow their suggestions, separating a piece of dough into three equal parts, carefully kneading each piece in the same way, but kneading one part for 5 minutes, the second for 10, and the third for 15, and baking them in the same oven. Then they check to see if there are differences in the way the different pieces look. Next they discuss their results and relate them to the hypothesis. They find that the pieces kneaded for 10 and 15 minutes each were the same height but were taller than the piece kneaded for only 5 minutes. There is a considerable amount of uncertainty about what those results actually mean, but they tentatively conclude that bread must be kneaded an adequate amount, but kneading beyond that amount doesn't matter.

"Before our time is all up, I'd like us to think a little about what we did and why. How did we get started on this problem? Who remembers? Anthony?"

"José asked why we had to knead the bread so long?"

"Good memory, Anthony. That's correct. Our inquiry started with a question. Then we had some tentative ideas or guesses. Who remembers what we call these tentative ideas? Shanda?"

"Hypotheses?"

"Fine, Shanda. Hypotheses are our best guesses about how the world works. And why was it important to cook all of the loaves . . ."

Just then the bell rings and Karen dismisses her class with a smile and, "Let's stop here. Good work, class. See you tomorrow."

Inquiry is *the process of asking questions and systematically answering them based on facts and observations.* Inquiry is central to scientific thinking and can play a powerful role in our everyday lives. The **Inquiry Model** is *a problem-based teaching strategy designed to involve students in the inquiry process.* When using the model, teachers' overriding goal is for students to learn how to systematically design investigations, such as the one we saw in Karen's class. The Inquiry Model is implemented in five phases:

Phase 1: Identify a question
Phase 2: Generate hypotheses
Phase 3: Gather data
Phase 4: Assess hypotheses
Phase 5: Generalize

When teachers use the Inquiry Model, they guide students through these steps as the students attempt to answer the question. For example, a *question* was identified in Karen's class when José asked about the length of time the dough had to be kneaded. This was followed by Jill's and Ed's *hypothesis* suggesting that kneading affected the way the dough would rise. The class then discussed ways of designing their investigation to ensure that they got valid information. Then, they baked the pieces and observed the results. This was all part of *data gathering.* Finally, students discussed the results and concluded that an optimum amount of kneading was necessary, which partially supported their hypothesis. This discussion and their tentative conclusion were all part of the *assessing hypothesis* phase. They then formed a tentative *generalization* relating the optimum amount of kneading to the amount the bread rose. Finally, Karen encouraged them to think about the inquiry process, making them more aware of the steps they had been following. Let's turn now to the process of planning for inquiry activities.

Planning for Inquiry Activities

Planning for inquiry lessons differs from planning for more content-oriented models, such as the Inductive Model or the Integrative Model, in at least three ways. First, because inquiry problems, hypotheses, and the data used to test them ideally come from students, teachers must design the lesson so they can provide enough guidance to keep the process moving but not so much that they intrude on students' initiatives and experiences. Keeping this balance requires sensitivity and professional judgment. Second, most inquiry lessons are ongoing, that is, they often require more than a single class period, so you should consider this factor when planning. Finally, inquiry lessons are designed to help students develop inquiry skills and self-directed learning, and planning should focus on those objectives.

The planning process for lessons using the Inquiry Model exists in four steps, which are illustrated in Figure 8.4 and discussed in the sections that follow.

Identifying Inquiry Topics and Learning Objectives. Identifying learning objectives when the Inquiry Model is used is relatively simple. Solving the specific inquiry problem and learning the critical-thinking skills associated with inquiry will always be the learning objectives. However, although content objectives are secondary in importance compared to developing inquiry skills, inquiry lessons can also help students find cause-and-effect relationships, which are important content objectives. In Karen's lesson, for example, students looked for a relationship between the amount of time bread was kneaded and the amount it rose. Most content areas have topics that contain cause-and-effect relationships. Some examples are outlined in Table 8.2.

After conducting inquiry investigations, students can construct generalizations, such as, "The higher the level of aerobic exercise the greater the cardiovascular fitness," or "Many wars are the result of economic problems." These occur in the last phase of inquiry

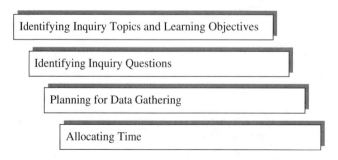

FIGURE 8.4   Planning Lessons with the Inquiry Model

TABLE 8.2   Cause-and-Effect Relationships in Different Content Areas

Content Area	Cause-and-Effect Relationship
English	How do authors' lives influence the content of their writing?
Science	How is plant growth affected by amount of sunlight, water, and type of soil?
Social studies	How do economics and religion influence the causes of wars?
Health	How do different types of exercise influence cardiovascular fitness?

lessons after students analyze data and assess hypotheses. As students' thinking improves they develop their abilities to assess these generalizations based on facts and observations. This illustrates the close relationship between content and critical thinking.

Although students are the primary investigators in an inquiry lesson, a teacher must carefully plan in order to facilitate the process. To conduct inquiry lessons, students need a focal problem or question to examine, and they must have access to data that allow investigation of the problem. Both of these require careful planning.

Identifying Inquiry Questions.   Having identified a topic or content area that can be investigated, the next task is to prepare an inquiry question. For instance, a question in the English example could be, "What factors in Poe's life may have impacted the style of his writing?" In the science class a question could be, "What factors affect plant growth?" Ideally, these problems grow spontaneously out of class discussions, as occurred in Karen's lesson, but they often have to be planned by the teacher in advance.

Preplanning can assist the teacher in guiding a class toward inquiry problems. For example, as students discuss different American authors, the teacher could introduce facts about one or two authors' lives. As these authors' works are discussed, the teacher could then raise a question, such as, "What impact do you think authors' lives in general have on their work?" Study of additional authors, their works, and their lives could then serve as the data-gathering phase for the inquiry problem.

As another example, a science teacher could embed an inquiry lesson on plant germination in a larger unit on plant growth. As the unit develops, the teacher could relate the investigation of plant germination, characteristics of different plants, plant growth and the environment, and plant nutrition.

Planning for Data Gathering.   Once you have planned the inquiry problem, you must consider how students will gather information to be used in assessing their hypotheses. Although suggestions for data-gathering procedures should ideally come from students, you often need to guide the process. Table 8.3 presents several examples of questions and potential data-gathering procedures.

Primary and Secondary Data Sources.   Learning to distinguish between primary and secondary sources of data can be an important learning objective, particularly for older students. **Primary data sources** are *individuals' direct observations of the events being studied.* Karen's students' observations of the baked bread, the observations of a pendulum

TABLE 8.3   **Questions and Procedures for Gathering Data**

Questions	Possible Data Sources
How are authors' works related to their personal lives? (English)	Author biographies and samples of their works
How is the road system in a city related to the city's traffic patterns? (Social studies)	Observations of traffic flow at different times of the day, city traffic reports
How is the type of shingle related to its durability? (Industrial technology)	Shingles subjected to different kinds of wear
What factors impact the growth rate of cities? (Social studies)	Geographical information, census data, and historical events
What factors influence the frequency of a simple pendulum? (Science/math)	Pendulums of different weights and lengths

swinging under different conditions, or interviews with people are primary sources. **Secondary data sources** are *other individuals' interpretations of primary sources.* Textbooks, encyclopedias, biographies, and other reference books are all secondary sources.

Because secondary sources have been screened through the perceptions and potential biases of others, primary sources are preferred. In some cases, such as Karen's lesson, using primary sources is possible. As an alternative, Karen could have referred the class to reference books on baking, but then the students would have had less opportunity to learn how to form hypotheses, control variables, and analyze data. In other cases, such as in a lesson on authors and their works, using primary sources is not possible and secondary sources are necessary. Also, an analysis of secondary sources for potential bias can, in itself, be a valuable learning experience.

Allocating Time.   Because inquiry lessons usually take more than a single class period, you should consider how the lesson will be integrated with other activities. For example, an English teacher initially might pose the question about authors' lives and their works. Discussion would then result in one or more hypotheses, for example, "Authors' personal lifestyles are reflected in their works" or "Authors' works reflect their personal beliefs and needs." Teams of students could then be assigned to gather personal information about different authors and report this information back to the class. As students complete their assignments, class time could be spent in discussing some other aspect of the curriculum, such as writing or even grammar. As students report, the class would revisit the problem, discuss the hypotheses, and form tentative conclusions about their validity.

Having determined how students will be guided into identifying problems, how data will be gathered, and how the lesson will be integrated with the rest of the curriculum, you are ready to implement the lesson.

Implementing Inquiry Lessons

To help students solve a specific inquiry problem and acquire the critical-thinking skills needed for the inquiry process, implementing inquiry lessons occurs in five phases. Because the Inquiry and Problem-Solving Models are both types of problem-based learning, their learning and motivation functions are similar. They are outlined in Table 8.4 and discussed in the sections that follow.

Phase 1: Identify a Question. An inquiry investigation begins when a question that is intended to attract attention and provide a challenge for the students is identified. As we saw in Karen's lesson, the question can grow naturally out of a class discussion or, as we said in our discussion of planning, you can think about problems in advance and guide the students into identifying the question.

To ensure that the question is clear, you should write it on the board or display it on an overhead and check to be sure that students understand concepts in it. Asking students to explain the question in their own words or relate it to prior discussions can help determine whether the students clearly understand it.

Phase 2: Generate Hypotheses. Once a question has been clarified, the class is ready to try to answer it. In providing a tentative answer, students are involved in the process of

TABLE 8.4 Learning and Motivation Functions for the Inquiry Model

Phase	Learning and Motivation Function
Phase 1: Identify question A question or problem is identified that provides the focal point for student investigation	■ Attracts attention ■ Capitalizes on the motivating effects of curiosity and challenge
Phase 2: Generate hypotheses Students generate hypotheses that attempt to answer the question	■ Activates background knowledge ■ Begins schema production
Phase 3: Gather data Students gather data related to the hypotheses	■ Develops metacognition ■ Promotes involvement
Phase 4: Assess hypotheses Students assess the validity of the hypotheses based on the data gathered	■ Promotes perceptions of competence ■ Achieves equilibrium
Phase 5: Generalize Students generalize based on their assessment of the hypotheses	■ Facilitates transfer ■ Advances schema production

hypothesizing. A **hypothesis** is *a tentative answer to a question or solution to a problem that can be verified with data.* A hypothesis can be considered a tentative generalization, and for young children it can be presented as a "hunch" or "educated guess."

Generating hypotheses activates the students' background knowledge and begins the process of schema production as they search their long-term memories for possible links or answers to the question. To facilitate the process you may ask students to brainstorm possible hypotheses. Initially, all ideas should be accepted and listed. Later, students can be asked to determine if each is relevant to the question or problem.

After students have developed a list of hypotheses, they should be prioritized for the purposes of investigation. For example, a science class investigating the problem, "What factors determine the frequency of a simple pendulum?" might suggest the following hypotheses:

> "The shorter the pendulum the greater the frequency."
> "The heavier the weight the greater the frequency."
> "The greater the initial angle, the greater the frequency."

While gathering data, students need to be clear as to which hypothesis they are investigating in order to know which variables they must control and how they will structure their investigation. After investigating the first, they can then move to the second, and then the third, but this must be done systematically. Once hypotheses have been stated and prioritized, the class is ready to gather data.

Phase 3: Gather Data.   Hypotheses guide the data-gathering process. The data-gathering process promotes metacognition as the students think about their strategies for gathering information. This phase also promotes high levels of student involvement as they gather their data.

The complexity of this process depends on the question they're attempting to answer. For example, in the investigation of plant growth, students could plant bean seeds, systematically vary growing conditions, and measure germination time and growth rate. To investigate the first hypothesis in the pendulum problem, students would systematically vary the pendulum length, keeping the weight and angle constant, and measure the number of swings in a specified amount of time for each length. To investigate the second hypothesis, they would systematically vary the weight and keep the length and angle constant, and for the third hypothesis, they would vary the angle keeping the length and weight constant.

For the lesson comparing authors' lives to their works, gathering data would be more complex, so this is a problem that would require developmentally advanced learners. They would use a variety of sources, such as the Internet, libraries that have biographical information about authors, and other sources that provide insight into the authors' lives. Then, they would have to carefully study the authors' works. In this case the teacher might have to provide considerable assistance.

Although they are demanding, these experiences help students develop skills far beyond the inquiry question. For example, they would learn Internet and library research skills, how to critically assess secondary sources, how to decide what information was important and what should be ignored, and they would develop tolerance for ambiguity when information in different sources is inconsistent. These are valuable experiences for all students.

TABLE 8.5   Data Gathered for the Pendulum Problem

Weight: two large paper clips
Time: 15 seconds
Angle: 45°

Length	Average Number of Swings for Three Trials
30 cm	12
40 cm	11
50 cm	10
60 cm	9
70 cm	8.5
80 cm	8
90 cm	7.5
100 cm	7

Displaying Data.   Organizing and presenting data is a major task for students during this phase. Initially, students will struggle with their abilities to display information clearly, but their skills will improve with practice.

Tables, matrices, or graphs are all effective ways to organize data. Table 8.5 shows a display of data gathered in the pendulum problem.

Teacher questioning helps students think analytically about what they're doing. For instance, we see that the students made three trials for each length and averaged the number of swings. The teacher could ask them to consider what they might do if two of the trials were identical and a third was quite different (suggesting experimenter error in the third trial), or why they chose a 15-second time trial, two paper clips, a 45° angle, and variations in length of 10 centimeters (probably arbitrary). The teacher might also ask if varying the length by the same amount (10 centimeters in this case) each time is necessary. Students could also be asked what improvements might be made in their data-gathering techniques. All of these questions encourage students to become more thoughtful about what they're doing, which is an important goal of inquiry activities.

In the lesson on authors and their works, the data might be displayed in a matrix similar to those we saw in Chapter 7 when we discussed the Integrative Model. An outline of the matrix might appear as follows:

Author	Personal Characteristics	Experiences	Samples from Works
Poe			
Faulkner			
Hemingway			
Fitzgerald			

As with the pendulum problem, a discussion of why certain information was included, and other information ignored, and why the matrix was organized the way it was helps students become metacognitive about the process. This process is valuable because it helps students understand the kinds of decisions journalists, historians, and scientists make when they are involved in inquiry activities in the real world.

Phase 4: Assess Hypotheses.   In this phase of the lesson, students are responsible for assessing their hypotheses on the basis of the data. This analysis is facilitated by the organization done earlier. For example, a casual glance at Table 8.5 comparing lengths of pendulums to the number of swings indicates that frequency decreases as length increases. Assessment of the other hypotheses in the case of the pendulum problem and in the case of plant growth can be facilitated with questioning.

In other instances, such as the problem with authors, the process will be more complicated. Clear and distinct patterns, such as the relationship between frequency and length of a pendulum, won't exist. Trends that do exist may be much more complex and subtle. Discovering that the data are inconsistent is, in itself, a valuable experience for students. Little in life is clear and unambiguous, and the more experience students have in dealing with ambiguity, which requires tentative rather than dogmatic conclusions, the better prepared they are for the real world. Analyzing and discussing the data as they relate to hypotheses may be the most valuable part of the inquiry process.

The process of assessing hypotheses can be rewarding because making decisions about the extent to which a hypothesis is valid promotes perceptions of competence and helps students achieve a sense of equilibrium. Concluding that a hypothesis is valid and providing data that support the conclusion can be an almost heady experience for a learner. This motivating function is one of the most important in the activity.

Phase 5: Generalize.   Content closure occurs in an inquiry lesson when students tentatively generalize about the results on the basis of the data. Generalizing promotes transfer and helps advance the process of schema production as the students mentally organize their understanding of the problem and its results. For example, in investigating the relationship between the frequency of a pendulum and its weight, the data indicate that weight does not impact the frequency. Students would reject the hypothesis, "The heavier the weight the greater the frequency," and would conclude, "The weight of a pendulum doesn't affect its frequency." Because the data are consistent, generalizing would be straightforward. This generalization could then be related to other scientific principles, such as "Falling objects accelerate at the same rate regardless of weight," which further advances the process of schema production.

In other cases, such as the problem with authors and their works, patterns in the data may be less apparent, accepting or rejecting the hypothesis may be less certain, and generalizing may be more tentative. In fact, generalizing may then lead to additional questions, setting the stage for new inquiry problems. This process occurs continually in science and the world at large. In developing the ability to generalize tentatively, students learn an important lesson about life. They begin to realize that the tidy, structured answers we all strive for often do not exist. Over time, they develop tolerance for complexity and ambiguity, which can help them understand and cope with the complexities of life.

This stage also provides opportunities to reflect on the process, so it is hoped students will be able to transfer the process to other classroom activities and to their daily lives, which is its own form of generalizing. Karen initiated this part of the activity when she said, "Before our time is all up, I'd like us to think a little about what we did and why." In response to this request, students identified how inquiry began and how hypotheses guided the inquiry process. By talking about inquiry processes in the context of lessons, teachers make abstract ideas become real and help students see how inquiry works in real life.

Spontaneous Inquiry

So far we have focused on carefully planned and systematic approaches to inquiry lessons. However, one of the greatest benefits of studying inquiry is an increased ability to capitalize on opportunities to conduct inquiry activities that occur spontaneously. This was the case in Karen's lesson. A question was posed by a student in the class, and she capitalized on the opportunity when it occurred.

Opportunities abound if teachers are aware of the possibilities. They commonly occur when students encounter situations that have no clear answers. For instance, consider the following simple science demonstration, in which students see an inverted cup of water covered by a card, and the card stays on the cup, preventing the water from spilling as shown in Figure 8.5. When presented to elementary students, they asked questions such as:

"What if the cup wasn't completely full?"
"What if the cup only had a small amount of water in it?"
"What if the cup was turned 90°?"
"What if we used a liquid other than water, such as milk or a soft drink?"

Each of these questions could be a starting point for an inquiry minilesson. Students could be asked to conjecture answers (hypotheses) to the questions and explain why they believed what they did. Then each could be systematically investigated. For example, the class could vary the amount of water to see if this variable makes a difference (it doesn't). Finding that the card stayed against the cup in each case, the class would eliminate

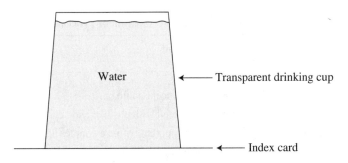

FIGURE 8.5   Simple Science Demonstration

"amount of water" as a variable causing the card to stay against the cup and would then pursue other variables.

Spontaneous inquiry lessons have at least four positive features. First, motivation is high because the students see that the investigation results directly from a question they (rather than the teacher) ask. Second, students often suggest creative ways to investigate a problem, and a classroom climate of teamwork and cooperation develops.

Third, the spirit of inquiry is effectively captured, yet very little time and effort are required from teachers. They merely have to guide students toward thinking about questions and how they could be investigated. And finally, spontaneous inquiry lessons allow students to see how the process directly relates to the subjects they study. The distinction between teacher-generated and student-generated questions is subtle but powerful. When students only pursue questions generated by others, they learn that knowledge is external rather than personal and functional. Content is often presented as preestablished truths to be memorized and repeated. Students are seldom asked to investigate or generate their own problems (Goodlad, 1984). The use of spontaneously generated student investigations can do much to help them understand how knowledge is produced and the relationship of that knowledge to themselves.

Inquiry and Concept Attainment

When we discussed the Concept Attainment Model in Chapter 6, we suggested that it also could be used to help students understand the process of inquiry and the scientific method. Based on the positive and negative examples, students hypothesize possible labels for the concept, and these hypotheses are analyzed based on additional examples. The examples and nonexamples then serve as the data used to analyze the hypotheses. Table 8.6 further outlines the comparisons between Inquiry and Concept Attainment activities.

The Concept Attainment Model can be an effective tool to introduce students to the processes of inquiry. Because it doesn't take a great deal of time to complete a lesson; students can see the entire process unfold in one lesson. However, it doesn't give students a totally valid picture of the process of inquiry because the teacher provides all the data—the examples and nonexamples. But it can be an effective way to introduce students to inquiry before they conduct "full-blown" inquiry investigations on their own.

TABLE 8.6   A Comparison of Inquiry and Concept Attainment Processes

Inquiry	Concept Attainment
1. Problem or question	What is the concept?
2. Hypothesizing	The name of the concept could be. . . .
3. Data gathering	Students are presented with positive and negative examples.
4. Analysis of hypotheses	Hypotheses not supported by the examples are rejected.
5. Generalizing	The concept is defined.

Using Technology to Support Problem-Based Learning

The success of problem-based learning depends on its ability to present realistic, motivating problems to learners. One goal in using this model is to bring the real world into the classroom for investigation, analysis, and reflection. Technology has the unique potential to accomplish this goal.

A number of technology supported problem-based learning programs exist. A simple Internet search provides outlines and reviews of many of these programs. One of the most widely known has been created by the Cognition and Technology Group at Vanderbilt (1992). Let's take a look at it.

Problem-Based Learning in Math: The Jasper Series

The mathematics curriculum includes a great many opportunities to promote problem solving, and reform efforts in math have targeted problem solving as an important vehicle to promote mathematical thinking (National Council of Teachers of Mathematics, 1989, 2000). However, many of the problems we give our students fail to capture the realism and complexity of real world math applications (Williams, Bareiss, & Reiser, 1996). To remedy this problem researchers have developed a video-based math series called *The Adventures of Jasper Woodbury*. Each problem begins with a 15- to 20-minute video scenario that reveals a challenge to the characters in the segment. The following condensed version gives us an idea of the types of problems found in these scenarios.

> Jasper has just purchased a new boat and is planning to drive it home. The boat consumes 5 gallons of fuel per hour and travels at 8 miles per hour. The gas tank holds 12 gallons of gas. The boat is currently located at mile marker 156. Jasper's home dock is at mile marker 132. There are 2 gas stations on the way home. One is at mile marker 140.3 and the other is at mile marker 133. They charge $1.19 and $1.25 per gallon, respectively. They don't take credit cards. Jasper started the day with $20. He bought 5 gallons of gas at $1.25 per gallon (not including a discount of 4 cents per gallon for paying cash) and paid $8.25 for repairs to his boat. It's 2:35. Sundown is at 7:52. Can Jasper make it home before sunset without running out of fuel? (Williams et al., 1996, p. 2)

The problem is purposefully left open ended to provide students with opportunities to solve it by first defining the problem, identifying subgoals (e.g., finding out how much money he has left), separating relevant from irrelevant data (e.g., is the time of day important?), and computing the final solution. Students are given an extended period of time, such as 3 to 4 days, to work on each problem, and they must solve it before they can see how the characters in the video solved the challenge. For additional information about the Jasper series, consult: http://peabody.vanderbilt.edu/projects/funded/jasper/preview/AdvJW.html.

The Jasper series is not the only technology-supported problem-based learning program. It is merely one of the most widely known. You should investigate other programs to determine which ones are most consistent with your learning objectives.

Increasing Motivation with Problem-Based Learning

Problem-based learning models can be effective for increasing student motivation because they capitalize on the motivating effects of curiosity, challenge, authentic tasks, involvement, and autonomy, all factors that increase students' motivation to learn (Pintrich & Schunk, 2002).

Researchers have found that the ability to arouse curiosity and present a sense of challenge are two characteristics of intrinsically motivating tasks (Lepper & Hodell, 1989). They arouse people's innate desires to understand how the world works. Because a problem, the solution of which isn't immediately obvious, is at the core of all problem-based learning activities, they capitalize on the capacity to increase intrinsic motivation.

Problem-based learning activities also capitalize on the motivating effects of **authentic tasks,** which are *learning activities that require understanding that can be used in the world outside the classroom* (Eggen & Kauchak, 2004). Authentic tasks are motivating because they help students see how abstract concepts and processes relate to the real world. Laura Hunter used an authentic task—finding the area of carpet in a classroom—to motivate her students to learn about area. Effective teachers make real-world linkages such as this all the time in their instruction.

In addition, problem-based activities capitalize on the motivating effects of involvement and autonomy. Student autonomy increases when students have choices in deciding what to do and how to do it, and involvement is high when students conduct their investigations (Pintrich & Schunk, 2002). Classrooms are often one-dimensional learning environments where student choice is minimized and everyone does the same thing at the same time. Teachers can increase student autonomy and involvement during problem-based activities by giving students choices about factors such as:

- What problem to pursue
- What hypotheses to generate
- How to investigate the problem
- How to report results

In addition to increasing motivation, student autonomy and involvement also increase students' abilities to direct their own learning, the essence of self-regulation.

Assessing Learning in Problem-Based Activities

As with all instructional models, the form that assessment takes should be determined by the learning objectives of the lesson. Problem-based learning has three interrelated learning objectives:

- To increase understanding of the processes involved in problem-based learning
- To develop students' self-directed learning
- To acquire content

The assessment of content acquisition in this model is similar to processes involved in other models, so we won't discuss this aspect of assessment further. Instead, we focus our discussion on how to assess the first two objectives of problem-based activities.

Alternate Assessment and Problem-Based Learning

Traditional assessments, most commonly in the form of objective tests, have a long history of criticism, with critics arguing that they are artificial and removed from the realities of learning (Kilbane & Herbert, 1998; Reckase, 1997). In response to these criticisms, the use of alternate assessments, or "direct examination of student performance on significant tasks that are relevant to life outside of school" (Worthen, 1993, p. 445) has been advocated. The term **alternate assessments** is used to describe *assessments that directly measure student performance through "real life" tasks* (Shepard, 2001; Wiggins, 1996/97). (Although the increasing emphasis on standards, high-stakes tests, and accountability has tempered alternative assessment efforts, it remains a viable tool for measuring learning objectives that are hard to measure with traditional tests.) Alternative assessments can be effective for measuring students' abilities to:

- Design a problem-solving strategy
- Conduct an inquiry investigation
- Generate hypotheses
- Gather data relevant to a hypothesis
- Work collaboratively in a group to solve a problem-based case

In addition to products, such as the answer or solution to a problem, teachers using alternate assessments are also interested in the processes students use to prepare the products, which emphasize higher-order thinking (Gronlund, 2003). Insights into these processes provide teachers with opportunities to assess student knowledge and correct student misconceptions (Parke & Lane, 1996/97). For example, a structured interview might be used to gain insights into students' thinking as they design science experiments.

Performance Assessments. **Performance assessments** are *tasks in which students demonstrate their levels of competence or knowledge or skill by carrying out an activity or creating a product* (Airasian, 2000; Valencia, Hiebert, & Afflerback, 1994). They attempt to increase validity by placing students in as lifelike a situation as possible and evaluating their performance against preset criteria. The term *performance assessment* originated in content areas such as science, where students were required to demonstrate a skill in a hands-on situation rather than recognizing a correct answer on a teacher-made or standardized test (Hiebert & Raphael, 1996).

For example, a middle school science teacher noticed that her students were having difficulties applying scientific principles to real-world events. In an attempt to improve this ability, every Friday she focused on everyday problems, for example, why an ice cube floated in one cup of clear liquid but sank in another, that students had to solve in groups and discuss as a class. On subsequent Fridays, she presented other problems. For example, she put two clear liquids of the same volume on a beam balance, and students had to explain why the beam became unbalanced (a beam balance measures mass). As they worked, she circulated among them, taking notes that would be used for assessment and feedback (Stiggins, 2001). Performance assessments allow teachers to assess their students' work while engaging in realistic problem-solving situations.

Systematic Observation.   Another way to evaluate the processes students use when they are engaged in problem-based learning is through systematic observation. **Systematic observations** require *teachers to specify criteria for the processes they are assessing and take notes based on the criteria.* A **rubric** is *a scoring scale that describes the criteria for grading* (Stiggins, 2001). For example, a science teacher attempting to teach her students the steps involved in scientific problem solving might use the following rubric.

1. States problem or question
2. States hypotheses
3. Identifies independent, dependent, and controlled variables
4. Describes the way data will be gathered
5. Orders and displays data
6. Evaluates hypotheses based on the data

By gathering data systematically while students are engaged in authentic learning activities, teachers are in better positions to assess students' strengths and weaknesses, and provide feedback.

Checklists.   Checklists are another way for teachers to make their assessments of students' thinking more systematic. **Checklists** are *written descriptions of dimensions that must be present in an acceptable performance.* When checklists are used, the desired performances are typically "checked off" rather than described in notes, as they would be with systematic observation. For example, the science teacher wanting to assess scientific problem-solving ability might use a checklist such as the one shown in Figure 8.6.

FIGURE 8.6   Checklist to Evaluate Scientific Problem Solving

DIRECTIONS: Place a check in the blank for each step performed.

_____   **1.** Writes problem at the top of the report.

_____   **2.** States hypothesis(es).

_____   **3.** Specifies values for controlled variables.

_____   **4.** Makes at least two measurements of each value of the dependent variable.

_____   **5.** Presents data in a chart.

_____   **6.** Draws conclusions consistent with the data in the chart.

Notes could be added to each dimension to combine the best of checklists and systematic observations.

Rating Scales. One of the limitations of checklists is they require a yes/no response from the evaluator and don't take into account degrees of success. Rating scales address this problem. **Rating scales** are *written descriptions of evaluative dimensions of an acceptable performance and scales of values on which each dimension is rated.* Rating scales, such as the one shown in Figure 8.7, can be used to evaluate the processes students use during problem solving or inquiry.

Rating scales can be designed to provide even more information to students by providing anchors for each of the numerical values. For example, how does one know whether "States problem or question clearly and accurately" warrants a rating of 3 or 4? To provide better feedback, definitions of values, such as the following, could be included.

Rating = 4

Problem is stated in clear, complete, and observable language; communicates clearly with reader; indicates understanding of content by specifying significance and importance of problem; provides a clear basis for hypothesizing solution.

Anchors such as these help teachers assess more systematically and also provide students with better quality feedback about their performances.

Group versus Individual Assessment. Throughout the text we have encouraged teachers to use student interaction as a learning tool. However, groupwork presents special challenges in the area of assessment. Research shows that group composition during collaborative group assessment can significantly influence both the process and the quality of the products (Webb, Neber, Chizhik, & Sugrue, 1998). As expected, high-ability students tend to increase performance of the group, whereas low-ability students tend to depress performance. Assessing a group's performance is problematic not only because it

FIGURE 8.7 Rating Scale for Evaluating Experimental Technique

DIRECTIONS: Rate each of the following items by circling 4 for an excellent performance, 3 for a good performance, 2 for fair, 1 for poor, and 0 for nonexistent.

4 3 2 1 0   **1.** States problem or question clearly and accurately.

4 3 2 1 0   **2.** States hypothesis that clearly answers the question.

4 3 2 1 0   **3.** Controls variables.

4 3 2 1 0   **4.** Uses appropriate data-gathering procedures.

4 3 2 1 0   **5.** Displays gathered data accurately and clearly.

4 3 2 1 0   **6.** Draws appropriate conclusions.

provides a potentially distorted picture of individual performance but also because it fails to provide helpful and informative corrective feedback that specific individuals can use to improve their performance.

This suggests that teachers should combine both group and individual assessments in evaluating problem-based learning. Group-based assessments provide the teacher with information about how well students and groups collaboratively work together. Individual assessments provide the teacher with information about individual student growth and progress.

Using Cases to Assess Student Understanding in Inquiry Lessons

Inquiry lessons provide unique assessment challenges to teachers. One of the most important goals of assessment in inquiry lessons is determining whether students can form hypotheses and relate data to explanations. Case studies provide one way of accomplishing this assessment goal. When case studies are used, students are given a problem and are asked to provide relevant hypotheses, data-gathering questions, and observations or data from the problem itself. As an example, consider the following item.

> For the following situation, develop a hypothesis for Joe's behavior, write two data-gathering questions that could be used to test this hypothesis, and list three observations that can be made from reading the passage.
>
> Two boys had been good friends throughout their childhood. One day the boys were diving from a tree into a swimming hole. As Lionel crawled out to the end of the tree branch and prepared to dive, Joe shook the branch and Lionel fell to the ground, suffering a permanent injury to his hip. Why did this happen?
>
> a. Hypothesis:
> b. Data-gathering questions:
> c. Observations:
>
> Following are potential responses to the questions.
>
> a. Hypothesis: Joe was jealous of Lionel's athletic ability.
> b. Data-gathering questions:
>   1. Is Joe the smaller of the two boys?
>   2. Are Lionel and Joe on an athletic team together?
> c. Observations:
>   1. The boys were good friends.
>   2. The boys went swimming together.
>   3. Joe shook the branch.

(This problem was adapted from John Knowles's novel, *A Separate Peace*.)

An alternate way of measuring students' inquiry skills is to provide them with the script from an inquiry session together with a possible explanation and ask them to determine the relationship of data to that explanation. As an example of this format, consider the following example based on a social studies problem concerning the unequal growth of two cities.

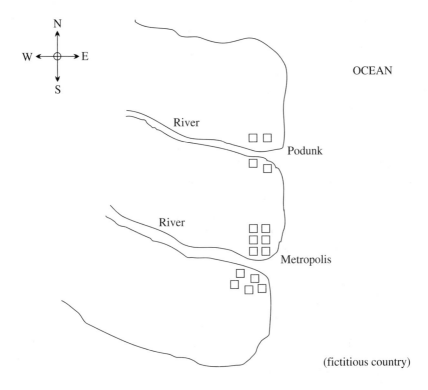

(fictitious country)

Both cities are on the coast and exist at the mouth of rivers. However, Metropolis is large and a busy transportation center, whereas Podunk is small and insignificant. The following is a proposed explanation for these differences in size and significance:

> Although both Podunk and Metropolis are on the coast and are at the mouths of rivers, the entrance to Podunk's harbor is quite small, and the prevailing winds and tricky currents made entrance dangerous in the early years when sailing ships were used. Further, a coast range of mountains isolated Podunk by land but became foothills by the time they reached Metropolis, leaving it freely accessible to overland shipping.

The following data were gathered. By each statement write S for support, NS for not support, or U for unrelated if the data respectively support the explanation, do not support the explanation, or aren't related to the explanation.

  a. The current along the coast runs from north to south.
  b. Metropolis's harbor is larger than Podunk's.
  c. Metropolis and Podunk are more than 100 miles apart.
  d. Approximately the same number of ships ran aground near Metropolis as did near Podunk in the sailing days.

    e. The river near Metropolis is capable of carrying heavier ships than is the river near Podunk.

    f. The mountains around Podunk are more rugged than the mountains around Metropolis.

    g. Both Metropolis and Podunk are in the meteorological belt of the prevailing westerly winds.

    h. The local winds are more variable around Podunk than they are around Metropolis.

As an additional measure of students' inquiry skills, the teacher may also choose to expand the measurement process by asking students to rewrite the explanation (hypothesis) in keeping with additional data.

With any format for measuring critical-thinking skills, you should be certain that the situation used in the measurement is one not previously presented. Otherwise, students may be merely recalling previous information.

As with all teaching and learning, assessment is an essential part of the process. Creating high-quality assessments and providing detailed feedback are essential for promoting as much learning as possible.

Summary

Problem-Based Learning: An Overview

Problem-based learning models begin with a problem or question: students assume primary responsibility for investigating the problem, and the teacher facilitates the process by guiding the students' efforts and providing support. When conducting problem-based learning activities, teachers want students to learn to systematically investigate a problem, learn to take control of their learning progress, and acquire a deep understanding of a specific topic. The first two goals are most important in problem-based learning activities.

Problem-Based Learning: Theoretical Foundations

Problem-based learning models are designed to teach students how to pursue problems in a systematic fashion, develop as independent learners, and acquire content in the process. The models in this group are based on John Dewey's views of meaningful learning as well as sociocultural views of how language and interaction facilitate learning. In addition, each of the models in this group begins with a problem and asks students to solve the problem using different strategies.

The Problem-Solving Model

The Problem-Solving Model has five sequential phases. In the first, students identify the problem, differentiating relevant from irrelevant information. In the second phase, students represent the problem, which helps them conceptualize different relationships within the problem. This leads to selecting a strategy, the third step, which leads naturally to the next, carrying out the strategy. In the final two phases of the model, students evaluate results and analyze the process.

Inquiry

Inquiry is a process of systematically answering questions based on evidence. The Inquiry Model begins with a question about a causal relationship. Tentative solutions or answers (hypotheses) to the question are offered, and data are then gathered, which allows an assessment of these solutions and answers. Then the hypotheses are assessed based on the available data, and generalizations are made about the conclusions. Finally, students are asked to reflect about their cognitive processes during inquiry.

Using Technology to Support Problem-Based Learning

Technology provides opportunities for teachers to bring aspects of the real world into the classroom for analysis and study. The Jasper Series presents students with a number of realistic, complex problems to solve. A number of technology-supported problem-based learning programs exist, and an Internet search provides access to these programs.

Increasing Motivation with Problem-Based Learning

Problem-based learning activities capitalize on the motivating effects of curiosity and challenge, authentic tasks, and involvement and autonomy. Beginning activities with a problem promote curiosity and challenge, authentic tasks link abstract content to the real world, and autonomy and involvement exist as the activities are conducted.

Assessing Learning in Problem-Based Activities

Alternate assessments are especially valuable in evaluating problem-based learning because they provide teachers with ways of assessing process outcomes. Performance assessments, systematic observation, checklists, and rating scales provide both teachers and students with informative feedback about learning progress.

Case studies provide an additional way to assess learning in inquiry lessons. By providing students with inquiry-based cases, teachers can assess the different component processes in inquiry.

IMPORTANT CONCEPTS

Alternate assessments (p. 273)
Authentic tasks (p. 272)
Checklists (p. 274)
Cognitive apprenticeship (p. 252)
Heuristics (p. 258)
Hypothesis (p. 266)
Ill-defined problems (p. 256)
Inquiry (p. 261)

Inquiry Model (p. 261)
Performance assessments
  (p. 273)
Primary data sources (p. 263)
Problem (p. 254)
Problem-based learning models
  (p. 248)
Rating scales (p. 275)

Rubric (p. 274)
Secondary data sources (p. 264)
Self-directed learning (p. 250)
Sociocultural theory (p. 251)
Systematic observation (p. 274)
Well-defined problems (p. 256)

E X E R C I S E S

1. Examine the following teaching episode and identify where these problem-solving steps occur.
   a. Identifying the problem
   b. Representing the problem
   c. Selecting a strategy
   d. Carrying out the strategy
   e. Evaluating results
   f. Analyzing the process

   The stray dog has been seen around the school for several days, and children would feed it scraps of food left over from their lunches. The situation comes to a head one cold, rainy day when the dog walks into Sherry Myers's fourth-grade social studies class.
   "Can we keep him for a pet?"
   "Can he be our class mascot?"
   After the class settles down, Sherry and the students talk about alternatives, with the dog curled up quietly in a corner of the room. The class concludes that he is a stray because he has no tags. After determining that the school cannot become a permanent home for the dog, the class considers the following alternatives: Find the original owner; find a new owner; seek outside help.
   The Humane Society and Animal Control Division are mentioned, but students are not quite sure who they are.
   In the next few days, a temporary home is found for the dog, but the problem of strays and unwanted animals is still a topic of interest to the class. To aid students, the teacher draws a diagram on the board showing the various facets of the problem. To research the problem, the class divides up into groups of four or five, each group targeting a different dimension of the problem. One group focuses on the general topic of pets in America. Another does research on the Humane Society, using printed information from the organization as a major source. A third group attacks the problem from a government perspective and arranges to have a speaker from the County Animal Control Division come and visit. Sherry assists by coordinating the various groups and helping them in their group tasks. After several weeks, the different groups report back to the class; the class then analyzes the recommendations in a whole-class discussion. Out of this discussion students decide to launch a public information campaign about the plight and problem of unwanted and stray pets. Afterward, Sherry encourages them to talk about what they have done and evaluate their actions.

2. Examine the following objectives and describe a problem that would allow the objective to be met using an inquiry activity.
   a. A music teacher wants students to understand the reasons why some sounds are considered music and others are considered noise.
   b. A teacher of literature wants to study the nature of social traditions and has chosen the story "The Lottery" as a vehicle for study.
   c. A social studies teacher wants students to know factors affecting the decision to drop the first atomic bomb on Hiroshima.
   d. A social studies teacher wants students to understand the factors involved in the astounding victory of Truman over Dewey in 1948.

    e. A science teacher wants students to understand that objects will float on a fluid if they are less dense than the fluid.

    f. An art teacher wants students to understand the factors that affect the price of a commercial painting.

3. Read the following teaching episode, which describes a teacher using the Inquiry Model, and answer the questions that follow.

Renee Stanley is beginning a unit on the newspaper in her high school journalism class. She wants students to understand factors that shape the form that newspapers take and the role that newspapers play in the total context of journalism. She begins her lesson saying, "Class, today we are going to begin our unit on the newspaper. As an introductory activity, I'd like us to take a look at some newspapers that I've saved from the past week and see what we can discover." With that she places newspapers from each day of the previous week on a table in front of the class and puts a little sign on each indicating the day of the week.

    "Class, what do you notice about these newspapers? Jill?"

    "The ones toward the end of the week are fatter than the ones toward the beginning."

    "Okay, anything else, Todd?"

    "Sunday looks to be the fattest and seems to have the most color photographs."

    "Does everyone agree? Any other observations, Mary?"

    "There seem to be more inserts in Wednesday's and Thursday's papers."

    "Those are all good observations, class. Now I'd like us to go one step farther with one of those, which is the size of the newspaper. I'd like us to investigate factors that influence the size and composition of our daily newspaper."

    Saying this, she then proceeds to write the following on the board: "What factors influence the size and composition of the daily newspaper?"

    She continues, "Any ideas, class? How about you, Rob? Do you have a hypothesis?"

    "It might be feature articles, such as things to do on the weekend or travel stuff. Maybe that's what makes some days fatter than others."

    "Okay, let's put that on the board under hypotheses. Any other ideas, Sally?"

    "It could also be advertising. People have more time to shop for things on the weekend."

    "All right, let's put advertising up there, too. Any others, Dave?"

    "Another factor could also be sports. There are more sports events on weekends, so that might be one reason why Sunday's is so fat."

    "That's a good idea, too. Let's stop there in terms of working on hypotheses, and let's spend a moment trying to figure out how we could gather some data related to our hypotheses. Any ideas, Susan?"

    "I'm not sure if this will work, but we could count the number of pages that have these different topics on them."

    "Interesting idea. Jim, did you have a comment?"

    "What about pages that have more than one thing on it? What would we do there?"

    The class continues to discuss the procedures they will use to analyze the newspapers and finally arrive at the following table.

National and international news, local news
No. of pages

> Features
> Sports
> Advertising
> Percentage
> Percentage of total

> Renee then assigns students to seven groups with each group responsible for analyzing a newspaper from a given day of the week. As each group completes its task, it puts its information in the form of a table on the board to share with others. When all the groups are finished, Renee continues.
> "Well, class, what do we have here? That sure is an awful lot of data. To make our job a little bit easier, I think we ought to analyze the data systematically. Let's take our hypotheses one by one and see what we find out. Can we look at the 'features' hypothesis first? What patterns do you see? Jackie?"
> "It looks like in terms of pages there are the most feature articles on Sunday."
> "Does everyone agree? Why do you think we see that pattern, Sam?"
> "I think it's because people have more leisure time on Sunday to read feature stuff."
> "Everyone agree? Joe, did you have a comment?"
> "But look at the percentage column for features on Sunday. It's no higher than any of the others. I can't figure that out."
> "Any ideas, class? I see that the bell is going to ring in a few minutes. Let's save the information on the board and continue our discussion tomorrow, beginning with Joe's comment."

Answer the following questions based on the information in the scenario.

a. Was Renee's inquiry lesson spontaneous or preplanned?

b. Were the data sources that students used to investigate their problem primary or secondary? Explain.

c. Identify in the teaching lesson where each of these phases occurred.
   1. Question identification
   2. Hypothesis generation
   3. Data gathering
   4. Assessment of hypotheses
   5. Generalizing

4. David Smith wants to measure his students' inquiry process skills, so he prepares a case study for students. The case study is composed of (a) a problem, (b) hypotheses suggested as explanations for the problem, and (c) data gathered to test the hypotheses. He then prepares several questions for his students. The case study appears as follows:

> There is a country that is shaped as it appears on the accompanying map. This country is unusual in that most of the population lives on the eastern coast. Why did this unequal distribution of population occur?

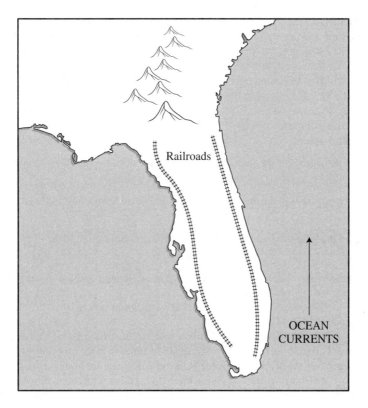

The following hypotheses were included with the case study.

1. There are more natural seaports on the east coast, which promotes shipping to that area, thus leading to a buildup in population.
2. A mountain range on the west coast prevents the area from being developed.
3. A railroad extends from the country to the north along the east coast, promoting immigration and commerce and leading to a buildup in the population in the east.

The data relating to the problem are as follows:

1. The number of seaports on the east and west coasts are approximately the same.
2. The country is flat throughout its area.
3. The climate conditions in all parts of the country are similar.
4. The ocean currents along the east coast run from south to north.
5. Railroads run north and south in the country on both coasts.
6. The first railroad was built on the east coast.
7. A mountain range runs from north to south in the country above the country in question, about 200 miles in from the coast.

David then prepares the following three questions. Your task as a reader is to analyze each question and determine if each is appropriate for measuring the inquiry process abilities of David's students.

a. Which of the following factors influence the location of cities?
   1. Rail line
   2. Currents
   3. Mountains
   4. Harbors

b. On the basis of the data, decide which of the three hypotheses can be accepted and which must be rejected, and explain the basis for the decision.

c. On the basis of the data, revise the hypotheses to form a final explanation for the problem.

5. Read the following anecdote and answer the questions that follow.

Two teachers, Susan and Bill, are sitting in the lounge one day discussing an incident between two other teachers.

"I've never seen Joan flare up that way," Susan says to Bill. "Why do you suppose she jumped all over Mary that way?"

"I don't know for sure," Bill responds. "But I think she's having some trouble at home. I notice that she's edgy when she first comes in in the morning but settles down as the day goes on. Also, she made some snide remark about her husband yesterday morning."

"Yes, I heard that too," Susan nods. "But I think it was all in fun. Also, she commented only last week how happy she was and how well things were going both at home and at school. I really don't think her home life would cause her to jump on Mary that way."

Joe was also in the lounge, saw the incident, and has been listening to Susan and Bill talking. "I think," he says, "that she's simply exhausted and her nerves are on edge. She's taking two classes at the university in addition to teaching, she's the annual and school paper advisor, and now that it's spring she's trying to help with the girls' tennis team. It's just too much."

"That's probably it," Susan agrees.

"She commented that she's averaged 5 hours of sleep since she started with the coaching. That's been three weeks, and she's probably exhausted."

"Also, her husband sells," Bill adds, "and they do an awful lot of entertaining of prospective buyers."

a. Identify the inquiry question in the anecdote.

b. Identify two hypotheses that were offered to answer the question.

c. Identify at least four comments in the anecdote that could be called items of data.

d. For each item of data, identify to which hypothesis it relates, and indicate whether it supports the hypothesis or detracts from it.

Feedback for these exercises begins on page 341.

DISCUSSION QUESTIONS

1. What are two areas of the curriculum that are well suited to problem-based learning activities? What are two areas of the curriculum in which it is difficult to implement problem-based learning activities? Explain the differences between the content areas.

2. Are problem-based learning activities more effectively taught at the beginning or end of a unit? Why?

3. From a developmental perspective, what would be an optimal sequence for introducing the Inquiry Model; Case-Based Problem Solving; and Concept Attainment I, II, and III?

4. What are the advantages and disadvantages of asking students to *independently* pursue a research topic using the Inquiry Model? If you did this, what would have to precede individual inquiry?

5. List as many primary data sources as you can in your area of the curriculum. Do the same with secondary data sources. How could these be used in problem-based learning? Compare your answers with others in your class.

CHAPTER

9 The Direct-Instruction Model

The Direct-Instruction Model is a widely applicable strategy that can be used to teach both concepts and skills. Also called *explicit instruction* (Pearson & Dole, 1987), this model derives from hundreds of studies that attempted to identify links between teacher actions and student learning (Brophy & Good, 1986; Rosenshine & Stevens, 1986). When you have completed your study of this chapter, you should be able to:

- Identify topics most effectively taught with the Direct-Instruction Model.
- Plan lessons using the Direct-Instruction Model.
- Implement Direct-Instruction lessons with your students.
- Assess learner understanding in lessons using the Direct-Instruction Model.

To begin, let's look at two teachers using the Direct-Instruction Model in their classrooms.

Tim Hardaway, a first-grade teacher, looks up from his planning book and stares out the window. "I wonder if they are ready?" he thinks. "We've been working on addition for weeks now and they understand the process and most even know their math facts, but is transition to addition with two-digit numbers going to be tough? I've got to make sure that we review place value before we begin. If they don't understand that, I'll lose them."

The next Monday Tim begins his math class by saying, "Please put away your reading books and take out your math pieces. Today we are going to learn a new way to add. This new way to add will help us solve problems like this one." With this, he displays the following problem.

> Sonya and Willy are working together to save soft drink cans, so they can get a free soccer ball. Sonya has thirteen cans and Willy has fourteen. How many did they have together?

After giving the children a few seconds to read the problem, Tim continues, "Problems like this are important in math because they help us in our everyday lives. When we're done with today's lesson, you'll be able to solve problems like this.

"Now let's review for a few minutes. Everyone do this problem." He writes the following problem on the board.

$$\begin{array}{r} 5 \\ +4 \\ \hline \end{array}$$

He quickly circulates around the room, and then comments, "Great! We really know how to do that . . . Now, I want you to try a slightly harder one, and I want you to use your math pieces for this one," as he writes the following problem on the board.

$$\begin{array}{r} 6 \\ +7 \\ \hline \end{array}$$

Again, Tim circulates around the room, offering brief suggestions and comments.

He then moves back to the front of the room and says, "Who would like to come to the flannel board to show us how they did this problem? . . . Antonio? . . . Good! Come on up here and use the same color pieces as you used at your desk."

Antonio walks up to the front of the room and starts arranging the pieces on the flannel board.

"Antonio, talk out loud while you're doing it and explain what you're doing so everyone can understand."

". . . Well, you take six of these . . . [unit pieces] here, and . . . you . . . add these . . . these seven . . . and thirteen, you get thirteen. . . . That's the answer."

"Excellent Antonio. Does everyone see how he did that? Now, Antonio, do you remember what we can do when we have ten unit pieces? How can we make the answer simpler?"

". . . We can . . . trade ten, . . . ten of these for that one" [a tens piece].

"Okay, go ahead and do that. Class, if you haven't already done that, do that at your desk."

Tim pauses for a few seconds while the class rearranges their counting pieces so that they have one ten piece and three unit pieces.

"Does everyone see how Antonio did that? He traded ten of his unit pieces for one of his ten pieces and still got thirteen. Good thinking, Antonio.

"Now, we are ready to learn something new today. Today we're going to learn how to add numbers that have tens in them. We already know how to add smaller numbers, and we know how to convert units to tens so this shouldn't be too difficult if we all work hard. When we add numbers with tens and units, we simply have to remember to add the units with units and the tens with tens. Let's begin by looking at our problem."

Again he displays the problem,

> Sonya and Willy are working together to save soft drink cans, so they can get a free soccer ball. Sonya has thirteen cans and Willy has fourteen. How many did they have together?

"Everyone look up here at the overhead. Good. Now what does the problem ask us? Shalinda?"

"How . . . many they have . . . together?" Shalinda responds hesitantly.

"Good. . . . So, how might we solve this problem? . . . Lakea?"

"I . . . I . . . think we could add them up."

"Good," Tim smiles. "Why do you think so?"

"It . . . says . . . how many do they have together, so if we added, we . . . would know that."

"Excellent," Tim nods. "Now let's put the problem on the board. What is one number that we add? Carlos?"

"Thirteen."

"Good, Carlos. And what's the other number we add, Cheryl?"

"Fourteen."

"Fine, so let's put the problem on the board like this," Tim continues, writing the following on the board.

$$\begin{array}{r} 14 \\ +13 \\ \hline \end{array}$$

"Now, what is this fourteen?" Tim asks pointing to the fourteen on the board.

". . . How many cans . . . Willy has," Leroy answers.

"Now, I'd like everyone to show me how to make a fourteen at your desk using both ten and unit pieces."

Tim pauses as the class works at their desks.

"Does everyone's look like this?" Tim asks as he does the same at the flannel board.

"Now I'd like you to do the same with thirteen. Everyone do that at your desk," Tim adds and then pauses for them to work.

"Here's what my thirteen looks like. Is that right? Good. Now we're ready to add them. When I add three and four what do I get? . . . Let me think about that . . . three and four are seven. Let's put a seven up on the board," Tim says as he walks to the board and adds a seven.

$$\begin{array}{r} 14 \\ +13 \\ \hline 7 \end{array}$$

"Now, we still have to add the tens. What do we get when we add two tens? . . . That should be easy. One ten and one ten is two tens. . . . Look where I have to put the two up here. It is under the tens column because the two means two tens." With that he writes the following on the board:

$$
\begin{array}{r}
14 \\
+13 \\
\hline
27
\end{array}
$$

"So how many cans did Sonya and Willy have together? Alesha?"

"Twenty-seven?"

"Good, Alesha. They had twenty-seven all together. . . . Show me the number with your pieces."

Tim watches as the children put seven of their units pieces in a group and place two of their tens pieces beside them. A few of the children are uncertain about how to represent the number, and Tim gives them enough help, so they are also able to correctly represent the number with their pieces.

He then continues, "Let's try another one."

Let's leave Tim and his children now and visit Karen Hendricks, a middle school science teacher, who is beginning a unit on plants.

"Class, that was the bell, so I need to have everyone's eyes up here," Karen announces loudly as she scans the room for silence.

"Thank you. Billy, . . . thank you. Sandra, we're waiting."

After a short pause, Karen continues, "As you'll recall, we've been studying different kinds of plants for the past several weeks. We talked about single-celled plants, algae, mosses, and ferns, and last week we talked about gymnosperms. Who can remember some plants that are gymnosperms? . . . Becky."

". . . Pine . . . trees and that funny one from China . . . Gink . . . Gingko."

"Good, Becky. Also last week we learned about angiosperms or flowering plants. Who can remember some examples of angiosperms? Wade?"

". . . Umm, roses and . . . maple . . . maple trees."

"Good, Wade. Today, class, we are going to learn about two kinds of angiosperms—monocotyledons and dicotyledons, or monocots and dicots for short. These are important members of the plant family because most of the food we eat comes from them. When we're all done, you'll be able to tell the difference between monocots and dicots and explain how they're related to angiosperms. Look up here on the overhead and you'll see these terms defined."

"Now first I'd like to focus on monocots. Look up here [holding up a grass plant]. This is a monocot that I found on our playground. Monocots are flowering plants that produce seeds with a single cotyledon. That's why we call them monocots—because *mono*

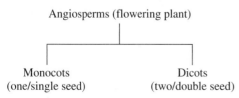

Angiosperms (flowering plant)

Monocots (one/single seed)   Dicots (two/double seed)

means one. If you will look up here at the overhead, you will see a cross-section of a corn seed. Note that it has a unitary construction—it isn't in halves, and there is only one leaf coming out of the seed. Corn and this grass plant are examples of monocots.

"The second type of angiosperm we are going to learn about today is dicots or dicotyledons. Who knows what *di* means? Maria?"

". . . If . . . the other stuff meant one, . . . it must mean two," Maria replies.

"Excellent, Maria. So dicots have two seed leaves. Look up here at a cross-section of a bean plant." Karen continues, pointing up at the overhead, "Can you see the two halves of the seed and the two seed leaves coming out? . . . Good.

"Now, besides the seeds, there is a second difference between monocots and dicots. Look at the leaves of this grass plant and this bean plant and see if you can tell. Clarice?"

". . . Well, the grass leaves are long and thin and the bean leaves are kind of round."

"Good, Clarice. And what about the leaf veins? Take a closer look. Alfredo, what do you see?" Karen asks, holding it close for Alfredo to see.

". . . The veins in the grass plant are long and narrow; the veins in the bean plant go all over and are hooked to each other."

"Good, Alfredo. So a second difference is in the shape of the leaves and the veins in the leaves. Let's add these to our diagram.

Angiosperms (flowering plant)

Monocots | Dicots
One-seed leaf | Two-seed leaves
Long parallel veins in leaves | Netlike veins in leaves

"Let's try another plant and see if these characteristics make sense," Karen continues, taking out a green onion and holding it in front of the class. "What kind of angiosperm do we have here and why?"

The class continues with Karen presenting pictures and overheads of rice, corn, daffodil, rose, and sunflower plants. In each instance, they talk about the plant structure and analyze the seeds, when available.

Finally, Karen brings the lesson to a close by saying, "Class, let's summarize what we learned today. . . . Cheryl, what is one thing you learned today?"

". . . About angiosperms and how they . . . like . . . have two families," Cheryl replies, pointing to the board.

"Good, what else? . . . Kenny?"

"We learned about monocots and dicots and how they're different," replies Kenny.

"Fine, and what is one difference between them? Trang?"

"Monocots have a one-seed leaf and they have long, parallel veins."

"Excellent, Trang. You were listening. And what about dicots? Kaylynne?"

". . . Um, dicots have two-seed leaves and their leaves are rounder and have lots of veins that go every which way."

"Good, Kaylynne. Class, it seems like you are understanding the differences between these two types of plants. What I would like you to do now is work on this handout that has some additional examples of plants. Your job is to classify them as monocots or dicots and explain why."

After Karen passes the worksheets to the students, she circulates around the class, answering questions. Toward the end of the class, Karen begins again, "Class, I have an assignment for each of you. I want you to go home tonight and look in your yards, or in your refrigerator or even a park and find one more example of a monocot or dicot. Bring it in if you can, but don't pull up somebody's flowers." She pauses as the class giggled and exchanges glances. "Make sure you write that assignment down and we'll discuss what you find first thing tomorrow morning."

The Direct-Instruction Model: An Overview

Direct-Instruction Model is *a model that that uses teacher explanation and modeling combined with student practice and feedback to teach concepts and procedural skills.* Examples of concepts include *monocots* and *dicots,* which Karen taught in her science lesson; *integer* and *imaginary roots* in math; *gerunds* and *participles* in language arts; *culture* and *economics* in social studies; and a variety of others. Procedural skills include examples, such as adding two-digit numbers, which Tim taught in his lesson; finding the longitude and latitude of various locations, writing essays using correct grammar, spelling, and punctuation; and writing chemical equations.

The teacher specifies learning objectives, explains and illustrates content, and models skills for the students. In effective direct-instruction lessons, students are active in responding to teacher questions, analyzing examples, and practicing skills to the point where they can be used with little or no mental effort.

The Direct-Instruction Model is well grounded in theory and research (Gersten, Taylor, & Graves, 1999). Let's look at this foundation.

The Direct-Instruction Model: Theoretical Foundations

The Direct-Instructional Model is built on research and theory from three areas:

- Teacher effectiveness research, which was described in Chapters 1 and 3
- Social Cognitive Theory, based on the work of Albert Bandura (1989, 1997) and his colleagues, which emphasizes the role of modeling on learning skills
- The influence of interaction in learning, based on the work of Lev Vygotsky (1978)

Teacher Effectiveness Research

We introduced teacher effectiveness research in Chapter 1 and discussed essential teaching skills derived from this research in Chapter 3. There we saw that teachers who, for example, use their time well, present high-quality examples, use clear language, provide effective feedback, and develop lessons with questioning increase student achievement more than teachers who have less expertise in these areas.

Researchers also found that these effective teachers followed a general pattern of instruction (Shuell, 1996). Different labels were used for this pattern, one of which was *direct instruction,* which Barak Rosenshine (1979), a prominent researcher, described as follows:

> Direct instruction refers to academically focused, teacher-directed classrooms using sequenced and structured materials. It refers to teaching activities where goals are clear to students, time allocated for instruction is sufficient and continuous, coverage of content is extensive, the performance of students is monitored . . . and feedback to students is immediate and academically oriented. In direct instruction the teacher controls instructional goals, chooses materials appropriate for the student's ability, and paces the instructional episode. Interaction is . . . structured, but not authoritarian. Learning takes place in a convivial academic atmosphere. (p. 38)

Direct instruction has six characteristics that are effective across grade levels and content areas:

- Reviewing the previous day's work
- Presenting new material in clear and logical steps
- Providing guided practice
- Giving feedback with correctives
- Providing independent practice
- Reviewing to consolidate learning (Rosenshine & Stevens, 1986)

These characteristics provide the structure for the Direct-Instruction Model.

Social Cognitive Theory: Learning by Observing Others

Social Cognitive Theory, which *describes changes in behavior, thinking, or emotions that result from observing the behavior of another person* (Bandura, 1989, 1997), is a second foundation for the Direct-Instruction Model. At the heart of Social Cognitive Theory is the concept of **modeling,** which is *the tendency of people to imitate behaviors they observe in others.* We have all seen little children imitate sounds and actions of their parents, and the tendency of teenagers to imitate the hair and fashion styles of rock and movie stars forms the basis for a multibillion dollar fashion industry.

The Direct-Instruction Model incorporates the benefits of modeling by having teachers demonstrate (model) the steps involved in learning a skill or the thinking involved in classifying examples of concepts. Tim used modeling when he demonstrated adding with two-digit numbers. Tim also used Antonio as a model when he asked Antonio to come to the flannel board and demonstrate the skill.

As Tim was modeling the process for adding two-digit numbers to the students, he said, "Here's what my thirteen looks like. Is that right? Good. Now we're ready to add them. When I add three and four, what do I get? . . . Let me think about that . . . three and four are seven. Let's put a seven up on the board. . . . Now we still have to add the tens. What do we get when we add two tens? . . . That should be easy. One ten and one ten is two tens. . . . Look where I have to put the two up here. It is under the tens column because the two means two tens."

By describing his thinking as he demonstrated the procedure, Tim was attempting to capitalize on **cognitive modeling,** which is *the process of verbalizing thinking as a person solves a problem.* Just as direct modeling is the display of behaviors intended to be imitated, cognitive modeling is the display of thinking also intended to be imitated. Tim also used cognitive modeling when he said, "Antonio, talk out loud while you're doing it [solving the problem] and explain what you're doing so everyone can understand."

Vygotsky: The Social Side of Skill Learning

Research on the social aspects of learning emphasizes the importance of verbal interaction in helping students learn (Cohen & Lotan, 1997; Wertsch, 1991), and much of the effectiveness of direct instruction results from the interaction between the teacher and students.

Two concepts from the work of Lev Vygotsky (1978) capitalize on this interaction. The first is **scaffolding** which is *the instructional support teachers provide as students learn skills.* Teachers can provide scaffolding in a variety of ways, including breaking complex skills into subskills, asking questions and adjusting their difficulty, presenting examples, modeling the steps in solving problems, and providing prompts and cues.

The second is the **zone of proximal development,** which is *the state of learning in which a student cannot solve a problem or perform a skill alone but can be successful with the help of a teacher.* The zone of proximal development is instructional paydirt; it is within the zone that teachers are most effective in aiding learning. Outside of the zone, students either don't need help (they have already mastered a new skill) or lack the prerequisite skills or background knowledge to benefit from instruction.

When using the Direct-Instruction Model, we attempt to implement lessons within students' zones of proximal development. For example, when Tim first introduced adding with two-digit numbers, most of his students were not able to perform this skill by themselves. However, by the end of the lesson, with his help, most of his students were able to perform the skill on their own. Tim had successfully helped his students proceed through the zone of proximal development.

Having examined the theoretical base of the Direct-Instruction Model, let's see how lessons with the model are planned and implemented.

Planning Lessons with the Direct-Instruction Model

The planning process for lessons using the Direct-Instruction Model involves four steps, which are illustrated in Figure 9.1 and discussed in the sections that follow.

Identifying Topics

In the introduction to the chapter we said that the Direct-Instruction Model is designed to teach concepts and procedural skills. We discussed concepts in detail in Chapter 5 and theories of concept learning in Chapter 6. To review these discussions, turn to pages 138 and 176.

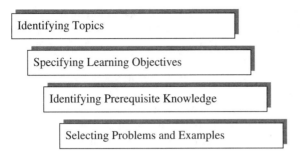

**FIGURE 9.1   Planning Lessons with the
Direct-Instruction Model**

Let's look at procedural skills in more detail.

Procedural Skills.   To begin this section consider the following problem:

$$\begin{array}{r} 987 \\ -788 \\ \hline \end{array}$$

Solving it is easy for most of us, but now let's consider how we would attempt to teach its solution to a child who understands simple subtraction but hasn't yet been introduced to regrouping. We need to explain the process so that children understand what they are doing and why. Ultimately they need to be able to perform the operations essentially automatically.

Solving problems such as this is **procedural skill,** which is a *cognitive operation that:*

- *Has a specific set of identifiable operations or procedures*
- *Can be illustrated with a large and varied number of examples*
- *Is developed through practice* (Doyle, 1983)

Skills are found across the curriculum and at virtually every grade level. For example, the language arts curriculum contains writing skills including general organizational strategies, as well as specific skills, such as capitalization, grammar, and punctuation. As we saw in Tim's lesson, math is replete with skills, ranging from basics, such as addition and subtraction, to those more complex, such as factoring and solving quadratic equations. Social studies and science also contain many skill areas. For example, students are asked to read maps and read and display information in charts and graphs in social studies, and science students conduct experiments and solve equations. Each includes a set of specific operations, each can be illustrated with a variety of examples, and in all cases practice leads to expertise.

Specifying Learning Objectives

We have two long-range learning objectives when we teach skills—automaticity and transfer. As we saw in Chapter 2, **automaticity** results from *overlearning a skill to the point that* *it can be performed with little conscious effort,* and it is important because it reduces the demand on our limited working memories. Word processing is an example. Once automaticity is achieved, we spend little effort thinking about what keys we will press; rather, we devote our working memory spaces to composing the document we're preparing. Similarly, in order to solve word problems in math, automaticity in basic operations—such as addition and multiplication—is important because it allows us to devote all of our limited working memory to solving the problem (Sweller et al., 1998).

Teachers promote automaticity by providing practice to the point of overlearning. This practice can occur under the guidance of the teacher or independently, and both are important.

Transfer is the second goal of skills instruction. **Transfer** occurs when *a skill or understanding acquired in one setting can be applied in a different setting.* For example, transfer occurs when students apply algebra to solve physics problems, or when students use math skills to determine which of two products is a better buy.

Teachers teach for transfer in three ways. The first is by ensuring that students understand the skill; the more students understand a skill, the better they will be able to use it across multiple situations. Tim had his students use their counting pieces to help reach this goal. The second is by providing a variety of problems or examples in which the skill is required, and the third is by giving students a chance to practice the skill on practical, real-world problems.

Having identified the concept or skill you want the students to learn, you are ready to identify prerequisite knowledge.

Identifying Prerequisite Knowledge

The Direct-Instruction Model focuses on teaching and learning specific concepts or skills. However, research on learning indicates that all new learning depends on what students already know—their prior knowledge (Eggen & Kauchak, 2004). Prior knowledge provides "hooks" for new learning, allowing students to connect new information with what they already understand. In planning for direct-instruction lessons, teachers need to think about how the concept or skill will be introduced and connected to what students already know.

Planning for accessing prerequisite knowledge is slightly different for teaching a concept than for teaching a skill. For concepts, the task usually involves identifying a superordinate concept to which the concept being taught can be linked. Karen used the superordinate concept *angiosperm* because she had previously taught the concept and it was meaningful to students. Though the goal in direct instruction may be to understand a specific concept (or concepts), such as *monocot* and *dicot* in Karen's lesson, a broader goal is for students to understand how the concept relates to other ideas.

Identifying prerequisites for a skills-oriented lesson is slightly more complicated because it involves identifying subskills that lay the foundation for the new skill. **Task analysis,** *the process of breaking a skill into its components,* can be helpful here. Tim did a task analysis when he determined that students first needed to understand place value before they could learn to do two-column addition.

Consider a second example from the area of writing. Our goal is for students to write well. What knowledge or skills are required to accomplish this goal? Among them are understanding what a sentence is, knowing the difference between sentence fragments and complete sentences, punctuating sentences correctly, and being able to use the specific punctuation symbols that are used with each sentence type. Once they are learned, these prerequisite skills provide a foundation that allows students to focus on the skill at hand.

Selecting Problems and Examples

The final step in planning for direct-instruction lessons is selecting examples or problems. A strength of direct instruction is the opportunities it provides for practice. Students practice concept learning when they relate examples to a definition or categorize examples themselves. Students practice skill learning when whey work sample problems on their own. In both instances, concrete examples and problems are essential for understanding.

In teaching concepts with the Direct-Instruction Model, the teacher has two tasks—selecting examples and then sequencing them. Examples are selected based on the extent to which they illustrate the concept's essential characteristics. In Karen's lesson, these characteristics included the number of seed leaves and the type of venation. Karen used a combination of real examples and pictures on overheads to illustrate these characteristics.

After selecting examples, the teacher then sequences them. Usually, the clearest and most obvious ones are presented first. For example, when teaching a simple concept, such as *mammal,* we would first use obvious examples, such as *dog, cat,* or *cow,* rather than less obvious examples, such as *whale, seal,* or *bat. Dog* and *cat* are good examples because they clearly illustrate mammalian characteristics, such as being furry, warm-blooded, and milk producers. Further, most students have had personal experiences with dogs or cats, which makes these examples more meaningful. Once learners begin to understand the concept, additional and less obvious examples can be used to enrich their understanding.

In selecting and sequencing examples and problems for skill acquisition, simpler problems are presented first. Problems should be selected and sequenced so that students can develop confidence quickly through successful practice with the skill.

Tim's lesson illustrates this process. He first used problems that involved single-digit addition without regrouping, then moved to single-digit addition with regrouping, proceeded to double-digit addition without regrouping, and finally arrived at double-digit addition with regrouping. By sequencing from simple to complex, Tim provided instructional scaffolding that ensured high success rates and minimized frustration and confusion.

Having identified topics and learning objectives, determined prerequisite knowledge, and selected and sequenced examples and problems, you are ready to conduct the lesson.

Implementing Lessons Using the Direct-Instruction Model

Implementing a lesson using the Direct-Instruction Model occurs in four phases, which are illustrated with their learning and motivation functions in Table 9.1 and discussed in the sections that follow.

TABLE 9.1 **Learning and Motivation Functions for the Phases of the Direct-Instruction Model**

Phase	Learning and Motivation Function
Phase 1: Introduction and review Students are drawn into the lesson	■ Attracts attention ■ Activates background knowledge
Phase 2: Presentation New content is presented and explained	■ Begins schema production ■ Promotes involvement
Phase 3: Guided practice Students practice the concept or skill under the teacher's guidance	■ Develops perceptions of competence ■ Ensures success
Phase 4: Independent practice Students practice using the concept or skill on their own	■ Advances schema production ■ Develops automaticity

Phase 1: Introduction and Review

In Phase 1, attempts are made to attract the students' attention and activate their background knowledge through a review of prerequisite knowledge or skills. Tim attempted to attract the students' attention with his sample problem, and he reviewed by having the students add one-digit numbers and regroup thirteen individual pieces into one tens piece and three unit pieces. He attempted to increase their motivation to learn by emphasizing that the new math skill would help them solve common, everyday problems.

Karen structured her lesson by first explaining that students would be able to differentiate between monocots and dicots when the lesson was over, and then she attempted to increase motivation to learn by explaining that monocots and dicots are important food sources.

Phase 2: Presentation

In Phase 2 the teacher attempts to begin the process of schema production by explaining and illustrating the concept or explaining and modeling the skill being taught. Although this phase appears simple and straightforward, research indicates that implementing it can be challenging. One of the problems is being able to anticipate how students might think so that we're able to present the content in a way that makes sense to them. Teachers describe the problem in this way:

> I've never thought through [how to teach a cognitive skill]. The most difficult thing is to think it through . . . Figuring out how to model [the skill] is a hard thing for me. . . . I have to really sit down and write it out. I mean, I am still doing that pretty much, like every day with that group. (Duffy & Roehler, 1985, p. 6)

Part of the difficulty stems from the fact that these concepts and skills are often so automatic for us that we have trouble verbalizing and modeling them for our students. For example, think about how you would explain and model tying a shoelace for a youngster. We might say something such as, "Well, first you take one of the laces in each hand, and then you put one lace over the other. . . . " and our modeling might be rushed and confusing. In reaction to this difficulty, teachers often rush through this phase of the lesson, providing too little explanation and modeling, and asking students to try the skill before they are ready.

Effective teachers, in contrast, spend a considerable amount of time on this phase, during which they provide a number of examples, and guide the students to an understanding of the concept or skill with questioning, as we saw in both Tim's and Karen's lessons. For example, Tim modeled a solution to the problem himself, and then he asked Antonio to demonstrate and explain how he solved his problem. Also, both Tim and Antonio used cognitive modeling while they were involved in problem solving, allowing others to share in their thinking.

Karen used several examples to make her presentation effective. As she introduced monocots and dicots, she shared examples of each with students, and, as she discussed the concepts' essential characteristics, she related them to both examples and overheads. She also wrote the characteristics and important information on the board.

Both Tim and Karen also promoted high levels of student involvement through questioning during this phase. This both increases student motivation and allows the teacher to continually assess learning progress.

Phase 3: Guided Practice

During Phase 3, the teacher attempts to help the students develop perceptions of competence by ensuring success. The students try out new content as the teacher carefully monitors their progress and provides support and feedback.

Teachers' and students' roles change during this phase. The teacher moves from information provider and model to coach, and students move from receiving information to testing their understanding with examples and problems.

During the early phases of guided practice, the teacher provides instructional scaffolding to ensure that students experience success. Gradually, teachers reduce their support and transfer more responsibility to students.

The kind and amount of teacher talk also shifts during this phase. Initially, the teacher gives cues and prompts that provide instructional scaffolding. Later, as students assume more responsibility for explaining problems and classifying examples, teachers' talk will be more probing, designed to raise the level of student thinking and application.

Guided practice occurred in Tim's lesson when he assisted his students in solving problems using their counting pieces and the flannel board. Karen provided guided practice when she presented pictures and overheads of plants, such as the rice and corn, and asked students to classify them and explain their answers. The objective in both cases was to provide opportunities for students to test their developing knowledge.

During guided practice teachers must decide when to make the transition to independent practice, when students try out the new skill on their own. Effective independent practice requires that students have enough expertise to be successful with little teacher assistance (Gersten et al., 1999).

Teachers can determine whether students are ready for independent practice in at least two ways. One is student success rates; when 80 to 90 percent of students' responses during guided practice are correct, the class is probably ready for independent practice. The quality of answers is a second measure. Quick, confident, and accurate answers signal that students are ready; hesitant or partially correct answers suggest the need for more guided practice.

As with the presentation phase, high levels of interaction between teacher and student are important during this phase. Teachers should ask clarifying and probing questions to determine if students truly understand the new content or are following a set of memorized procedures. Research indicates that effective teachers ask three times as many questions during this phase than do their less effective counterparts (Evertson, Anderson, Anderson, & Brophy, 1980). Teacher–student interaction also provides teachers with access to student thinking, allowing them to understand and "debug" student errors and misconceptions.

Phase 4: Independent Practice

Independent practice is the final phase of direct-instruction lessons. During this phase, students practice the new skill or concept on their own, developing both automaticity and the ability to transfer their understanding to new contexts (Gersten et al., 1999).

Ideally, independent practice occurs in two stages. During the first stage, students practice in class under the supportive umbrella of the teacher. Later, students work on their own on a homework assignment.

Independent practice in the classroom is important because it allows the teacher to monitor learning progress and provide assistance if needed. Student success rates and the learning problems students encounter both help the teacher in diagnosing learner problems. If few students are having problems, the teacher can work with individuals or small groups of students. If a number of students are having the same problems, it may be necessary to pull the class back together and reteach the parts of the topic that students don't understand (Good & Brophy, 2003).

Students began independent practice in Karen's lesson when she passed out the worksheets and had each student classify additional examples of monocots and dicots. We left Tim's lesson before it progressed to independent practice, but he provided independent practice by giving the students several problems that they were to solve on their own.

Increasing Motivation with the Direct-Instruction Model

Though teacher directed, the Direct-Instruction Model provides many opportunities to increase student motivation. This increased motivation can result in improved learning when the model is being used as well as improved attitudes about learning in general.

In Chapter 2 we saw that the need for competence is basic according to motivation theorists (Ryan & Deci, 2000). The need for competence helps explain why young children practice a developing skill, such as tying a shoe or zipping a coat, over and over. It also helps explain why adults will work countless hours getting better at sports, such as playing tennis and golf or struggling to improve their running times. People feel a sense of accomplishment when they get better at something (Good & Brophy, 2003; Ryan & Deci, 2000).

Developing perceptions of competence is the primary motivation function of the guided practice phase of direct-instruction lessons. Students attempt to solve problems, and teachers provide only enough support (scaffolding) to ensure that students are successful. The more nearly students are able to perform the skill or apply the concept *on their own,* the greater their perceptions of competence.

As learning progresses, teachers can praise students for their genuine accomplishment, which can increase both intrinsic motivation and motivation to learn. Praise for genuine accomplishment is motivating because it communicates to students that their competence is increasing (Deci & Ryan, 1991).

In communicating information about increasing competence, teachers should emphasize individual learning progress rather than competition with others; research suggests that competition can have negative effects on learning, especially for low-ability students or students who don't fare well in competitive situations (Pintrich & Schunk, 2002; Stipek, 2002).

Teachers can also contribute to motivation by emphasizing the influence of effort on increasing competence. Comments, such as, "Nice job, your hard work is paying off" and "I can really tell you're trying hard; you are understanding this stuff better and better," on both written work and answers in class help students attribute their increasing competence to personal effort. Understanding that hard work leads to increased learning can also spread to other areas of the curriculum as well (Pintrich & Schunk, 2002; Stipek, 2002).

The Direct-Instruction Model: Variations

We have described direct instruction as a model designed to teach concepts and skills. However, it can be used to teach generalizations, principles, and academic rules as well.

Using Direct Instruction to Teach
Generalizations, Principles, and Rules

In Chapter 5, we saw that generalizations, principles, and rules are similar in that each describes a relationship between concepts. Some examples include:

- A diet high in saturated fat raises a person's cholesterol level. (generalization)
- The greater the unbalanced force on an object, the greater the object's acceleration. (principle/law)
- A pronoun must agree with its antecedent in number and gender. (academic rule)

Generalizations, principles, and academic rules are similar to concepts in that high-quality examples are the key to successful learning in all cases, and the process of planning and implementing lessons in which a principle, generalization, or rule is taught is similar to the processes involved in teaching a concept.

Let's look at an example of a teacher using the Direct-Instruction Model to teach the law of supply and demand.

Tamra Evans, a high school social studies teacher, wants to teach her students the generalization, "If demand stays constant, price is inversely related to supply."

She begins her lesson by stating, "We have been studying the economics of different countries for several lessons, so let's review what we've done so far. What do we mean by economics? . . . Jacinta?"

"Economics sort of deals with money," she responds.

"Good, and what particular aspects of money? . . . Antonio?"

". . . Well, it tells how money is made and how it is spread around," Antonio answers.

"Excellent, Antonio," Tamra smiles. "Now, everyone, today we're going to deal with a particular law in economics. This law states that 'when demand stays constant, price, and supply are *inversely* related,'" and as she states the generalization, she writes it on the chalkboard.

"This law is important," she continues, "because it helps us understand why the prices of things we buy in stores go up or down. Supply, as we'll see in today's lesson, is a major factor influencing price."

"Now, . . . how do supply, demand, and price relate to the larger topic of economics? . . . Cheryl?"

". . . I think . . . price relates to money and . . . how someone would make money," Cheryl answers hesitantly.

"Yes! Very good, Cheryl. Now let's look at the terms *supply, demand, price, and inversely*. What does the word inversely mean? . . . Mike?"

". . . It means something like when one thing gets bigger, another gets smaller," Mike responds.

Tamra continues the discussion of each term until she is satisfied that the students' understanding of each is correct. At this point, she continues: "Look up at the overhead. The paragraph on it illustrates the generalization we're learning today." She shows the students the following example.

As I drove into a city of approximately a half million people in August of 2003, I filled my car with gas at an independent station for $1.94 per gallon. In March of 2004, I made a trip into the same city. I looked at a pump which said $2.09 for unleaded. When I asked the attendant about the big price jump, he explained that problems at local refineries had made gas hard to get.

After allowing the students time to read the anecdote, she asks, "How does the example relate to our generalization? . . . Judy?"

". . . The problem would mean that the supply was reduced, I guess."

"Yes, good. You've identified a key variable in the example, Judy. What else? . . . David?"

"The price shot up," David answers quickly.

"And what do we call that kind of relationship?"

". . . Oh. That's what inverse means," David answers after thinking a moment.

"And the amount people wanted to buy stayed about the same," Anna volunteers.

"Very well done," Tamra smiles. "We see how the example illustrates that price and supply are inversely related if the demand stays the same.

"Now look at another example and tell me if it illustrates the law," she proceeds. She then shows them the following example.

Jimmy decided to put up a lemonade stand. He charged 4 cents a cup, and people were buying lemonade at the corner of his father's lot faster than he could make it. Jimmy decided, "I'll bet they'll still buy my lemonade if I charge 5 cents a glass." So he did.

Two days later Joey, who saw how well Jimmy was making out, decided to open up his own lemonade stand across the street from Jimmy's. He charged 3 cents a glass, and soon most of the people who had been stopping at Jimmy's stand were going to Joey's instead. Jimmy then lowered his price to 3 cents a glass, and both the boys sold lemonade.

"How does this example illustrate the principle we've been discussing?" Tamra asks. ". . . How is the demand affected by Joey opening his stand? . . . Jason?"

"I guess it isn't. It should be about the same."

"Very good, Jason. There is no reason to think that Joey's stand would have any affect on the amount people wanted to buy.

"Yes, Kristy," Tamra smiles in response to Kristy's waving hand.

"I've got it," Kristy says excitedly. "Because the demand was the same and Joey's stand increased the supply, the price had to go down, which is an inverse relationship."

"Excellent analysis, Kristy. So does the example illustrate the principle?"

"Yes," Kristy replies confidently.

"Let me show you one more," Tamra says as she displays the following example on the overhead.

In the early 1990s, with the boom in Asian trade, many universities dramatically expanded their international trade preparation programs, and a campaign was on to try and maintain a lead over other industrialized countries, such as Germany and Japan. At that time, Ph.D.s in Asian business trade could virtually name their salaries at most universities.

As the country moved into the late 1990s, a great many students took majors in Asian business trade, but with the slump in the economies of many Asian countries, the emphasis on this aspect of international trade was reduced somewhat.

In the late 1990s, many business majors in Asian trade were unable to get jobs, and those that were employed received lower comparative salaries than those trained 10 years earlier.

"Does this example illustrate the law we're discussing?" Tamra queries. "Karen?"

". . . I'm . . . I'm not sure," Karen answers.

"Let's look carefully," Tamra suggests. "What has happened to the price?"

". . . Their salaries were lower," Karen tentatively suggests.

"Yes they were. That's good, Karen. Now, how about the supply? . . . Jan?"

"It doesn't look to me as if it's changed that much."

"Aha! But the demand has gone down!" Kwan adds with a look of insight on his face. "The example doesn't illustrate the idea we're discussing, because our generalization says the demand stays constant."

"Excellent, everyone!" Tamra praises. "That is real good thinking. Because you've done so well, think now and see if you can create some more examples that illustrate the generalization."

The students, with Tamra's help, then generate additional examples, which they analyze as they did for the first three.

She then continues, "Class, I have some additional cases that I'd like you to do now. In each case if it does illustrate the generalization, explain *how* it's illustrated by identifying each part—supply, demand, and price—in the generalization, and if it doesn't illustrate it, explain why. I'd like you to start on these with the time remaining, and I'll come around to see if you have any questions. Whatever you don't finish, take home for homework and we'll discuss them tomorrow."

As we can see, using the Direct-Instruction Model to teach generalizations, principles, and rules is very similar to procedures used in teaching concepts. During planning, the teacher identifies the topic and specifies learning objectives, establishes prerequisite knowledge, and finds or creates examples.

When the lesson is implemented the teacher attempts to attract the students' attention and reviews during Phase 1, presents information and promotes high levels of student involvement during the presentation phase (Phase 2), and provides practice in the final two phases by having the students analyze additional examples. Tamra used case studies to illustrate the law and to help students see how it relates to the real world, and she used her examples in the presentation phase and both of the practice phases.

In summary, the Direct-Instruction Model provides an effective and time-efficient way to teach generalizations, principles, and rules. As with concept teaching, the essential ingredients for successful lessons are the liberal use of examples, and teacher–student and student–student interaction that involves learners in making sense of these examples.

Direct Instruction and Learners from Diverse Backgrounds

Although research has shown direct instruction to be effective with students in general, additional research indicates that direct instruction is especially effective with students from diverse backgrounds (Gersten et al., 1999). This explicit approach to teaching concepts and skills provides culturally and linguistically diverse students with additional structure, which facilitates learning. In addition, the interactive nature of direct-instruction lessons provides opportunities for teachers to link new ideas to students' varying background knowledge and to continually assess learning progress. Let's see how.

Structure is important for all students. It organizes ideas and procedures, making them understandable and predictable, and helps establish a sense of equilibrium. Structure is especially important to culturally and linguistically diverse students because school can be confusing and chaotic for them (Peregoy & Boyle, 2001). Additional research in basic skills areas, such as reading and math, suggest that a structured approach, such as direct instruction, facilitates learning in these areas (Gersten et al., 1999).

A second reason that direct instruction is effective with students of diverse backgrounds is that it provides opportunities for academically focused interaction between teacher and students. These interactions are important because they help reduce cross-cultural and linguistic boundaries (Gersten et al., 1999). Problems and examples make sense to teachers, which is why they're chosen. However, these same problems and examples may not be meaningful to students. Interactions within the Direct-Instruction Model provide opportunities to clarify examples and elicit culturally relevant examples from students.

Direct instruction can also be effective with English language learning (ELL) students and in sheltered English instruction. In these classes teachers have the dual goals of teaching content while building on students' developing English skills. Experts in the area (Gersten et al., 1999; Peregoy & Boyle, 2001) recommend the following elements of effective ELL instruction:

- Specific targeting of key concepts or skills
- Activation of students' prior knowledge
- Extensive use of demonstrations and modeling
- Emphasis on students' active involvement
- Opportunities for extensive practice

Each of these recommendations is an integral component of direct instruction, making this strategy optimally suited for linguistically diverse students.

Assessing Student Understanding

The assessment of content outcomes in a direct-instruction lesson is similar to the process with the Inductive Model and the Concept Attainment Model. This process was discussed in detail in Chapter 5 and reinforced in Chapter 6. You may want to review those sections at this time.

To illustrate the assessment process with the Direct-Instruction Model, let's look again at Karen's lesson on plants. She has several options to choose from in assessing her students. For example, she could:

1. Have the students define monocots and dicots.
2. Give them pictures of monocots and dicots and ask them to identify each.
3. Give them actual examples of monocots and dicots and ask them to classify and explain their classifications.
4. Have them bring in their own examples of monocots and dicots and explain the examples in each case.

Having the students define these concepts is a very superficial measure of their understanding of the concept because it basically involves memorizing a string of words—something that may or may not involve meaningful learning. Each of the other strategies would be a more valid indicator of their understanding, with the demands on the students being progressively greater in each case.

An effective measure of concept learning in general is to have students classify examples and nonexamples of the concept. For example, in a lesson on adjectives, the teacher could present students with the following item:

Circle each of the following words that could be adjectives.
  a. pretty
  b. go
  c. ball
  d. early
  e. big
  f. crazily
  g. event

An item such as this is easy to prepare and score. However, this efficiency comes at a price. In the real world, we want students to be able to write using adjectives appropriately. A more valid item would require students to write a paragraph and identify the adjectives within it. Alternative assessments such as these attempt to place students in more realistic and lifelike settings to make the assessment process as similar as possible to real-life situations (Airasian, 2000; Stiggins, 2001).

However, scoring such an item can be time consuming. A reasonable compromise could be to present the students with an already prepared passage and have them identify the adjectives within it. Although this is not as effective as having them write their own, the passage could be scored efficiently. Determining the appropriate compromise between the validity of the assessment and the demand on the teacher is a matter of professional judgment. Only you, the teacher, can make that decision.

Assessing students' understanding of procedural skills is straightforward; students are provided with problems that they must solve on their own. However, even this process isn't as simple as it appears on the surface. If the problems used for assessment are too similar to those used in instruction, students may simply demonstrate their ability to memorize a set of procedures rather than demonstrate genuine understanding. This means that you must use careful judgment in selecting the problems you're using for assessment. As with assessing concept learning, only you can make that decision.

Summary

The Direct-Instruction Model: An Overview

The Direct-Instruction Model is a teacher-directed strategy that can be used to teach concepts and skills. It does this through strategic use of problems and examples and through structured interactions between teacher and students.

The Direct-Instruction Model: Theoretical Foundations

The Direct-Instruction Model is derived from several sources, including teacher effectiveness research, which looked into actual classrooms to document the strategies of effective teachers. It is also based on observational learning theory, which emphasizes the importance of modeling for the acquisition of complex behaviors. In addition, direct instruction is based on the work of Lev Vygotsky, who pointed out the importance of dialogue and social interaction in learning.

Planning Lessons with the Direct-Instruction Model

Planning with this model begins with the identification of a specific concept or skill. This is followed by identifying prerequisite knowledge that serves as the conceptual foundation for new learning. Finally, teachers need to carefully select examples and problems to illustrate important ideas.

Implementing Lessons Using the Direct-Instruction Model

The Model exists in four sequential phases—introduction, presentation, guided practice, and independent practice. The use of well-thought-out examples and problems is the key to the success of learning activities in which the model is used.

Though it is strongly teacher directed, effective use of the Direct-Instruction Model requires high levels of interaction between the teacher and students. The patterns in this interaction shift as a lesson develops. Initially, the teacher presents information and strongly guides students as they work with examples and problems. Later, students work more and more independently until they are able to analyze examples and solve problems without the teacher's help.

Increasing Motivation with the Direct-Instruction Model

Motivation theory suggests that the need for competence is innate. The guided practice phase of direct-instruction lessons helps meet this need as students practice their understanding of concepts and skills with the support of the teacher. As competence increases, teachers provide less support, and feedback indicating that competence is increasing can increase both intrinsic motivation and motivation to learn.

The Direct-Instruction Model: Variations

Although the model is designed specifically to teach skills and concepts, it can be modified easily to teach principles, generalizations, and academic rules.

The model is especially effective in teaching students of diversity because of its structure and opportunities for interaction. The structure provides a familiar learning landscape for students; the interaction provides opportunities for teachers and students to identify mutually meaningful examples.

Assessing Student Understanding

The key to effective assessment with this model is to ensure that students learn content at a meaningful level. This requires that students work actively with examples and concepts, linking them to the abstraction being taught.

IMPORTANT CONCEPTS

Automaticity (p. 295)
Cognitive modeling (p. 294)
Direct-Instruction Model (p. 292)
Modeling (p. 293)

Procedural skill (p. 295)
Scaffolding (p. 294)
Social Cognitive Theory (p. 293)
Task analysis (p. 296)

Transfer (p. 296)
Zone of proximal development
  (p. 294)

EXERCISES

1. Consider the following list of goals. Identify those most appropriately taught using the Direct-Instruction Model.
   a. To understand *prime number*
   b. To simplify arithmetic expressions that follow the rule, "Multiply and divide left to right and then add and subtract left to right"
   c. To understand *square*
   d. To understand *major scale*
   e. To understand "For substances that don't mix, less dense materials float on more dense materials"
   f. To understand *gerund*
   g. To identify the relationships between the economy and geography of the North and South prior to the Civil War and how these factors impacted the outcome of the war

2. Select a topic in your teaching area. Then prepare a set of examples that could be used to effectively teach the topic.

3. Read the following description of a teacher using the Direct-Instruction Model and then answer the questions that follow.

Kathy Lake begins her language arts class with, "Today, class, we're going to talk about a different kind of word pair. Who remembers what other word pairs we've been studying? . . . John?"

". . . Synonyms," John answers.

"Good, and who knows what a synonym is? . . . Maria?"

". . . They . . . like . . . mean the same, their meanings are the same, like . . . big and large."

"Very good, Maria. How about another example? . . . Toni?"

". . . Fast and speedy."

"Super! And one more? Roberto?"

". . . Skinny . . . and thin?"

"Yes, very good example, Roberto. Well, today we're going to study a different kind of word pair called *antonyms*. When we are done with the lesson today, you will be able to give me some examples of antonyms. Also, when I give you a word you will be able to give me an antonym for it."

She then writes the following on the board.

Synonyms   *Antonyms*
(Same meaning)   (Opposite meaning)

"Antonyms are word pairs that have opposite meaning. What do we mean by word pairs?" Kathy asks.

Susan hesitates and then says, "Like . . . two words."

"Good, Susan," Kathy nods with a smile. "So *word pair* means two words. Now, what does *opposite* mean?"

"Not . . . the same," Joe volunteers.

"That's very close, Joe," Kathy continues. "Let me give you an example. Big and small have opposite meanings and they're two words, so they're antonyms. *Opposite* means having a different, or almost a reversed, meaning as with *big* and *small*."

With this, she writes *big* and *small* under the term *Antonyms*.

"Another example of antonyms is *up* and *down*. They are antonyms because they're a pair of words whose meanings are opposite. So let's put them up here under the antonyms column. Let me try another one. Are *happy* and *glad* antonyms? Antonio?"

". . . No," replies Antonio.

"Why not?" Kathy asks.

"Because, . . . because their meanings are the same . . . not opposite."

"So what are they, Antonio?"

". . . Synonyms."

"Fine, Antonio. Let's put them under the synonym column. Now let's try another one. Are *cold* and *hot* antonyms? Ted?"

". . . Yeah, . . . they're a word pair, and the words have opposite meanings."

"So, let's put them over here on the board. And what about *alive* and *dead*? . . . Pat?"

"Those . . . are antonyms, too; they're the opposite."

"Fine. Now I want to see if you can give me some examples of antonyms. Think real hard. . . . Anyone? . . . Lynn?"

"How about *in* and *out*?"

"Good, Lynn. Anyone else? . . . Clarissa?"

"How about *high* and *low*?"

"And why are those antonyms?" Kathy probes.

". . . 'Cuz . . . they're . . . a word pair that is opposite . . . have opposite meanings."

"Real fine. Now one last test. Remember we had the word pair *happy* and *glad* and you said that they weren't antonyms? Can anyone think of antonyms for these words? . . . Juan?"

". . . How about . . . *happy* and *sad*?"

"Good. Sam, do you have another one?"

"*Glad* and *upset*."

"Those are both excellent antonyms. I think you've all done a good job today in learning about this new kind of word pair. Now someone tell me what we learned today. . . . Susan?"

". . . Well, we learned about antonyms."

"Good. Go on," Kathy smiles.

"Antonyms . . . mean . . . opposite."

"Yes, excellent! And one more thing. . . . Brad?"

"They're word pairs."

"Exactly. Very good, Brad."

She then closes the lesson by saying, "Remember, word pairs that mean the same are . . . class?"

"Synonyms!" they all respond in unison.

"Fine, and word pairs that are opposite are . . . ?"

"Antonyms!" they answer again.

"Excellent. Now I have some exercises that I would like you to do individually." She then distributes worksheets among the students and circulates as they begin working on them.

a. Identify each of the phases of the Direct-Instruction Model in Kathy Lake's lesson.

b. Consider assessing the concepts Kathy taught. Prepare an assessment item that could be used to evaluate students' understanding of the concepts.

c. While Kathy's instruction technically followed the Direct-Instruction Model, we might criticize it on one important basis. Offer that criticism. (*Hint:* Think about the idea of meaningfulness.)

Feedback for these exercises begins on page 341.

DISCUSSION QUESTIONS

1. Compare the Direct-Instruction Model to the Inductive and Concept Attainment Models. What similarities and differences do they share? What are advantages and disadvantages of each?

2. How does the Direct-Instruction Model differ from a typical lecture? What are its advantages and disadvantages compared to the lecture method?

3. The Direct-Instruction Model is heavily teacher centered. What advantages are there to this? What disadvantages?

4. Consider content goals again. How do these goals affect the decision to select the Inductive or Direct-Instruction Model? Discuss this question in terms of the abstractness of the concept or generalization, how "vague" the topic is, and the backgrounds of the students.

5. What alternative does the teacher have if he or she reaches the end of a direct-instruction lesson and the students still do not understand the abstraction? How would this compare to an inductive lesson?

6. Compare the amount of teacher talk and student talk in a direct-instruction lesson compared to an inductive lesson. What conditions could cause these amounts to vary?

As we saw in Chapter 9, the Direct-Instruction Model is designed to teach concepts and skills, with emphasis on active teaching and high levels of student involvement. However, as we saw in Chapter 7, teachers often have goals, such as understanding the Revolutionary War in social studies or the respiratory system in health, that involve understanding organized bodies of knowledge. There we discussed the Integrative Model, a learner-centered strategy designed to teach these topics, and in this chapter we examine the Lecture-Discussion Model, a teacher-centered approach to helping students understand organized bodies of knowledge. When you have completed your study of this chapter, you should be able to:

- Describe the theoretical foundation of the Lecture-Discussion Model.
- Use the Lecture-Discussion Model to plan for teaching organized bodies of knowledge.
- Construct different kinds of advance organizers.
- Implement effective lecture-discussion lessons.
- Assess content acquisition in lecture-discussion lessons.

Let's begin our study of the Lecture-Discussion Model by looking at a teacher using this model to teach a lesson on *reinforcement schedules* from a unit on behaviorism in a high school psychology class.

Lorrie Martello has covered both classical and operant conditioning and begins her class by reviewing the two concepts. "Explain how the two ideas are similar. . . . Antonio."

". . . Well, with classical conditioning, the response is out of the person's control, like learning to fear dogs, because they got bit by a dog, and . . . with operant conditioning the response is voluntary, like my dad picks up the stuff around his chair better now because my mom kisses him when he does it."

"Very good response, Antonio, and what do we call the kiss Antonio's dad is receiving? . . . Sherilyn?"

". . . A reinforcer," Sherilyn responds after hesitating for a couple seconds.

"Exactly," Lorrie smiles. "And that's where we're heading today."

With that she displays the following on the overhead.

Reinforcement schedules are applications of operant conditioning in which the frequency of rewards differs. This difference can be based on time or the behaviors that are displayed. When I periodically write comments on your papers for particularly good responses, I am using a reinforcement schedule.

"Now, let's look at this statement. . . .The first concept we should focus on is *reinforcement.* Remember we said that reinforcement results in an increase in behavior as a result of some desired consequence, such as a compliment for a person or a treat for a dog. . . . Now, when someone displays a behavior, we can reinforce it every time, some of the time, or not at all. So, for example, if your little brother volunteers to help you take the dishes out of the dishwasher, you can compliment him every time he does it, some of the time, or you may not compliment him at all. That's what we mean by a reinforcement schedule. . . . So, we can represent what we've just said with this outline," and Lorrie then displays the following diagram on the overhead.

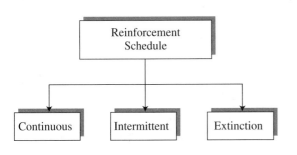

"Now, let's take a look at the diagram," Lorrie continues. "What do you suppose *continuous* means? . . . Jim?"

". . . Well, continuous must mean when we compliment him every time."

"Good, and how about *extinction?* . . . Delcia?"

". . . That must mean never . . . no compliments."

"Exactly," Lorrie smiles, ". . . and *intermittent?* . . . Candy?"

"Must be some of the time, but not all of the time."

"Good, all of you," Lorrie nods. ". . . Now, let's look back at classical and operant conditioning. . . . Are we talking about operant or classical when we talk about reinforcement schedules? . . . Juan?"

". . . I think, operant."

"And, why do you think so."

". . . Helping unload the dishwasher is a voluntary behavior. He can control whether he helps."

"And what else is a key idea? . . . Mike?"

". . ."

"What do we call the compliment you give your little brother?"

"Oh, a reinforcer."

"Good. . . . Now, let's go on. . . . Let's focus on the intermittent schedule, where we said that we compliment him some of the time but not all the time. This is called a *ratio schedule* because the compliments depend on his behavior. By that I mean, he gets complimented right after he helps with the dishes, but he doesn't get complimented every time.

"The other type of intermittent schedule is called an *interval schedule,* which depends on time. For example, sometimes when you're working in your groups, I'll come around and comment on the work you're doing. My comments are reinforcers, but they don't depend on a particular behavior . . . rather they depend on time. . . . So, let's add them to our diagram."

Lorrie then adds the terms to the diagram, so it appears as follows:

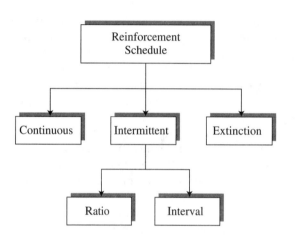

"So, when I periodically write comments on your papers, is that a ratio schedule, or an interval schedule? . . . What do you think? . . . David?"

". . . I think . . . ratio schedule."

"Why do you think so?"

". . . The comment depends on what we write. It doesn't depend on time."

"Excellent thinking, David," Lorrie smiles.

"So, how about our quizzes in here? We have a quiz nearly every Thursday. . . . Ratio or interval? . . . Lisa?"

". . . Interval."

"Okay, explain."

". . . We get reinforced when we get the quiz back on Friday, which depends on time."

"Very good everyone. . . . So, now let's keep our diagram in mind and go back to the statement we saw at the beginning of the lesson. . . . How does the diagram relate to it? . . . Kathy?" and Lorrie then briefly displays the description of reinforcement schedules on the overhead, and then puts the diagram back up.

". . . All of these are applications of operant conditioning," Kathy responds, pointing to the different parts of the diagram.

"And, how are continuous, intermittent, and extinction related to each other? . . . Disideria?"

". . . They tell how much . . . or how many reinforcers are given."

"Go ahead and add a little more to that. . . . What do you mean?" Lorrie probes.

". . . Well, *continuous* means a lot of reinforcers are given, . . . actually every time, and *intermittent* means some of the time, . . . and *extinction* means not at all."

"Good explanation, Desideria," Lorrie smiles.

"Now, we're going to switch gears for a few minutes. . . . I want you to work with your partner and write three different summary statements about what we discussed today. When you're finished, we'll discuss them and then I want you to hand them in. Go ahead and get started. You have 10 minutes.

As the name implies, the Lecture-Discussion Model derives from lectures, which have always been the most widely used teaching methods that exists (Cuban, 1984), and no evidence indicates that this has changed. Before we discuss the model, let's briefly examine lectures.

Lectures: Teacher Monologues

A **lecture** is *a form of instruction in which students receive information delivered in a verbal and (presumably) organized way by teachers.* The popularity of lectures can be traced to three factors (Eggen & Kauchak, 2004):

- Lectures are easy to plan; the planning process is reduced to organizing the content.
- Lectures are flexible; they can be applied to virtually all content areas.
- Lectures are simple to implement; they reduce the load on teachers' working memories, so novice teachers can use them. Most people can learn to deliver acceptable lectures. More sophisticated instruction is much more demanding.

In spite of their popularity, lectures are ineffective for many, if not most students. First, they put learners in passive roles by encouraging them to merely listen to and absorb information. We saw in Chapter 2 that social interaction is one of the principles of cognitive learning theory, and research on young (Berk, 2003) and poorly motivated students (Brophy, 1986) helps us understand why. If, for example, we observe a class of young children, we see that they sit quietly for the first few minutes of a teacher's explanation but soon start to fidget and look around. If the monologue continues, they not only tune out but also start talking and poking each other, seeking some type of activity.

Older students are usually less disruptive, but little learning takes place. Because they've learned that fidgeting and talking can get them into trouble, some prop their heads on their hands and attempt to appear interested. Others give up completely and work on homework for other classes, read, or put their heads down on their desks. Unfortunately, some teachers continue lecturing despite these clear signs that few are listening or learning.

Second, lectures can, and often do, overload students' working memories. As we also saw in Chapter 2, the capacity of working memory is limited, and the amount of information presented in lectures commonly exceeds its capacity. This helps us understand a common lament from teachers: "I explained it so carefully; it's as if they didn't hear a word I said." It is more likely that the students couldn't process and encode the information quickly enough, so much of it was lost.

Third, lectures don't allow teachers to assess learning progress. During interactive lessons, answers to teachers' questions give them information about student understanding. If understanding is inaccurate or incomplete, teachers can adjust by providing additional examples and asking more questions to remedy the problem. Because communication is one way in lectures, teachers have no way of making these assessments and adapting their instruction.

The ineffectiveness of lecture is well documented. In seven comparisons of lecture to discussion, discussion was superior in all seven on measures of retention and higher-order thinking. In addition, discussion was superior in seven of nine studies in terms of student attitude and motivation (McKeachie & Kulik, 1975).

The Lecture-Discussion Model is designed to overcome these deficiencies by combining brief presentations with discussions that actively involve learners. Let's look at an overview of the model.

The Lecture-Discussion Model: An Overview

In the lesson we just saw, Lorrie used the Lecture-Discussion Model to help her students understand connections among concepts within the topic *behaviorism*. In implementing the model, she first provided an overview that served as a framework for the lesson and then presented information in a brief lecture. She followed this presentation with questions that helped ensure that the students understood the information, a process called *comprehension monitoring*. Comprehension monitoring was followed by more questioning to promote *integration* of the new information with their existing background knowledge.

Lorrie employed the essential teaching strategies, discussed in Chapter 3, throughout the lesson. She was well organized, her lesson was aligned, she communicated clearly, and her diagrams provided a form of focus. She guided the entire process with questioning, and she brought the lesson to closure by having the students summarize what they had learned. As we said earlier, lecture-discussions are intended to capitalize on the strengths of lectures but overcome their weaknesses by actively involving students.

The Lecture-Discussion Model: Theoretical Foundations

The effectiveness of the Lecture-Discussion Model is grounded in two theoretical sources. First, it is designed to capitalize on the way our cognitive architecture processes information. Second, based on the work of David Ausubel (1963, 1968), teachers using the model present information in a systematic way, which helps students construct an organized understanding of the topic.

Information Processing

In Chapter 2 we saw that stimuli from the environment enter sensory memory, we select those stimuli that attract our attention and organize the information in working memory as we construct meaning from the experience. In the process of constructing understanding we retrieve information from long-term memory and integrate the new information with what we already know. The more extensive and better organized the networks we retrieve, the more effective the integration will be because more locations exist to connect new information to old. (As we saw in Chapter 7, these organized networks of information are called *schemas,* and *integration* is the fundamental process described in schema theory.)

Our new understanding is then encoded in long-term memory in networks that are more complex and better organized than those that existed prior to having the new experiences (Ormrod 2004; Schunk, 2004). These processes are outlined in Figure 10.1.

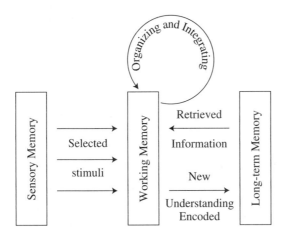

**FIGURE 10.1   Integrating New Knowledge
with Prior Understanding**

Let's see how they worked in Lorrie's lesson. She first presented the students with information in a brief lecture. She then asked the students questions to determine if they had selected the desired information and organized it accurately in their working memories. This process also helped ensure that the students' working memories were not overloaded.

She also attempted to help the students organize the information by providing diagrams that illustrated the conceptual structure of the content. (We should emphasize that, because learners construct their own understanding, the way the information is organized in their working memories and stored in their long-term memories may not be the way that Lorrie organized it. This is the reason that Lorrie's questioning to check their comprehension was so essential.)

After checking to ensure that the students' comprehension of the material she presented was accurate, Lorrie then asked additional questions that helped them integrate the new information with what they already knew. After promoting integration, she started a new cycle by presenting additional information, again checking comprehension, and again promoting integration. The process then repeats itself as many times as necessary until the lesson comes to closure.

We see this process illustrated in both the real world and in school. A person who has read extensively about a topic, for example, has an advantage compared to a person who has less experience. In this regard, "the more you know, the more capacity you have for knowing" because you have more background knowledge with which new information can be integrated.

The patterns we see in schools support this notion. Students who come to us with a wealth of past experiences typically learn more and faster than those who have not had such experiences (Eggen & Kauchak, 2004). This premise is a fundamental principle that supports early enrichment programs for disadvantaged students.

Our goal as teachers should be to help learners encode information in logical relationships. Research indicates that information logically organized in long-term memory results in:

- Increased initial learning
- Better memory and retention
- Improved transfer to new contexts (Mayer, 2002; Ormrod, 2004; Schunk, 2004)

Meaningful Verbal Learning: The Work of David Ausubel

One of the most influential people in bringing the ideas behind schema theory to classrooms was a psychologist named David Ausubel. Beginning with studies done in the early 1960s and captured in his book, *The Psychology of Meaningful Verbal Learning* (1963), Ausubel stressed the importance of organized information in long-term memory as an aid to further learning.

According to Ausubel, **meaningful verbal learning** is *the acquisition of ideas that are linked to other ideas.* In contrast, **rote learning** is *the memorization of specific items of information isolated from other items.* Meaningful learning occurs when the ideas in a new schema are connected both to each other and to previously established schemas.

Though Ausubel favored teacher-directed instruction, he was strongly opposed to putting students in passive roles. Consistent with Ausubel's views, Lorrie used questioning to involve the students, and her goal throughout was to help the students find relationships in the information they were studying. One of the most prominent ideas to emerge from Ausubel's work is the concept of *advance organizers.*

Advance Organizers. **Advance organizers** are *verbal or written statements at the beginning of a lesson that preview and structure new material and link it to the students' existing schemas.* Advance organizers are like cognitive roadmaps; they allow students to see where they have been and where they are going. Effective advance organizers are:

- Presented prior to learning a larger body of information
- More general than the content that follows
- Presented in paragraph form
- Illustrated with a concrete example that helps learners identify the relationship between the ideas in the organizer and the information to follow (Corkill, 1992)

To illustrate how advance organizers work, let's look again at the way Lorrie began her lesson. She displayed the statement

> Reinforcement schedules are applications of operant conditioning in which the frequency of rewards differs. This difference can be based on time or the behaviors that are displayed. When I periodically write comments on your papers for particularly good responses, I am using a reinforcement schedule.

This was her advance organizer. It was a short paragraph, she presented it at the beginning of her lesson, and she used a concrete and personalized example to illustrate it. We will examine advance organizers in more detail when we discuss planning for lecture-discussion lessons. Let's turn to it.

Planning for Lecture-Discussion Lessons

The planning process for lessons using the Lecture-Discussion Model involves four essential steps, which are illustrated in Figure 10.2 and discussed in the sections that follow.

Identifying Topics

As we've seen in each of the earlier chapters, planning for lessons with the Lecture-Discussion Model begins with a topic. If the topic is an organized body of knowledge, the model is an effective counterpart to the Integrative Model, which you studied in Chapter 7.

The Lecture-Discussion Model can be used to organize topics in two ways. First, it can help organize an entire course or a unit within the course. You can use it to make decisions about the scope and sequence of the content, and it can guide students in their progress though the material over an extended period of time. The second use of the model is to structure content within a lesson. Used in this way, the model provides direction in beginning, developing, and ending lessons.

Lorrie used the model to organize a series of lessons on behaviorism, one of which we saw at the beginning of the chapter. These dual levels of organization apply in a variety of content areas. How this might look in a geography class is illustrated in Figure 10.3.

We see the two planning functions illustrated in the diagram. First, it helped plan the year's work in geography and a smaller unit on elements of the physical environment. Second, it was used to relate concepts in a single lesson on landforms. The focus of the lesson was to understand the characteristics of the different landforms and how they related to each other.

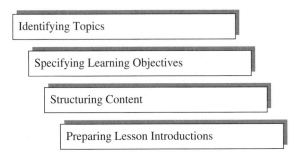

FIGURE 10.2   Planning for Lecture-Discussion Lessons

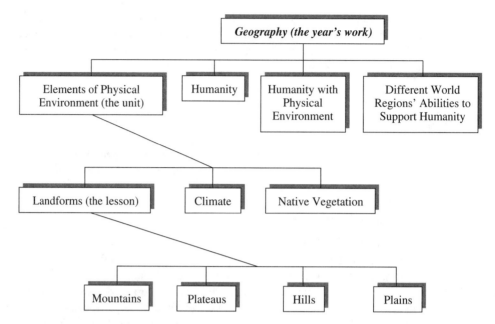

FIGURE 10.3   Organization of Content in Geography

Specifying Learning Objectives

Having identified a topic, you next consider learning objectives. In Lorrie's case, she wanted the students to understand specific similarities and differences between continuous and intermittent reinforcement schedules and how they related to extinction. She also wanted the students to understand differences between ratio and interval intermittent schedules.

Note here that Lorrie's objective was for the students to understand the *relationships* among the concepts, not the concepts themselves. If her focus had been on a single concept, such as *continuous reinforcement,* a different approach, such as using the Inductive Model or the Direct-Instruction Model, would have been more appropriate.

Structuring Content

After learning objectives for the lesson have been identified, the content must be structured so that it can be presented in an organized way. Research indicates that organization is essential for promoting meaningful learning and retrieval (Bruning et al., 2004; Durso & Coggins, 1991).

Hierarchies can often be used effectively for organizing content. Preparing hierarchies is reasonably easy, and the relationships in them are clear. We saw how Lorrie used a hierarchy to structure the content for her lesson. As another example, a lesson on mammals could be structured according to taxonomic description. The structure of such a lesson might appear as shown in Figure 10.4.

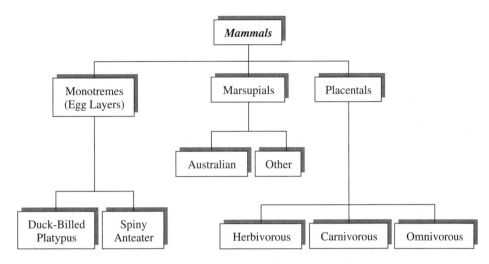

FIGURE 10.4   Hierarchy for Organizing Information on Mammals

In cases where the material doesn't have a natural structure, you can impose structure on it. For example, a social studies unit on community helpers might be structured as shown in Figure 10.5. Organizing content in this way allows students to see how different community helpers relate to each other and how they relate to the general idea of community helpers.

Another way of imposing a hierarchy on the content is through the use of interrelated generalizations. For example, a lesson based on the generalization, "America has expanded

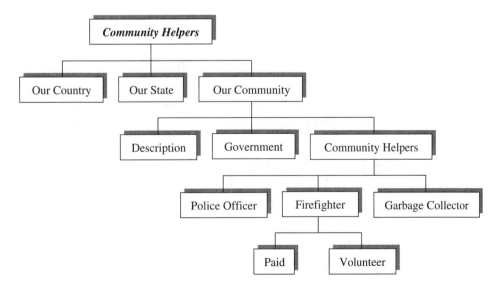

FIGURE 10.5   Hierarchy for Organizing Community Helpers

because of natural resources, form of government, and a unique mixture of people," might be structured as appears in Figure 10.6. In this structure, the generalization is divided into narrower topics, which are either illustrated with examples or further broken down into subordinate concepts.

Although hierarchies are often effective, content can be structured in other ways as well. Outlines, concept maps, models, graphs, geographic maps, and matrices all impose structure on content. For example, the outlines included at the beginning of each chapter of this book are attempts to structure the content of each chapter to make the topics meaningful and interconnected. The matrices you encountered in Chapter 7 are also forms of structuring content.

In many cases, teachers combine different structures to organize their lessons. For instance, a teacher preparing a unit on the Civil War might use a hierarchy that includes elements such as causes of the war, significant battles and events, outcomes from the war, and how the war still affects us today as a structure for the unit. A lesson on the causes of the war could include a map that shows the northern and southern colonies, together with a matrix that includes information about the geography and economics of the North and the South. Significant battles and events could be structured with a matrix, and outcomes might be structured with a matrix or an outline. There is no single best way to structure content, and the form you use depends on your professional judgment. The key to structuring content is to make the relationships between ideas as clear as possible, which makes the topic meaningful for students.

In all cases, when teachers structure their material, they should keep students' background knowledge in mind. For example, if "modern capitalist democratic countries" are part of the content, and students don't understand the terms *capitalist* and *democratic,* the teacher's planning must include ways of illustrating these concepts. Otherwise, the lesson will be less meaningful to students.

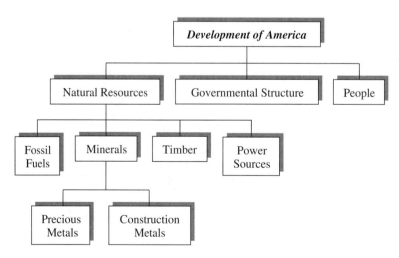

FIGURE 10.6   Hierarchy for Organizing Generalizations

Preparing Lesson Introductions

When we begin lessons or make transitions from one lesson to another, we often incorrectly assume that students are able to quickly focus on the topic at hand. In one study of elementary classrooms, researchers found that only 5 percent of teachers made an explicit effort to introduce lessons in a way that would draw students into them (Anderson, Brubacker, Alleman-Brooks, & Duffy, 1985), and as a result, less learning took place.

To draw students into a lesson, teachers use the essential teaching skill **focus,** which we described in Chapter 3 as *the set of teacher actions at the beginning of lessons that attracts students' attention and maintains their attention during learning activities.* Focus alerts students that a transition is taking place and provides something tangible and interesting to which to attend.

Although focus is important for any teaching strategy, it is particularly important when the Lecture-Discussion Model is used because, unlike the Inductive, Concept Attainment, and Integrative Models, which immediately put students in active roles, the learning activity in the Lecture-Discussion Model begins with the teacher presenting information. If students are not focused on the topic at the beginning of the lesson, the information that follows will be less meaningful.

Preparing lesson introductions that provide focus for the students can be accomplished in several ways. Some types and examples are outlined in Table 10.1.

In addition to the forms of focus outlined in Table 10.1, advance organizers can be effectively used as lesson introductions. Let's look at them in more detail.

Preparing Advance Organizers. The characteristics of advance organizers were outlined earlier in the chapter, and we saw an example with Lorrie's lesson. Let's look at hers again.

> Reinforcement schedules are applications of operant conditioning in which the frequency of rewards differs. This difference can be based on time or the behaviors that are displayed. When I periodically write comments on your papers for particularly good responses, I am using a reinforcement schedule.

TABLE 10.1   Different Types of Focus

Type of Focus	Example
Discrepant events	An ice cube is placed in a glass of water and floats, and a second cube is dropped in pure alcohol (which, because it is a clear liquid, students believe is water) and it sinks.
Problems	A lesson on genetics begins with the teacher asking why one of the students in the class has blue eyes whereas another has brown eyes.
Demonstrations	A teacher begins a lesson on magnetism by demonstrating that the magnet will pick up a paper clip but not a piece of aluminum foil.

As we saw earlier, an advance organizer precedes the lesson; it is more general than the content that follows; it is written in paragraph form; and it includes a concrete example. These characteristics were included in Lorrie's advance organizer.

As another example, consider the following, which could be used with the lesson on landforms mentioned earlier in the chapter.

> Landforms are the geographical features of our planet. They differ in age, elevation, and the types of materials that make them up. The mountains our town is in is one type of landform.

Again we see that the advance organizer is a general statement in paragraph form that includes a concrete example.

When the content is unfamiliar or abstract, analogies can be effectively used as advance organizers. The following is an example.

> An electric circuit is like the water system in your house. The wires are like your water pipes, the battery is like a pump, and the water flowing through the pipes is the current. For the circuit to work, all the parts must be connected, just as your pipes must be connected if you are to get water.

Analogies are used to help students connect unfamiliar content to what they already know. In this regard, the entire advance organizer is a form of concrete example, so it doesn't necessarily include a specific additional one.

Each of these advance organizers is intended to provide a framework to which the content of the lesson will be linked. When links are made in content, it becomes more meaningful for students.

Regardless of the type of lesson introduction that is prepared, each is designed to attract students' attention and provide an umbrella for the lesson.

Implementing Lecture-Discussion Lessons

Having identified learning objectives, structured content, and prepared a lesson beginning, you are now ready to implement the lesson. A lecture discussion lesson exists in five phases, which are outlined with their learning and motivation functions in Table 10.2 and discussed in the sections that follow.

Phase 1: Introduction

Phase 1 of a lecture-discussion lesson begins when the teacher reviews to activate learners' background knowledge and presents the advance organizer or other form of lesson beginning to attract attention and provide a framework for the lessons. As we said earlier in the chapter, lesson beginnings are important when the Lecture-Discussion Model is used because the

**TABLE 10.2   Learning and Motivation Functions for the Phases
of the Lecture-Discussion Model**

Phase	Learning and Motivation Function
Phase 1: Introduction Review and present a form of focus for the lesson	■ Attracts attention ■ Activates background knowledge
Phase 2: Presentation Organized information is presented	■ Provides background knowledge ■ Begins schema production
Phase 3: Comprehension monitoring Questions check students' understanding of the presented material	■ Checks perception ■ Puts learners in active roles
Phase 4: Integration New learning is connected to existing understanding	■ Elaborates schemas ■ Achieves equilibrium
Phase 5: Review and closure	■ Completes schema production ■ Promotes perceptions of competence

teacher presents information in Phase 2, so Phase 1 is intended to put learners in roles that are as cognitively active as possible.

An oversight teachers commonly commit is to present the advance organizer or other form of lesson introduction at the beginning and then ignore it as the lesson develops. If our goal is to have students understand relationships among ideas, these relationships should be emphasized throughout the lesson. Periodically referring to the advance organizer, problem, or demonstration throughout the lesson helps students organize (mentally) and encode the content. Lorrie displayed her advance organizer at the beginning of the lesson, and later in the lesson she said, "So, now let's keep our diagram in mind and go back to the statement we saw at the beginning of the lesson. . . . How does the diagram relate to it? . . . Kathy?" as she displayed her advance organizer again. This is important if the lesson introduction is to be effective.

Phase 2: Presentation

After introducing the lesson, the teacher presents information designed to develop students' background knowledge. Including the hierarchy or other form of lesson organizer as part of the presentation is important in this process because it helps students see the structure in the content and promotes schema production. Lorrie displayed her advance organizer at the beginning of the lesson and then described continuous and intermittent reinforcement, and extinction, and included an example in her presentation. She then displayed her hierarchy, which outlined what she had said.

The value of this presentation format can be explained with schema theory and Ausubel's meaningful verbal learning. Broader concepts are used as the foundations for new concepts, and as students learn new concepts, they are connected to those that are broader and more general. The most important aspect of this process is that ideas are not learned in isolation; knowledge is cumulative and the outcome is an interconnected set of ideas.

As we look back at Lorrie's presentation, we see that it was very short—literally no more than a few minutes. Teachers commonly overestimate the listening capacities of their students. Before a recent Superbowl football game, advertisers were concerned whether 90-second commercials would be too long to hold viewers' attention. Ninety seconds! Compare this with the length of many lectures. Research indicates that retention rates drop sharply a few minutes after the beginning of a lecture (Gage & Berliner, 1992). Our cognitive architecture discussed in Chapter 2 helps us understand why. First, attention quickly wanes during lectures, and information obviously must be attended to or it can't be processed. Second, the capacity of our working memories is limited, and lengthy explanations quickly overload them. Comprehension monitoring through teacher questioning is one way to prevent or minimize this problem.

Phase 3: Comprehension Monitoring

Comprehension monitoring is *the process of informally assessing student understanding in lecture-discussion lessons,* and it is most commonly accomplished through teacher questioning. Comprehension monitoring is essential because it promotes student involvement and provides students with feedback about their understanding.

How often should comprehension monitoring occur? Although the answer depends on the difficulty of the content and the development of the students, *it almost cannot be overdone.* First, there is a tendency for lecture-discussion lessons to disintegrate into teacher monologues; comprehension monitoring prevents this. Second, it's virtually impossible for students to be too involved in a lesson; questioning provides opportunities for students to be cognitively engaged. Third, students need constant feedback and teachers need to continually assess their students' understanding; comprehension monitoring provides opportunities for both. To see how quickly Lorrie moved to the comprehension-monitoring phase of the lesson, let's look again at some dialogue in her lesson.

> **LORRIE:** Now, let's take a look at the diagram. . . . What do you suppose *continuous* means? . . . Jim?
>
> **JIM:** . . . Well, continuous must mean when we compliment him every time.
>
> **LORRIE:** Good, and how about *extinction?* . . . Delcia?
>
> **DELCIA:** . . . That must mean never . . . no compliments.
>
> **LORRIE:** Exactly . . . and *intermittent?* . . . Candy?
>
> **CANDY:** Must be some of the time, but not all of the time.

With this set of questions Lorrie was able to informally assess the extent to which the students understood the information in her presentation (which is the source of the term *comprehension monitoring*). The questions came immediately after a short presentation, and they took only a matter of minutes.

Information processing theory and schema theory both help us understand the importance of comprehension monitoring. First, the way students perceive information is the way it will be transferring into working memory for further processing. If their comprehension of the material that is presented is incomplete or inaccurate, the information that is processed in working memory, and ultimately encoded into long-term memory, will also be inaccurate, and the schemas that are constructed will be incomplete or invalid. Second, comprehension monitoring moves students into active roles, and being cognitively active is a crucial factor in accurately encoding information in long-term memory.

Schema theory also helps us understand why comprehension monitoring is important. Learners bring individual and varying schemas to the learning activity, and new learning will be interpreted based on prior understanding. If their prior understanding is incomplete or invalid, the new schemas they construct will be distorted or inaccurate. Comprehension monitoring helps prevent this from happening.

Although questioning is most common, other ways of monitoring comprehension exist. They include:[*]

- *Question/write.* The teacher poses a question, asks all students to write down an answer, and then asks for volunteers to share.
- *Examples.* The teacher asks students to give examples or explain ones provided by the teacher.
- *Think-pair-share.* The teacher poses a question, ask students to individually come up with an answer, share with a partner, and finally share with the class.
- *Voting.* When questions are controversial or require a judgment call, the teacher asks students to form an opinion and then vote with their hands and share their thinking with the group.
- *Choral response.* When a question has a single right answer choral responses can be used to involve the whole class (Harmin, 1994).

These response variations can provide the teacher with feedback about the extent to which students comprehend the content and also promote their deep processing of information.

Phase 4: Integration

To begin this section, let's look at some additional dialogue from Lorrie's lesson, beginning with the Candy's comment at the end of the last dialogue we read.

> **CANDY:** Must be some of the time, but not all of the time.
>
> **LORRIE:** Good, all of you. . . . Now, let's look back at classical and operant conditioning . . . Are we talking about operant or classical when we talk about reinforcement schedules? . . . Juan?
>
> **JUAN:** . . . I think, operant.
>
> **LORRIE:** And, why do you think so?
>
> **JUAN:** . . . Helping unload the dishwasher is a voluntary behavior. He can control whether he helps.

> **LORRIE:**   And what else is a key idea? . . . Mike?
>
> **MIKE:**   . . .
>
> **LORRIE:**   What do we call the compliment you give your little brother?
>
> **MIKE:**   Oh, a reinforcer.

Here we see that Lorrie continued her questioning, but the questions didn't focus on reinforcement schedules; rather, they asked the students to connect their understanding of reinforcement schedules to their understanding of classical and operant conditioning. This illustrates **integration,** which is *the process of linking new information to prior understanding.* If new and prior understanding are not connected, the goal of constructing interrelated schemas will not be reached.

Integration is a natural extension of comprehension monitoring. The difference between the two lies in the focus of the questions. During comprehension monitoring questions attempt to determine whether students understand the individual ideas presented; during integration, questions focus on relating new information and prior understanding as well as relating the new ideas to each other. In the dialogue Lorrie's focus was on relating reinforcement schedules to the students' prior understanding of operant and classical conditioning. Questions that asked students to find similarities and differences in the types of reinforcement schedules would also have been a form of integration.

The exact type of question depends on the content being taught, and the line between comprehension monitoring and integration will sometimes be blurred. The essential characteristic of integration is that the questions cause students to search for links with other ideas in the lesson.

Notice also, that integration won't always be smooth and effortless. We saw this illustrated in the dialogue when Lorrie had to prompt Mike. In classrooms, much more prompting will probably be required, but the effort will be more than worth it in the learning it produces.

This process is supported by research (Cruikshank, 1985; Eggen & Kauchak, 2004), and it makes intuitive sense. When parts of a lesson are interrelated, deeper understanding results. Links help ensure that the new content is being learned as an interconnected body.

Schema theory and information processing both help us understand the importance of integration. First, the more interrelated a schema, the more meaningful it becomes, which contributes to learners' equilibrium. Second, as we saw in Chapter 2, interrelating schemas reduces the load on students' working memories. As information becomes increasingly related, more information is encoded and available for retrieval without an increase in load on working memory.

Lecture-Discussion Cycles: The Building Blocks of Lessons

What you saw illustrated in the previous sections was one **lecture-discussion cycle** which is *a recurrent sequence of presenting information, monitoring comprehension, and integration.* It is at the heart of lecture-discussion lessons. After one cycle is completed, a second occurs, then a third, and so on until the lesson is complete. Each cycle includes a brief presentation, followed by comprehension monitoring, and integration.

Integration is the essential link in lecture-discussion cycles. With each cycle integration becomes broader and deeper as the information in one cycle is integrated with content from earlier cycles. To illustrate, let's look at some more dialogue from Lorrie's lesson. In the first cycle Lorrie presented some information about reinforcement schedules, checked the students' comprehension of continuous reinforcement, intermittent reinforcement, and extinction, and helped them integrate their understanding with their prior understanding of operant and classical conditioning. She then began a second cycle by presenting some additional information. Let's look at some additional dialogue.

LORRIE: Good. . . . Now, let's go on. . . . Let's focus on the intermittent schedule, where we said that we compliment him some of the time but not all the time. This is called a *ratio schedule* because the compliments depend on his behavior. By that I mean, he gets complimented right after he helps with the dishes, but he doesn't get complimented every time.

The other type of intermittent schedule is called an *interval schedule,* which depends on time. For example, sometimes when you're working in your groups, I'll come around and comment on the work you're doing. My comments are reinforcers, but they don't depend on a particular behavior . . . rather they depend on time. . . . So, let's add them to our diagram. [Lorrie then added the items to the diagram.]

So, when I periodically write comments on your papers, is that a ratio schedule, or an interval schedule? . . . What do you think? . . . David?

DAVID: . . . I think . . . ratio schedule.

LORRIE: Why do you think so?

DAVID: . . . The comment depends on what we write. It doesn't depend on time.

LORRIE: Excellent thinking, David. . . . So, how about our quizzes in here? We have a quiz nearly every Thursday. . . . Ratio or interval? . . . Lisa?

LISA: . . . Interval.

LORRIE: Okay, explain.

LISA: . . . We get reinforced when we get the quiz back on Friday, which depends on time.

LORRIE: Very good everyone. . . . So, now let's keep our diagram in mind and go back to the statement we saw at the beginning of the lesson. . . . How does the diagram relate to it? . . . Kathy? [Lorrie then displays her advance organizer and diagram again.]

KATHY: . . . All of these are applications of operant conditioning.

LORRIE: And, how are continuous, intermittent, and extinction related to each other? . . . Disideria?

DISIDERIA: . . . They tell how much . . . or how many reinforcers are given.

LORRIE: Go ahead and add a little more to that. . . . What do you mean?

DISIDERIA: . . . Well, *continuous* means a lot of reinforcers are given, . . . actually every time, and *intermittent* means some of the time, . . . and *extinction* means not at all.

LORRIE: Good explanation, Desideria.

The dialogue we've just seen represents a second lecture-discussion cycle. It began when Lorrie presented information about ratio and interval intermittent schedules, moved to comprehension monitoring with Lorrie's question to David about her comments on their papers, and shifted to integration when Lorrie asked how the information and her advance organizer related to the diagram she had presented.

Two aspects of the second cycle are significant. First, she monitored the students' comprehension by asking them to identify examples as ratio or interval schedules. Being able to classify examples is one of the most effective forms of comprehension monitoring that exists. Second, the integration in her second cycle was simultaneously broader (linking the information to the diagram and advance organizer) and more specific (comparing continuous and intermittent reinforcers and extinction). The result was a more organized and interrelated body of knowledge.

Linking Lecture-Discussion Cycles. Each lecture discussion cycle takes only a few minutes, and by stringing several of these cycles together, the teacher can consolidate the ideas in an organized body of knowledge into an effective lesson. This process is outlined in Figure 10.7. We saw two of the cycles illustrated in Lorrie's lesson and the process continues until the entire body of knowledge identified in the teacher's learning objectives has been taught.

Phase 5: Review and Closure

As we saw in Chapter 3, review and closure are essential teaching skills. They are particularly important when the Lecture-Discussion Model is used because they further promote the integration of ideas. **Review** *summarizes the topic, emphasizes important points, and provides a link to which new learning can be attached.* Although effective at any point in a learning activity, it is most effective at the beginnings and ends of lessons. Lorrie reviewed

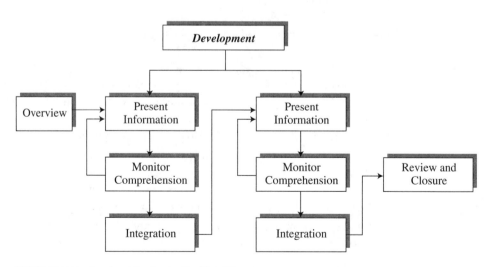

FIGURE 10.7 Lecture Cycles in the Total Lesson

at the beginning of her lesson to remind students of the larger topic of behaviorism and to ensure that new information was embedded in that content. We also saw that review is an essential component of Phase 1 of the model. As we saw in Chapter 3, **closure** is *a form of review that occurs at the end of a lesson*; it summarizes, structures, and completes the topic. Lorrie brought her lesson to closure when she asked her students to write summary statements about the information that had discussed that day.

Schema theory and motivation theory both help us understand the importance of closure. When a lesson comes to closure, students' schemas will be as complete, organized, and interrelated as they're going to be at that point in their understanding. This understanding is what they take away from the lesson and bring to the next lesson.

Motivation theory also helps us understand the importance of closure. As students see connections among the topics they're studying, their perceptions of their own competence increase, and, as we saw in Chapter 2, the need for competence is basic according to motivation theory.

Variations of the Model

In the preceding sections we saw that the primary purpose of the Lecture-Discussion Model is to help students construct interrelated schemas by finding relationships between old and new learning and among the different parts of an organized body of knowledge, such as the relationships among reinforcement schedules and how they relate to operant conditioning in Lorrie's lesson. In this section we examine some additional ways of organizing content within lecture-discussion lessons and strategies for increasing motivation when using the model.

Additional Ways of Organizing Content

Within the general framework of lecture-discussion lessons, content can be organized in a number of ways. One of these is the use of *minihierarchies* to supplement other models. For example, recall Jim Rooney's lesson on the rules for forming singular and plural possessives in Chapter 5. At some point in the lesson, a hierarchy identifying the relationships among the different parts of the rules would have made the material more meaningful for the students. The hierarchy might appear as shown in Figure 10.8.

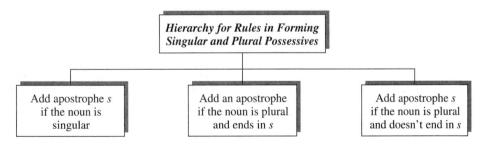

FIGURE 10.8   Hierarchy for Rules in Forming Singular and Plural Possessives

This hierarchy helps students see the relationships among the different parts of the rule because it gives a visual illustration of when the apostrophe appears before the *s,* when it is used after the *s,* and why no apostrophe is used in some cases.

As another example, consider a teacher discussing the topic of closure in mathematics. (An operation is considered to be closed if the outcome of the operation produces a number that belongs to the same set as the numbers combined in the operation.) A discussion of the topic could be supplemented with a brief hierarchy such as the one shown in Figure 10.9.

This outline is effective because it illustrates a pattern; the number of closed operations increases as we go from counting to rational numbers. Students could then be encouraged to hypothesize on the basis of the pattern and test their hypotheses with other numbers and sets. In addition to helping make the concepts more meaningful, the hierarchy provides an avenue for promoting deeper understanding of the ideas being discussed.

A second option that takes advantage of the organizing powers of the Lecture-Discussion Model uses hierarchies in conjunction with matrices. (Recall some of the matrices we saw in Chapter 7.) As an example, consider the outline in Figure 10.10 used with a unit of study on the novel.

The advantage of an outline such as this is that it shows at a glance the superordinate, coordinate, and subordinate relationships contained in the content. However, diagrams can become cluttered, and when they do, the information in them is harder to use. In this case a matrix, such as the one shown in Figure 10.11 could be used as a supplement. Matrices illustrating salient aspects of closely related concepts can help students organize similarities and differences in their minds, keeping the concepts distinct but connected. This is illustrated in Figure 10.11.

The use of a matrix as a supplement to a hierarchy has two advantages. One is that a chart allows the teacher to include and organize data for a lesson; the second is that it helps promote thorough integration of ideas. The structural outline graphically illustrates how the concepts are differentiated; the chart, in turn, ensures their integration through an analysis of the data in it.

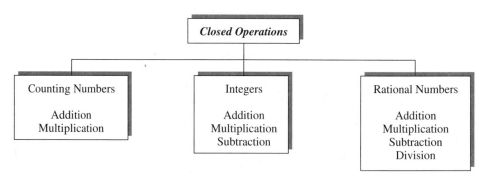

FIGURE 10.9   Hierarchy for Representing Closure in Mathematical Operations

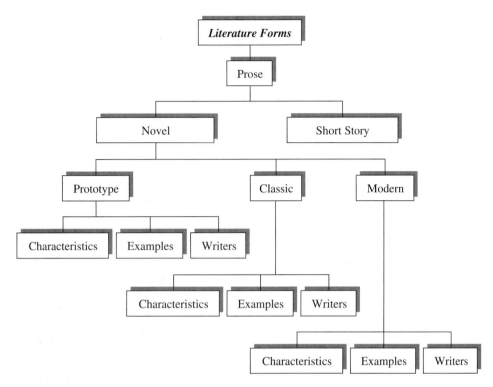

FIGURE 10.10   Hierarchy for Organizing Information on the Novel

TYPES OF NOVELS

	Characteristics	Examples	Writers
Prototypes			
Classic			
Modern			

FIGURE 10.11   Matrix Used as a Supplement for Organizing Content

Increasing Motivation and Learning through Group Interaction

The need to involve students is a principle of motivation theory, and it is emphasized in all of the models discussed in this text. This is a particularly important issue for this chapter, because students can become cognitively passive during the presentation phase of lecture-discussion lessons. Although questioning is the primary way of promoting involvement, groupwork can also be used to increase involvement and motivation in lecture-discussion lessons.

Group interaction provides students with opportunities to think about and clarify their own ideas about a topic, articulate them, compare their views with those of other students, and generate new ideas through dialogue and verbal give and take.

Research supports the effectiveness of group interaction as a motivational tool. In one study of elementary and secondary teachers' motivational practices, group tasks were reported as a major motivational strategy by 55 percent of the teachers (Zahorik, 1996). This same group of teachers recommended avoiding sedentary activities, including lectures and passive listening. Observations in classrooms also support the motivational effectiveness of groupwork; researchers found engagement rates above 90 percent in the majority of small groups they studied (Emmer & Gerwels, 1998). Teachers attributed these high engagement rates to high student active involvement in groupwork learning tasks.

Groupwork is compatible with lecture-discussion lessons, particularly in the comprehension-monitoring and integration phases. For example, during the comprehension-monitoring phase of her second lecture-discussion cycle, Lorrie could have had the students work together to decide if her comments on their papers and the quizzes they took in class were ratio or interval schedules. This phase was particularly appropriate for groupwork because specific answers were required, they were conceptual rather than memorized, and the co-construction of understanding could have occurred during the discussions. More students being involved during groupwork is an advantage. Although effective questioning is essential, students not directly involved in answering the question can become passive, particularly if several minutes go by before they're called on.

Groupwork can also be used during the integration and review and closure phases of the lesson. Teachers can ask small groups to relate concepts and present their ideas to the class as a whole. Different groups often come up with varying descriptions of relationships and conclusions, and these variations provide opportunities to compare perspectives and clarify differences. Asking students to summarize ideas also has motivational benefits because students feel greater ownership of the ideas discussed, which contributes to their sense of personal control and autonomy, both essential factors in motivation.

Assessing Student Understanding in Lecture-Discussion Lessons

The Lecture-Discussion Model is designed to teach relationships in organized bodies of knowledge. This is similar to the goals for the Integrative Model but different from those for the Inductive, Concept Attainment, and Direct-Instruction Models, which are designed to teach specific topics in the form of concepts, generalizations, principles, rules, and procedural skills.

Assessing understanding of these specific forms of content has been discussed in earlier chapters, so we won't examine it further here. Instead, because the Lecture-Discussion Model is designed to teach relationships among them, we want to focus on the decisions teachers make in assessing students' understanding of these relationships.

The ability to relate different topics depends on an understanding of the topics themselves, so assessment should involve both the specific topics and the relationships among them. As an example, consider the following item that might be used to assess Lorrie's students' understanding of reinforcement schedules.

Read the following anecdote and answer the questions that follow:

> Mrs. Cortez collects homework on Mondays, Wednesdays, and Fridays, whereas Mrs. Amato collects it periodically but doesn't announce when she will collect it. (She averages 3 days a week on different days.) Both teachers score and return the homework each day after giving it.
>
> 1. Identify the type of reinforcement schedule each teacher is using.
> 2. Explain why it is that type in each case.
> 3. Based on our understanding of reinforcement schedules, which teacher is likely to be most effective in promoting students' efforts on homework?

This item is designed to accomplish three goals:

- It measures students' understanding of the concepts of fixed-interval and variable-interval schedules of reinforcement.
- It measures their understanding of the differences between the two concepts.
- It shows students how the topics they're studying can be applied to the real world.

In addition, being able to explain *why* the first was fixed-interval and the second was variable-interval requires higher-order thinking. Ideally, assessments should accomplish all of these goals.

Items that ask students to apply information to new situations are important for both motivation and transfer. They show how ideas relate to the real world and encourage students to apply information to new settings. As another example of asking students to apply information to a new situation, consider the following item:

> Describe how the staging for the Greek play, *Oedipus Rex,* would be different if it were done in an Elizabethan theater.

In order to answer this question correctly, students must know the characteristics of Elizabethan theater and apply them to a Greek play. This information provides the teacher with a measure of the extent to which the schemas for theater in the two eras had been integrated with the students' prior knowledge.

Understanding the relationships between concepts is an important goal in lecture-discussion lessons. One way of measuring students' understanding of subordinate, coordinate, and superordinate relationships is to provide them with a list of concepts and ask them to arrange the concepts hierarchically. Research indicates that students' abilities to relate concepts hierarchically is an effective way to measure relationships between concepts (Winitzky, Kauchak, & Kelly, 1994). As an example, consider a lesson on vertebrates in a high school biology class. The teacher would provide the students with the following list of concepts related to vertebrates and ask the students to organize them hierarchically.

Reptiles	Birds	Vertebrates
Fish	Warm-blooded	Mammals
Snakes	Monotremes	Placentals
Frogs	Salamanders	Cold-blooded
Marsupials	Turtles	Lizards
Amphibians		

The hierarchy that students create might then appear as shown in Figure 10.12.

The examples we've given are only a few of the ways that learners' understanding of relationships among ideas can be assessed. Many more exist. With effort and with a learning focus in mind, you can continually improve your assessments, and with them the quality of your students' learning.

Summary

Lectures: Teacher Monologues

Lectures, forms of instruction in which teachers verbally present information to students, are popular because they're easy to plan, they're flexible, and they're simple to implement. However, they are often ineffective, particularly for young and poorly motivated students, because they put learners in passive roles, they commonly overload students' working memories, and they don't allow teachers to informally assess learning progress.

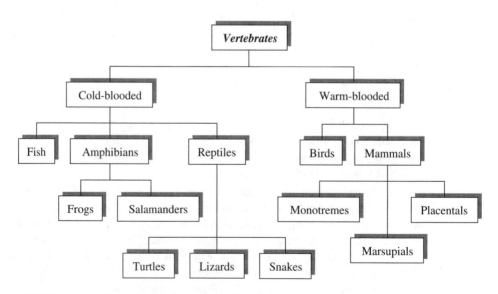

FIGURE 10.12   Hierarchy for Organizing Vertebrates

The Lecture-Discussion Model: An Overview

The Lecture-Discussion Model is a teacher-directed model designed to help learners understand relationships in organized bodies of knowledge. As opposed to content-specific models, which focus on individual concepts, the Lecture-Discussion Model helps students understand not only concepts but also how they are related.

The Lecture-Discussion Model: Theoretical Foundations

Grounded in schema theory and David Ausubel's concept of meaningful verbal learning, the model is designed to help learners link new information with prior learning and relate the different parts of new learning to each other. The model is designed to overcome some of the most glaring weaknesses of the lecture method by strongly emphasizing teacher questioning and learner involvement in the learning process.

Planning for Lecture-Discussion Lessons

Planning for lecture-discussion lessons involves identifying goals, assessing students' backgrounds, structuring content, and preparing advance organizers. The goal of teacher planning in this model is to ensure that new content is learned in a meaningful, related manner and integrated with previously learned ideas.

Implementing Lecture-Discussion Lessons

Lecture-discussion lessons begin with an introduction that draws students into the lesson and provides an overview of the lesson's focus. During the presentation stage, the teacher shares new information, linking it to students' schemas. Comprehension monitoring ensures that students understand new ideas; integration links these ideas to each other and to previously learned content. In the final phases, review and closure, students are further encouraged to integrate ideas.

Variations of the Model

Matrices provide alternate ways of representing and organizing content. One of their advantages is that they can store information that students can use in constructing new ideas.

Group processes can complement lecture discussions by providing increased opportunities for student involvement and dialogue. Teacher planning is required to ensure that the groups function smoothly and that group tasks are integrated into the structure of the model.

Assessing Student Understanding in Lecture-Discussion Lessons

Assessment with this model focuses on students' understanding of relationships among the topics they study and application of those topics to new situations. This requires alternate items that extend beyond the measurement of specific concepts.

I M P O R T A N T   C O N C E P T S

Advance organizers (p. 318)
Closure (p. 331)
Comprehension monitoring
(p. 326)

Focus (p. 323)
Integration (p. 328)
Lecture (p. 315)
Lecture-discussion cycle (p. 328)

Meaningful verbal learning
(p. 318)
Review (p. 330)
Rote learning (p. 318)

E X E R C I S E S

1. Read the following case study and answer the questions that follow.

> Iris Brown is teaching her English class about parts of speech. She wants them to understand the functions of different parts of speech in the total communication process. She also wants them to understand the relationships between the different parts of speech. She begins her class with a review of previously discussed material.
>
> "Who can remember how we started our unit on communication and parts of speech?" Iris asks.
>
> ". . . We said communication is . . . the . . . two-way sending back and forth of information that usually is done with language, . . . and we said that the parts of speech and the way we punctuate are . . . parts of . . . the whole process," Steve says haltingly.
>
> "Good Steve, and what did we say about parts of speech yesterday?" Iris continues.
>
> After thinking for a few seconds, Quiana replies, "We said that parts of speech are like building blocks in a house. The parts of speech are sort of like the . . . like the building blocks for the way we communicate, and the way the blocks are put together determines the form of the message and what it means."
>
> "We also said words could be divided into naming words, action words, describing words, and other words," Evelyn adds.
>
> "That's good," Iris smiles. "Now how did we describe these groups?"
>
> The lesson continues with a discussion of each of these parts of speech.

a. Describe the scope of the teacher's planning for the lesson.

b. Identify and describe the two advance organizers in the case study.

c. Diagram the organization of the material illustrated in the episode.

2. The following is a description of a college class involved in a discussion of teaching models. This is the last day of a 3-day presentation.

> 1. Phyllis Confrey begins her Friday class with a review of the two previous sessions.
> 2. "How did we begin the Monday session?" she asks.
> 3. "Well," Ron begins, "you said a teaching model is like a conceptual blueprint in that both are used to achieve some purpose. A blueprint is used as a guide for an engineering objective, whereas a teaching model is a guide to achieving content and process objectives."

4. Arlene adds, "You noted that models can be grouped according to whether they emphasize cognitive, affective, psychomotor, or a special kind of cognitive goal called information processing."

5. "You said that our emphasis in here would be on information processing," Mary adds.

6. "Wednesday you began to deal with the information processing family," Bob interjects.

7. "And you said you wanted to deal with each of the models separately so that they would remain clear and distinct in our minds," Martha adds.

8. Then George says, "You began the lesson on information processing models by stating that they are designed to help students handle information from the environment and transform it into more meaningful ideas."

9. "You then went on to say that the models are grouped according to whether they are primarily deductive, primarily inductive, or oriented toward problem solving," Kay notes.

10. "You further broke the inductive models into the Integrative Model, the Inductive Model, and the Concept Attainment Model, and the deductive models into Direct-Instruction, which teaches concepts and skills, and the Lecture-Discussion Model," Russ adds.

11. "You also noted that although the Lecture-Discussion Model is primarily expository and deductive and the Integrative Model is inductive, they aren't as unrelated as you would expect because they can be used to process large amounts of information, but the way in which this is done differs."

12. "We also added that the Integrative Model is much more process oriented than is the Lecture-Discussion Model," Carol comments.

13. "You also suggested," Linda notes, "that Ausubel sees the nervous system as an information processing mechanism, analogous to a discipline, which organizes concepts hierarchically."

14. "Excellent," Phyllis comments. "You seem to have formed stable concepts of the ideas that we've discussed so far. Today, I want to consider a new model. This information processing model is the Problem Solving Model, designed to help students develop their abilities to solve problems in the classroom and in the real world.

15. "This model combines both inductive and deductive modes of thinking. The first part of the model involves identification of some kind of a problem, and the rest of the model involves gathering information to explain or solve the problem."

16. Wayne raises his hand and asks, "We learned that there are primarily three forms of knowledge we try to teach: concepts, generalizations, and facts. Which of these is the Problem Solving Model designed to teach?"

17. "That's a good question," Phyllis notes. "But before I answer that, I'd like to show you some examples of the Problem Solving Model and see if you can answer that question yourself." The class then proceeds to analyze the examples presented and ultimately determines the answer to Wayne's question.

a. Identify the advance organizers in the lesson (some may be from previous lessons).

b. Draw a hierarchy of the content contained in the lesson.

c. Identify in the lesson where integration took place.

Feedback for these exercises begins on page 341.

DISCUSSION QUESTIONS

1. How are schemas acquired? Give at least three examples from common experience.

2. Though schema theory was described as one theoretical foundation for the Lecture-Discussion Model, it could be described as a framework for the other models presented to this point as well. Why then would it have been described specifically as the theoretical foundation for this chapter?

3. The Inductive Model was described as being based on constructivist views of learning. Is the Lecture-Discussion Model also based on constructivist views of learning? Explain why or why not.

4. What are the particular strengths of the Lecture-Discussion Model? What are its primary weaknesses?

5. What conditions might influence the effectiveness of advance organizers? Are they more effective with younger students or older? Are they more effective with new material or old? Are they more effective with abstract or concrete material?

EXERCISE FEEDBACK

Chapter 2

1. Kevin's lesson was more nearly based on behaviorism than on cognitive learning theory. For example, he had the students complete exercises such as, "Did you get the card from Kelly and (I, me)?" Responses to the exercises were observable, that is, Kevin could directly observe whether the students selected "I" or "me." If they selected "me" for this exercise, they were reinforced, and if they selected "I," they were punished; they were told no, which decreased the likelihood of a similar response in the future.

2. Suzanne's lesson was more nearly based on cognitive learning theory than on behaviorism. With respect to the principles of cognitive learning theory, she first provided a concrete and real-world example of the grammar rule. Second, she promoted high levels of social interaction, and third, using the examples and through the interaction, the students were able to construct an understanding of the rule. Fourth, the examples provided the students with experience, which helped develop their background knowledge, and finally she had the students practice. All of the principles of cognitive learning theory were illustrated in her lesson.

3. Kevin applied some of the factors that increase motivation to learn but not others. For example, he promoted success, and he appeared to be enthusiastic and caring. His classroom environment was safe and orderly.

   His primary weaknesses were in the instructional factors that increase motivation to learn. For example, he provided no feedback about the students' understanding other than telling the students that their answers were correct or incorrect. His examples were abstract, out of context (isolated sentences rather than in paragraphs), and they weren't personalized. Challenges that lead to perceptions of competence, control and autonomy, and equilibrium were largely absent.

4. Suzanne applied most of the characteristics that increase motivation to learn. As with Kevin, she appeared to be enthusiastic and caring, and she demonstrated positive expectations. Her classroom was safe and orderly. The way she began and conducted her lesson created a sense of challenge for the students that leads to perceptions of competence, control and autonomy, and equilibrium. She promoted success with her open-ended questions; her students were highly involved, both in the whole-group and small-group portions of the lesson; she used concrete examples; and she provided informative feedback about the students' learning progress.

Chapter 3

1. *Organization.* She had her materials ready—her chart was displayed for the students when they came into the room; her routines were well established—the students had

their books on their desks and were waiting without being told to do so; and she began her lesson very nearly at the time it was scheduled to begin.

2. *Review.* Kathy began, "We began talking about the northern and southern colonies yesterday. Let's see what we remember. . . ." (She used questioning and clear communication throughout, but her purpose in this set of paragraphs was to review.)

3. *Focus.* At this point in the lesson Kathy said, "Today, we want to see what some of these specific differences are and why the two economies are so different. So, remember as we go through the lesson that we're talking about the way the colonies made their money, and we're trying to figure out why they are so different. . . ." This statement was designed to attract and maintain the students' attention and provide a conceptual umbrella for the lesson.

4. *Questioning; prompting.* She asked Ann Marie a question in Paragraph 15, Ann Marie didn't answer, and Kathy prompted her in 17, so she was able to give an acceptable answer in 18.

5. *Review and closure; closure.* Kathy said, "Now, everyone, get with your partner, take 2 minutes and write two or three summary statements about what we've learned here today. . . ." Summarizing what they learned in the lesson is a form of closure.

6. *Questioning; equitable distribution.* Kathy called on a variety of students, and in each case she called on the student by name. (She also waited before calling the student's name, so *questioning–wait-time* would also be an acceptable answer.)

7. *Feedback.* In each case Kathy provided the students with information about their responses.

8. Calling on a student who isn't paying attention is a good idea. If the student doesn't hear the question (because he isn't paying attention), he will hear his name. The teacher can then simply repeat the question. The student knows he got "nabbed," and he knows that the teacher knows he wasn't paying attention. Yet, nothing bad happened to him. He wasn't admonished or reprimanded in any way. The teacher simply brought him back into the lesson by calling on him.

9. These are open-ended questions, which are questions that have a variety of acceptable answers. Some of the reasons they're effective include the following: (a) Because a variety of answers are acceptable, student success is virtually assured; (b) open-ended questions are easy to ask, so teachers can involve a number of students in a short time with little effort; (c) open-ended questions are effective for diagnosing students' background knowledge because the comments the students make reflect their perceptions; and (d) because open-ended questions have a variety of acceptable answers, they can be effectively used as prompting questions.

10. The best example of a question that required critical thinking was in Paragraph 19 where Kathy asked, "Now why might that have been the case?" This question required the students to provide an explanation, and explanations should be based on evidence.

Chapter 4

1. Jim Felton used Group Investigation to help his students learn about nutrition. To do this he divided students into teams and made each team responsible for investigating different topics; he then asked each team to report on their findings.

   Jesse Kantor used Jigsaw II to help her students learn about amphibians. Different members of each team were responsible for different topics (e.g., circulatory system). These "experts" then taught other members of the team, and all members of the team were evaluated with a quiz covering all the topics.

2a. Knowledge of multiplication facts is convergent information best taught using STAD.

2b. Analyzing social issues suggests that the teacher is interested in process in addition to content. Designing a research project on voting would best be taught using the Group Investigation Model.

2c. This objective is content oriented and involves learning large bodies of interconnected information rather than discrete bits of information, so this learning objective would best be reached using Jigsaw II.

2d. Studying pollution through group projects would best be taught using Group Investigation.

2e. Helping students learn to research a topic would best be taught using Group Investigation.

2f. Knowing and understanding the four major food groups suggests that the teacher not only wants his students to understand basic facts about nutrition but also the interconnections between the facts. This suggests Jigsaw II.

2g. Knowing the names of capitals of states involves the learning of facts. Facts are best taught using STAD.

3a. The targeting of group goals was suggested when Anya said, ". . . we're going to work on them in groups." Group goals were also suggested when she said, "I'll be giving you a quiz in a week, and your team's score will depend in how well *all* the team members do—not just score. Any question? . . . Hakeem?"

3b. Individual accountability was suggested by Anya saying, ". . . your team's score will depend upon how well *all* the team members do—not only some."

3c. Anya worked on her students' collaboration skills in several ways. First, she had team members spend time getting to know each other. She also modeled effective small-group behaviors. In addition, as she circulated around the room, she specially targeted some students dominating groups.

3d. Anya didn't do as good a job here as with the other components. She did call the class's attention to one group's productive procedure of doing the first three problems together. However, she didn't debrief at the end, asking each group to reflect on their group's effectiveness.

4a. One way to form teams is to divide students into quartiles and take the top and bottom students from the lowest and highest quartiles, and add them to the top and bottom students in the middle quartiles. Doing this, the first group would be composed of Juan, Ted, Kim, and Joan; the second group would have Bettina, May, Henry, Heather, and Lisa, and so on.

4b. Other factors to consider include gender, ethnicity, and ability to work together in groups. For example, note that the second group formed was composed of all females. If one of the teacher's goals was to teach boys and girls to work together cooperatively, then a better gender mix would be desired.

Chapter 5

1. First each of the teachers used examples to illustrate the content they taught. For instance, Judy Nelson used her ball and globe, Sue Grant used her demonstration and drawings, and Jim Rooney used his passage with the rules for forming possessives.

Second, each of the teachers diagnosed the students' existing knowledge by asking open-ended questions.

Third, each of the teachers put the students in active roles in the learning process by encouraging them to discuss their developing understanding.

Finally, each of the activities involved real-world tasks.

2. Judy's comment, "When we're done, we'll be so good at this that we'll be able to pinpoint any city in the world. Keep this in mind as we work today," was an attempt to establish positive expectations in her students.

3a. Generalization

3b. Rule

3c. Generalization

3d. Principle

4a. Immigration and economics

4b. Number and verb form

4c. Type of diet and cholesterol level

4d. Polarity and attraction

5a. Brief case studies could be used to illustrate this generalization. An example might be the following:

Enrique Rodriguez came home exhausted from a long day in the fields. The third year of drought had nearly destroyed his small farm in northern Mexico, and now he could barely grow enough corn and beans to feed his family of five.

"We must do something," his wife said with concern as they sat quietly one evening. "The children are hungry."

"I will go to the city," Enrique finally said with determination. "I will get the papers and see if we can go north of the border to find better work."

Cases, such as this one, illustrate the relationship between immigration and economics and could be effectively used with the Inductive Model. An alternative would be to use historical data displayed in charts that showed how immigration was related to economics.

5b. Ideal examples would be sentences in the context of a reading passage. Some of the sentences would be written so that the subjects and verbs agree in number and others would have subjects and verbs that disagree. The teacher would then guide the students to identify the differences in the sentences.

5c. As with the generalization relating immigration and economics, brief cases describing people and their diets together with their cholesterol counts would be good choices for examples. In addition, charts or graphs showing this relationship could also be used.

5d. To illustrate this principle, the teacher could have students experiment with actual magnets, calling their attention to the fact that some ends are labeled "S" and some "N."

6. A concept analysis might appear as follows:

Definition	A quadrilateral with opposite sides equal in length and all angles 90°
Characteristics	Opposite sides equal in length 90° angles
Examples	(Another example that appears at an angle)
Superordinate	Quadrilateral, parallelogram
Superordinate	Square
Coordinate	Rhombus

7a. Jim Rooney's passage was a type of concrete materials.

7b. Judy Nelson's beach ball was a model.

7c. Maps are also forms of models. We don't typically think of them that way, but they allow us to visualize what is too vast to be directly observed.

7d. Sue Grant's balloons were a form of concrete materials.

7e. Sue Grant's drawings were models.

8a. The teacher used one example. The vials on the balance only established that the water was more dense than the oil. The water poured on the oil established that the less dense material floated.

8b. They were concrete materials.

8c. The teacher would have to prompt the students to conclude that the water was more dense than the oil. She would need to get them to say that the volumes were the same, but that the mass of the water was greater, so the water was more dense. The students would readily see that the oil floated on the water.

   The teacher would then have to prompt the students to articulate the relationship between density and flotation, that is, "Less dense materials float on more dense materials."

8d. The teacher would present the students with additional examples and have the students explain what they saw. For instance, the teacher might drop an ice cube in water. Because it floats, we know that ice is less dense than water. She might also drop an ice cube in alcohol. Since the ice sinks in the alcohol, ice is more dense that alcohol. (We can also conclude from these examples that alcohol is less dense than water.)

Chapter 6

1. Objectives a, b, and d are all concepts and would be appropriate for the Concept Attainment Model.

   Objectives c and e would not be appropriately taught with the Concept Attainment Model. Let's see why.

   Objective c: A teacher wanting students to know why two coffee cans roll down an incline at different rates has an objective that requires an explanation. Explanations include concepts but are broader than the concepts themselves. As such, they are not appropriately taught with the Concept Attainment Model. A problem-based learning model, such as those presented in Chapter 8 would be appropriate.

   Objective e: A literature teacher who wants her students to know the time period during which Poe wrote has an objective that calls for factual information; "Poe wrote in the first half of the nineteenth century" is a fact. Facts are not taught as the content goal in a Concept Attainment activity.

2. Let's now consider sequences of examples for the concepts *gerund, soft,* and *miscible fluids.*

   (a) For the concept *gerund* a sequence might be the following: (The positive examples are in italics. The sentences not italicized are the negative examples.)

Hunting is a popular sport in many parts of the country. Walking is a major part of hunting, and hunters get a lot of exercise.

   Susan and Jimmy were hunting together. Suddenly, glancing to the side of the road, they saw another hunter chasing a deer out of the woods. Their hunting dog, Ginger, jumped out of their truck and also gave chase. *Running off the road isn't a good idea,* but this is what Jimmy did when he saw the bizarre events in front of him. Jimmy stared very disgustedly as he looked at his crumpled fender. He didn't know what to do.

   Obviously, there are many ways that a sequence of examples could be prepared to allow attainment of the concept *gerund.* The prepared sequence illustrates only one possibility. The sequence does, however, illustrate how the examples can be embedded in the context of a short passage instead of being presented as a list of unrelated sentences. The important point is that each of the *yes* examples contains a gerund, whereas none of the *no* examples contains a gerund.

(**b**) A sequence of examples for the concept *soft* might be the following:

1. Piece of terry cloth   Yes
2. Piece of sandpaper   No
3. Chamois skin   Yes
4. Diaper   Yes
5. Drinking glass   No
6. Sponge ball   Yes
7. Toy car   No
8. Wadded facial tissue   Yes
9. Piece of chalk   No

The positive examples could be indicated by smiling faces, plus signs, or the word *yes*. Note again that the *yes* and *no* examples do not always alternate. There is no rule that says every *yes* must be followed by a *no* or vice versa. As with the number of examples, the ordering of the examples depends on the judgment of the teacher.

(**c**) An appropriate sequence to teach *miscible fluids* might appear as follows. Notice that the actual fluids should be used if the examples are to be most effective. Using the actual fluids (a form of concrete materials) would allow students to directly observe the characteristics of the concept. If a compromise is required, a combination of actual fluids for some examples and models for other examples would be the next most effective method. The least effective form of example would be the use of words alone. Following is a possible sequence.

1. Water and alcohol   Yes
2. Alcohol and cooking oil   No
3. Benzene and gasoline   Yes
4. Water and cooking oil   No
5. Benzene and alcohol   No
6. Water and hydrochloric acid   Yes
7. Oil and sulfuric acid   No
8. Water and motor oil   No
9. Vinegar and water   Yes

In some cases—water, cooking oil, alcohol, gasoline, motor oil, and vinegar—the actual liquids are easy to obtain, and in these cases they should be used. For the others, models are a reasonable compromise. The model could represent the different sizes of the respective elements and could show the mixing process. Although words are commonly used in an instance such as this, a model would be vastly superior.

3. The examples and sequences will be highly individual depending on background knowledge and experience. Check with a fellow student or your instructor for feedback. Keep in mind as you design the sequence that *all* the positive examples must illustrate the concept and *none* of the negative examples can illustrate it. Also, use your imagination, and try to design the sequence cleverly to promote critical skills in the students.

4a. The examples of the concept in the anecdote are:

German shepherd   Fox
Collie   Wolf
Beagle

The other examples cited in the anecdote, such as Siamese cat, were the nonexamples (negative examples). The negative examples further clarify the concept by showing what it is not, whereas the positive examples show what the concept is.

4b. The characteristics cited in the anecdote are:

Four legs   Prominent teeth
Barks   Hair

Note that none of these attributes alone is sufficient to describe the concept. However, together they provide an adequate description for the purposes of the teacher's lesson.

4c. The hypotheses that students offered were:

   1. "It's an *animal.*"
   2. "It could be *pet.*"
   3. "I think it's *mammal.*"
   7. "I think it's *dogs.*"
 12. "Maybe it's *dog family.*"

4d. Michele's sequence was presented as follows:

Yes	1. German shepherd	No	6. Siamese cat
No	2. Oak tree	Yes	7. Fox
Yes	3. Collie	No	8. Leopard
No	4. Magnolia tree	Yes	9. Wolf
Yes	5. Beagle		

Consider now a second partial sequence.

Yes	1. German shepherd
No	2. Siamese cat
Yes	3. Wolf
No	4. Leopard

The sequence Michele used allowed students much more opportunity to practice their thinking skills than would the second because the first few examples she used were more general and allowed for a variety of hypotheses. In the second sequence, "Siamese cat" as the first negative example would eliminate "animal" or "pet" as initial hypotheses, and "wolf" as the second positive example would probably cause the students to immediately identify the concept. The first sequence, in contrast, allowed many hypotheses that were successively narrowed until the concept was isolated.

4e. Michele could have further enriched the concept by including other positive examples, such as "jackal" and "coyote," to broaden the concept for the students.

4f. Michele presented examples two at a time rather than singly. This is not critical and demonstrates the flexibility in the procedure. The only argument against this practice is that it might increase the cognitive load on young or inexperienced students to the point where they have some difficulty processing the information.

4g. There were several points (e.g., Paragraphs 9 and 10) in the lesson where students voluntarily made the logic behind their answers explicit. Michele made a conscious effort to encourage this when she asked Phyllis to explain her hypothesis in Paragraph 4.

Chapter 7

1. Phase 1: Asking for similarities is part of Phase 1.

2. Phase 1: The teacher continues to ask for similarities.

3. JT: Providing an example based on the information in the matrix supplies evidence for the earlier statement.

4. Phase 3: The teacher asks students to consider different conditions and suggest the outcomes of those conditions, which is a call for hypothetical reasoning.

5. JT: In asking, "What makes you say that?" the teacher asks the students to justify their thinking.

6. Phase 1: By again asking for similarities or differences the teacher returns to Phase 1.

7. JT: Asking, "What makes you say that?" is another way of requiring students to justify their thinking.

8. Phase 2: "Why do you suppose idealism appears as a theme?"

9. Phase 4: Describing general patterns near the end of the lesson is a form of summarizing used to bring the lesson to closure.

10. Phase 4: The teacher continues to ask the students for summarizing statements.

11. JT: Again the teacher asks the student to justify her thinking by providing an example.

12. A variety of responses are possible. The following questions and answers are offered as illustrations. They are not the only possible answers, and they are not necessarily the best possible answers.

    Phase 1
    a. Look at the diameters of the planets. What do you notice here?
       Answer: The diameters of Jupiter, Saturn, Uranus, and Neptune are dramatically bigger than those of the other planets.
    b. How do the planets' densities compare to their diameters?
       Answer: The planets with large diameters have low densities compared to the other planets.

    Phase 2
    a. Why do you think the planets with large diameters have low densities?
       Answer: They are composed of materials that aren't very dense, such as gases.

b. Why do you suppose that Mercury's temperature varies so much—from 300° below zero to 800° above zero?
    Answer: It rotates very slowly on its axis, so one side faces the sun for a long time and gets very hot, whereas the other side faces away from the sun for a long time and stays very cold.

c. It is generally believed that Earth is the only planet in the solar system that supports life as we know it. Why might that be the case?
    Answer: Earth is the only planet with liquid water, and it is the only planet that has a livable average temperature—with the possible exception of Mars.

d. In spite of its large diameter, Saturn's gravity isn't much greater than Earth's. Why might that be the case?
    Answer: The density of Saturn is very low, so its gravity would be lower than would be expected for its size.

Phase 3

a. Suppose Mercury rotated on its own axis much more rapidly than it presently does. How might that affect its ability to support life?
    Answer: It still wouldn't support life. It has no atmosphere. It is close to the sun, so it would still be very hot. It has no water.

b. Suppose that Saturn was a solid planet like Earth. How would that effect its gravity?
    Answer: Its gravity would be much greater than it now is.

Phase 4

a. What kinds of general descriptions can we make about the planets in the solar system?
    Answer: The planets with large diameters have generally low masses and densities, so their gravities are lower than would be expected for their large size.
    Answer: The farther away the planets are from the sun the colder they are.
    Answer: The farther away a planet is from the sun, the longer its year.
    Answer: All the planets rotate on their own axes.
    Answer: All the planets except Mercury and Venus have at least one moon.

Chapter 8

1a. The problem for the class was stray and unwanted pets.

1b. In representing the problem the class decided on the following topics: pets in America, the Humane Society, and the County Animal Control Division.

1c. The strategy that the class adopted was primarily fact finding or informational.

1d. They carried out the strategy by seeking information through interviews and printed materials.

1e. In evaluating their results the class decided to launch a public information campaign about the problem of unwanted and stray pets.

1f. After the investigation Sherry encouraged the class to analyze the process by talking about what they had done and evaluate their actions.

2a. An event that the teacher could present might appear as follows:

He could play excerpts of sounds considered musical and excerpts of sounds considered noise. After playing the excerpts, the teacher might say something such as, "Why was the first selection considered music and the second selection considered noise?"

2b. The teacher might begin the description of the event in either verbal or written form in this way:

Mrs. Jones was a typical housewife in the town of Stevensville. She was married to a respected citizen, was the mother of three children, was active in civic groups, and she attended church regularly. However, on Saturday, June 17, the day of the annual community picnic, Mrs. Jones was taken aside and stoned to death by the rest of the people in the town. Mrs. Jones had done nothing to deserve this execution and yet it was performed by most of the townspeople in front of the rest of the citizens who did nothing to prevent it. Why would this happen?

2c. The teacher's description of the event might appear as follows:

Hiroshima, a city of approximately 250,000 people, was located at the end of the main island of the Japanese chain. Hiroshima was not the largest city, nor was it the city with the bulk of the military supplies on the Japanese mainland. It was not the main cultural center of Japan. Yet, this city was selected as the target for the dropping of the first atomic bomb in World War II. Why was Hiroshima selected as the first target when other places would seem to be more desirable?

2d. A description of the event could be:

Prior to the 1948 presidential election, which pitted Truman against Dewey, public polls favored Dewey by a wide margin. In fact, on the night of the election, one prominent newspaper's headlines reported a victory for Dewey. According to the preelection polls, Dewey was more popular, was believed to be better qualified for the presidency, and had powerful people on his side. Yet, when the final tally was taken, Truman had won a tremendous upset victory. How could this have happened?

2e. One possible description of an event is the following:

The teacher places two beakers of colorless liquid (water and alcohol) on a demonstration table for the children to observe. The teacher then puts an ice cube into each of the containers of fluid. The ice cube floats on one of the fluids and sinks in the other. The two fluids appear to be the same, and the ice cubes are the same or nearly identical. The teacher would then ask why the object floats on one of the fluids and sinks in the other.

2f. In this case the teacher might show the students pictures of apparently similar paintings. They could be similar in style, coloring, and framing. The teacher might say something similar to the following: "The painting on the right sold for $5,000, whereas the painting on the left sold for $25. When the paintings appear to be similar, why should the one be so much more valuable than the other?"

3a. Renee's actions in the lesson suggested that the lesson was preplanned rather than spontaneous. She had a content objective in mind (for students to understand factors that shaped the form that newspapers took) and came to class with the materials necessary for the activity.

3b. Students used primary data sources in pursuing their problem. An alternative secondary source would be to have students look up the information in a textbook.

3c. (1) Question identification began when students compared the various newspapers. This phase of the model concluded when the teacher wrote "What factors influence the size and composition of the daily newspaper?" on the board. (2) Hypothesis generation took place when students offered their ideas (sports, advertising) about factors affecting newspapers and when Renee wrote these on the board. (3) Data gathering occurred in small groups as each group analyzed their individual newspapers. (4) The data analyses were just beginning as time ran out. This is not an atypical problem for inquiry lessons, and teachers need to simply adjust to it. (5) After having examined the hypotheses, students would cautiously generalize to include other instances.

4. Question A would be inappropriate for measuring process skills because it primarily covers content that has already been discussed in class. Consequently, what is being measured here is recall of information rather than process skills.

An important factor in measuring for process is whether students are asked to analyze a problem not previously discussed. If the problem has not been previously discussed, students' abilities to analyze are being measured. If the problem has been discussed, the problem measures recall or comprehension of content rather than process abilities.

Question B is appropriate and directly measures students' abilities to relate explanations and data. The question could probably have been specified more accurately to provide better directions to students. For example, the illustrated item with the population distribution in the given country is clearer and more specific. Again, however, the reader is reminded that the explanation and the data regarding the population must be unfamiliar to students or the teacher will be measuring recall of previously covered content.

Question C is also appropriate and measures students' abilities to apply the information they've analyzed to develop a revised explanation. A combination of Questions 2 and 3 would be excellent for measuring students' process abilities.

5. The anecdote illustrated an inquiry problem as well as the hypothesizing—data gathering—hypothesizing cycle. (a) The problem needing explanation was why Joan flared up at another teacher. (b) The first hypothesis suggested to explain this phenomenon was that Joan was having marital problems. Our inquirers then formed a hypothesis suggesting fatigue as a cause for Joan's behavior. Subsequent data seem to support this hypothesis but the reader should note that no formal closure was reached. (c) Comments that are items of data include:

1. ". . . she's edgy when she first comes in in the morning but settles down"
2. ". . . she made some snide remark about her husband"
3. ". . . she commented only last week how happy she was"
4. "She's taking two classes at the university"
5. ". . . she's the annual and school paper advisor, and . . . [helping] with the girls' tennis team"
6. "She commented that she's averaged 5 hours of sleep"
7. ". . . her husband sells and they do an awful lot of entertaining"

(d) The first two items of data could support the first hypothesis. The third one refutes this hypothesis. All the rest supported the second hypothesis.

Chapter 9

1. Choices A (prime number), C (square), D (major scale), and F (gerund) are all concepts and can be taught with the Direct-Instruction Model. Choice B (to simplify arithmetic expressions following the rule: "Multiply and divide left to right and then add and subtract left to right") is a skill and is also effectively taught with the Direct-Instruction Model. Choice E (to understand that for nonmixing substances, less dense materials float on more dense materials) is a principle, and the model can be modified to effectively teach it. Choice G (to identify the relationships between the economy and geography of the North and South prior to the Civil War and how these factors impacted the outcome of the war) is an organized body of knowledge. A model such as the Lecture-Discussion Model, discussed in Chapter 10, would be more appropriate for teaching it. The reason the Direct-Instruction Model would be less appropriate is because the content described in the goal cannot be illustrated with a variety of examples or problems as can skills or concepts, and as a result, teaching the topic requires a different form of organization and presentation.

2. Responses to this item will vary widely. Select the topic and discuss the examples with your instructor or a colleague. The criteria for good examples are the same for the Direct-Instruction Model as they would be for the Inductive or Concept Attainment Models.

3a. The four phases of the Direct-Instruction Model appeared in the lesson in the following ways.

   Introduction: The introduction to the lesson occurred when Kathy linked the concept *antonym* to the superordinate concept *word pairs* and to the coordinate concept *synonyms,* which they had previously learned. Note that the introduction didn't contain any motivational component.

   Presentation: This phase of the lesson occurred when Kathy defined the concept and illustrated it with examples.

   Guided practice: Guided practice occurred when Kathy presented examples and nonexamples of the concept and asked students for their own examples.

   Independent practice: The final phase of the model consisted of the students working on exercises that contained additional examples of antonyms.

3b. The most effective form of assessment would be to have the students write a paragraph in which a specified number of antonyms would be embedded and identified.

3c. The lesson might be criticized in two ways. First, the concept *antonyms* was presented out of context. A better way of presenting the examples would have been to have them embedded in the context of a passage. A second criticism is that Kathy might have more actively involved more students through groupwork and interaction.

Chapter 10

1a. The Lecture-Discussion Model was used to plan in two ways. The first was to organize a unit of study on communication, and the second was to organize the lesson on parts of speech.

1b. There were two advance organizers illustrated in the anecdote. The first advance organizer was used to organize the unit on communication and was a definition (communication is the two-way transmission of information that typically takes place through language). The second advance organizer was an analogy comparing parts of speech to building blocks and was used to organize the lesson on parts of speech.

1c. The organization for the unit as well as the lesson can be diagramed as follows:

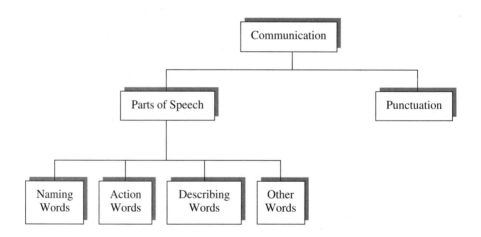

2a. There were four advance organizers mentioned in the lesson. Paragraphs 3 and 13 contained analogies, and Paragraphs 8 and 14 contained descriptions.

2b. A hierarchical outline for the content presented might look like this:

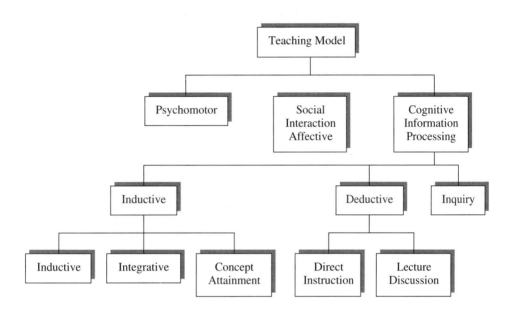

2c. Integration took place in Paragraphs 11 and 12 where the Integrative and Lecture-Discussion Models were compared and contrasted.

GLOSSARY

Academic rules. Relationships between concepts arbitrarily derived by people.

Advance organizers. Verbal or written statements at the beginning of a lesson that preview and structure new material and link it to students' existing schemas.

Affective domain. The learning domain that focuses on attitudes and values and the development of students' personal and emotional growth.

Alternative assessment. Direct measurement of student performance using tasks similar to those that are found in "real life."

Attention. The cognitive process of consciously focusing on a stimulus.

Authentic tasks. Learning activities that require understanding that can be used in the world outside the classroom.

Automaticity. The ability to perform a skill or action with little conscious effort.

Base score. A student's average on past tests and quizzes, or a score determined by a previous year's or term's grade.

Callouts. Answers given by students before the students have been recognized by the teacher.

Characteristics (sometimes called attributes or features). A concept's defining features.

Checklists. Written descriptions of dimensions that must be present in an acceptable performance.

Classroom climate. Teacher and classroom characteristics that promote students' feelings of safety and security, together with a sense of success, challenge, and understanding.

Closure. A form of review that occurs at the end of a lesson.

Cognitive apprenticeship. An approach to instruction in which students work with an expert to learn both how to perform cognitive tasks and why they perform certain tasks in certain ways.

Cognitive domain. The learning domain that focuses on objectives addressing the development of students' intellect and understanding.

Cognitive modeling. The process of verbalizing thinking as a person solves a problem.

Cognitive processes. Intellectual actions—attention, perception, encoding, and retrieval—that transform information and move it from one information store to another in our information processing system.

Combining pairs. A groupwork strategy in which learning pairs share their answers with other pairs.

Comprehension monitoring. The process of informally assessing student understanding in lecture-discussion lessons.

Concept analysis. The process of describing a concept using its characteristics, related concepts, examples, and definition.

Concept mapping. A strategy that helps learners construct visual relationships among concepts.

Concepts. Mental categories, sets, or classes with common characteristics.

Connected discourse. A type of teacher presentation that is clear, thematic, and leads to a point.

Cooperative learning. A group of teaching models that provide structured roles for students while emphasizing social interaction.

Coordinate concepts. Related concepts, all of which are subsets of a superordinate concept.

Critical thinking. The ability and disposition to make and assess conclusions based on evidence.

Curiosity motivation. Motivation to understand experiences that can't be immediately explained with existing background knowledge, such as problems and discrepant events.

Databases. Computer programs that allow users to store, organize, and manipulate information, including both text and numerical data.

Definition. A statement that includes the name of a concept, a superordinate concept, and the concept's characteristics.

Direct-Instruction Model. A teaching model that uses teacher explanation and modeling combined with student practice and feedback to teach concepts and procedural skills.

Discussion Model. A teaching model designed to promote critical thinking and develop social skills through the process of group interaction.

Emphasis. The use of verbal statements, vocal inflection, or repetition to alert students to important information in a lesson.

Encoding. The process of representing information in long-term memory.

Equal opportunity for success. The feature of cooperative learning that provides for all students, regardless of ability or background, being recognized for their efforts.

Equitable distribution. A questioning pattern in which all students in the class are called on as equally as possible.

Essay items. Assessment items that require students to make extended written responses to questions or problems.

Essential teaching strategies. The teacher attitudes and skills necessary to ensure that all students learn as much as possible.

Exemplars. The most highly typical members of a class of objects or events.

Extrinsic motivation. Motivation to engage in an activity as a means to an end.

Feedback. Information about current behavior that can be used to improve future performance.

Focus. The set of teacher actions at the beginning of lessons that attracts students' attention and maintains their attention during learning activities.

General pedagogical knowledge. A type of teacher knowledge that represents an understanding of general principles of instruction and classroom management that transcends individual topics or subject matter areas.

Generalizations. Descriptions of general patterns with known exceptions.

Generative knowledge. Knowledge that can be used to interpret new situations, to solve problems, to think and reason, and to learn.

Group goals. Incentives within a learning environment that help create a team spirit and encourage students to help each other.

Group Interaction Models. Models that involve students working collaboratively to reach common goals.

Group Investigation. A cooperative learning strategy that places students in groups to investigate an identified topic.

Groupwork. An instructional strategy in which students work together to supplement other models.

Heuristics. General, widely applicable problem-solving strategies.

Hypothesis. A tentative answer to a question or solution to a problem that can be verified with data.

Ill-defined problems. Problems with more than one acceptable solution, an ambiguous goal, and no generally agreed-on strategy for reaching a solution.

Information stores. Repositories that hold information in our cognitive information processing system.

Inquiry. The process of asking questions and systematically answering them based on facts and observations.

Inquiry Model. A problem-based teaching strategy designed to involve students in the inquiry process.

Instructional alignment. The congruence among objectives, learning activities, and assessments.

Integration. The process of linking new information to prior understanding in lecture-discussion lessons.

Intrinsic motivation. Motivation to be involved in an activity for its own sake.

Jigsaw II. A form of cooperative learning in which individual students become experts on subsections of a topic and teach those subsections to others.

Learning (behaviorism). A change in observable behavior that occurs as the result of experience.

Learning (cognitive). A change in an individual's mental structures and processes that may or may not result in an immediate change in behavior.

Lecture. A form of instruction in which students receive information delivered in a verbal and (presumably) organized way by teachers.

Lecture-discussion cycle. A recurrent sequence of presenting information, monitoring comprehension, and integration in lecture-discussion lessons.

Long-term memory. The permanent information store in our information processing system.

Meaningful verbal learning. The acquisition of ideas that are linked to other ideas (in contrast with rote learning, which is memorizing ideas in isolation).

Meaningfulness. A description of the number of connections or links between an idea and other ideas in long-term memory.

Metacognition. The component of our information processing system that represents an awareness of and control over our cognitive processes.

Modeling. The process of imitating behaviors people observe in others.

Models. Representations that allow us to visualize what we can't observe directly, such as the model of the atom.

Models (teaching). Specific approaches to instruction that are designed to help students acquire deep understanding of specific forms of content and to develop their critical-thinking abilities, that include a series of specific steps intended to help students reach objectives, that are grounded in learning theory, and that are supported by motivation theory.

Monitoring. The process of continually checking students' verbal and nonverbal behavior for evidence of learning progress.

Motivation. A force that energizes, sustains, and directs behavior toward a goal.

Motivation to learn. A student's tendency to find academic activities meaningful and worth-while and to try and get the intended learning benefits from them.

Open-ended questions. Questions for which a variety of answers are acceptable.

Organized bodies of knowledge. Topics that combine facts, concepts, generalizations, and the relationships among them.

Pairs check. A groupwork strategy that involves student pairs in seatwork activities focusing on problems or questions with convergent answers.

Pedagogical content knowledge. A type of knowledge that describes the teacher's ability to represent content in ways that are understandable to learners and the teacher's understanding of what makes learning a specific topic easy or difficult.

Perception. The cognitive process people use to attach meaning to stimuli.

Performance assessments. Tasks used for assessment in which students demonstrate their levels of competence or knowledge or skill by carrying out an activity or creating a product.

Personal teaching efficacy. The belief that teachers can help all students learn, regardless of their backgrounds or abilities.

Personalization. The process of using intellectually and/or emotionally relevant examples to illustrate a topic.

Precise terminology. Teacher language that eliminates vague terms from presentations and answers to students' questions.

Primary data sources. Individuals' direct observations of the events being studied.

Principles. Relationships among concepts accepted as valid for all known cases.

Problem. A cognitive state that differs from a desired end state, including some uncertainty about reaching the end state.

Problem-based learning models. Teaching models designed to develop problem-solving skills and self-directed learning.

Procedural skill. A cognitive operation that has a specific set of identifiable operations or procedures, can be illustrated with a large and varied number of examples, and is developed through practice.

Productive learning environments. Classrooms that are orderly and focus on learning.

Prompt. A teacher question or directive that elicits a student response after the student has failed to answer or has given an incorrect or incomplete answer.

Prototype. The best representative of a category or class of objects or events.

Psychomotor objectives. Learning objectives that include the acquisition of manipulative and movement skills.

Questioning frequency. The process of describing the number of questions teachers ask.

Rating scales. Written descriptions of evaluative dimensions of an acceptable performance and scales of values on which each dimension is rated.

Relatedness. The feeling of connectedness to others in one's social environment resulting in feelings of being worthy of love and respect.

Retrieval. The process of pulling information from long-term memory back into working memory in our information processing system.

Review. The process of summarizing previous work and forming a link between prior learning and the present topic.

Rote learning. The memorization of specific items of information isolated from other items.

Rubric. A scoring scale that describes the criteria for grading.

Scaffolding. Instructional support teachers provide as students learn skills.

Schemas. The forms of understanding that represent the way knowledge is organized in long-term memory.

Scientific method. A pattern of thinking that emphasizes forming conclusions based on observation, developing hypotheses, and testing the hypotheses with additional observations.

Secondary data sources. Other individuals' interpretations of primary sources, such as are typically found in textbooks, encyclopedias, and biographies.

Self-directed learning. Students' abilities to take control of their learning progress.

Self-efficacy. Individuals' beliefs about their capabilities of accomplishing specific tasks.

Self-regulation. An individual's conscious use of mental strategies designed to improve thinking and learning.

Sensory memory. The part of our information processing system that briefly holds information until we attend to it.

Short-answer items. Assessment items that require students to make brief written responses to specific questions.

Social Cognitive Theory. A learning theory that describes changes in behavior, thinking, or emotions that result from observing the behavior of another person.

Sociocultural Theory. A cognitive learning theory that emphasizes the essential role that social interaction and language, embedded within a cultural context, have on learning and development.

Standards. Statements that describe what students should know or be able to do at the end of a prescribed period of study.

Strategies. General approaches to instruction that apply in a variety of content areas and are used to meet a range of learning objectives.

Student Teams Achievement Divisions (STAD). A form of cooperative learning that uses multiability teams to teach facts, concepts, and skills.

Subordinate concepts. Subsets or examples of a category or class of objects or events.

Superordinate concept. A larger category into which a category or class of objects or events fits.

Systematic observations. A form of assessment in which teachers specify criteria for the processes they are assessing and take notes based on the criteria.

Task analysis. The process of breaking a skill into its smaller components.

Task specialization. A component of Jigsaw II that requires different students to assume specialized roles in reaching the objectives of a learning activity.

Teacher-effectiveness research. A description of the teacher skills and strategies that increase learning for all students in all subject matter areas.

Teacher expectations. Inferences that teachers make about the future behavior, academic achievement, or attitudes of their students.

Teammates consult. A form of the combining pairs groupwork strategy that requires discussion before students write down an answer.

Think-pair-share. A groupwork strategy in which individual students in learning pairs first answer a teacher-initiated question and then share it with a partner.

Think-pair-square. A variation of the groupwork strategy think-pair-share that substitutes a team discussion for the dyadic interaction.

Think-write-pair-share. A variation of the groupwork strategy think-pair-share in which students write down their answers before comparing them with a partner.

Transfer. The ability to take understanding acquired in one context and apply it in a new context.

Transition signal. A form of communication in which a teacher uses a verbal statement to indicate that one idea is ending and another is beginning.

Vignettes. Short case studies used for the purposes of illustrating an abstract idea.

Wait-time. A period of silence in a question-and-answer session both before and after a student responds that gives the student time to think about his or her answer.

Well-defined problems. Problems with only one correct solution and a certain method for finding the solution.

Working memory. Historically called short-term memory, it is the conscious, "thinking" part of our information processing system.

Zone of proximal development. The state of learning in which a student cannot solve a problem or perform a skill alone but can be successful with the help of a teacher or other more knowledgeable individual.

REFERENCES

Airasian, P. (2000). *Classroom assessment* (4th ed.). New York: McGraw-Hill.

Amrein, A., & Berliner, D. (2002). High-stakes testing, uncertainty, and student learning. *Education Policy Analysis Archives, 10*(18). Retrieved October 1, 2002, from http://epaa.asu.edu/epaa/v10n18/

Anderson, L., Brubaker, N., Alleman-Brooks, J., & Duffy, G. (1985). A qualitative study of seatwork in first-grade classrooms. *The Elementary School Journal, 86,* 123–140.

Anderson, L., & Krathwohl, D. (Eds.). (2001). *A taxonomy for learning, teaching, and assessing: A revision of Bloom's taxonomy of educational objectives.* New York: Addison Wesley Longman.

Anderson, R. (1959). Learning in discussions: A resume/The authoritarian-democratic studies. *Harvard Educational Review, 29,* 201–216.

Anderson, R., Nguyen-Jahiel, K., McNurlen, B., Archodidou, A., Kim, S., Reznitskaya, A., Tillmanns, M., & Gilbert, L. (2001). The snowball phenomenon: Spread of ways of talking and ways of thinking across groups of children. *Cognition and Instruction, 19*(1), 1–46.

Aronson, E., Blaney, N., Stephan, C., Sikes, J., & Snapp, M. (1978). *The Jigsaw classroom.* Beverly Hills, CA: Sage.

Ashcraft, H. (2002). *Cognition* (3rd ed.). Upper Saddle River, NJ: Prentice Hall.

Ausubel, D. (1963). *The psychology of meaningful verbal learning.* New York: Grune and Stratton.

Ausubel, D. (1968). *Educational psychology: A cognitive view.* New York: Holt, Rinehart & Winston.

Babad, E., Bernieri, F., & Rosenthal, R. (1991). Students as judges of teachers' verbal and nonverbal behavior. *American Educational Research Journal, 28*(1), 211–234.

Bandura, A. (1986). *Social foundations of thought and action: A social cognitive theory.* Upper Saddle River, NJ: Prentice Hall.

Bandura, A. (1989). Social cognitive theory. In R. Vasta (Ed.), *Annals of child development* (Vol. 6, pp. 1–60). Greenwich, CT: JAI Press.

Bandura, A. (1997). *Self-efficacy: The exercise of control.* New York: Freeman.

Banks, J. (2001). *Cultural diversity and education.* Boston: Allyn & Bacon.

Banks, J. (2002). *An introduction to multicultural education* (3rd ed.). Boston: Allyn & Bacon.

Bennett, S. (1978). Recent research on teaching: A dream, a belief, and a model. *British Journal of Educational Psychology, 48,* 27–147.

Berk, L. (2003). *Child development* (6th ed.). Boston: Allyn & Bacon.

Berk, L. (2004). *Development through the lifespan* (3rd ed.). Boston: Allyn & Bacon.

Bertman, S. (2000). *Cultural amnesia: America's future and the crisis of memory.* Westport, CT: Praeger.

Bishop, J. (1998). The effect of curriculum-based external exit systems on student achievement. *Journal of Economic Education, 29,* 171–182.

Bloom, B. (1986). Automaticity. *Educational Leadership, 43*(5), 70–77.

Bloom, B., Englehart, M., Furst, E., Hill, W., & Krathwohl, O. (1956). *Taxonomy of educational objectives: The classification of educational goals: Handbook 1. The cognitive domain.* White Plains, NY: Longman.

Blumenfeld, P. (1992). Classroom learning and motivation: Clarifying and expanding goal theory. *Journal of Educational Psychology, 84*(3), 272–281.

Borko, H., & Putnam, R. (1996). Learning to teach. In D. Berliner & R. Calfee (Eds.), *Handbook of educational psychology* (pp. 673–708). New York: Macmillan.

Bourne, L. (1982). Typicality effects in logically defined categories. *Memory & Cognition, 10,* 3–9.

Boyer, E. (1983). *High school: A report on secondary education in America.* New York: Harper & Row.

Bransford, J., & Stein, B. (1984). *The IDEAL problem solver.* New York: Freeman.

Bransford, J., Brown, A., & Cocking, R. (Eds.). (2000). *How people learn: Brain, mind, experience, and school.* Washington, DC: National Academy Press.

Brenner, D. (2001, April). *Translating social constructivism into methodology for documenting learning.*

Paper presented at the annual meeting of the American Educational Research Association, Seattle.

Brophy, J. (1986). Research linking teacher behavior to student achievement: Potential implications for instruction of Chapter 1 students. In B. Williams, P. Richmond, & B. Mason (Eds.), *Designs for Compensatory Education Conference proceedings and papers* (pp. IV-121–IV-179). Washington, DC: Research and Evaluation Associates.

Brophy, J. (1987a). On motivating students. In D. Berliner & B. Rosenshine (Eds.), *Talks to teachers* (pp. 201–245). New York: Random House.

Brophy, J. (1987b). Syntheses of research on strategies for motivating students to learn. *Educational Leadership, 45*(2), 40–48.

Brophy, J. (1992). Probing the subtleties of subject-matter teaching. *Educational Leadership, 49*(7), 4–8.

Brophy, J. (1998). *Motivating students to learn.* Boston: McGraw-Hill.

Brophy, J., & Good, T. (1986). Teacher behavior and student achievement. In M. Wittrock (Ed.), *Handbook of research on teaching* (3rd ed., pp. 328–375). New York: Macmillan.

Brown, A. (1994). The advancement of learning. *Educational Researcher, 23,* 4–12.

Bruer, J. (1993). *Schools for thought: A science of learning for the classroom.* Cambridge, MA: MIT Press.

Bruner, J., Goodenow, J., & Austin, G. (1956). *A study of thinking.* New York: Wiley.

Bruning, R., Schraw, G., Norby, M., & Ronning, R. (2004). *Cognitive psychology and instruction* (4th ed.). Upper Saddle River, NJ: Prentice Hall.

Burbules, N., & Bruce, B. (2001). Theory and research on teaching as dialogue. In V. Richardson (Ed.), *Handbook of research on teaching* (4th ed., pp. 1102–1121). Washington, DC: American Educational Research Association.

Carlsen, W. (1987, April). *Why do you ask? The effects of science teacher subject-matter knowledge on teacher questioning and classroom discourse.* Paper presented at the annual meeting of the American Educational Research Association, Washington, DC.

Case, R. (1978). Intellectual development from birth to adulthood: A neo-Piagetian interpretation. In R. Siegler (Ed.), *Children's thinking: What develops?* (pp. 37–71). Hillsdale, NJ: Erlbaum.

Cazden, C. (2001). *Classroom discourse* (2nd ed.). Portsmouth, NH: Heinemann.

Chomsky, N. (1959). A review of Skinner's verbal behavior. *Language, 35,* 25–58.

Clark, C., & Peterson, P. (1986). Teachers' thought processes. In M. Wittrock (Ed.), *Handbook of research on teaching* (3rd ed., pp. 255–296). New York: Macmillan.

Clifford, M. (1990). Students need challenge, not easy success. *Educational Leadership, 48*(1), 22–26.

Cognition and Technology Group at Vanderbilt. (1992). The Jasper Series as an example of anchored instruction: Theory, program description, and assessment data. *Educational Psychologist, 27,* 291–315.

Cohen, E. (1994). Restructuring the classroom: Conditions for productive small groups. *Review of Educational Research, 64,* 1–35.

Cohen, E. (1998). Making cooperative learning equitable. *Educational Leadership, 56*(1), 18–21.

Cohen, E., & Lotan, R. (Eds.). (1997). *Working for equity in heterogeneous classrooms: Sociological theory in practice.* New York: Teachers College Press.

Coleman, J., Campbell, E., Hobson, D., McPartland, J., Mood, A., Weinfield, F., & York, R. (1966). *Equality of educational opportunity.* Washington, DC: U.S. Department of Health, Education and Welfare.

Connell, J., & Wellborn, J. (1990). Competence, autonomy, and relatedness: A motivational analysis of self-system processes. In M. Gunnar & L. Sroufe (Eds.), *The Minnesota Symposia on Child Psychology* (Vol. 22, pp. 43–77). Hillsdale, NJ: Erlbaum.

Corkill, A. (1992). Advance organizers: Facilitators of recall. *Educational Psychology Review, 4,* 33–67.

Covington, M. (2000). Intrinsic versus extrinsic motivation in schools: A reconciliation. *Current Directions in Psychological Science, 9,* 22–25.

Crooks, T. (1988). The impact of classroom evaluation practices on students. *Review of Educational Research, 58,* 438–481.

Cruickshank, D. (1985). Applying research on teacher clarity. *Journal of Teacher Education, 35*(2), 44–48.

Cuban, L. (1984). *How teachers taught: Constancy and change in American classrooms: 1890–1980.* White Plains, NY: Longman.

Curwin, R. (1992). *Rediscovering hope: Our greatest teaching strategy.* Bloomington, IN: National Education Service.

Deci, E., & Ryan, R. (1991). A motivational approach to self: Integration in personality. In R. Dienstbier (Ed.), *Nebraska Symposium on Motivation, 1990* (Vol. 38, pp. 237–288). Lincoln: University of Nebraska Press.

Dempster, F. (1991). Synthesis of research on reviews and tests. *Educational Leadership, 48*(7), 71–76.

Dewey, J. (1902). *The child and the curriculum.* Chicago: University of Chicago Press.

Dewey, J. (1916). *Democracy in education.* New York: Macmillan.

Dillon, J. (1987). *Classroom questions and discussions.* Norwood, NJ: Ablex.

Doyle, W. (1983). Academic work. *Review of Educational Research, 53,* 159–199.

Duffy, G., & Roehler, L. (1985). *Constraints on teacher change.* East Lansing: Michigan State University Institute for Research on Teaching.

Duffy, T., & Cunningham, D. (1996). Constructivism: Implications for the design and delivery of instruction. In D. Jonassen (Ed.), *Handbook of research for educational communications and technology* (pp. 170–195). New York: Macmillan.

Dunkle, M., Schraw, G., & Bendixon, L. (1995, April). *Cognitive processes in well-defined and ill-defined problem solving.* Paper presented at the annual meeting of the American Educational Research Association, San Francisco.

Dunkin, M., & Biddle, B. (1974). *The study of teaching.* New York: Holt, Rinehart, and Winston.

Durso, F., & Coggins, K. (1991). Organized instruction for the improvement of word knowledge skills. *Journal of Educational Psychology, 83,* 108–112.

Educational Testing Service. (1999). *Principles of learning and teaching test bulletin.* Princeton, NJ: Author.

Eggen, P. (2001, April). *Constructivism and the architecture of cognition: Implications for instruction.* Paper presented at the annual meeting of the American Educational Research Association, Seattle.

Eggen, P., & Austin, C. (2004, April). *Teachers' and educational leaders' conceptions of classroom interaction.* Paper presented at the annual meeting of the American Educational Research Association, San Diego.

Eggen, P., & Kauchak, D. (2004). *Educational psychology: Windows on classrooms* (6th ed.). Upper Saddle River, NJ: Merrill/Prentice Hall.

Emmer, E., Evertson, C., & Worsham, M. (2003). *Classroom management for secondary teachers* (6th ed.). Boston: Allyn & Bacon.

Emmer, E., & Gerwels, G. (1998). *Classroom management tasks in cooperative groups.* Paper presented at the annual meeting of the American Educational Research Association, San Diego.

Evertson, C., Anderson, C., Anderson, L., & Brophy, J. (1980). Relationship between classroom behaviors and student outcomes in junior high mathematics and English classes. *American Educational Research Journal, 17,* 43–60.

Evertson, C., Emmer, E., & Worsham, M. (2003). *Classroom management for elementary teachers* (6th ed.). Boston: Allyn & Bacon.

Florida Educational Tools, Inc. (2003–2004). *Middle school geography standards.* Author.

Foos, P. (1992). Test performance as a function of expected form and difficulty. *Journal of Experimental Education, 60*(3), 205–211.

Forcier, R., & Desci, D. (2002). *The computer as an educational tool: Productivity and problem solving.* Upper Saddle River, NJ: Prentice Hall.

Gage, N., & Berliner, D. (1992). *Educational psychology* (5th ed.). Boston: Houghton-Mifflin.

Gage, N., & Giaconia, R. (1981). Teaching practices and student achievement: Causal connections. *New York University Education Quarterly, XII,* 2–9.

Gagne, E., Yekovich, C., & Yekovich, F. (1993). *The cognitive psychology of school learning* (2nd ed.). New York: HarperCollins.

Geography Education Standards Project. (1994). *Geography for life: National geography standards.* Washington, DC: National Geographic Research and Exploration.

Gersten, R., Taylor, R., & Graves, A. (1999). Direct instruction and diversity. In R. Stevens (Ed.), *Teaching in American schools* (pp. 81–102). Columbus, OH: Merrill.

Gillies, R., & Ashman, A. (1998). Behavior and interactions of children in cooperative groups in lower and middle elementary grades. *Journal of Educational Psychology, 90*(4), 746–757.

Good, T. (1987). Teacher expectations. In D. Berliner & B. Rosenshine (Eds.), *Talks to teachers* (pp. 159–200). New York: Random House.

Good, T., & Brophy, J. (1986). School effects. In M. Wittrock (Ed.), *Handbook of research on teaching* (3rd ed., pp. 570–604). New York: Macmillan.

Good, T., & Brophy, J. (2003). *Looking in classrooms* (9th ed.). New York: Longman.

Goodenow, C. (1993). Classroom belonging among early adolescent students: Relationships to motivation and achievement. *Journal of Early Adolescence, 13,* 21–43.

Goodlad, J. (1984). *A place called school.* New York: McGraw Hill.

Grabinger, R. (1996). Rich environments for active learning. In D. Jonassen (Ed.), *Handbook of research for educational communications and technology* (pp. 665–692). New York: Macmillan.

Graham, S., Berninger, V., Weintraub, N., & Schafer, W. (1998). Development of handwriting speed and legibility in grades 1–9. *Journal of Educational Research, 92*(1), 42–49.

Greene, R. (1992). *Human memory: Paradigms and paradoxes.* Mahwah, NJ: Erlbaum.

Greeno, J., Collins, A., & Resnick, L. (1996). Cognition and learning. In D. Berliner & R. Calfee (Eds.), *Handbook of educational psychology* (pp. 15–46). New York: Macmillan.

Gronlund, N. (2003). *Assessment of student achievement* (7th ed.). Boston: Allyn & Bacon.

Hall, R., Hall, M., & Saling, C. (1999). The effects of graphical postorganization strategies on learning from knowledge maps. *Journal of Experimental Education, 67,* 101–112.

Hampton, J. (1995). Testing the prototype theory of concepts. *Journal of Memory and Language, 32,* 686–708.

Harmin, M. (1994). *Inspiring active learning: A handbook for teachers.* Alexandria, VA: Association for Supervision and Curriculum Development.

Hiebert, E., & Raphael, T. (1996). Psychological perspectives on literacy and extensions to educational practice. In D. Berliner & R. Calfee (Eds.), *Handbook of educational psychology* (pp. 550–602). New York: Macmillan.

Hirsch, E. (2000). The tests we need and why we don't quite have them. *Education Week, 19*(21), 40–41.

Hmelo, C. (1995, April). *The effect of problem-based learning on the early development of medical expertise.* Paper presented at the Annual Meeting of the American Educational Research Association, San Francisco.

Hmelo, C., & Lin, X. (1998). Becoming self-directed learners: Strategy development in problem-based learning. In D. Evensen & C. Hmelo (Eds.), *Problem-based learning: A research perspective on learning interaction.* Mahwah, NJ: Erlbaum.

Holt, J. (1964). *How children fail.* New York: Putnam.

Interstate New Teacher Assessment and Support Consortium. (1992). *Model standards for beginning teacher licensing, assessment and development: A resource for state dialogue.* Available online at www.ccsso.org/content/pdfs/corstrd.pdf.

Jacobsen, D. (2003). *Philosophy in classroom teaching: Bridging the gap* (2nd ed.). Upper Saddle River, NJ: Prentice Hall.

Jencks, C., Smith, M., Acland, H., Bane, M., Cohen, D., Gintis, H., Heyns, B., & Michelson, S. (1972). *Inequality: A reassessment of the effect of family and schooling in America.* New York: Basic Books.

Johnson, D., & Johnson, R. (1994). *Learning together and alone: Cooperation, competition, and individualization* (4th ed.). Boston: Allyn & Bacon.

Joyce, B., & Weil, M. (1972). *Models of teaching.* Englewood Cliffs, NJ: Prentice Hall.

Kagan, D. (1992). Implications of research on teacher beliefs. *Educational Psychologist, 27,* 65–90.

Kagan, S. (1986). *Cooperative learning.* San Juan Capistrano, CA: Resources for Teachers.

Kagan, S. (1994). *Cooperative learning.* San Juan Capistrano, CA: Resources for Teachers.

Kauchak, D., & Eggen, P. (2003). *Learning and teaching: Research-based methods* (4th ed.). Boston: Allyn & Bacon.

Kauchak, D., & Eggen, P. (2005). *Introduction to teaching: Becoming a professional* (2nd ed.). Upper Saddle River, NJ: Prentice Hall.

Keislar, E., & Shulman, L. (Eds.). (1966). *Learning by discovery: A critical appraisal.* Chicago: Rand McNally.

Kent, M., Pollard, K., Haaga, J., & Mather, M. (2001). *First glimpse from the 2000 U.S. census.* Retrieved October 1, 2002, from www.prb.org/AmeriStat-Template.cfm

Kerman, S. (1979). Teacher expectations and student achievement. *Phi Delta Kappan, 60,* 70–72.

Kilbane, C., & Herbert, J. (1998). *Judging the merits of case-based instruction on the Internet.* Paper presented at the annual meeting of the American Educational Research Association, San Diego.

King, A. (1999). Teaching effective discourse patterns for small-group learning. In R. Stevens (Ed.), *Teaching in American schools* (pp. 121–139). Upper Saddle River, NJ: Merrill/Prentice Hall.

Klausmeier, H. (1992). Concept learning and concept thinking. *Educational Psychologist, 27,* 267–286.

Knowles, J. (2003). *A separate peace.* New York: Scribner.

Kozulin, A. (1990). *Vygotsky's psychology: A biography of ideas.* Cambridge, MA: Harvard University Press.

Krajcik, J., Blumenfeld, P., Marx, R., & Soloway, F. (1994). A collaborative model for helping middle grade science teachers learn project-based instruction. *Elementary School Journal, 94,* 483–497.

Kuhn, D. (1999). A developmental model of critical thinking. *Educational Researcher, 28*(2), 16–26, 46.

Lambert, N., & McCombs, B. (1998). Introduction: Learner-centered schools and classrooms as a direction for school reform. In N. Lambert & B. McCombs (Eds.), *How students learn: Reforming schools through learner-centered education* (pp. 1–22). Washington, DC: American Psychological Association.

Langer, J., Bartolome, L., Vasquez, O., & Lucas, T. (1990). Meaning construction in school literacy tasks: A study of bilingual students. *American Educational Research Journal, 27,* 427–471.

Lave, J. (1988). *Cognition in practice: Mind, mathematics, and culture in everyday life.* New York: Cambridge University Press.

Lave, J. (1990). The culture of acquisition and the practice of understanding. In J. Stigler, R. Schweder, & G. Herdt (Eds.), *Cultural psychology* (pp. 309–327). Cambridge, England: Cambridge University Press.

Leont'ev, A. (1981). The problem of activity in psychology. In J. Wertsch (Ed.), *The concept of activity in Soviet psychology* (pp. 37–71). Armonk, NY: Sharpe.

Lepper, M., & Hodell, M. (1989). Intrinsic motivation in the classroom. In C. Ames & R. Ames (Eds.), *Research on motivation in education* (Vol. 3, pp. 73–105). San Diego, CA: Academic Press.

Maehr, M. (1992, April). *Transforming the school culture to enhance motivation.* Paper presented at the annual meeting of the American Educational Research Association, San Francisco.

Marzano, R. (2003). *What works in schools.* Alexandria VA: Association for Supervision and Curriculum Development.

Maslow, A. (1968). *Toward a psychology of being* (2nd ed.). New York: Van Nostrand.

Maslow, A. (1970). *Motivation and personality* (2nd ed.). New York: Harper & Row. (Original work published 1954.)

Mason, L., & Boscolo, P. (2000). Writing and conceptual change. What changes? *Instructional Science, 28,* 199–226.

Mayer, R. (1983). Can you repeat this? Qualitative effects of repetition and advance organizers from science prose. *Journal of Educational Psychology, 75,* 40–49.

Mayer, R. (1996). Learners as information processors: Legacies and limitations of educational psychology's second metaphor. *Educational Psychologist, 31*(4), 151–161.

Mayer, R. (1998). Cognitive theory for education: What teachers need to know. In N. Lambert & B. McCombs (Eds.), *How students learn: Reforming schools through learner-centered instruction* (pp. 353–378). Washington, DC: American Psychological Association.

Mayer, R. (2002). *The promise of educational psychology: Volume II. Teaching for meaningful learning.* Upper Saddle River, NJ: Prentice Hall.

Mayer, R., & Wittrock, M. (1996). Problem-solving transfer. In D. Berliner & R. Calfee (Eds.), *Handbook of educational psychology* (pp. 47–62). New York: Macmillan.

McCombs, B. (1998). Integrating metacognition, affect, and motivation in improving teacher education. In N. Lambert & B. McCombs (Eds.), *How students learn: Reforming schools through learner-centered education* (pp. 379–408). Washington, DC: American Psychological Association.

McCutchen, D. (2000). Knowledge, processing, and working memory: Implications for a theory of writing. *Educational Psychologist, 35*(1), 13–23.

McDermott, P., Mordell, M., & Stoltzfus, J. (2001). The organization of student performance in American schools: Discipline, motivation, verbal learning, and nonverbal learning. *Journal of Educational Psychology, 93*(1), 65–76.

McDevitt, T., & Ormrod, J. (2002). *Child development and education.* Upper Saddle River, NJ: Merrill/Prentice Hall.

McDougall, D., & Granby, C. (1996). How expectation of questioning method affects undergraduates' preparation for class. *Journal of Experimental Education, 65,* 43–54.

McGreal, T. (1985, March). *Characteristics of effective teaching.* Paper presented at the first annual Intensive Training Symposium, Clearwater, FL.

McKeachie, W., & Kulik, J. (1975). Effective college teaching. In F. Kerlinger (Ed.), *Review of research in education* (Vol. 3, pp. 24–39). Washington, DC: American Educational Research Association.

Medin, D., Proffitt, J., & Schwartz, H. (2000). Concepts: An overview. In A. Kazdin (Ed.), *Encyclopedia of psychology* (Vol. 2, pp. 242–245). New York: Oxford University Press.

Meter, P., & Stevens, R. (2000). The role of theory in the study of peer collaboration. *Journal of Experimental Education, 69*(1), 113–127.

Miller, G. (1956). Human memory and the storage of information. *IRE Transactions on Information Theory, 2*(3), 129–137.

Missouri Department of Elementary and Secondary Education. (1996). *The Show Me standards: Science.* Jefferson City, MO: Author. Retrieved February 2004 from www.dese.state.mo.us/standards/science.html

Moreno, R., & Mayer, R. (2000). Engaging students in active learning: The case for personalized multimedia messages. *Journal of Educational Psychology, 92*(4), 724–733.

Morine-Dershimer, G. (1987). Can we talk? In D. Berliner & B. Rosenshine (Eds.), *Talks to teachers* (pp. 37–53). New York: Random House.

Morine-Dershimer, G., & Vallance, C. (1976). *Teacher planning* (Beginning Teacher Evaluation Study, Special Report C). San Francisco: Far West Laboratory.

Morrison, G., & Lowther, D. (2002). *Integrating computer technology into the classroom* (2nd ed.). Upper Saddle River, NJ: Prentice Hall.

Nathan, M., Koedinger, K., & Alibali, M. (2001, April). *Expert blind spot: When content knowledge eclipses pedagogical content knowledge.* Paper presented at the annual meeting of the American Educational Research Association, Seattle.

National Association for Sport and Physical Education. (1995). *Moving into the future, national standards for physical education: A guide to content and assessment.* St. Louis, MO: Mosby.

National Board for Professional Teaching Standards. (2004). *What teachers should know and be able to do.* Available online at www.nbpts.org/pdf/core-props.pdf.

National Council of Teachers of Mathematics. (2000). *Curriculum and evaluation standards for school mathematics.* Reston, VA: Author.

National Parent Teacher Association. (2000). *Standards for parent/family involvement programs.* Retrieved October 1, 2002, from www.pta.org/programs/INVSTAND

National Standards in Foreign Language Education Project. (1999). *Standards for foreign language learning in the twenty-first century.* Lawrence, KS: Author.

Nisan, M. (1992). Beyond intrinsic motivation: Cultivating a "sense of the desirable." In F. Oser, A. Dick, & J. Patry (Eds.), *Effective and responsible teaching: The new synthesis* (pp. 126–138). San Francisco: Jossey-Bass.

Noblit, G., Rogers, D., & McCadden, B. (1995). In the meantime: The possibilities of caring. *Phi Delta Kappan, 76,* 680–685.

Noddings, N. (1999, April). *Competence and caring as central to teacher education.* Paper presented at the annual meeting of the American Educational Research Association, Montreal.

Ormrod, J. (2004). *Human learning* (4th ed.). Upper Saddle River, NJ: Merrill/Prentice Hall.

Paris, S. (1998). Why learner-centered assessment is better than high-stakes testing. In N. Lambert & B. McCombs (Eds.), *How students learn: Reforming schools through learner-centered education* (pp. 189–209). Washington, DC: American Psychological Association.

Parke, C., & Lane, S. (1996/97). Learning from performance assessments in math. *Educational Leadership, 54*(4), 26–29.

Pearson, D., & Dole, J. (1987). Explicit comprehension instruction: A review of research and a new conceptualization of instruction. *Elementary School Journal, 88*(2), 153–165.

Peregoy, S., & Boyle, O. (2001). *Reading, writing, and learning in ESL* (3rd ed.). New York: Longman.

Perkins, D. (1992). *Smart schools.* New York: Free Press.

Perkins, D., & Blythe, T. (1994). Putting understanding up front. *Educational Leadership, 51,* 4–7.

Perry, N. (1998). Young children's self-regulated learning and contexts that support it. *Journal of Educational Psychology, 90*(4), 715–729.

Peterson, P. (1988). Teachers' and students' cognitional knowledge for classroom teaching and learning. *Educational Research, 17,* 5–14.

Peterson, P., & Walberg, H. (1979). *Research on teaching.* Berkeley, CA: McCutchan.

Peterson, P., Marx, R., & Clark, C. (1978). Teacher planning, teacher behavior, and student achievement. *American Educational Research Journal, 15,* 417–432.

Piaget, J. (1952). *Origins of intelligence in children.* New York: International Universities Press.

Piaget, J. (1959). *Language and thought of the child* (M. Grabain, Trans.). New York: Humanities Press.

Pintrich, P., Marx, R., & Boyle, R. (1993). Beyond cold conceptual change: The role of motivational beliefs and classroom contextual factors in the process of conceptual change. *Review of Educational Research, 63,* 167–199.

Pintrich, P., & Schunk, D. (2002). *Motivation in education: Theory, research, and applications* (2nd ed.). Upper Saddle River, NJ: Prentice Hall.

Poole, M., Okeafor, K., & Sloan, E. (1989, April). *Teachers' interactions, personal efficacy, and change implementation.* Paper presented at the annual meeting of the American Educational Research Association, San Francisco.

Prawat, R. (1992). From individual differences to learning communities—Our changing focus. *Educational Leadership, 49,* 9–13.

Putnam, R., Borko, H. (2000). What do new views of knowledge and thinking have to say about research on teacher learning? *Researcher, 29*(1), 4–15.

Reckase, M. (1997, March). *Constructs assessed by portfolios: How do they differ from those assessed by other educational tests?* Paper presented at the annual meeting of the National Educational Research Association, Chicago.

Reisberg, D. (1997). *Cognition: Exploring the science of the mind.* New York: Norton.

Resnick, L., & Klopfer, L. (1989). Toward the thinking curriculum: An overview. In L. Resnick & L. Klopfer (Eds.), *Toward the thinking curriculum: Current cognitive research* (pp. 1–18). Alexandria, VA: Association for Supervision and Curriculum Development.

Robinson, D., Katayama, A., Dubois, N., & Devaney, T. (1998). Interactive effects of graphic organizers and delayed review on concept application. *Journal of Experimental Education, 67*(1), 17–31.

Roblyer, M. (2003a). *Integrating educational technology into teaching* (3rd ed.). Upper Saddle River, NJ: Prentice Hall.

Roblyer, M. (2003b). *Starting out on the Internet: A learning journey for teachers* (2nd ed.). Upper Saddle River, NJ: Prentice Hall.

Rose, L., & Gallup, A. (2002). The thirty-fourth annual Phi Delta Kappa/Gallup poll of the public's attitudes towards public schools. *Phi Delta Kappan, 84,* 41–46, 51–56.

Rosenshine, B. (1979). Content, time and direct instruction. In P. Peterson & H. Walberg (Eds.), *Research on teaching.* Berkeley, CA: McCutchan.

Rosenshine, B., & Stevens, R. (1986). Teaching functions. In M. Wittrock (Ed.), *Handbook of research on teaching* (3rd ed., pp. 376–391). New York: Macmillan.

Ross, B., & Spalding, T. (1994). Concepts and categories. In R. Sternberg (Ed.), *Handbook of perception and cognition* (Vol. 12). New York: Academic Press.

Ross, S. (1992). (Producer). Direct instruction in fifth-grade social studies. [Video Episode]. Upper Saddle River, NJ: Prentice Hall.

Rowe, M. (1974). Wait-time and rewards as instructional variables, their influence on language, logic, and fate control: Part I—Wait time. *Journal of Research in Science Teaching, 11,* 81–94.

Rowe, M. (1986). Wait-time: Slowing down may be a way of speeding up. *Journal of Teacher Education, 37*(1), 43–50.

Rutter, M., Maughan, B., Mortimore, P., Ouston, J., & Smith, A. (1979). *Fifteen thousand hours.* Cambridge, MA: Harvard University Press.

Ryan, R., & Deci, E. (2000). Intrinsic and extrinsic motivations: Classic definitions and new directions. *Contemporary Educational Psychology, 25,* 54–67.

Sadoski, M., & Paivio, A. (2001). *Imagery and text: A dual coding theory of reading and writing.* Mahwah, NJ: Erlbaum.

Schmuck, R., & Schmuck, P. (1997). *Group processes in the classroom* (7th ed.). Madison, WI: Brown & Benchmark.

Schmuck, R., & Schmuck, P. (2001). *Group processes in the classroom* (8th ed.). Madison, WI: Brown & Benchmark.

Schraw, G., & Lehman, S. (2001). Situational interest: A review of the literature and directions for future research. *Educational Psychology Review, 13*(1), 23–52.

Schunk, D. (1994, April). *Goal and self-evaluative influences during children's mathematical skill acquisition.* Paper presented at the annual meeting of the American Educational Research Association, New Orleans, LA.

Schunk, D. (2004). *Learning theories: An educational perspective* (4th ed.). Upper Saddle River, NJ: Merrill/Prentice Hall.

Schwartz, B., & Reisberg, D. (1991). *Learning and memory.* New York: Norton.

Serafini, F. (2002). Possibilities and challenges: The National Board for Professional Teaching Standards. *Journal of Teacher Education, 53,* 316–327.

Sharan, Y., & Sharan, S. (1992). *Expanding cooperative learning through group investigation.* New York: Teachers College Press.

Shepard, L. (2001). The role of classroom assessment in teaching and learning. In V. Richardson (Ed.), *Handbook of research on learning* (4th ed., pp. 1066–1101). Washington, DC: American Educational Research Association.

Shuell, T. (1996). Teaching and learning in a classroom context. In D. Berliner & R. Calfee (Eds.), *Handbook of educational psychology* (pp. 726–764). New York: Macmillan.

Shulman, L. (1986). Those who understand: Knowledge growth in teaching. *Educational Researcher, 15*(2), 4–14.

Shulman, L. (1987). Knowledge and teaching: Foundations of the new reform. *Harvard Educational Review, 57,* 1–22.

Skinner, E., & Belmont, M. (1993). Motivation in the classroom: Reciprocal effects of teacher behavior and student engagement across the school year. *Journal of Educational Psychology, 85,* 571–581.

Slavin, R. (1986). *Using student team learning* (3rd ed.). Baltimore, MD: The Johns Hopkins University, Center for Research on Elementary and Middle School.

Slavin, R. (1995). *Cooperative learning: Theory, research, and practice* (2nd ed.). Boston: Allyn & Bacon.

Slavin, R. (2003). *Educational psychology: Theory and practice* (7th ed.). Boston: Allyn & Bacon.

Slavin, R., Madden, N., Dolan, L., & Wasik, B. (1994). Roots and wings: Inspiring academic excellence. *Educational Leadership, 52,* 10–14.

Smith, L., & Cotten, M. (1980). Effect of lesson vagueness and discontinuity on student achievement and attitude. *Journal of Educational Psychology, 72,* 670–675.

Snyder, S., Bushur, L., Hoeksema, P., Olson, M., Clark, S., & Snyder, J. (1991, April). *The effect of instructional clarity and concept structure on students' achievement and perception.* Paper presented at the annual meeting of the American Educational Research Association, Chicago.

Stepien, W., & Gallagher, S. (1993). Problem-based learning: As authentic as it gets. *Educational Leadership, 50*(7), 25–28.

Sternberg, R. (1998). Principles of teaching for successful intelligence. *Educational Psychologist, 33*(2/3), 65–72.

Stiggins, R. (2001). *Student-centered classroom assessment* (3rd ed.). Upper Saddle River, NJ: Merrill/Prentice Hall.

Stipek, D. (1996). Motivation and instruction. In D. Berliner & R. Calfee (Eds.), *Handbook of educational psychology* (pp. 85–113). New York: Macmillan.

Stipek, D. (2002). *Motivation to learn: Integrating theory and practice* (4th ed.). Boston: Allyn & Bacon.

Sweller, J., van Merrienboer, J., & Paas, F. (1998). Cognitive architecture and instructional design. *Educational Psychology Review, 10,* 251–296.

Taba, H. (1965). Techniques of inservice training. *Social Education, 29,* 44–60.

Taba, H. (1966). *Teaching strategies and cognitive functioning in elementary school children* (Project No. 2404). Washington, DC: USOE.

Taba, H. (1967). *Teachers handbook to elementary social studies.* Reading, MA: Addison Wesley.

Tennyson, R., & Cocchiarella, M. (1986). An empirically based instructional design theory for teaching concepts. *Review of Educational Research, 56*(1), 40–71.

Thelen, H. (1960). *Education and the human quest.* New York: Harper & Row.

Valencia, S., Hiebert, E., & Afflerback, P. (Eds.). (1994). *Authentic reading assessment: Practices and possibilities.* Newark, DE: International Reading Association.

Vygotsky, L. (1978). *Mind in society: The development of higher psychological processes* (M. Cole, V. John-Steiner, S. Scribner, & E. Souberman, Eds. and Trans.). Cambridge, MA: Harvard University Press.

Vygotsky, L. (1986). *Thought and language.* Cambridge: MIT Press.

Wang, M., Haertel, G., & Walberg, H. (1993). Toward a knowledge base for school learning. *Review of Educational Research, 63*(3), 249–294.

Webb, N., Baxter, G., & Thompson, L. (1997). Teachers' grouping practices in fifth-grade science classrooms. *Elementary School Journal, 98*(2), 107–111.

Webb, N., Farivar, S., & Mastergeorge, A. (2002). Productive helping in cooperative groups. *Theory into Practice, 41*(1), 37–44.

Webb, N., Nemer, K., Chizhik, A., & Sugrue, B. (1998). Equity issues in collaborative group assessment: Group composition and performance. *American Educational Research Journal, 35*(4), 607–652.

Weiner, B. (1990). History of motivational research in education. *Journal of Educational Psychology, 82,* 616–622.

Weiner, B. (1994a). Ability versus effort revisited: The moral determinants of achievement evaluation and achievement as a moral system. *Educational Psychologist, 29,* 163–172.

Weiner, B. (1994b). Integrating social and personal theories of achievement striving. *Review of Educational Research, 64,* 557–573.

Weinstein, R. (1998). Promoting positive expectations in schooling. In N. Lambert & B. McCombs (Eds.), *How students learn: Reforming schools through learner-centered education* (pp. 81–111). Washington, DC: American Psychological Association.

Wertsch, J. (1991). *Voices of the mind: A socio-cultural approach to mediated action.* Cambridge, MA: Harvard University Press.

White, R. (1959). Motivation reconsidered: The concept of competence. *Psychological Review, 66,* 297–333.

Wigfield, A., & Eccles, J. (2000). Expectancy-value theory of achievement motivation. *Contemporary Educational Psychology, 25,* 68–81.

Wiggins, G. (1996/97). Practicing what we preach in designing authentic assessment. *Educational Leadership, 54*(4), 18–25.

Williams, S., Bareiss, R., & Reiser, B. (1996, April). *ASK Jasper: A multimedia publishing and performance support environment for design.* Paper presented at the annual meeting of the American Educational Research Association, New York.

Wilson, S., Shulman, L., & Richert, A. (1987). 150 different ways of knowing: Representations of knowledge in teaching. In J. Calderhead (Ed.), *Exploring teacher thinking* (pp. 104–124). London: Cassel.

Winitzky, N., Kauchak, D., & Kelly, M. (1994). Measuring teachers' structural knowledge. *Teaching and Teacher Education, 10*(2), 125–139.

Worthen, B. (1993). Critical issues that will determine the future of alternative assessment. *Phi Delta Kappan, 74,* 444–454.

Zahorik, J. (1996). Elementary and secondary teachers' reports of how they make learning interesting. *The Elementary School Journal, 96*(5), 551–564.

INDEX